Persuasion Ethics Tod

Persuasion Ethics Today explores persuasive communication in the fields of advertising, promotions, public relations, and integrated marketing communication and is designed for course use in advertising curricula.

Ethical questions have become increasingly important in today's media landscape, and issues of regulation, privacy, and convenience are the subjects of heated debate among consumers, industry professionals, policy makers, and interest groups. With the explosion of social media, mobile devices, tracking technologies, and behavioral targeting, the ethical issues about persuasion continue to increase in importance.

This book's goal is to offer a broad introduction to the ethical standards, challenges, understanding, and decision-making strategies involved in the practice of persuasion. *Persuasion Ethics Today* links real-world persuasive communication activities to fundamental philosophies of ethics. It also offers tools for students and practitioners to engage with ethical dilemmas in a systematic way and jump-start debates about the right ethical choices in an increasingly complex media and social environment.

Margaret Duffy is Professor and Chair of the Strategic Communication Faculty at the Missouri School of Journalism, University of Missouri, USA. An author, consultant, and award-winning scholar, Duffy's research focuses on visual communication, narrative theory, digital media, news, and persuasion ethics. She is a former marketing executive and serves on the board of the Institute for Advertising Ethics.

Esther Thorson is Professor, Associate Dean for Graduate Studies, and Director of Research at the Missouri School of Journalism, University of Missouri, USA. She has published extensively on the news industry, advertising, news effects, and health communication. Her scholarly work has won many research and writing awards and she serves on an extensive list of journal editorial boards.

Persuasion Ethics Today

Edited by Margaret Duffy
and Esther Thorson

Routledge
Taylor & Francis Group

NEW YORK AND LONDON

First published 2016
by Routledge
711 Third Avenue, New York, NY 10017

and by Routledge
2 Park Square, Milton Park, Abingdon, Oxon OX14 4RN

Routledge is an imprint of the Taylor & Francis Group, an informa business

Library of Congress Cataloging-in-Publication Data
Persuasion ethics today / edited by Margaret Duffy & Esther Thorson.
    pages cm
  Includes bibliographical references and index.
  1. Advertising—Moral and ethical aspects.   2. Advertising—
Psychological aspects.   3. Persuasion (Psychology)   I. Duffy, Margaret
(Professor of Communications), editor.   II. Thorson, Esther, editor.
    HF5381.P44 2015
    174'.4—dc23
    2015026470

ISBN: 978-0-765-64471-8 (hbk)
ISBN: 978-0-765-64472-5 (pbk)
ISBN: 978-1-315-65130-9 (ebk)

Typeset in Times New Roman
by Apex CoVantage, LLC

Printed and bound in Great Britain by
TJ International Ltd, Padstow, Cornwall

Contents

Figures and Tables

Figures

Tables

Contributors

Richard F. Beltramini (Ph.D., University of Texas, Austin) is Professor of Marketing in the School of Business Administration at Wayne State University and served on the faculty of Arizona State University for 15 years. His primary research focus is in the believability of marketing communications information, and he has published in the *Journal of Advertising, Journal of Advertising Research, Journal of Consumer Research, Journal of Marketing*, and a variety of other journals, conference proceedings, and books, as well as coediting *Gift Giving: A Research Anthology*. Prior to academe, Dr. Beltramini worked for Texas Instruments, Inc. and The Drawing Board, Inc. both in Dallas, and he has also worked as Visiting Research Professor for J. Walter Thompson Advertising in Chicago, Honeywell Information Systems in Phoenix, and the Federal Trade Commission in Washington, D.C.

Tom Bivins (Ph.D., University of Oregon) is the John L. Hulteng Chair in Media Ethics, the Area Director in Media Studies, and the head of the Graduate Certificate Program in Communication Ethics in the School of Journalism and Communication at the University of Oregon. His research focuses on media ethics with a concentration in persuasion and strategic communications. Bivins is the author or coauthor of five books and numerous research articles in both media ethics and media history. He also has a published book of poetry and several illustrated children's books.

Renita Coleman is Associate Professor at the University of Texas in Austin. Her research focuses on visual communication and ethics. She is co-author of the book *The Moral Media: How Journalists Reason About Ethics* (Erlbaum, 2004, with Lee Wilkins) and has published articles in numerous journals including *Journalism & Mass Communication Quarterly, Journal of Communication*, and *Journalism Studies*. She is associate editor of the *Journal of Mass Media Ethics*. She was a newspaper journalist for 15 years.

Katherine T. Frith (Ed.D., University of Massachusetts) is a Professor in the School of Journalism at Southern Illinois University. She received her doctorate in education at the University of Massachusetts and has taught at Iowa State University, Pennsylvania State University, and Nanyang

Technological University in Singapore. She has been the recipient of two Fulbright Awards to teach in Malaysia in 1987 and Indonesia in 1993. She is the author/editor of four books and numerous book chapters and research publications. Her areas of research interest are gender and advertising and the global beauty industry.

Stephanie Geise currently works as a postdoctoral researcher and Assistant Professor at the Department of Methods of Empirical Communication Science at the University of Erfurt, Germany. She holds a German equivalent (Diplom) of an MBA in economics and a master's in communication science, sociology, and art history. As a research and teaching assistant, she has worked at the universities of Augsburg and of Hohenheim in southern Germany, where she finished her dissertation, "Vision that Matters," on the functional logic and the media effects of visual communication using the example of election posters in 2010. For this work Geise was honored with the DGPuK Dissertation Award in 2012, a distinction presented by the German Communication Association for the best Ph.D. thesis in the field of communication science over two years. Geise's research interests are media effects and empirical methods with a special focus on visual communication. She is chair of the Visual Communication Division of the German Communication Association (DGPuK).

Gene R. Laczniak (Ph.D., University of Wisconsin-Madison) is the Sanders Professor of Business Emeritus at the Graduate School of Management, Marquette University (WI). Laczniak is coauthor of five books on marketing ethics and has published numerous articles on public policy, corporate social responsibility, and ethical business practice. In 2012, Laczniak received a lifetime achievement award from the American Marketing Association (Marketing & Society SIG) for his scholarly contributions to the marketing and social issues dialogue.

Carrie La Ferle (Ph.D., University of Texas at Austin) is a Professor and Director of Graduate Studies in the Temerlin Advertising Institute at SMU. For the past 15 years she has been teaching classes in International Advertising and Advertising Ethics. She has worked and lived in a variety of places from Toronto to LA, Tokyo, Singapore, and Hong Kong. Her research examines how culture impacts advertising and consumer behavior. Dr. La Ferle's work has resulted in over 40 publications including articles published in the *Journal of Advertising, Journal of Advertising Research, International Journal of Advertising,* and *Journal of Business Research,* among many others.

Seow Ting Lee has been examining ethics issue since the days of her dissertation. She has discussed the teaching of mass media ethics (Lambeth et al, 2004). She has explored corporate ethics issues (Lee & Cheng, 2012; Lee, 2011), ethical issues in marketing to children (Lee & Nguyen, 2013; 2015), ethics issues related to health communication (Cheng & Lee, 2012; Lee,

2011), and issues with journalist truth (Lee, 2004, 2005). All of this work means that Dr. Lee is one of the major authorities on ethics issues as related to a variety of messaging channels.

Marlene S. Neill (Ph.D., University of Texas at Austin) is an Assistant Professor at Baylor University. Her research interests include public relations management in terms of organizational power and influence, integrated communication, and ethics. Neill serves on the Board of Ethics and Professional Standards for the Public Relations Society of America (PRSA).

Janis Page (Ph.D., Missouri School of Journalism) joined New Mexico State University in 2015. Her research and consulting expertise focuses on the visual rhetoric of strategic and political communication. In her prior 20-year executive career, she directed strategic communication, marketing, public relations, and creative services for U.S. business and consumer magazine publishers, including Cahners Publishing and Emmis Communications, and Sunset and Chicago magazines. She continues to be partner in MediaWerks, a public relations consultancy. Since beginning her academic career in 2005, Dr. Page has taught as a full-time faculty member at the University of Florida, Purdue University, Florida Institute of Technology, and Zayed University, Abu Dhabi; and as an adjunct for Medill School of Journalism, Northwestern University and for the Graduate School of Political Management, George Washington University. Dr. Page is the author of 40 book chapters, journal articles, and conference papers. Her research on political campaign visual messaging and issue advertising in social media won "top faculty paper" in the visual communication division at AEJMC both in 2013 and 2014.

Jef I. Richards (Ph.D., University of Wisconsin; J.D., Indiana University) is Professor and Chair of the Department of Advertising and Public Relations at Michigan State University. His research interests revolve around ethics, public policy, and regulation of marketing communications. He serves on the Board of Directors of the Advertising Educational Foundation, as well as on the Advisory Council of the Institute for Advertising Ethics and as a panel member of the National Advertising Review Board.

Chris Roberts (Ph.D., University of South Carolina) is an Associate Professor of Journalism at The University of Alabama. His research interests include media ethics, media and politics, journalism, and the intersection of journalism and public relations. Roberts is the coauthor (with *Journal of Mass Media Ethics* cofounder Jay Black) of *Doing Ethics in Media: Theories and Practical Applications* (Routledge, 2011); he joined academia after decades as a reporter and editor.

Erin Schauster (Ph.D., University of Missouri) is Assistant Professor of the Advertising, Public Relations and Media Design Department at University of Colorado Boulder. Schauster uses qualitative methods to examine the relationship between advertising ethics and organizational culture. Her research also examines changing organizational structures and practices of advertising and public relations industries, and the implications for advertising education. Schauster's work is published in multidisciplinary books and journals including *Ethical Issues in Communication Professions: New Agendas in Communication, Journal of Advertising Education*, and *Journal of Mass Media Ethics*, among others. Between earning her bachelor's degree from Southern Illinois University Carbondale, a master's degree from Southern Illinois University Edwardsville and her doctorate at the Missouri School of Journalism, Schauster worked at advertising agencies in St. Louis and Nashville.

Heather Shoenberger, JD (Ph.D., University of Missouri) is Assistant Professor of Advertising at the School of Journalism and Communication at the University of Oregon. Her research interests include interest-based advertising and consumer privacy issues as they pertain to such advertising. Shoenberger has co-authored and presented several research papers on the topic of consumer privacy concerns as they pertain to interest-based advertising.

Wally Snyder, Esq. (J.D., University of Iowa) serves as Executive Director of the Institute for Advertising Ethics; Chair of National Advertising Review Board; Distinguished Visiting Professor, Missouri School of Journalism; Professor and Senior Advisor for Advertising Ethics, Michigan State University; and President Emeritus, American Advertising Federation. His research interests include the value and trust consumers place on truthful and ethical advertising and its impact on professional development and advancement. Snyder has written articles appearing in *Business and Professional Ethics Journal* and the *Journal of Advertising Research*; he was presented the Kim Rotzoll Award for Advertising Ethics by the American Academy of Advertising in 2009; and he was inducted into the Advertising Hall of Fame in 2010.

Fred Vultee (Ph.D., University of Missouri) is an Associate Professor of Journalism in the Department of Communication at Wayne State University in Detroit. He teaches news editing, political communication and research methods, and his research focuses on the role of media in conflict and crisis communication, particularly how perceptions of national and cultural security are created and maintained. Before falling into academia, he was a copy editor, news editor, and occasional writer at newspapers for 25 years.

T. J. Weber (M.B.A., Marquette University) is a Ph.D. student in marketing at Washington State University. His research focuses on the intersection of marketing and public policy, with the aims of encouraging consumer behavior that benefits society and discouraging consumer behavior detrimental to society. In 2015, Weber was chosen as Washington State University's presenter at the Robert A. Mittelstaedt Doctoral Symposium at the University of Nebraska-Lincoln to present research on the effects of unregulated corporate political activity.

Lee Wilkins teaches and studies media ethics and media coverage of hazards and disasters. She is co-author of one of the most widely used college media ethics texts, *Media Ethics: Issues and Cases*, in its 8th edition, and has written books and scholarly articles on how journalists and public relations professionals make moral decisions. In 2010 her work on ethical thinking by public relations professionals received the PRIDE Award as the best research in public relations by the National Communication Association. In 2009 her co-edited book *Handbook of Mass Media Ethics* was named the best edited book by the ethics division of the National Communication Association.

Section I

Introductory Issues

1 Why Is Persuasion Ethics So Important to All Communication Students Today? How Does this Book Help You Develop Your Own Perspective?

Margaret Duffy and Esther Thorson

Introduction

Every day we experience a deluge of media messages from our social networks, advertisers, news media, and our favorite Internet sites ranging from celebrity gossip to news of the world to streaming video of favorite programs. Consider this: Facebook has 1.317 billion monthly active users, if Twitter were a country it would be the fourth largest in the world, and more than five million photos were uploaded to Instagram daily in 2014 (IACP, 2014).

We welcome some of the thousands of messages we get. Our friends send us amusing videos, product warnings, and recommendations for products we might like. Along the way, however, we have to make judgments. Is this a credible source? Can I trust this news program to give me accurate information? Is this ad deceptive? Can I be confident that the health messages I'm receiving are safe and effective? Will I be interested in reading this story my friend sent?

Some of the questions we ask ourselves about media products involve issues of ethics. Regardless of your career or career goals, you're part of a vast interlocking media landscape. And whether you're a creator or consumer of media or both, it's important to consider issues of right and wrong. These issues aren't easy or simple and, as you'll see, there's considerable room for disagreement. Nevertheless, we hope you'll find that the chapters in this book illuminate the issues and suggest processes for navigating the world of contemporary media ethics.

Many of you are in or will go into careers in strategic communication, news and information, nonprofits, photography, video production, teaching, or one of many other communication-centered occupations. If you're a part of such professions, it is important that you understand persuasion ethics, not only because issues of morality are important but because ethical and legal breaches pose significant threats to individuals, organizations, and society.

Furthermore, as social networks and technologies springing up every day become even more widely used for news, entertainment, and strategic communication, ethical challenges become more and more common because of the complex interconnectedness of the world. The web of communication we each participate in means that actions in one area are likely to have effects in many other areas. Some of those effects involve injuring individuals and groups psychologically and even physically. You've seen the effects of a misplaced Tweet, perhaps seen cyberbullying in action, and learned to fear having your identity stolen.

An example seen from an ethical perspective may clarify this: ads that look like news content. This is relevant to both news professionals and strategic communicators. Various names for these ads are "advertorials," "branded news," "sponsored content," or "native advertising." "Native" is meant to indicate that the ad conforms to the style and content where the reader/user encounters it. Such ads "look and feel like natural content" (*Native Advertising Insights*, 2015).

Advertorials do provide content and have the look of journalistic stories but are actually paid for by advertisers, sometimes written by advertisers, and now sometimes written by employees of news organizations. The *New York Times*, *Huffington Post*, and *Wall Street Journal* have developed brand content studios housed separately from the news writers but tasked with writing content that is sponsored (Bilton, 2014).

In the heyday of print, advertorials appeared, much as they do today in print, as content that looked like a news story, but they almost always featured a label identifying the content as an advertisement. In digital media, native advertising is identified in a variety of ways, some of it quite clear, but often it is not labeled or is labeled in a deceptive way. However, today's digital native content has much in common with the advertorials of yesterday as in this 1950s ad for Guinness created by advertising giant, David Ogilvy (Ogilvy, 1950). Ogilvy developed a whole series of guides to dining, including oysters, cheese, and game birds, all built around Guinness beer (Ogilvy, 1978).

Why would an advertiser want to pay for advertorial content rather than a regular advertisement? Research has shown that that many people mistakenly believe the stories are actually news, not advertising. In a classic experiment, (Cameron & Curtain, 1995) showed that two weeks after people viewed content labeled as an "advertisement" and content not labeled, they couldn't remember whether the content was labeled or not. In other words, it is easy to confuse advertorials with editorial content. *Forbes*, a publication that both praises the benefits of sponsored content for marketers and also makes extensive use of sponsored content on its own site, defines it as "a paid-for placement on a digital screen or within a content stream that promotes a brand's content marketing much the same way editorial content is promoted." This in-content placement is contrasted with more traditional display ads, such as banners and pop-ups, which are "disruptively placed and transport consumers away from the site they came to visit in the first place" (DVorkin, 2013).

Sharethrough, an online advertising exchange and native content provider, also commissioned an eye-tracking study in 2013 to determine the effectiveness of native advertising. The study concluded "consumers visually engage with native ads more frequently than traditional banner ads and in an equivalent

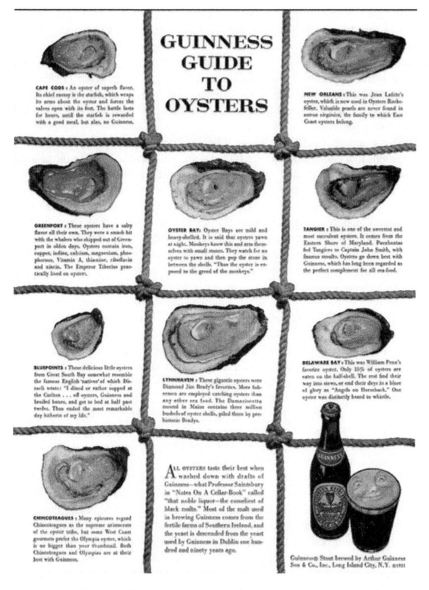

Figure 1.1 Ogilvy's native content ad for Guinness beer, courtesy of Guinness Storehouse, Dublin

way to editorial content." (*Native Advertising Insights*, 2015). In fact, consumers looked at native ads 53% more frequently than at banner ads. The study also found that a slightly higher percentage of viewers looked at native ads than original editorial content.

Is it ethical to use promotional approaches such as advertorials that are clearly used to confuse consumers? They represent paid commercial content as the same as content written by those on the editorial staff of the publication or website. Those defending the practice insist that the content is accurate and useful for readers and viewers and is (mostly) properly labeled as "sponsored content." Others point out that for decades, lifestyle and women's magazines have featured products and services in editorial content, often positioning related advertising adjacent to that content and giving advertisers input into the editorial material. Still others say the practice is deceptive and unethical by its very nature.

This example is particularly useful because it exemplifies the kind of ethics questions that communicators must deal with, and because it shows the blurred lines between advertising, news, and public relations. A video or print news release can be picked up nearly verbatim by a reporter and be presented as a news story. This frequently happens, and the practice of using news releases as "news" has been around for a very long time. Careful analysis, however, would show clearly that it is not news in the sense that a reporter independently researched and reported the content. Running a news release as a story means that the news organization has no firsthand knowledge of whether the "story" is true or not. A native advertiser can write a "story" that is really intended to promote (advertise) a brand. What is native advertising in comparison to these two examples? PR or advertising? As will be seen in this book, there are many cases where it is not useful to distinguish advertising and public relations. To complicate matters further, Chapter 2 suggests that all human communication is, at some level, "intentional" persuasion. Nevertheless, there is decided value to consumers to know where the information they are receiving and perhaps relying on actually comes from.

Another important perspective involves understanding how high-level, strategic communication executives think about the importance of media ethics. Drumwright and Murphy (2009) interviewed many high-placed executives and found that in terms of the content of advertising, they believed it was important to communicate true information about products and services while promoting them. The industry leaders believed this is a relatively easy task. In contrast, when it came to use of new media and the complexity that digitally based environments create, these same professionals were much more concerned with potential ethical challenges. The active role of consumers in the digital universe was seen to reduce control over messaging on the parts of promoters and lead to greater possibilities of unethical messages. Another area of concern involves privacy issues about people's personal data being subject to all kinds of unknown and perhaps problematic uses. Practices that fake or exaggerate the size of audiences using bots to increase traffic and false viral responses to messages were also seen as posing increased ethical dangers for professional persuaders. The particular concern about what happens in the digital environment demonstrates how important it is for students of persuasion to be sensitive to and able to deal with ethical questions.

Of course it is beyond the scope of this book to cover all the ethics topics in communication. Instead we focus on some of the most important questions in the field, providing a brief but useful review of the study of advertising, public relations, and general communication ethics. Drumwright and Murphy (2009) distinguish between two perceptions of persuasion ethics. The first concerns what is legal for strategic communication functions, specifying advertiser rights and restrictions. The second channel explores broader questions about the morality and ethics of strategic communication practices in society. This book tends to focus more on the second approach.

Before we get started, it is important to settle on a definition of strategic communication ethics. We borrow from a 1999 definition of advertising ethics and expand it to refer to all of strategic communication. Strategic communication ethics is "what is right or good in the conduct of the strategic communication" function. It is concerned with questions of what ought to be done, not just with what legally must be done" (Cunningham, 1999). Notice that this definition places greater emphasis on the moral than the legal.

Overview of the Book

Section I of the book sets the stage for our study of ethics. In Chapter 2, Thorson and Duffy explore the fundamental question of the nature of persuasion in human life. Most of us think of advertising and public relations as intentional efforts by marketers to persuade people to buy their products and services, and we think of news more as information, imparting knowledge about people, places, things, and events. Many claim that information can be factual, unbiased, and objective, and not persuasive in nature. On the other hand, it is said that while persuasion may or may not be factual, it is inevitably biased and certainly not objective. Chapter 2 argues that all human messages are inherently persuasive. When we communicate, we have intentions and expectations about our messages and their likely effects. Journalists intend to motivate people to read their information and find it credible. Advertisers' messages intend to sell products and services and to convince others that their information about promoted brands is credible. If all messages are persuasive in intention, how then is news different from public relations and advertising? How could "news" be considered ethically superior to public relations and advertising? Can news be intentionally false or misleading? Where, if anywhere, is "objectivity" located? These are important issues to understand, because often practitioners of strategic communication encounter ethical critiques simply because they engage in strategic communication. Understanding persuaders' societal function as simply another instance of "inevitable persuasion" provides a useful perspective on how communication works. It lessens what many argue to be the inherent "moral superiority" of news activities over strategic communication activities.

Chapter 3 provides philosophical background for thinking and problem solving in strategic communication. Author Lee Wilkins, one of the leading news ethicists in the United States, explains why Utilitarian Theory ("the greatest good for the greatest number") is not sufficient for decision making about strategic communication ethics. Instead of relying on utilitarianism, Wilkins suggests combining two ethical philosophies, Ross's moral theory and feminist theory. Wilkins discusses feminist theory in terms of the fundamental value of "ethical choice." This ethical choice allows "all involved to flourish and to attain those capabilities—for example, free speech—without which our common humanity is diminished."

Scottish philosopher W. D. Ross based his approach on the need to make decisions based on five central "duties". These include: 1) The duty of keeping promises; 2) the duty of reparation—that is, attempting to pay reparations for the harm we do to others; 3) the duty of gratitude, to return favors and services given to us by others; 4) the duty of beneficence, to maximize the good (things of intrinsic value); and 5) the duty to refuse to harm others. Wilkins demonstrates the usefulness of these two approaches in an analysis of the ethics of advertising one of America's newest legal products—marijuana.

In Chapter 4, authors Neill and Schauster discuss the relationships of public relations and advertising. Both authors have extensive experience in advertising and public relations and have witnessed the changes that technology has brought to theory and practice. As integrated marketing communication has become more prevalent, brands are using a toolbox of promotional techniques. Thus campaigns that deploy both advertising and public relations tactics need to be assessed in a holistic way, accounting for their interactions with each other as they encounter new potential ethical dilemmas.

Section II of the book focuses on some of the main criticisms leveled at advertising and public relations practice. Schudson (1982), summarizing the case against advertising, wrote that brands are portrayed as having only positive attributes or they are shown offering consumers only positive outcomes from using products and services. Characters in video commercials are not "real people," but representatives of categories of people, such as wives, children, wealthy men, glamorous women, and so on. Thus in commercials, consumers see abstractions of humans presented in idealized ways. Although usually advertisers do not intend to present fraudulent depictions, they often present a "better" reality than reality. They offer stereotypes and models who people want to emulate. These models are typically shown as thinner, richer, and happier than most people.

Chapters 5 and 6 exemplify the ethical issues involved in stereotyping and specifically the representation of women and men. Bivins looks at portrayals of males in commercials and finds that stereotypical images of men as competent, tough, and in control have been displaced with much different roles. He is concerned with ads that show men as confused, bumbling husbands and dads showing little sense of responsibility or capability, especially in family or household settings. Potentially, young men will assume society sets low expectations, and Bivins cites significant research showing how stereotypes can negatively affect audiences through a variety of mechanisms.

Frith points out that advertising and commercial messages are only a part of a complex media environment. Television, films, magazines, and other media as well as advertising representations function to "teach" women and men about standards of beauty, behavior, and attractiveness. In Frith's view, unattainable beauty standards suffuse media and society, and it is important to understand advertising's role in these processes in a holistic way.

While Chapters 5 and 6 describe how promotions and advertising portray stereotypical or idealized versions of people, Chapter 7 explores how adults interpret advertising and whether they see certain ads as problematic. Ads are frequently criticized by policy makers and individuals who argue that many ads show stereotypes, glamorize dangerous behaviors, or are in bad taste. The results of this study may surprise you. Different people viewing the same commercial have very different interpretations of its meaning. It appears that our personal worldviews make a big difference in our reactions. Some people are offended by "sexist" commercials, while others report enjoying the same sexy commercial. For still others, their response depends largely on how they feel about the celebrity starring in the spot. This chapter suggests that ethicists need to consider people's widely varied interpretations when considering whether a commercial has breached ethical standards.

Chapter 8 takes on the challenges of negative political advertising. More than four billion dollars were spent on advertising in the U.S. 2014 off-year elections (Open Secrets, 2014). In spite of, or perhaps because of the huge amount of political advertising, one of the least popular types of commercials in the United States is political advertisements. Chapter 8 investigates the problems of negative political ads from an ethical point of view. Some critics argue that such messages increase cynicism and discourage citizens from participating in civic life and voting. However, other research shows that negative advertising spurs political discussions. While negative messages, even if they are untrue are permissible because of the First Amendment, Weber and Laczniak call for "moral courage" on the part of political marketers.

Chapter 9 builds on the research of Ivan Preston (1975), who argued that in addition to persuasive messages being either true or false, many of them could be identified as "puffery." One of Preston's best-known students, Jef Richards, is the author of Chapter 9. Richards explains that puffing is exaggerating, usually with subjective opinions and superlatives, and is often used in promoting events, brands, and services. To say that Budweiser is the King of Beers is to puff. In what sense is the beer a "king"? Presumably, anyone could claim kingship for a beer (or a burger or a watch) because everyone knows this is not "true," in the sense that the brand is number one nationally or has the best taste test scores. Defenders of such advertising insist that a reasonable person understands that terms like "King of Beers" or videos of animals talking are entertaining fictions that dramatize the brand. The problem, however, is that these puffs are actually quite persuasive. This chapter looks at how puffery, figurative language, and exaggerations are treated by the courts and suggests a definition clarifying instances when puffery is deceptive and should be prohibited.

Chapter 10 concerns one of the newest and most rapidly growing genres of advertising: "online behavioral advertising." These are ads delivered to you based on your online activities, including searches, social network activity, and your shopping behavior. You may welcome these online ads and recommendations because they are relevant to what you want or prefer. The Internet knows your friends on Facebook, whether you've gotten a speeding ticket, and people who have tagged you in their own social network sites. Most people readily agree to give up their information and quickly check "agree" without reading the terms of service. This is an ethics issue, because in most Western societies, people believe information about their lives belongs to them and should not be sold to others to make promotional targeting more effective. In addition, many critics are concerned about governmental surveillance of online activities and other potential misuse of such information.

Chapter 10 considers both sides of the privacy controversy associated with online behavioral advertising. Author Heather Shoenberger examines the nature of privacy and how it should best be defined. While it may seem obvious, courts and individuals have struggled with definitions. Traditionally, one's home or office constituted a zone of privacy, a concept derived from the Fourth Amendment of the Constitution prohibiting the government from unreasonable searches or seizures. As early as 1890, judges and critics became concerned that technology threatened people's privacy. Today much of the discussion centers on the notion that individuals should have control over their own data similarly to the control they exercise over the privacy of their own home.

Section III addresses special topics in advertising ethics. In Chapter 11, Carrie La Ferle provides insight into cultural influences in play in international advertising and marketing. Many corporations are multinational, and while they may have a familiar name, they may be based or have significant operations in countries around the world. Cultural dilemmas emerge in business practices, marketing approaches, and promotions. Some cultures accept practices of payment for doing business, while in other cultures such payments are labeled as kickbacks and are illegal. In addition, advertising and promotions that are considered to be clever and ethically acceptable in one culture may be seen as deeply offensive in others. The chapter points out that cultural values can often conflict and notions of Western individualism, Eastern collectivism, Confucian philosophy, and Islam-based religions mean that what is acceptable will vary widely. Planning and sensitivity to these differences are crucial to successful international promotional campaigns. Most important, the chapter attempts to derive a universally cultural ethics of advertising.

Chapters 12 and 13 move our attention from text to visual representations in persuasive messages. Together these two important chapters demonstrate that often the visual image carries more complex and problematic ethics issues than those of text. Chapter 12 begins with a discussion about how communicators construct messages, choosing certain elements over others, downplaying or omitting some aspects of a phenomenon. This activity is called framing, and it's a useful way to think about how communicators make decisions about how to talk about brands. You've probably heard about journalists saying they need an "angle" in how to effectively tell a news story. That angle and frame will help make a story more interesting and readable. But in creating frames, communicators may intentionally or unintentionally alter how audiences will interpret the story's meanings and its characters. That clearly introduces an ethical dimension to the discussion. Persuaders, of course, seek to find the best frame that will encourage audiences to adopt a certain point of view. Those in the health communication field hope to create messages that will move people to adopt healthy lifestyles and avoid dangerous behaviors. Communicators use framing both for textual messages and for visual and audiovisual storytelling. Nevertheless the potential for deception via an effective frame is often troublingly easy.

In Chapter 13, Page and Duffy offer an extended discussion of visual persuasion ethics, providing examples that illustrate some of the challenges. Many observers have discussed how in contemporary society, the influence of visuals now dominates textual messages. Visuals communicate quickly and viscerally and do not require sophisticated language literacy skills for interpretation. In addition, often visuals communicate more powerfully and memorably than texts. Visual ethics issues are not limited to strategic communication, as ethical problems arise in photo manipulation in all kinds of media as well as depictions of violence and trauma, and of criminals and victims in news stories. The authors also explain how the ease of creating and disseminating visual memes, videos, and other images through social media has expanded the potential of visually based ethical problems.

In Chapter 14, Seow Ting Lee considers the ethical intersections among advertising, public relations, and health communication efforts. In evaluating ethics in these fields, she applies the TARES model for analysis. TARES has five dimensions for assessing persuasion messages: the truthfulness of the message, authenticity of the persuader, respect for the person being persuaded, the equity or fairness of the appeal, and social responsibility for the common good. Lee explains that health communication often escapes ethical scrutiny because its goals of changing people's health behaviors for the better seem to be intrinsically beneficent. However, she points out that many health campaigns sometimes stigmatize certain beliefs and behaviors and set out expectations that many people will be unable to meet.

Regulation of Advertising Messages

Wally Snyder, lawyer and former executive director of the American Advertising Federation (AAF) provides an overview of self-regulation efforts in corporate and agency ethics practices in Chapter 15. Industry leaders in public relations and advertising have long advocated measures encouraging organizations to monitor their own behaviors and make changes when problems or ethical issues arise. The AAF and the Missouri School of Journalism partnered to develop the Institute for Advertising Ethics (IAE) to conduct research and educate students and professionals. Part of this effort has led to firms creating ethics codes and initiating training for employees and students throughout the United States.

In Chapter 16, Chris Roberts offers a critical analysis of existing corporate codes of ethics and points out the numerous gray areas in persuasion. He finds that many codes contradict themselves, are unclear, and sometimes simply pay lip service to ethical conduct. However, despite the limitations of many of these codes, he cautions that they can often serve important purposes. Codes can educate new employees, remind current employees of a firm's standards, and spur discussion about the difficult and often challenging dilemmas practitioners face. Furthermore, he writes that codes can distill the values of an organization and raise the consciousness of employees to act in accordance with those values.

The final chapters in the book return to a perspective about you, the student of persuasion. In Chapter 17, longtime business school professor Richard Beltramini reports on his work of tracking the attitudes of business students toward business ethics for 20 years. Business ethics is closely synonymous with persuasion ethics (Open Secrets, 2014). Beltramini's chapter provides a good opportunity to see what other students think about these issues and how their attitudes and beliefs have changed over the years. From our point of view, the most encouraging finding is that across his three studies, Professor Beltramini reports that overall interest in ethics has increased each time. Students are highly concerned about ethics. Students express the fear that their own values and ethics will become irrelevant or dishonored when they join the career ranks. We think this finding suggests there needs to be more concern on the part of American corporations to talk about their ethics codes with new employees and invite them to speak up when faced with hard decisions. Second, the studies found that in all three surveys, women were more concerned than men about business ethics. This finding is important for what you're going to find in your working life. Are gender differences likely to appear in the workplace as well as in the classroom? Are women's perspectives on ethics ignored or downplayed? Do different levels of concern with ethics create workplace conflict? We suggest you compare how you would have answered the questions in Beltramini's survey to how students nationwide responded.

Chapter 18 provides a wrap-up of what these chapters can mean to youth who are about to enter the persuasive communication fields. Duffy and Thorson provide examples of new questions that are being raised in the ethics domain and point out gain how the complexity of digital communication makes ethical issues more frequent and sometimes difficult to identify. Regardless of your career choices and experiences, you'll have ever-changing situations and opportunities that will offer ethical dilemmas, conflicts of interest, and questions of loyalty to different parties. We hope the ideas in this book offer perspectives on how you can stay true to your own values and standards while meeting the challenges of a dynamic communication landscape.

References

Bilton, R. (2014). Meet the publishers who ask their reporters to write native ads. *Digiday*, June 5. http://digiday.com/publishers/publishers-enlist-reporters-write-native-ad-content/

Cameron, G. T., & Curtin, P. A. (1995). Tracing sources of information pollution: A survey and experimental test of print media's labeling policy for feature advertising. *Journal and Mass Communication Quarterly*, 72(1), 178–89.

Cunningham, A. (1999). Responsible advertisers: A contractualist approach to ethical power. *Journal of Mass Media Ethics*, 14(2), 82–94.

Drumwright, M. E., & Murphy, P. E. (2009). The current state of advertising ethics. *Journal of Advertising*, 38(1), 83–107.

Dvorkin, L. (2013). Inside Forbes: Controversy gives way to market realities. *Forbes*, July 8. Retrieved March 15, 2015 from http://www.cios.org/EJCPUBLIC/004/2/004220.html

IACP Center for Social Media IACP (2014). Fun facts. Retrieved March 5, 2015 from http://www.iacpsocialmedia.org/Resources/FunFacts.aspx

Native Advertising Insights (2015). Sharethrough. Retrieved March 9, 2015 from https://www.sharethrough.com/nativeadvertising/#intro

Ogilvy, D. (1950). *Guinness guide to oysters*. Retrieved July 1, 2015 from http://swiped.co/file/guinness-guide-to-oysters-by-david-ogilvy/

Ogilvy, D. (1978). *Confessions of an Advertising Man*. New York: Atheneum.

Open Secrets (2014). Election to cost nearly $4 billion, CRP topping previous midterms. Retrieved July 1, 2014 from http://www.opensecrets.org/news/2014/10/election-to-cost- nearly-4-billion-crp-projects-topping-previous-midterms/

2 All Communication Is Persuasive

Exploding the Myth of Objectivity

*Margaret Duffy, Esther Thorson,
and Fred Vultee*

CHAPTER SUMMARY

If you're like most people, your defenses go up when you think someone is trying to persuade you of something. You're skeptical of advertising claims, sales people, or news that appears to be biased. You suspect that people trying to talk you into something are likely doing it to benefit themselves, not you.

Most people draw distinctions between persuasion and information, and their everyday working theories often characterize persuasion as unethical— or at least suspect—while "information" is believed to be factual, unbiased, and objective. In this chapter, we introduce a controversial view that persuasion is not inherently unethical, but it is inherently inevitable. Put differently, we argue that every instance of human communication is persuasive in nature and those messages can never be purely informational or objective. Every day you practice persuasion, sometimes intentionally and often simply as part of human interaction, through a whole range of influence strategies. You try to get your friends to go to the movie you want to see, you greet others you like or want to impress with a smile and a compliment, you update your social network profiles and photos to present yourself more positively. You may not consciously realize that you're engaged in persuasion, but nevertheless, that's what's going on. Persuasion is crucial to community life and democracy. Responsible persuasion helps us work together to solve problems rather than resorting to coercion. It helps us connect with each other, forge relationships, and develop shared understanding. In the world of professional persuasion, advertising and public relations help people learn about products and services they might need or like. They encourage competition, foster innovation, and help keep prices down. Of course, not all persuasion is ethical, and those are the issues we're going to sort out in this book. At this point, you're probably protesting that persuasion and information are different and that you can tell the difference. You may also think that other people are more susceptible to influence than you yourself. We'll talk more about that later. But try to keep an open mind regarding our very clear effort to persuade you.

Ethics and Objectivity in Journalism

Many people—journalists in particular—characterize "objective" journalism as informational and advertising or other sponsored messages as persuasive. Journalists are often highly critical of advertising and PR as manipulative and deceptive, while characterizing their own work as high-minded and free of bias. We think this is an inaccurate view of the relationship between persuasion and information, and we believe that any message, whether spoken, appearing in a newspaper, in a television commercial, or a social media site of a consumer product is a persuasive message. In this chapter, we're going to try to persuade you of that very notion.

Journalists insist that objectivity is not only crucial for ethical and responsible journalism, but it is possible to achieve. *New York Times* Public Editor Margaret Sullivan wrote (2013) that reporters can and should check their prejudices and biases at the door and help readers find the truth about an event, an individual, or a phenomenon. Many reporters think that they can write stories that are free of their own biases and beliefs and that fairly present opposing viewpoints—different sides of the story. Similarly, most members of the public desire and expect the journalism they read and view to be free of bias, political slant, or agendas. But oddly, many people also think that the journalism they consume tends to be biased—and usually is perceived to be biased against their own points of view (Vallone, Ross, & Lepper, 1985).

Before we get into specific examples and evidence, let's talk about the concept of persuasion in more depth. As we suggested earlier, arguing about its nature is nothing new. Plato disdained the Sophists for using flattery, cajoling, and other strategies to influence people, claiming that the Sophists (teachers who taught courses in how to influence and persuade audiences in speeches) sought power, not truth. Critics of the Sophists said that only rational, emotion-free messages constituted ethical communication. This viewpoint emerges from the idea that information can, at least potentially, be free of human bias and provide an accurate reflection or mirror of events. Why then is it that different people and groups can have widely conflicting understanding of events and phenomena? Why can't we all agree that Event X happened and this is what Event X means?

Let's start with the idea of frames of reference and experience. Consider your own life. What values and beliefs do your family and friends hold? What were you taught about how people should behave and what constitutes good and moral actions? Did you learn that small towns nurture solid citizens or that they nurture small-mindedness? Were you taught that practical training and hard work trump airy-fairy theories and impractical schemes? Did you grow up around people who looked like you and valued similar things? Did you see different expectations for proper behavior for men and women? Young people? Elderly people?

This is just a brief list of the differences in how people's worldviews and perspectives must be different based on their life experiences. If people see the world differently and have somewhat differing values, they are likely to interpret events differently.

Why is this important? Following the lead of philosopher Kenneth Burke, we argue that all language is rhetorical, value-laden, and persuasive, including scientific treatises and journalistic stories. Second, we note that as revealed in textbooks, creeds, and mottos, journalism clearly stakes out a value proposition in its goals. Its ethical claims themselves are "a form of persuasive, rhetorical speech" (Ward, 2004, p. 3). The admonition to "comfort the afflicted and afflict the comfortable" is a call to arms. Walter Williams's famous Journalist's Creed is focused on humanism, public service, and promoting equality among citizens (Williams, 1908). These are noble goals but manifestly are not neutral or objective. Third, we conduct brief analyses of several recent news stories to identify rhetorical elements they share. We need to recognize that no account of an event can include everything about any phenomenon and that certain elements will be downplayed while others will be highlighted. This is as true in a 30-second spot as in a news article.

An understanding of rhetoric can be helpful at this point. When many people hear that term, they think of high-flown speech that's flowery and not reality based. In fact, the classic definition of rhetoric is persuasion and the use of symbolic language that people use to make sense of the world. Far from being a mere bag of linguistic tricks, rhetoric is a form of "interactive, social argumentation" that lies at the center of ethical deliberation (Ward, 2004, p. 29). Kenneth Burke, the philosopher and rhetorical theorist, explains, "Rhetoric as such is not rooted in any past condition of human society. It is rooted in an essential function of language itself, the use of language as a symbolic means of inducing cooperation in beings that by nature respond to symbols" (Burke, 1969, p. 43).

Larson (1995) draws on Burke for a nuanced understanding of rhetoric and persuasion. He writes that persuasion "is the co-creation of a state of identification or alignment between a source and a receiver that results from the use of symbols" (p. 9). Larson's point is that when an individual identifies with a certain presentation of events through spoken, written, or visual narratives (wholly fictional or based on real events), she has been persuaded. She has accepted as "real" a value-laden narrative that offers a world in which certain attitudes, beliefs, behaviors, and lifestyles are appropriate or inappropriate. She has, to paraphrase Ettema and Glasser (1990), participated in a "moral universe." Ettema and Glasser cite Hayden White saying that stories "permit us to 'judge the moral significance of human projects . . . even while we pretend to be merely describing them'" (1987, p. 270).

Certain types of communication, such as scientific articles, are often thought to be immune from persuasive or rhetorical elements. But many authors have pointed out that the form and content of scientific writing are also rhetorical. Rhetoric is thus not to be condemned but understood as inevitable: "An economist or historian cannot avoid writing rhetorically since any argument has a rhetoric, a style of argument, taking 'argument' to mean 'any designs on the reader'" (McCloskey, 1990, p. 56). Any story that presents a certain version of reality through story form and content is rhetorical. In fact, as McCloskey writes, the "just the facts" model (similar to traditional journalistic styles) is in itself a rhetorical construction. Moreover, the style of the story and its "poetics" or artistic elements are critical to its success in being a persuasive and powerful representation of events (McCloskey, 1990). Again, these are influence strategies.

Cheseboro's (1990) discussion of the rhetoric of computer science illuminates our argument. Like the scientist, the journalist has been portrayed as "exploring and describing 'what is'" (p. 156). If science, with its orientation toward systematic and replicable procedures can be identified as rhetoric, so can journalism. Cheseboro goes on to say that scientific rhetoric is "a powerful set of humanly created concepts and symbols which constitute a way of 'talking to others-which has gained respect and power because of its persuasive use of language, its strategies and tactics, and its appeals to human values" (p. 156–57). He argues that computer science rhetoric (and by extension, other types of rhetoric) is epistemic and involves how we know rather than the nature of reality. In fact, he suggests that scientists' claim to ontological status for their work is itself a rhetorical act. They are emphasizing "the symbols of computer science to convince others of its own universality power and significance" (p. 167).

That understanding illuminates Tuchman's (1972) description of the "strategic rituals" that distance reporters from the claims they report (Tuchman, 1972). Nylund (2003) goes further in suggesting that using quotations, for example, "co-constructs the controversial news story as knowledge" and thus "implies that the newspaper is a legitimate institution that serves an important democratic (rather than, say, commercial) function for society" (p. 850).

Early on, scholars of news work began to understand the rhetorical and narrative qualities of the work itself. Sociologist Robert Park, writing in 1940, argued "news . . . has tended to assume to character of literature, so fiction— after the newspaper the most popular form of literature—has assumed more and more the character of news" (Park, 1940, p. 686). Consumers of news media see "an artistic, interpretive, organized portrayal of social reality" (Bormann, 1982, p. 145). The frames or story structures and words selected by those creating stories have profound implications for the meanings intended by reporters and interpreted by readers. Many studies of journalistic content demonstrate this. Condit and Selzer (1985) show how coverage of a murder trial was biased toward the prosecution, demonstrating how dramatic emphasis in news stories challenges the concept of journalistic objectivity. Brooks, Kennedy, Moen, and Ranly (2008) acknowledge that news work itself has built-in biases such as preferences for novelty, conflict, questioning of authority, and skepticism toward sacred cows of society that may lead politically conservative individuals to assume a liberal media bias.

Schudson (1982) points out that the conventions of news story forms limit what may be told. Implicit in the form of the news story are key assumptions.

For example, we take it for granted that it is appropriate for journalists to select and repackage elements of "reality" in a conventional news narrative. Schudson argues that that form of news inevitably carries with it instructions about what is most important for the reader. In Carey's analysis, news is as much drama as information: It "does not describe the world but portrays an arena of dramatic forces and action; it exists solely in historical time; and it invites our participation on the basis of our assuming, often vicariously, social roles within it" (1989, p. 21).

Narrative theory illuminates the frames embedded in news stories. Many studies of news-as-narrative have demonstrated the dramatic, mythic, and cultural aspects of journalism. Narrative and dramatistic theories propose that people use symbols to make sense of what William James called the "blooming, buzzing confusion" that the everyday world presents (Meyers, 2001). News products are just one example. Walter Fisher, theorist of the narrative paradigm, writes, "even scientific (technical) discourse, which is a form of literature, is informed by metaphor (and myth), contains 'plots,' and is time bound" (p. 243). But journalism's core values are particularly caught up in narrative. Ettema and Glasser (1987) assert that investigative news stories "issue a compelling summons to participate in a moral universe, a summons to confront very real and terrible injustices" (p. 270). Their critique suggests the narrative form of investigative journalism may actually lessen the potential for more complete societal deliberation.

Traditional rhetoric has terms for story elements that we can apply to journalistic rhetoric. News stories call upon ethos (the character of the speaker or source), logos (the logical arguments or reasons cited in the story), and pathos (emotional appeals embedded in the story.) The journalist's credibility and ethos traditionally rested on her role as a reporter and the news "brand" of her paper. Some news stories rely on the analysis of data and thus fall into the logos category. Breaking news, investigative stories, and feature stories use pathos and other strategies to help the reader share in the outrage, anger, pity, fear, joy, and celebration. Many news stories are a blend of the three strategies, but all lead to a particular and persuasive worldview: "The task is accomplished by cueing the audience's response to these characters through the emplotting of events as recognizably moralistic stories and, more specifically, through the skillful use of such story elements as a point of view, ironic detail, and ritual denial" (Ettema & Glasser, 1990, p. 270)

Burke (1969) suggests "Perhaps the sturdiest modern variant of epideictic rhetoric is 'human interest' stories depicting the sacrificial life of war heroes in war times" (p. 70). Epideictic rhetoric is communication that praises or places blame and is seen in ceremonial events such as funeral orations, praise for the Navy Seals who killed Osama Bin Laden, the Olympic Games, or following events such as the 9/11 attacks. Deliberative rhetoric is aimed at discussions about decisions that should be made that will affect the future. Forensic rhetoric looks backward and assigns guilt or innocence. Journalistic genres can be categorized along these lines as well, though many employ all three types of rhetoric in telling the story. The investigative story identifies guilty parties and their victims; political stories, for example, will investigate, through interviews and other methods, what policies may be enacted that will affect groups and individuals.

Contemporary Analyses of Media Rhetoric and Frames

Framing is one of several theoretical approaches that are useful in explaining and understanding the value propositions and ideology of journalistic stories, including framing. Put simply, news frames are ways of organizing experience that shape and guide our interpretations of reality; such scholars as Goffman (1974), Entman (1991, 1993), Reese (2001), and De Vreese (2004) have applied framing to a range of social artifacts. Frames are powerful because they are usually deployed and consumed without much conscious effort. High-profile arguments about "terrorists" and "insurgents" are the most visible examples of framing, but commonplace newsroom choices about whether the victim, the damage, or the time of year should be the dominant element of a house-fire story are equally elements of framing. As unremarkable as those decisions seem, research offers many examples of persuasive effects of framing that go well beyond the routine concerns of the newsroom. DeVreese (2004) found that the same set of facts could elicit different responses when an event is portrayed as a matter of conflict rather than as an issue of pocketbook impact. Price (1989) found that the introduction of a group conflict tended to support a "social identification" model in which group membership became more salient to audiences. Anastasio, Rose, and Chapman (1999) suggested that such media reports might both reinforce inaccurate pictures of the world and encourage low-effort shortcuts in processing of information about outgroups. It is hard to think of an aspect of framing that does not serve to reinforce or challenge some attitude of the receiver's.

Journalists' choices of personalized or broad-brush frames have consequences for viewers' perceptions. Iyengar and Kinder (1987) found that personalized, "vivid" frames can encourage television viewers to attribute responsibility to the individual featured in the story rather than to broader social factors or governmental policy failures. Because "statistical representations are, almost by definition, collective or thematic rather than individual or episodic" (Goshorn & Gandy, 1995, p. 135), the journalistic mandate to tell a good story by putting a human face to it poses a particular problem in framing—and thus implicitly in persuasion. The "people-make-news" approach has effects beyond audience appeal. Keum et al. (2005) found that individual and group frames in national security reports can produce distinct outcomes, with individual frames tending to increase attitude polarization and group framing tending to attenuate it. While the individual news focus may help create compelling stories, it clearly entails persuasive effects. Those effects might be drastically different from what the journalist intended but they are nonetheless real.

Some framing choices are cast as mandates of news practice. A dictum often found in stylebooks as well as journalism textbooks is the need to translate "euphemisms": turning "withdrawal" into "retreat," for example (Baskette et al., 2001).

Constructing Reality: Selection Processes

A group of journalists assembled at random from around the country could probably agree quickly on the "facts" relevant to reporting something as mundane as a car crash: location, damage or injuries, identities of drivers and passengers, the weather, and so forth. Other elements, though equally "true," might face greater debate about whether and how they are incorporated into the narrative: distractions to drivers, the age and gender of those involved, disruptions to traffic, the involvement of alcohol or seat belts. Depending on how those elements are chosen and ordered, a report "about" the crash is in the larger sense "about" age, infrastructure maintenance, drunk driving, and the like. Those are clear, if simple, examples of the ways in which news makes facts be more than simple recitations of events. The deliberate framing of journalism clearly reflects the functions Entman (2003) outlined: defining problems, identifying their causes, "conveying a moral judgment of those involved," and "endorsing remedies or improvements" (p. 417). Even when it hews strictly to verifiable facts, framing conveys values and moral judgments.

Framing decisions do not need to be made at the highest levels after consultation with the publisher or lawyers. They happen routinely at many levels of the newsroom and reflect the ideology of news work. For example, in describing ways to begin a report of a small house fire, some textbooks suggest that both prominence (if the mayor's house is involved) and public awareness may be significant. During a fire safety campaign, the driving factor might be "the need for fire safety in a community where awareness of the problem had already been heightened" (Brooks et al., 1992, p. 59). These decisions illuminate the ways in which persuasive effects can be brought about by the normal discourse of news—by an intentional rhetoric, in other words, that produces unintended effects.

Despite academic and professional attention to the objectivity question, news organization policies, day-to-day commentary, and audience expectations take the possibility and desirability of objectivity as a reasonable and achievable goal. For instance, the Corporation for Public Broadcasting's website asserts its "strict adherence to objectivity and balance in all programs or series of programs of a controversial nature" (Corporation for Public Broadcasting, 2010). A Pew study noted that Americans are migrating to many clearly opinionated outlets for the news. The headline read: "Americans Spending More Time Following the News: Ideological News Sources: Who Watches and Why." The subhead itself implies that nonideological news sources exist. Examples of the matter-of-fact acceptance of the objectivity standard abound.[1,2,3] Readers and viewers themselves are selecting sources they perceive as aligning with their own ideological positions (Latham & Laxson, 2006).

Intentional Persuasion in News

What is a front-page box reminding voters of the countdown to election day if not an effort to persuade them to vote? What is the purpose of reporting on whether auto accidents involved alcohol or text messaging if not to change or reinforce attitudes toward traffic safety behavior or to place blame or identify the innocent? Still, the idea of justifying a powerful persuasive tool such as fear or disgust as a means to journalistic ends remains commonplace; it was how *Time* magazine explained its 2010 cover photo of a mutilated Afghan woman (Stengel, 2010). Such practices are worth mentioning precisely because they are so ordinary. They are no more unusual than the exclamation points that decorate headlines after a dramatic win by the home team.

Investigative journalism is important and clearly persuasive journalism, the type of journalism that is most often rewarded with national recognition and renown. The verbs alone make clear the importance that journalism places on its role as investigator. News organizations expose wrongdoing and "issue a compelling summons to participate in a moral universe" (Ettema & Glasser, p. 270). This crusading zeal is echoed in journalism textbooks. The days of the "muckrakers" are cited as evidence that "investigative reporting has a rich tradition in the history of American journalism" (Brooks et al., 1992, p. 422). A journalism of public service is one in which journalists "are revealing campaign finance abuses and the lax law enforcement of polluters and health care profiteers" (Mencher, 2000, p. xi). These are goals to which the rituals of objectivity can be applied, but they are realized through rhetorical practices that point directly to persuasive outcomes.

Analyzing News Stories Through a Persuasive Lens

A glance at any newspaper reveals the narrative loading and literary artistry that go into a news story. When an airline pilot landed his crippled airliner in the Hudson River with no loss of life in mid-2009, the *Los Angeles Times* celebrated with this headline and subhead:

> Pilot gets a hero's welcome on return home to California: US Airways' Capt. Chesley 'Sully' Sullenberger III is hailed by cheering Danville residents for his quick thinking and heroism in landing crippled jet on the Hudson River, saving 155 lives.
>
> (Dolan, 2009)

When a worker is denied compensation for illnesses he likely contracted while he spent "more than two decades up to his elbows in a drum of the solvent, trichloroethylene" the *New York Times* dramatizes the "hurdles" he faces in trying to get compensation (Barringer, 2009). When a foster parent makes a plea for an increased clothing allowance saying, "these [foster] children are in crisis," the journalist highlights a social problem, bringing it to the attention of larger publics (Ganey, 2009). When viewers of CBS Channel 5 in San Francisco were asked to put themselves in the place of a 90-year-old man who lost his life savings in the Madoff fraud, the reporter evoked pity, anger, and goodwill. The poignant story dramatically depicts a man who has been victimized, yet remains plucky and optimistic in going to work as a grocery store greeter. It depicts a business manager who generously offers an elderly man a job and gives him a day off and a chair from which to greet the public: "'This is not a, woe is me, kind of man,' said Barbara Laffer of Ben Lomond Market. 'This is a community coming together and helping each other out in times of need,'" (Do, 2009).

These are good stories, interesting and well told. The reporters created compelling narratives that are important to communities and even the nation, narratives that are replete with rhetorical devices. They celebrate our shared humanity and the accomplishments of special and worthy individuals. They are persuasive in promulgating worldviews and understandings that showcase what most of us believe are the best (and worst) of human beings and society. They are never neutral.

There is ample evidence that audiences are not averse to messages that come with a viewpoint. This is clear not just from the elements of real news that a viewer of Jon Stewart's "fake news" gets as part of the bargain. Detailed research from Spain (Barnhurst, 2000) suggests that two elements U.S. editors tend to consider unacceptable, a clear ideological line and a willingness to talk about the competition, are actually attractive to readers. While European press models have experienced some setbacks, they are, overall, far more robust than most American news organizations (CBS News, 2010).[4] We do not propose that journalists simply promote their own views and opinions. On the contrary—having an opinion is not in itself persuasive. Acknowledging that one does, indeed, have an opinion, offers transparency.

The Journalist on the Job

Journalism textbooks provide additional insights and show the contradictions of so-called objectivity. For example, an investigative reporter's job is not just to gather facts but also "to tell the reader what they add up to" and "satisfying readers' demands by going beyond exposure in search of solutions" (Brooks et al. 1992, p. 429). Rallying the public around a wrong that must be righted is clearly a persuasive function. It becomes even more so when a skeptical establishment must first be convinced that the wrong even exists, as in the Watergate case (Downie & Kaiser, 2002, p. 5). Others, however, suggest that the reporter's job is "to describe an action or situation rather than to examine it in a critical sense" (Agee, Ault, & Emery, 1983, p. 10). Textbooks contend not only that "the reporter must write objectively, scrupulously avoiding any expression of personal opinion" (Agee, et al., 1983, p. 10), but that "most journalists know they can get their points across much more effectively through careful reporting than through news slanting" (Ryan & Tankard, 1977, p. 162).

Textbook prescriptions for how journalism should use language struggle with the inherent contradictions of a discipline that is supposed to be objective but cannot be. "Loaded or emotion-charged words should not be used in journalistic writing as a substitute for creative thought" warns one text (Ryan & Tankard, 1977, p. 162). Writers should prefer "words that correspond to specific objects and identifiable feelings and ideas" rather than "vague terms" on the order of progress, freedom, or patriotism (Mencher, 2000, p. 172). At the same time, writers should "use vigorous action verbs and nouns" and to "seek originality in phraseology," since "apt figures of speech and clever turns of phrase give writing flair and zest" (Agee et al., 1983, p. 114). Analogies are particularly important: "With similes and metaphors, writers draw word pictures . . . . The techniques set the pages of a scrapbook of images turning" (Brooks et al., 1992, p. 91). Elsewhere, the same techniques raise concern: "Similes and metaphors can cause trouble because their use sometimes leads the reporter to inject his or her feelings into a piece" (Mencher, 2000, p. 58). Yet it is hard on any real semantic grounds to distinguish the example of an offensive simile offered here ("looking as though he would be more comfortable in a scarlet bowling shirt than in the business suit he wore") from the metaphors and analogies praised just as vigorously in other texts.

Many textbooks advise personalization because, for example: "Those to whom unemployment rates are meaningless may eagerly follow a story about the jobless as told through the eyes of a factory worker who was laid off because the company shut down rather than comply with anti-pollution standards" (Brooks et al., 1992, p. 380). Another author suggests that writers should "focus on a person to explain impact" (Rich, 2003, p. 412) and yet another advises that a "high-quality example, incident or anecdote . . . amplifies and humanizes the story theme" (Mencher, 2000, p. 170). While the prescriptions for writing compelling and accurate news stories show some contradictions, they clearly seek to create a product that will draw and hold audiences, just as advertisers do.

This emphasis on strong statements, combined with elements of news routines that emphasize the importance of explaining the impact of news on audiences, has produced concerns from the study of science coverage. The idea that journalistic language evenhandedly presents all sides of a controversy has been questioned and referred to as "false equivalency" (Garfield, 2013). For example, almost all credible scientists think that the evidence for human contributions to climate change is strong. Frequently, however, journalists show a curious—and from the perspective of this chapter, inappropriate— evenhandedness toward such issues. In earlier decades, "evenhanded" reporting about the health risks posed by tobacco did not provide public service when reporters sought out representatives from the industry and tobacco-producing states to provide a "balanced" view. News organizations also use strategies to increase their brand's identification and affiliation with audiences. These are very similar to the strategies sales people and advertisers use to establish common ground with customers.

First, journalists should accept that an accurate statement of where they stand on basic issues must provide the context of their news. Kennedy & Cameron

(2007) write that there is "bias built into the practice of journalism" (p. 14). They argue that journalists challenge the status quo, seek social change for the better, uncover and try to right injustices:

> This built-in bias lies in the very job description of journalism-to remain apart from the power structure, to question and when necessary challenge authority, to expose injustice and wrong-doing, and to protect the powerless from the powerful.
>
> (p. 14)

They go on to say that these types of activities are more likely to be labeled as "liberal" than "conservative."[5] The values of the journalist should be upfront and central in news vehicles, and this information needs to be repeated—both in general and within the context of individual stories. Given that many people already perceive biases, it is damaging to pretend they are not present.

Second, journalism is never a mirror of reality but always is a constellation of assumptions, values, and perceptions. News values are just that: human constructions and guides. An awareness of the persuasive implications of news work and news routines should not scare journalists away from doing their jobs. The intended effects of an investigative series are not invalidated because their routes of appeal are known. News writers who want to be understood should know how their audiences listen and read and, increasingly, why those audiences are dissatisfied with the product they are offered.

Our focus on the inevitability of persuasion in human communication sets the stage for the chapters that follow. The extended example examining journalistic practices sought to highlight that, despite the efforts of individuals and institutions, news organizations cannot achieve objectivity or avoid influence strategies. This underscores the importance of in-depth understanding of how persuasion works in today's increasingly diverse and dynamic communication environment.

Notes

1. Recent curriculum changes at Northwestern's Journalism School have begun to consider some aspects of audience development. However, our present argument about journalism curriculum is more extensive and substantively different from their initiatives. See "J-Schools play catch up" by Brian Steltzer, April 14, 2009. Available at http://www.nytimes.com/2009/04/19/education/edlife/journ-t.html
2. For a useful summary of studies of news-as-narrative, see *A Companion to Media Studies* (2005) by A.N. Valdivia.
3. Following are examples of the stated commitment of journalists and their organizations to neutrality and objectivity. The University of Wisconsin's Global Journalism ethics identifies its mission, in part, thusly:

   > Journalism should work against a narrow ethnocentrism or patriotism. What do these three imperatives imply for specific standards of journalism, such as objectivity? Under global journalism ethics, objectivity becomes the ideal of

informing impartially from an international stance. Objectivity in journalism has usually been understood as the duty to avoid bias toward groups within one's own country.

(Ward, 2010)

In day-to-day comments by journalists, the assumption of their own objectivity is common. The American Society of Newspaper Editors (ASNE) aggregates the codes of ethics and behaviors of many news organizations. Hearst's statement of professional principles states

> While we encourage all of our employees to be good public as well as private citizens, employees should avoid any active involvement in partisan politics. Employees should also avoid active involvement in community issues or organizations to the extent that their participation might cause the paper's objectivity to come into question.

Reuters advises its employees to be sure a "story is balanced, fair and neutral; watch for phrases that might suggest we are taking sides (e.g. 'fears' or 'hopes'). Be careful with words like 'claimed' and phrases such as 'according to' which suggest we doubt what is being said" (ASNE, 2010). On the Sept. 17, 2010 episode of the Bill Maher *Real Time* show, ABC senior foreign correspondent Martha Raddatz declined responding to a question about the motives of a conservative politician saying "I'm the objective reporter in the middle" (Maher, 2010). Similarly when network anchorman Charles Gibson retired, he was quoted saying "Objectivity is not universally in favor in our business these days, but it is critically important" Rosenthal (2009). The *Washington Post* issued a Twitter policy that said,

> When using these networks, nothing we do must call into question the impartiality of our news judgment. We never abandon the guidelines that govern the separation of news from opinion, the importance of fact and objectivity, the appropriate use of language and tone, and other hallmarks of our brand of journalism.

(Alexander, 2009)

4. While many factors are at work, European newspapers are far more robust in maintaining circulation and revenues, in part because of structural differences in revenue sources. Are newspapers dying? Not in Europe (2010). CBS News, June 14. Retrieved from http://www.cbsnews.com/stories/2010/06/14/business/main6581833.shtml.
5. It should not be assumed that this orientation produces "liberal" journalism; a crude shorthand summary of decades of work on news sociology and demographics, ownership patterns, and such theories as indexing, framing, and agenda setting would be that center-left journalists cover the activities of tenured political and economic elites for center-right ownership.

References

Agee. W. K., Ault, P. H., & Emery, E. (1983). *Reporting and Writing the News.* New York: Harper & Row.

Alexander, A. (2009). Post editor ends tweets as new guidelines are issued. *The Washington Post.* Retrieved July 9, 2014 from http://voices.washingtonpost.com/ombudsman-blog/2009/09/post_editor_ends_tweets_as_new.html

Anastasio, P. A., Rose, K. C., & Chapman, J. (1999). Can the media create public opinion? A social-identity approach. *Current Directions in Psychological Science*, 8(5) 152–55.

ASNE (2010). Ethics codes. Retrieved September 15, 2015 from http://asne.org/key_initiatives/ethics/ethics_codes.aspx

Barnhurst, K. G. (2000). Political engagement and the audience for news: Lessons from Spain. *Journalism & Communication Monographs*, 2.1.

Barringer, F. (2009). Exposed to solvent, worker faces hurdles. *New York Times*. Retrieved September 15, 2015 from http://www.nytimes.comI2009/01/25/us/25toxic.html.

Baskette, F. K., Sissors, J. Z., & Brooks, B. S. (2001). *The Art of Editing*. 7th ed. Boston: Allyn and Bacon.

Bormann, E. G. (1982). A fantasy theme analysis of the television coverage of the hostage release and the Reagan inaugural. *Quarterly Journal of Speech*, (68), 133–45.

Brooks, B. S., Kennedy, G., Moen, D. R., & Ranly, D. (1992). *News Reporting and Writing* (6th ed.). Boston: Bedford/St. Martin's.

Brooks, B. S., Kennedy, G., Moen, D. R., & Ranly, D. (2008). *News Reporting and Writing* (9th ed.). Boston: Bedford/St. Martin's.

Burke, K. (1969). *A Rhetoric of Motives*. Berkeley & Los Angeles: University of California Press.

Carey, J. W. (1989). A cultural approach to communication. In *Communications as Culture: Essays on Media and Society* (pp. 13–36). Boston, MA: Unwin Hyman.

CBS News (2010). Are newspapers dying? Not in Europe. CBS News. Retrieved June 14, 2010b from http://www.cbsnews.com/stories/2010/06/14/business/main6581833.shtml

Cheseboro, J. W. (1990). Computer science as rhetoric. In B. L. Brock, R. L. Scott, & J. W. Cheseboro (Eds.) *Methods of Rhetorical Criticism* (3rd ed.) (pp. 156–69). Detroit: Wayne State University Press.

Condit, C. M., & Selzer, J. A. (1985). The rhetoric of objectivity in the newspaper coverage of a murder trial. *Critical Studies in Mass Communication*, 2(3), 197–216.

Corporation for Public Broadcasting (2010). CPB's commitment to objectivity and balance. Retrieved September 15, 2015 from http://www.cpb.org/aboutcpb/goals/objectivity/

DeVreese, C. H. (2004). The effects of frames in political television news on issue interpretation and frame salience. *Journalism and Mass Communication Quarterly*, 81, 1, 36–52.

Do, K. (2009). Ben Lomond, Madoff Victim, 90, returns to work. CBS 5 News, San Francisco. Retrieved October 10, 2009 from http://cbs5.com/local/elderly.madoff.victim.2.929316.html

Dolan, M. (2009). Pilot gets a hero's welcome on return home to California. Retrieved September 15, 2015 from http://www.latimes.com/news llocallla-me-pilot25¬2009jan25.0.1469278.story.

Downie, L., & Kaiser, R. G. (2002). *The News About the News: American Journalism in Peril*. New York: Alfred A. Knopf.

Entman, R. (1991). Framing U. S. coverage of international news: Contrasts in narratives of the KAL and Iran air incidents. *Journal of Communication*, 41(4), 6–27.

Entman, R. M. (1993). Framing: Toward clarification of a fractured paradigm. *Journal of Communication*, 43(4), 51–8.

Entman, R. M. (2003). Projections of Power: Framing News, Public Opinion, and U.S. Foreign Policy. Studies in Communication, Media, and Public Opinion. Chicago: University of Chicago Press.

Ettema, J. S., & Glasser, T. L. (1990). Narrative form and moral force: The realization of innocence and guilt through investigative journalism. In B. L. Brock, R. L. Scott, & J. W. Cheseboro (Eds.) *Methods of Rhetorical Criticism* (3rd ed.) (pp. 256–72). Detroit: Wayne State University Press.

Fisher, W. (1990). The narrative paradigm: An elaboration. In B. L. Brock, R. L. Scott, & J. W. Cheseboro (Eds.) *Methods of Rhetorical Criticism* (pp. 234–255). Detroit: Wayne State University Press.

Ganey, T. (2009). Foster parent says state aid must increase: Higher allowance left out of budget. *Columbia Daily Tribune*. Retrieved March 24, 2009 from http://www.colum biatribune.com/news12009/mar123/foster-parent-says¬state-aid-must-increasel.

Garfield, B. (2013). False equivalence: How 'balance' makes the media dangerously dumb. *The Guardian,* Oct. 11. Retrieved September 15, 2015 from http://www.the guardian.com/commentisfree/2013/oct/11/false-equivalence-balance-media.

Goffman, E. (1974). *Frame Analysis: An Essay on the Organization of Experience.* New York, NY: Harper & Row.

Goshorn, K., & Gandy, O. H. (1995). Risk, race and responsibility: Editorial constraint in the framing of inequality. *Journal of Communication,* 45(2) 133–51.

Iyengar, S., & Kinder, D. R. *News That Matters.* Chicago, University of Chicago Press.

Kennedy, G., & Cameron, G. (2007). Americans and journalism: We value but criticize it. In G. Kennedy & D. Moen (Eds.) *What Good is Journalism?* (pp. 8–17). Columbia: University of Missouri Press.

Keum, H., Hillback, E. D., Rojas, H., De Zuniga, H. G., Shah, D., & McLeod, D. M. (2005). Personifying the radical: How news framing polarizes security concerns and tolerance judgments. *Human Communication Research,* 31(3), 337–64.

Larson, C. U. (1995). *Persuasion: Reception and Responsibility.* Belmont, CA: Walsworth Press.

Latham, S., & Laxson, T. (2006). Audience Perceptions of the *Objectivity* Norm. Paper presented at the annual meeting of the International Communication Association.

Maher, B. (2010). Real Time with Bill Maher. Retrieved September 17, 2010 from billmaher.com.

McCloskey, D. N. (1990). *If You're So Smart: The Narrative of Economic Expertise.* Chicago: University of Chicago Press.

Mencher, M. (2000). *News Reporting and Writing.* Boston: McGraw Hill.

Meyers, G. E. (2001). *William James: His Life and Thought.* New Haven: Yale University Press.

Nylund, M. (2003). Quoting in front-page journalism: Illustrating, evaluating and confirming the news. *Media, Culture & Society,* 25, 844–51.

Park, R. (1940). News as a form of knowledge: A chapter in the sociology of knowledge. *American Journal of Sociology.* July, 1939–May, 1940, 669–86.

Perloff, R. (2003). *The dynamics of Persuasion: Communication and Attitudes in the 21st Century.* Mahwah, NJ: Lawrence Erlbaum.

Price, V. (1989) Social identification and public opinion: Effects of communicating group conflict. *Public Opinion Quarterly,* 53, 197–224.

Reese, S. D. (2001). Framing public life: A bridging model for media research. In *Framing Public Life: Perspectives on Media and our Understanding of the Social World.* S. D. Reese, O. H. Gandy, & A. E. Grant (Eds). Mahweh, NJ: Lawrence Erlbaum Associates.

Rich, C. (2003). *Writing and Reporting news: A Coaching Method.* Belmont, CA: Wadsworth.

Rosenthal, P. (2009). ABC's Charles Gibson says farewell: "Objectivity is not universally in favor in our business these days, but it is critically important." *Chicago Tribune*. Retrieved December 19, 2009 from http://newsblogs.chicagotribune.com/tow erticker/2009/12/abcs-charles-gibson-says-farewell-objectivity-is-not-universally-in-favor-in-our-business-these-days.html

Ryan, M., & Tankard, J. W., Jr. (1977). *Basic News Reporting*. Palo Alto, CA: Mayfield.

Schudson, M. (1982). The politics of narrative form: The emergence of news conventions in print and television. *Daedulus*, 111(4), 97–112.

Smith, C. (1996) Reporters, news sources, and scientific intervention: The New Madrid earthquake prediction. *Public Understanding of Science*, 5, 205–216.

Steltzer, B. (2009). J-Schools play catch up. *The New York Times*, 14 April. Retrieved September 15, 2015 from http://www.nytimes.com/2009/04/19/education/edlife/journ-t.html

Stengel, R. (2010). The plight of Afghan women: A disturbing picture. Time.com. Retrieved July 29, 2010 from http://www.time.com/time/world/article/0,8599,2007 269,00.html

Tuchman, G. (1972). Objectivity as strategic ritual: An examination of newsmen's notions of objectivity. *American Journal of Sociology*, 77, 660–79.

Valdivia, A. N. (2005). *A Companion to Media Studies*. Malden, MA: Blackwell.

Vallone, R. P, Ross, L., & Lepper, M. R. (1985). *Journal of Personality and Social Psychology*, 49(3), 577–85.

Ward, S.J.A. (2004). *The invention of journalism ethics*. Montreal: McGill-Queen's University Press.

Ward, S.J.A. (2010). Global Journalism Ethics. Retrieved September 17, 2010 from http://www.journalismethics.ca/global_journalism_ethics/index.htm

Williams, W. (1908). The Journalist's Creed. Retrieved September 15, 2015 from http://journalism.missouri.edu/about/creed.html

3 Advertising Ethics

Applying Theory to Core Issues and
Defining Practical Excellence

Lee Wilkins

CHAPTER SUMMARY

This chapter, by a noted journalistic ethicist, starts with the declaration that advertising is essentially information, and therefore its ethical challenges are directly comparable to those of journalism. Note the consistency of this stance with Chapter 2's suggestion that all communication operates on a continuum of "persuasive intent." Wilkins then asks, why is "theory" about ethics so important to efforts toward professional persuasion ethics?

Application of utilitarianism demonstrates this importance, but the author argues that utilitarianism is not sufficient for developing a theory of ethical persuasion. Therefore, to some of the assumptions of utilitarianism, the author adds W. D. Ross's moral theory and feminist theory. The chapter closes with application of these two theories to the question of whether or not, and if so how, ethical professionals should design advertising for marijuana.

Introduction

This chapter is going to begin with a statement that will seem like gospel to advertising practitioners but may be accepted only grudgingly by journalists: advertising, like news, is information. This premise is important ethically for several reasons. First, if advertising is information, then assertions that the entire practice is unethical are unsustainable. Information is essential to human society and to individual well-being. Second, if advertising is information, then, just like news, both the message content and how advertising is "practiced" can become the focus of ethical thinking and subject to ethical evaluation. How such evaluation might be conducted is the focus of this chapter. Finally, and just as is the case with news, the impact of advertising on democratic societies can also be the subject of ethical analysis. That's where this chapter will conclude—with a discussion of why market language—the sort of language that the ubiquitous nature of advertising promotes—may not be the best way to describe and promote some sorts of human activity.

To make sense of the ethical questions surrounding advertising, it is important to understand the central issues for the profession and to unpack some philosophical theory that may help with thinking about them. Why ethical theory? Because if both news and advertising are information, then ethical standards by which we evaluate both are shared. There is not one set of ethical rules for scribes and another set for denizens of the market. There are common standards by which both activities can be judged and by which exceptional professional performances can be evaluated. Theory also promotes consistent decision making. It means that the standards that advertising practitioners employ on Monday are the same ones they use on Tuesday. Even seemingly novel issues—for example, the appropriate way to advertise weed (or marijuana)—find commonality with similar issues that practitioners have already reasoned through. And theory provides a systematic way to show us how these comparisons can be enlightening.

Advertising ethics—in the real world—has traditionally relied on one particular theory: utilitarianism. And it has sometimes applied that theory in a remarkably ham-handed way. Utilitarianism, crudely phrased, says that we will know what is good—what is ethical—if it does the greatest good for the greatest number of people. Advertising has taken that very rough summary and translated it into "advertising is good if it sells the most . . . gets the most votes . . . gets the most positive response for a brand . . . makes the most consumers feel better about their purchasing decisions." Right now—not six months or a year from now. Of course, this is utilitarianism wrongly applied. For one thing, the "greatest good for the greatest number" slogan ignores some of the most important things that John Stuart Mill (1859) and Jeremy Bentham (1789) wrote when they developed that theory. Mill articulated utilitarianism as the greatest good for the greatest number of people who live in a community. Maintaining that community was the central goal of Mill's work, which after all was a political treatise about democracy. Mill believed that people were connected, and hence he made the community itself a stakeholder in ethical decisions. Omitting community robs utilitarianism of much of its political power. The greatest good for the greatest number without considering community disconnects people from one another and from the shared results of their acts. This approach to utilitarianism also privileges short-term thinking. What's "good" right now is not necessarily "good' six months from now. Thinking about "the good" only in terms of the greatest number means that majorities can trump minorities, even when violating minority viewpoints and rights causes serious short-term and long-term harm to that minority—which of course is a part of that community. There is also another persistent question that utilitarianism has no ready answer for: If what I do causes great harm to just a few people (or institutions) and relatively modest good for many others, can the action truly be considered ethical? The greatest good for the greatest number conceptualization too often tends to reduce ethics to an oversimplified math problem.

It is not that utilitarianism is a "bad" ethical theory; it has great power and, in fact, is the central ethical justification for activities as varied as investigative reporting or placing grocery ads in the local newspaper. But relying on a

single ethical theory—and applying that theory poorly—leads to flawed decisions. So to encourage better thinking, this chapter will review two additional
theories and demonstrate how they also can be applied to some of the central
ethical questions in advertising.

Persistent Ethical Issues in Advertising

Advertising has been around for hundreds of years, and during that time, four
categories of issues have persisted (Patterson & Wilkins, 2013). Some of them
have provoked such significant public consternation and debate that they have
become the subject of government regulations. In the United States, those regulations are enforced at the federal level by agencies such as the Federal Trade
Commission and on rare instances have been the subject of U.S. Supreme
Court decisions. In Europe, many questions about advertising are regulated by
the European Union and its various policy-making bodies. Some governments,
for example China, retain a tight control on what may be advertised and how;
government in such countries is among the biggest advertisers. But in all these
instances, advertising is what theorists call an "instrumental" activity—it is a
means to an end, whether that is selling goods and services or molding public opinion and actions to conform to government decisions. The instrumental
nature of the advertising message also can make it particularly problematic
when messages that would be well understood as persuasive in one culture are
placed in a culture that understands them quite differently (Wilkins & Christians, 2001; also see Chapter 11). Within this global context, the following are
the persistent issues that advertising has raised for decades:

First, there is the set of issues that focus on whom should be the target of
advertising messages—advertising to vulnerable audiences—children, racial
and ethnic minorities, the elderly, and children in school. Vulnerability here
means that audience members do not have the knowledge or cognitive ability to logically evaluate the claims made in advertising. Keep in mind that
some kinds of knowledge are based in culture. All parents want their children
to be healthy and well fed—but that very human desire can mean something
quite different when baby formula is advertised in the United States (where
there are many competing messages about infant nutrition) and sub-Saharan
Africa (where poor women chose to abandon breast feeding because they were
malnourished themselves and did not grasp the long-term expense of infant
formula and having access to enough clean water to mix it properly). Or how
about the Detroit teens who stand in line for two or three days to buy the latest
pair of $500 Air Jordans when they and their families are underemployed and
struggling to pay bills? Here vulnerability is all about being a teenager, and the
ethical question is, do advertisers and marketers need to take special care when
targeting messages to these groups?

Second, there is a set of issues that cluster around what to advertise. These
questions have traditionally focused on "sin" products, such as hard liquor,
beer, or tobacco in its various forms. Prescription drugs are not considered a

"sin" product, but direct-to-consumer advertising of drugs raises the same set of issues. Advertising for these categories of products is among the most regulated in developed societies. And sometimes advertising for such products is the focus of self-censorship. Condom advertising, for example, although it has never been illegal, was very difficult to place until two events—the fragmentation of the media audience first through cable television and then through the Internet and the AIDS epidemic—made magazine editors and broadcasters rethink their decisions not to allow condom ads in their publications or on many television channels. In American culture, sex was the "sin." In other cultures, for example, the Scandinavian countries, condom advertising was much more readily accepted, because public health—not sin—was involved.

The third and largest set of ethical questions focus on the nature of advertising appeal itself. Advertisers often employ what is called creative vagueness as part of advertising campaigns. If advertising is information, then the vague claims made in ads should still be subject to standards of truth telling and verification. What is Nike claiming, for example, when its ads say "Just do it" or have the nonverbal claim embedded in the Nike swoosh? What does McDonald's mean when it says, "Give yourself a break today" as part of its ads? As the Nike example suggests, claims in an ad can be both visual and verbal. How consumers and those who produce ads evaluate the truthfulness of images is a sophisticated question requiring considerable thought (see Chapter 13 for further analysis of this question). Then there is the nature of the appeal. Sex sells, but is using sex or sexuality to sell a product such as life insurance ethical (also see Chapter 7 for elaboration of this question)? Should appeals stereotype their target markets—for example, portray the elderly as frail and weak—to sell a product (see Chapters 5 and 6)? Is it okay to be deceptive in an ad, for example, to put marbles at the bottom of a cereal bowl so the cereal itself floats to the top, looking delicious. (Hint: the Federal Trade Commission has ruled that this practice is illegal, a good indication that it is probably unethical as well.) And what about an ad camouflaged as entertainment in things like films and television shows. Do we really care that Superman eats Cheerios or that ET drinks Coors beer? How consumers interact and decode advertising messages probably represents the single biggest category of ethical problems the industry—and consumers—face.

Finally, there is the special nature of political advertising, particularly in democratic societies (see Chapter 8). Some, for example those in the United Kingdom, limit political advertising of any sort to within a few months of an election. Others, especially the United States, have opened the floodgates for political advertising. Campaign seasons can go on forever, and there are few limits in how much money can be raised and used in campaigns. One basic question surrounding political ads is whether candidates or political issues should be marketed in the same way, using the same techniques as selling consumer goods (e.g., see Thorson, Christ, & Caywood, 1991). A second set of questions emerges surrounding how to get candidates to be responsible and accountable for the claims made in their advertising—or advertising on their behalf—without restricting political speech. A third set of issues focuses on whether the money that it takes to buy the necessary advertising to get elected drowns out competing points of view, thus restricting the political speech of those who lack access to money raised in a variety of ways.

This common core of questions also raises questions about who we are as people and how it is that we flourish—the fundamental end of ethical thinking, decision making, and behavior. Ads tap not just our rational selves but also our emotions. Traditional ethical theory has assumed that people are completely rational, yet purchasing a specific kind of deodorant because you do not want to be a social outcast is not an entirely rational act. Thinking about advertising ethics requires that we think about who we are as humans. Advertising ethics also asks us to think deeply about what it means to flourish—which is how philosophers describe people who are living the best, most productive, joyful, and even loving life they can.

So in addition to utilitarianism, this chapter introduces two additional philosophical approaches and uses them to puzzle out some potential answers to the core issues that emerge when discussing advertising ethics. The first of these is what philosophers call a duty-based approach, and it will rely on 20th century philosopher W. D. Ross (1930) for application. The second is feminist philosophical theory, a theoretical approach that allows for discussion of emotion and connection, two of the qualities that advertising seeks to maximize and evoke. We look first at duty.

Multiple Duties: Balancing Client, Community, and Consumers

Philosopher William David Ross based his ethical theory on the notion that human beings shoulder duties that compete simultaneously for preeminence in ethical decision making. Ross's theory suggests (1930) that ethical thinking takes place within a tension between "the good" and "the right." Not coincidentally, that was the name of Ross's first book, and as contemporary philosopher Christopher Meyers (2003) notes, that title represents the tension that Ross tried to balance rather than resolve.

> Ross distinguished between the right and the good. The latter refers to an objective, if indefinable, quality present in all acts. It is something seen, not done. Rights, on the other hand, refer to actions. A right action is something undertaken by persons motivated by correct reasons and on careful reflection.
> (Meyers, 2003, p. 84)

Because there is always a tension between the good and the right, Ross's theory proposed six duties, three of which were labeled "prima facie duties" and three of which were labeled "duty proper," or the duties that arise from specific acts. These duties were affirmative—they were duties that we, as humans, should act to uphold. The seventh duty, and the only one that was not affirmative, was negative: Do no harm. The emphasis on affirmative duties—on requiring people to act in specific ways—also sets Ross's theory apart from many others in that the average person thinks of ethics as something that prohibits specific responses rather than encouraging them. For Ross, duty gains its moral weight not from consequences but from the highly personal nature of duty itself. For Ross, and for many other philosophers who emphasize duty as one way of thinking about ethics, duty arises from how individuals in specific circumstances choose to respond to—or fail to respond to—specific duties. Duty becomes personal when the individual responds to it in a specific situation, even though duty itself is broadly shared. For example, one of Ross's affirmative duties is fidelity: People can be faithful to each other (as in friendship or marriage) or faithful to an idea (as in truth telling) or faithful to an employer (doing your best on every account, even the ones that are not as much fun). How you choose to be faithful—and in what circumstances—is personal. But the duty—fidelity—is shared among people, regardless of specific circumstance.

Ross proposed the following duties. In professional life, the initial seven duties probably also imply two others.

1. Duties of fidelity that arise from making an implicit or explicit promise;
2. Duties of reparation, which arise from correcting a previous wrongful act;
3. Duties of gratitude, which rest on the previous acts of others;
4. Duties of justice, which arise from the necessity to ensure the equitable and meritorious distribution of pleasure and happiness;
5. Duties of beneficence, which rest on the fact that there are others in the world whose lot we can better;
6. Duties of self-improvement that rest on the fact that we can improve our own condition;
7. And the negative duty not to cause harm.

These seven duties imply two others, the duty of veracity or truthfulness, which can arise from the duty of fidelity, and the duty to nurture, which arises equally from the negative duty not to harm and the affirmative duty of beneficence.

Ross's concept of multiple duties works well for professionals who must often balance competing roles; for example, loyalty to a client that must be balanced with loyalty to an employer that must also be balanced with loyalty to the consumer. Ross's thinking about duty also allows those making ethical decisions to place community (the affirmative duty to promote justice) on an equal footing with self (the duty for self-improvement). Ross's thinking allows us to acknowledge that a specific set of circumstances, what philosophers call the morally relevant facts, demand an emphasis on a particular set of duties, while another set of circumstances might summon a different balance. The duties themselves do not change but how they are applied and balanced vary depending on the morally relevant facts.

Ross's conceptualization of duty, for example, allows advertising practitioners to think—and decide—differently about different categories of products or different kinds of appeals or even the different purposes to which advertising is put. For example, Ross's theory allows both practitioners and voters to make the claim that political advertising is a special case of persuasive information because it balances the duties of justice and beneficence in a way distinct from product advertising, which balances fidelity and self-improvement. Both kinds of advertising, however, must take into account the negative duty to cause no harm.

Ross's notions of fidelity and beneficence would suggest that the claims made in advertising should be true (you really can buy chicken for $1.99 per pound at the local grocery store), and there are others whose lot we can better by making this information widely known. However, an ad that stereotypes a certain group of people—for example, men who are portrayed as competent only in the workplace and not as parents or partners—does not meet either the duty of beneficence or self-improvement. Thus Ross's conceptualization of duty allows us to suggest that certain categories of advertising be treated differently than others, because they balance—or fail to balance—the multiple duties to which advertising professionals respond on a daily basis. Ross's theory also allows us to evaluate how products, services, and brands are advertised.

Thus the first set of issues that arise from advertising—advertising products and services to vulnerable audiences—can be evaluated by a thorough examination of which duties ads do and do not fulfill. The more vulnerable the audience—children; people who are disadvantaged by virtue of income, class, or caste; and those who are cognitively compromised or the focus of messages that do not account for cultural understanding and standards—the more all of Ross's duties will need to be balanced in the information provided. Buying a specific product should allow an individual to seek self-improvement, but it also should not harm other individuals, and it should consider justice within a community. Under Ross's test, international corporations would have to consider these distinct questions, and provide answers to them, as they initiate ad campaigns, think about target audiences, and develop ads themselves. Such an approach, for example, would probably have cautioned Nestle that advertising baby formula in Africa would be a potentially lethal move for the consumers it sought to attract. Thinking about advertising through the lens of duty gives professionals some powerful ways to persuade clients that just because a particular appeal will boost sales in the short run, it will not be in the client's best interest in the longer term.

Feminist Theory: The Ethics of Care

Duty is a way of thinking about ethics that has been around—in a formal, philosophical sense—for at least three hundred years. Feminist theory, on the other hand, is a 20th century insight, and it takes issue with some of the thinking that has dominated ethical theory for more than two thousand years.

Classical ethical theory asserts that ethical thinking can be derived from a set of principles. The principles are established first; the thinking and decision making come second. This is a top-down approach, and the emphasis is always on principles.

Feminist theory emerges differently. Feminist philosophers argue that ethical thinking begins in the "lived experience"; it is in the process of trying to live a flourishing life that ethical principles emerge. Principles come second, experience first. Thus feminist theory involves a bottom-up approach to doing ethics.

Carol Gilligan first articulated that bottom-up approach in her book *In a Different Voice* (1982), which began as an empirical study of how women make the decision to abort. Gilligan's interviews with these women, relationships that lasted in some cases for many weeks, suggested to Gillian that the women, instead of reasoning from principles, allowed their experiences to inform their decisions and that those decisions revolved around an ethics of connection. The experiences came first, before the "principle" that ethical decision making begins with a consideration of connection and care, which came second. Gilligan's later work, which explores why caring can be so difficult in contemporary society, is particularly critical of patriarchal thinking and organization. Relationships that are more equal in terms of power—whether that is in a corporation where there is a single boss and lots of "sub bosses" and then the workers, or whether it is advertising copyrighters who assume that they are smarter and cleverer than the consumers they want to reach—run afoul of this concept. Working in teams, among the most common organizational structures in strategic communication, and thinking about a commercial from the information receiver's point of view adopts some aspects of feminist philosophical approach, even though it may never have been labeled as such.

Gilligan's thinking was at once controversial and provocative. Other philosophers, among them Nel Noddings (1984), argued that care was not a virtue but the source of other virtues. Nussbaum (2000) pioneered the "human capabilities" approach to feminist ethics, in other words that the ethical choice was one that allowed all involved to flourish and to attain those capabilities—for example, free speech—without which our common humanity is diminished. Noddings's initial metaphor, that the ethics of care could be best understood by looking at the relationship between mother and infant, highlighted the caring approach that dominates some feminist thinking. Unfortunately, that metaphor shortchanged the "learning to be cared for" part of feminist ethics, which was every bit as essential (Nussbaum 2006). Maternal care, as all teenagers know, can sometimes be more oppressive than helpful—or at least it feels that way. A better metaphor for care is the role that both parents play during the teen years, when young people are becoming adults and testing, often in very uncomfortable ways, the limits of parental bonds and hence the boundaries of caring. Caring is now conceptualized as "everything we do directly to help others to meet their basic needs, develop or sustain their basic capabilities, and alleviate or avoid pain or suffering, in an attentive, responsive and respectful matter

(Engster, 2005, p. 55). This sort of caring is based on human beings' dependency on one another in community.

In some ways, caring may seem hostile to the entire strategic communication enterprise. After all, if strategic communication is about selling and persuading, then one reasonable inference is that care happens only at the swipe of a debit or credit card. But if adverting is conceptualized as information that is necessary for human flourishing, then feminist ethics can be exceptionally helpful. For example, feminist ethics encourages professionals—whether in strategic communication or news—to take their audiences and their communities seriously. That means thinking about the message from the audiences' point of view, both in the short and in the long run. It means thinking about how to help communities and promote strategic communication for enterprises such as nonprofit groups or foundations.

Feminist ethics also allows professionals to rethink how they create messages. An ethics of care, for example, would argue against advertising messages that stereotype or deceive, but it would encourage creative thinking as part of professional flourishing because it addresses the human capacity for free speech. An ethics of care promotes creativity and exploration as much as it says "don't do that"—too often how advertising professionals conceptualize the results of ethical thinking.

Feminist ethics also reminds practitioners that we care deeply about what we do. For the first two thousand years of writing about ethics, with some notable exceptions such as Hume (1739), emotion was considered an impediment to solid ethical thinking. But feminist ethics incorporates emotion into ethical thought, although it is a particular quality of emotion that is emphasized. Care, by its very nature, does not privilege one group or one approach over another. It encourages authenticity and condemns objectification and commodification—issues that conclude this chapter. But feminist ethics also provide a good analytic tool, and when combined with Ross's insights, it can help professionals make solid ethical decisions. It is to that effort that this chapter now turns.

Whether and How to Advertise Weed

If you did not quite understand what is meant by the concept that advertising arises within a culture, marijuana provides a good illustration. Getting high is hardly novel in human affairs—after all, the Greeks invented the term debauchery, but they did their debauching mostly with the aid of wine and beer. Other drugs also have been used for such purposes. But weed—what previous generations have referred to as marijuana or hemp—was initially used in the United States by African-Americans and was adopted by mainstream culture in the 1960s where it became the drug of choice for baby boomers (Weisman, 2014), particularly those boomers who called themselves hippies. Song lyrics touted the virtues of "Mary Jane," getting stoned included "smoking dope," and because of its association with marginal and countercultures, as well as its intoxicating effects, possessing, growing, and selling marijuana was criminalized. Internationally, Denmark took a much different approach with very different results. The Danish experience with decriminalizing drugs such as marijuana has been used as empirical evidence in policy debates regarding the same questions in the United States.

But in the United States during the 1960s—and in an example of how cultures grow and change—there was a small but vocal movement that favored legalizing the drug, arguing that its intoxicating effects were not more serious than those produced by alcohol (a legal drug providing you are not a minor), much less harmful to health than tobacco (also legal) or heroin (which was frequently placed in the same class of drugs as marijuana in criminal statutes). Proponents of legalization also noted that marijuana was the focus of selective enforcement (more people of color were arrested for marijuana violations than were Caucasians, even though many more Caucasians used the drug), and it might actually have health benefits (although in the 1960s there was no evidence to support this claim).

As the decades rolled forward, and the children of the '60s moved into positions of power and authority, having smoked dope in adolescence or young adulthood became more acceptable. Democratic presidents Bill Clinton and Barack Obama both admitted to smoking weed, although Clinton claimed he "never inhaled." Marijuana itself blossomed into a major contributor to an underground economy—a cash crop in geographic areas as distinct as California, Oregon, and southern Missouri. And actual research began to arrive: Marijuana was found to reduce the pain of cancer, sometimes when other drugs would not, and extracts of the plant (which did not produce a high for the average person) were prescribed for people with certain sorts of seizure disorders. Decades of experience as well as scientific studies began to provide evidence that marijuana could have medicinal impact. People for whom other forms of pain management failed to work found that often marijuana made their lives more bearable. At the same time, governments began to look for additional sources of revenue—alcohol and tobacco were already heavily taxed, why not weed? And, as younger generations know, the plant itself, which was the subject of genetic manipulation just as corn and wheat were, changed. In the 21st century, weed is stronger, more expensive, more profitable, and in many circles just as socially acceptable and sometimes as medically necessary as other drugs, including alcohol and tobacco. Plus, keeping all those people in prison for possessing or smoking small amounts of weed was getting very expensive. All these factors coalesced early in the second decade of the 21st century when first municipalities and then states began to legalize marijuana use—first for medical purposes—and then for recreation. By 2014, recreational marijuana was legal in two states, and as of this writing, it looks as if others will soon follow. Strategic communicators were confronted with a problem: What was an ethical approach to advertising weed?

Weed is the sort of product that spans three of the four traditional sets of ethical issues that confront strategic communication professionals. Weed is a "sin" product—or at least it used to be—and hence it raises initial questions of whether it should be advertised at all. Weed is also complicated, because it remains sinful in some governmental jurisdictions and among some subgroups of the population, while it is socially acceptable among others and even legal in some places. Advertising weed also raises the issue of vulnerable audiences. Like alcohol, what is the responsibility of the advertiser if children see—and respond to—weed promotions? Are people in great pain—from cancer or other diseases—capable of making the same sort of rational choices about weed as those who seek the drug for recreational purposes? Any ethical advertising appeal will have to consider harm as well as profit and enjoyment where vulnerable potential consumers are the focus. And weed certainly raises questions of what constitutes an ethically appropriate appeal. Portraits of all-out, weed-induced debauchery should probably be rejected, but what about weed appeals that parallel appeals for the highs provided by beer or by running? The weed advertising industry is truly in its infancy—how should it proceed in an ethical manner?

This is where theory comes in. Under Ross's conceptualization of duty, advertising weed would seem to be ethical within a limited framework. Certainly the product itself, if used for medical purposes, would fulfill the duty of beneficence. In some ways, weed advertising also could fulfill the duty of gratitude—it could repair the previous harm done by criminalizing the drug. Ross also would caution that weed advertising, just like advertising for other drugs, would need to account for doing no harm—any advertising would have to include the appropriate cautions just as direct-to-consumer advertising of drugs is required to. And some restrictions clearly would apply. Weed advertising, whether on Saturday mornings or imbedded as product placement in entertainment programming or as native advertising on the web, could inappropriately target vulnerable audiences (children) and thus fail to fulfill the affirmative duties of beneficence and nurture. Native advertising or product placement also involves significant levels of deception, thus failing to fulfill the affirmative duty of fidelity. Ross's theory suggests that advertising weed is, in and of itself, an ethical act providing that any such advertising campaign considers ways to protect vulnerable audiences and that the persuasive information itself balances the duty to do no harm with the duties of fidelity and beneficence. Creating such a campaign is entirely possible for competent professionals.

What might feminist ethics add? When constructing the advertising appeal, feminist ethics, because it arises from connection, would reinforce the notion of appropriate cautions, not just for the good of the individual but also for the good of the community. Feminist ethics also would suggest that medical marijuana, because it is an emotional issue for those who need the drug as well as those who oppose its use for this purpose, needs to be founded in rationality and evidence precisely because emotions are already at play. Feminists would suggest that one appropriate approach might be to advertise using the "real stories" of real consumers—advertising that arises from life. Such ads would rely less on slogans and catch phrases, and the visual information provided would need to be analyzed carefully. But personal stories—sometimes called testimonials—have a long and successful history in advertising, including some recent and nontraditional campaigns, such as the Dove Campaign for Real Beauty. Like that campaign, any ad developed under this theoretical approach would eschew commodification of the consumer and embrace the authenticity of the lived experience of those who have used the product. A feminist approach might go one step further, noting that the capabilities approach—encouraging free speech and adult flourishing—might suggest advertising practitioners consider whether they want to affirmatively seek to have weed advertising regulated in the same way that alcohol, tobacco, and prescription drugs currently are. The industry usually opposes such regulation; a collaboration with regulators in the specific instance of weed might allow the advertising industry to promote ethical practice thus forestalling what may be some "far out" demands by weed producers and distributors founded in utilitarianism where "the greatest good for the greatest number" is really translated as "do what looks the most profitable right now and just ignore both the subtle and long-term consequences.

Thus applying theory to this seemingly novel—if fun—problem actually results in some ways to go forward. Those insights allow for a thoughtful discussion of appeals that might work and even provide some guidance on ad buys and other forms of campaign planning that are currently essential elements of the business. These insights on how to proceed are every bit as important as the potential limitations that the theory also suggests. Perhaps the most important result of applying theory in this one specific instance is that it is consistent with best practices in the industry—a good place to start at the beginning of your career.

The Commodification of Life: The Ethical Limits of the Language of Sales

In 1831, Frenchman Alex De Tocqueville (2003) toured the eastern United States and wrote *Democracy in America*, which remains one of the most insightful discussions about the American democratic experiment ever written. In that book, De Tocqueville also examined what we have come to call the American character, and although much of what he said is laudatory, there were some uncomfortable insights. One of those focused on money and wealth. In a political culture that prided itself on economic egalitarianism, De Tocqueville said that Americans ran the risk of confusing—even substituting—money for excellence. He worried that the acquisition of great wealth would become a pernicious equivalent for everything from intellectual and creative achievement to an ethical character and a flourishing life.

Fast forward to this century and you have to wonder what sort of crystal ball De Tocqueville actually was gazing into. In our everyday conversations, we ask what relationships—as fundamental as lifelong partnerships—are "worth." We "incentivize" everything, from participating in public opinion polls to being a "loyal" customer at the grocery store, the department store, and the airline you fly most frequently. In many places, it is possible to pay people to stand in line for you. At Disney World, it's possible to pay a higher ticket price and move right to the front of the line. We say "money talks." We expect many social and cultural institutions—from public schools and universities to our prisons and even the military—to be "run like a business." In 2014, only two U.S. Senators were not millionaires in terms of net worth. And when it came to going to college, the higher the tuition, the more elite the student body, regardless of efforts to recruit a diversity of students to campus or the enormous endowments that elite universities cultivate. We monetize Facebook and our friendships—there's even an app called Klout that uses an algorithm to determine the quality of your "followers," and if your Klout score moves above 50, corporations want to "give" you stuff—providing you will post about it.

What is wrong with all of this? Who gets hurt if you pay someone—particularly a homeless person—to stand in line for you so you'll get a seat for a Congressional debate while being able to continue with your daily activities? What is so unacceptable about getting free stuff because you are popular in the Twitterverse?

A lot, says political philosopher Michael Sandel who in his 2012 book *What Money Can't Buy: The Moral Limits of Markets* argues that economic language has not only crowded out moral thinking but also sometimes changes our conception of what it means to have a good life. Whether it is paying kids to get good grades, selling everything from blood to kidneys, or celebrities getting millions from news organizations for exclusive rights to wedding or newborn photos, Sandel argues that there are places in life where the market simply does not belong. Sandel is hardly the first. The Protestant Reformation occurred in part because the Roman Catholic Church had monetized forgiveness, even though the Christian god and beneficence could not be bought.

Sandel notes two basic objections to the idea that everything can be commerce. The first is the notion of fairness and is illustrated by jumping a line—even if you pay for the privilege. Paying for the privilege of "coming first" is coercive, both for the people who pay and for those who cannot afford it. And for those who cannot afford it, there is no way to change such a system in which they have become unwilling participants. Being coerced in this way is a small but fundamental assault on individual autonomy, a necessary element of human capabilities as defined by feminist ethics and a foundational component of praiseworthy ethical decision making. Those who are coerced are not ethically responsible; just as important, they are often angry at the unwilling substitution of one person's judgment and acts for their own.

The second objection is that "marketizing" everything leads to corruption. People tend to think "things" can be bought, not just goods and services but the intangibles of life. The market tends to look at everything through the lens of scarcity and that includes traits such as generosity, solidarity, and civic duty. But there is empirical evidence that attempts to substitute the market for such human qualities is ineffective. Students who were offered a monetary incentive to raise money for a charity raised less money than those who were not paid.

Citizens in a Swiss community volunteered to become the locus of a nuclear waste repository, but when presented with the same choice plus an economic inducement, they turned it down. Sandel argues that when the language of the market is substituted for the language of ethics, our conceptualization of the good life itself becomes degraded. People become separated into those who have money and the things it can buy and those who do not. Further, those who have money may confuse their positive net worth with their own individual virtues and capabilities, which is precisely what De Tocqueville feared.

Sandel ends his book with the following: "The disappearance of the class-mixing experience once found at the ballpark represents a loss not only for those looking up but also for those looking down. Something similar has been happening throughout society. At a time of rising inequality, the marketing of everything means that people of affluence and people of modest means lead increasingly separate lives . . . Democracy does not require perfect equality, but it does require that citizens share in a common life . . . For this is how we learn to negotiate and abide our common differences, and how we come to care of the common good" (Sandel, 2012, p. 203).

At the beginning of this chapter, advertising was equated with information, something that we need to flourish in daily life. Information is instrumental—it is something human beings use to achieve important ends. Making everything about the market, and particularly about selling, privileges one category of ends, material well-being, for other kinds of ends—often those that are expressed in the language of connection. Perhaps as pernicious, the language of the market pretends to tell us—despite our authentic individual experiences—that connection, too, can be achieved through material success or, in some cases, actually bought. The art of professional practice is knowing the distinction and not confounding the ends toward which the language of the market can be employed. A truly ethically excellent ad—or campaign—is characterized by providing consumers with the right reasons for doing something to promote worthy ethical ends, including the duty of self-improvement. Advertising that achieves this standard will not only sell, it will remind consumers that the information that advertising provides is one component of human flourishing in the 21st century.

References

Bentham, J. (1789). An introduction to the principles of morals and legislation. In A. De Tocqueville (Ed.) 2003/1834. *Democracy in America*. New York: Penguin.

Engster, D. (2005). Rethinking care theory: The practice of caring and the obligation to care. *Hypatha*, 20(3), 50–74.

Gilligan, C. (1982). *In a Different Voice: Psychological Theory and Women's Development*. Cambridge, MA: Harvard University Press.

Hume, D. (1739/1977). *A Treatise of Human Nature*. Oxford: Oxford University Press.

Meyers, C. (2003). Appreciating W.D. Ross: On duties and consequences. *Journal of Mass Media Ethics*, 18(2), 81–97.

Mill, J. S. (1859). *On Liberty*. London: J. W. Parker.

Noddings, N. (1984). *Caring: A Feminine Approach to Ethics and Moral Education*. Berkeley: University of California Press.

Nussbaum, M. (2000). *Women and Human Development: The Capabilities Approach*. Cambridge: Cambridge University Press.

Nussbaum, M. C. (2006). *Frontiers of Justice*. Cambridge, MA.: Harvard University Press.

Patterson, P., & Wilkins, L. (2013). *Media Ethics: Issues and Cases* 8th ed. New York: McGraw Hill, pp. v–328.

Ross, W. D. (1930). *The Right and the Good*. Oxford, England: Clarendon Press.

Sandel, M. (2012). *What Money Can't Buy*. New York: Macmillan.

Thorson, E., Christ, W. G., & Caywood, C. (1991). Selling candidates like tubes of toothpaste: Is the comparison apt? In F. Biocca (Ed.), *Television and Political Advertising: Vol. 1 Psychological Processes*. Hillsdale, NJ: Lawrence Erlbaum.

Weisman, R. (2014, April 13). Are baby boomers ready to give marijuana a second change? *Boston Globe*. Retrieved September 15, 2015 from https://www.bostonglobe.com/business/2014/04/12/baby-boomers-who-moved-may-ready-give-marijuana-second-chance/8UcflcGP1dKkanaLuX6wOM/story.html

Wilkins, L., & Christians, C. (2001). Philosophy meets the social sciences: The nature of humanity in the public arena. *Journal of Mass Media Ethics*, 16(2, 3), 99–120.

4 Organizational Crossroads

The Intersection of PR and Advertising Ethics

Marlene Neill and Erin Schauster

CHAPTER SUMMARY

The roots of advertising and public relations are intertwined both historically and in contemporary practice. In fact, with the rise of integrated marketing communication (IMC) that suggests campaigns and programs should be coordinated using a range of tools depending on the target audience and the campaign goals, linkages are even more apparent. Frequently, a campaign will use both PR and advertising techniques to accomplish goals. Technology and increased complexity add to the challenges firms and individuals face when establishing ethical guidelines and norms.

Crucial factors in an organizations' ethical performance involve its culture and climate including behavioral expectations, role models, and historical anecdotes that give people frameworks for decision making. In addition, an agency's stated policies and procedures establish and define ethical behaviors. Many firms have formal training programs to emphasize their values and mission. In PR, many practitioners see themselves as the conscience of the organization, counseling senior management on ethical decisions and explaining the potential consequences for inappropriate actions. Practitioners are often also leaders in "employer branding" in which a company communicates to employees about its values and why it's a good place to work.

Advertising has long been criticized for being intrusive and ubiquitous, invading privacy, using sexual appeals and stereotypes to sell, and targeting vulnerable audiences. While some of these charges are certainly accurate, firms and industry associations make strong efforts to regulate themselves and give members tools for ethical decision making. For both advertising and public relations, trends in technology and social media are transforming practice and the way brands communicate with customers and stakeholders. And for both, strategies for improving ethical awareness and behavior are similar. They require education, role models, clear core values, and the genuine commitment of top management to hew to these values.

Introduction

Advertising and public relations share a common history in the field of mass communication. The ethical foundations of journalism on which the mass communication industry is based include values such as objectivity, truth, and fairness (Barney & Black, 1994; McBride, 1989). Unlike journalists, however, advertising and public relations practitioners are not only focused on distributing information to inform their audiences but also assume the responsibility of persuading them in order to achieve objectives for their organizations or clients. The nature of their jobs opens the potential for ethical dilemmas, because advertising and public relations practitioners have loyalties to their employers and clients, and they also need the trust of the public to perform their jobs effectively. Almost all discussion of ethics examines public relations and advertising as markedly different disciplines. However, in today's world of integrated marketing communication, as well as marketing communications (marcom), traditional roles and activities are increasingly overlapping and often synergistic. This chapter identifies the similarities and differences of ethical considerations in theory and practice.

Role Conceptions and Moral Justifications

Bivins (2004) applied moral philosopher William Davis Ross' prima facie duties to persuasive communications associated with both advertising and public relations. Bivins (2004) suggested that some of the conflicting loyalties someone working in these industries may face include duties of fidelity in respect to honoring a contract; fidelity to the profession by adhering to ethical standards, justice, and noninjury to people who may be impacted by the organization's decisions; and fidelity to those they are communicating with by telling the truth. As further support, Fitzpatrick and Gauthier (2001) suggested that professionals have obligations beyond profitability and that "responsibility to the public must be balanced with responsibility to a client or employer" (p. 203).

The degree of ethical conflict that persuasive communicators perceive is based in part on their role conceptions and use of moral justifications. Baker (1999) suggested there are five moral justifications that advertising and public relations practitioners can use to support their decisions in persuasive communications. At the lowest level is self-interest, which Baker (1999) described as looking "out for number one" (p. 71). At the next level is entitlement, which includes a focus on legal rights, such as the First Amendment and a perception that if something is legal, it is ethical. The entitlement justification may involve an advocacy role perspective similar to a lawyer who suggests the role of a communicator is to represent the client even in situations when personal values may conflict (Baker, 1999). Scholars have found this client-centric perspective in both public relations and advertising, with practitioners perceiving their roles as an advocate for the client even when the work involves compromising their own ethical values (Bowen, 2008; Drumwright & Murphy, 2004). Drumwright and Murphy (2004) found evidence that some advertisers based their decisions solely on what was legal by relying heavily on the First Amendment. Bowen (2008) similarly found that public relations practitioners said ethics analysis was not necessary if their organizations followed the law, and they perceived ethical issues as best addressed by the legal department. Fitzpatrick and Gauthier (2001) pointed out the weakness of the attorney-adversary model is that "in the court of public opinion, there is no guarantee that all interested parties will be represented or heard," (p. 197); but in the judicial courts, the assumption is that all parties will be well represented and the truth will emerge.

At a higher moral level is enlightened self-interest, which is based on the assumption that ethical behavior is good for business (Baker, 1999). At this level, philanthropy and good environmental practices are enacted to increase profitability and avoid government regulations. At the highest levels are social responsibility and kingdom of ends, which focus on obligations to society and moral ideals (Baker, 1999). Consistent with these perspectives, scholars have found some advertising and public relations practitioners who view their role as a strategic adviser rather than simply an advocate for their clients (Bowen, 2008; Drumwright & Murphy, 2004; Neill & Drumwright, 2012). This strategic role involves asking tough questions and anticipating potential consequences of actions, a role some senior practitioners described as the opposite of a "yes man" or woman (Neill & Drumwright, 2012). Fitzpatrick and Gauthier (2001) suggested that persuasive communicators' greatest loyalty is to their clients, but practitioners should ensure that their employers hear and consider stakeholders' interests and make efforts to minimize harm. Neill and Drumwright (2012) found evidence of this "dual loyalty—to their employers on the one hand and to the public interest on the other" which "was a mandatory professional obligation" (p. 224).

Baker and Martinson suggested that "advertisers and public relations practitioners act unethically if they utilize methods intended to manipulate, exploit, or both, listeners and persuadees [rather] than to respect them" (2001, p. 158). In juxtaposition to Baker's moral justifications for practitioners' moral reasoning, Baker's and Martinson's TARES test evaluates the ethics of a message. Using this model, practitioners evaluate persuasive messaging based on five principles, including truthfulness of the message, authenticity and sincerity of the persuader, respect for the one being persuaded, equity of the appeal, and social responsibility (Baker & Martinson, 2001). The TARES test has assessed the message ethics of fast food ads (Lee & Nguyen, 2013) and anti-smoking ads (Lee & Cheng, 2010). Lee and Cheng (2010) found that the source of the ad (e.g., CDC vs. other), thematic frame (e.g., smoking is health related), appeal (e.g., humor), and target audience influenced the ethicality of the message in addition to the five principles proposed by Baker and Martinson. Patterson and Wilkins (2011) noted the importance of sincerity and disclosure when evaluating the authenticity of a persuasive message. For example, practitioners can apply the TARES test to evaluate the authenticity of "ghost blogging" since the actual author is not the person listed in the blog's byline (Gallicano, Cho, & Bivins, 2014). Equity has been conceptualized as a "level playing field" between receiver and sender (Patterson & Wilkins, 2011). A practitioner might ask, does the receiver need to be well informed to interpret the ad accurately? Finally, Patterson and Wilkins (2011) suggested practitioners apply the principle of social responsibility to evaluate the consequences of using the product advertised. A practitioner would ask, is the product harmful or helpful to society if everyone were to use it?

Organizational Factors Impacting Ethical Decision Making

Scholars suggested advertising and public relations practitioners often find that their employers can either support or hinder ethical decision making based on the organization's climate, culture, policies, and procedures (Bowen, 2004; Drumwright, 2007; Neill & Drumwright, 2012; Neill, in press). Across marcom industries, PR and advertising professionals learn to use similar resources for completing their work, and their tasks tend to look similar. However, each organization has a unique culture based upon shared assumptions of how work is done (Keyton, 2005). Organizational culture is deeply held and shared, giving employees a frame of reference through beliefs, values, and expressive symbols (Alvesson, 2002). Schein (2010) argues that the beliefs, values, and assumptions of leadership, or the founder(s) of an organization, play a crucial role in sourcing organizational culture. Furthermore, culture defines an "agency's style, sense of values, ethical principles, atmosphere, and standing in the business community, as well as the (stated or unstated) norms of behavior that an agency expects of its employees" (Jones, 1999, p. 135).

Organizational culture's influence on ethical issues is dynamic and changing. Situational influences exerted by an organization and by the organizational environment can simultaneously shape and are shaped by its employees (Donnelly, 1995; Huff, Barnard & Frey, 2008; Schauster, in press). Ethical climate refers to dimensions such as behavioral norms, role models, and historical anecdotes, such as times when the company chose to do the right thing, even at a high cost (Cohen, 1993). An advertising agency, for example, resigned one of its largest accounts when the client asked the agency to do something that the CEO believed was unethical (Drumwright & Murphy, 2004). Another account of an ethical role model involved a senior officer at an energy company publicly apologizing at a news conference following an explosion, which several employees retold as evidence that their company was committed to doing the right thing and empowered them to raise ethical concerns (Neill, 2012).

Organizational culture can impact advertising and public relations executives' ethical decision-making power. Companies and organizations characteristic of McGregor's Theory Y (participatory) management style use decentralized management, allow for autonomy in decision making, and use cross-departmental teams to solve problems, (Bowen, 2004; Redmond & Trager, 1998). Participatory management, therefore, empowers public relations and advertising practitioners to serve as strategic advisers. In contrast, Theory X (authoritarian) management has been described as the "command and control approach," suggesting that employees need to be "coerced, controlled, directed, threatened with punishment" in order to achieve company objectives (Redmond & Trager, 1998, p. 43). The authoritarian leadership style involves a top-down decision-making and power-distance relationship between leadership and subordinates

(Bowen, 2004; Redmond & Trager, 1998). In addition, formal authority and hierarchical standing are preferred over expertise when determining committee or leadership teams (Bunderson, 2003), so if advertising and public relations practitioners are positioned lower in the hierarchy, they have less opportunity to provide strategic counsel. As further support, Ryan (1987) identified four organizational constraints that could prevent public relations managers from providing ethics counsel, including lack of access to management; the limited collection of information through budget constraints; barriers to dissemination of timely, accurate information; and perceptions that limit public relations to a more technical role or publicity model.

Organizational policies and procedures also impact ethical decision making. Vidaver-Cohen (1997) suggested that organizations can encourage ethical behavior by focusing on long-term rather than short-term goals, offering training in role taking and ethical decision making, offering rewards for morally imaginative decisions and imposing sanctions for unethical decisions. In a study of an ethically exemplar organization, Bowen (2004) identified the following characteristics as essential: an ethics statement, ethics training materials, and employee training programs emphasizing the organization's values and mission. Consistent with those recommendations, Neill (2015) found evidence that employers were using the following resources to promote ethics: a code of conduct, storytelling, reward systems in the form of annual award programs, ethics hotlines, and an ombudsperson.

The Intersection of Public Relations and Advertising Ethics

Both the public relations and advertising industries have taken proactive actions in support of ethical communication. The Public Relations Society of America (PRSA) and International Association of Business Communicators (IABC) offer members accreditation programs, and ethics comprises 15 to 20% of the questions on the accreditation exams (Wilcox & Cameron, 2012). Both PRSA and the IABC have established codes of ethics for their members that encourage truthful, accurate communication and avoiding deceptive practices. PRSA also recognizes the month of September as ethics month each year and encourages its chapters to offer professional development programming focused on ethics.

In 2010, the American Advertising Federation (AAF) established the Institute for Advertising Ethics (IAE) in partnership with the Reynolds Journalism Institute (RJI) and the Missouri School of Journalism to focus on advertising ethics research and education. The IAE established eight principles and practices for advertising ethics, which address issues of truth, disclosure, fairness, and consumer privacy (Neff, 2011). The IAE begins with the premise that self-regulation, spearheaded by industry leaders, is the best option for complying with ethical standards (Neff, 2010). The American Association of Advertising Agencies (4A's), a national trade association founded in 1917, adopted "Standards of Practice" based upon the belief that "sound and ethical practice is good business" ("Standards of Practice of the 4A's," 4A's,1924). The 4A's Standards of Practice outline five creative codes: do not knowingly create 1) false or misleading messages, 2) false testimonials, 3) misleading price claims, 4) distorted professional or scientific claims, or 5) offensive statements or images. Above all, the standards hold advertising agencies responsible and accountable to their clients, the public, media, and each other.

Issues in Public Relations

There are many definitions of public relations in part because it can involve so many different goals and processes, including issues management, crisis communication, publicity, and philanthropy. Wilcox and Cameron (2009) offer this definition:

> Public relations is "the strategic management of competition and conflict for the benefit of one's own organization—and when possible—also for the mutual benefit of the organization and its various stakeholders or publics.
>
> (Wilcox and Cameron, 2009)

This definition acknowledges the practitioner's role as an advocate for her organization or client but also acknowledges that establishing positive relationships and programs that also benefit publics is important. A key role for practitioners in well-managed firms is serving as a counselor and adviser for top management and various divisions of the organization.

Rooted in the perception of public relations practitioners as strategic advisers is the expectation of practitioners serving as an ethical conscience. For decades, industry leaders and scholars have called for public relations professionals to serve as the consciences of their organizations and provide ethics counsel to senior management (e.g., Bowen, 2008; Ryan & Martinson, 1983). During a speech, then PRSA president John Paluszek (1989) urged public relations professionals to serve as the consciences of their organizations adding "if not us, who? If not now, when?" (p. 750)

Public Relations' Role as Ethical Conscience

Scholars have found varied acceptance among public relations practitioners regarding the role of ethical conscience. Based on a multinational study, Bowen (2008) reported "a pronounced state of neglect" among public relations professionals "in areas related to ethical understanding, ethics counsel, and the ability to enact the role of ethical counsel" (p. 271–72). At the same time, Bowen (2008) found that some PR professionals do indeed provide ethics counsel and assume the role of ethical conscience. Neill and Drumwright (2012) found support for the role of ethical conscience among more senior-level practitioners. Regarding motives for providing ethics counsel, the authors found that due to public relations practitioners' roles as spokespersons, the voice and face of the organization, practitioners perceived that their personal reputations were on the line, which served as motivation for ethical communication (Neill & Drumwright, 2012). As one participant said,

> I can't afford to lose my credibility . . . As PR professionals, it's all we have. And if I lose my credibility here, it's not like [I] can just go start over with someone else, somewhere else. Credibility is something that you can't afford to lose.
>
> (Neill & Drumwright, 2012, p. 225)

The role of ethical conscience was also associated with public relations' reputation management or issues management role, which involves predicting potential problems, anticipating threats to the organization, minimizing surprises, resolving any issues that do arise, and preventing crises (Wilcox & Cameron, 2012). As one practitioner said,

> I find myself being the one that is raising the alarm about simple things that might have consequences either down the road or immediately. I have to quickly pull things together to figure that out.
>
> (Neill & Drumwright, 2012, p. 226)

Much of the ethics counsel practitioners discussed involved communication issues such as disclosure and addressed questions such as: What do you say, when do you say it, do you not say it, or do you hold it back? However, Neill and Drumwright (2012) found public relations practitioners:

> provided ethics counsel on issues that extended far beyond communication and traditional public relations responsibilities to include general management and strategic issues—issues of financial transparency, faulty product design, security breaches and human resource issues related to inappropriate sexual conduct.
>
> (p. 224)

Public relations practitioners also provided insight into the creative approaches they used to raise ethical concerns to senior management. Some of the techniques included staging a mock news conference, using "the headline test" (envisioning the best and worst potential newspaper headline reporting the action), providing viable alternatives, and assuming the role of a devil's advocate (Neill & Drumwright, 2012).

Public Relations' Role in Values Communication

Public relations practitioners also are being called upon to reinforce their employers' values in routine communication through a new trend called "employer branding," which involves "a company's efforts to communicate to existing and prospective staff that it is a desirable place to work" (Lloyd, 2002, p. 64). The efforts often focus on experiential benefits such as education and training opportunities, advancement potential, and culture (Moroko & Uncles, 2008). Employer branding relates to another trend in internal communications, which is employee engagement. Through employer branding programs, companies and organizations hope to improve employee engagement defined as "the ability to capture the heads, hearts, and souls of your employees to instill an intrinsic desire and passion for excellence" (Fleming & Asplund, 2007, p. 2). Engagement focuses on motivating the "discretionary effort exhibited by employees," (Saks, 2006, p. 601) or the willingness to go beyond the minimal efforts required to keep a job. Scholars suggested that internal communications could influence employee engagement, specifically communication about the values and goals of the organization (Welch, 2011)

In a recent study involving in-depth interviews with 32 executives working in 26 companies and organizations, Neill (2015) found that practitioners often included company/organizational values in routine communication and even scheduled content regarding values as part of their editorial calendar. Leading companies, those listed among the best places to work, also tied their values to their annual awards program, recognizing employees who exemplified their core values. One of the practitioners, an external communications consultant, warned about the distinction between aspirational and core values (Lencioni, 2002):

> It would be nice if we could be brought in earlier with the values discussion because . . . some of them have way too many, and then some of them have aspirational values; they're not core . . . and so there's a little bit of an eye roll even with what's listed as their values.
>
> (Neill, 2015, p. 14)

Lencioni (2002) defined aspirational values as those a company needs for the future but currently lacks, while core values are deeply ingrained and consistently guide a company's actions. Some of the more common approaches for communicating core values are employee testimonials and videos about the history of the company/organization. It should be noted that while public relations practitioners are often charged with reinforcing core values through routine communication, human resources executives are often responsible for initially introducing those values in recruitment messages and new employee orientation (Neill, 2015).

Issues in Advertising

Advertising ethics is the determination of what is right or good in advertising, defined as the paid placement of persuasive messages (Cunningham, 1999). Advertising ethics identifies processes for decision making when moral values conflict (Patterson & Wilkins, 2008) and when legality is insufficient for making judgments (Preston, 2010). Special issues in academic journals have been dedicated to the topic of advertising ethics (e.g., *Journal of Business Ethics* 48(3); *Journal of Advertising* 23(3)), as well as books and book chapters (e.g., Bishop, 1949; Bonifield & Cole, 2007; Drumwright, 2007; O'Guinn, 2007; Patterson & Wilkins, 2008; Wilkie & Moore, 2007). Ethical problems change as the industry changes. From January 1987 to June 1993, advertising ethics scholarship focused on the four topics of healthcare advertising, tobacco and alcohol advertising, the professional services of advertising, and advertising agencies (Hyman, Tansey, & Clark, 1994). More recently, authors suggested that new issues related to transparency and privacy have emerged due to new technology and new, nontraditional media (Drumwright & Murphy, 2009).

Advertising has been criticized for being intrusive and inescapable while reinforcing materialism (Pollay, 1986). Advertising practitioners are criticized for creating dishonest and misleading messages, targeting vulnerable segments, using sexual appeals and stereotypes to persuade audiences, and promoting the use of harmful products. These ethical problems are categorized as business ethics, which relate to the day-to-day operations in an agency and the issues practitioners face (Drumwright & Murphy, 2009). Ethical problems practitioners have reported facing include creating honest and effective ads and treating clients, employees, and other agencies fairly (Hunt & Chonko, 1987). In part, these problems are due to the multiple players involved in the practices of advertising (Patterson & Wilkins, 2008). Beyond agency practitioners, media and client representatives are also involved in the creation of persuasive messages. Today, large global networks contribute to the multitude-of-players complexity. Murphy (1998) contended that there are so many players involved in the advertising function that no one industry (i.e., media, client, agency) takes responsibility over questionable practices.

Ethical problems in advertising are also categorized as message ethics, which are concerned with the advertisement, including the creation and delivery of the ad (Drumwright & Murphy, 2009). Truth and deception are ongoing problems in advertising (Cunningham, 1999; Drumwright, 2007; O'Barr; 2007; O'Guinn, Allen, & Semenik, 2009). Truth in advertising refers to being sincere in action and utterance and avoiding deception (Baker & Martinson, 2001). Not providing full disclosure of a product's attributes, using ambiguous phrases that mislead audiences, and disguising advertisements as news are examples of deception (O'Barr, 2007). Regarding the latter, some advertisements are intentionally disguised. Native advertising, also known as advertorials or branded content, is paid content designed and written to match the editorial standards of a printed or digital publication. In 2013, 73% of online publishers offered native advertising (Marvin, 2013). When readers of Copyblogger (mostly marketers) were asked about their feelings toward native advertising, 51% of 2,088 respondents said they were "skeptical" yet 61% said native advertising does not deceive audiences (Marvin, 2014).

The law continues to change in an effort to adapt to new methods of advertising and to protect consumers against deception (Richards & Petty, 2007). Recently the Truth in Advertising bill, which regulates Photoshopping of beauty images, has been under consideration by Congress. Advocates of the bill purport that unrealistic depictions of the human body in the media result in eating disorders and that Photoshopped images are both deceptive and damaging (Dumenco, 2014). Along with the many potential opportunities for deception in advertising comes distrust for advertising practitioners. On a scale of trustworthy professionals, consumers have ranked advertising practitioners third to last, just above car salesmen and telemarketers (O'Barr, 2006).

Advertising is also criticized for intentionally reaching vulnerable audiences. Bonifield and Cole (2007) suggested that consumers become vulnerable due to conditions beyond their control, which are those related to physical, cognitive, motivational, or social characteristics. Vulnerable segments include older adults, children, and teenagers (Bonifield & Cole, 2007). Advertising intended to reach a targeted audience has the ability to unintentionally reach vulnerable segments, such as alcohol billboard advertising to which teenagers are exposed. Advertising also reaches across nations and cultures. Furthermore, advertising created in one country may reach, either intentionally or unintentionally, other nations and cultures with different views, tastes, values, and behaviors, and it may be deemed inappropriate (Douglas & Craig, 2007).

Ethical issues are often examined from the consumer or practitioner's perspective. It has been argued that problems in advertising may continue to exist because the previous approaches to advertising ethics often look at the micro-level (Baker & Martinson, 2001). A macro-level view focuses on advertising's effects on society, while a micro-level view affords attention to the individual consumer (Drumwright, 2007). Rather than focusing on an individual's perspective of ethics, Hackley (1999) suggested that ethics could be better understood as socially constructed in a mutualistic process with audiences and advertisers. Similarly, Drumwright (2007) recommended an organizational, meso-level of analysis, which acknowledges the role of organizational culture on ethical decision making among practitioners. Schauster (2013a) proposed that the organizational context is directly related to ethical problems that arise, "therefore having an influence on the ways in which these problems are acknowledged and resolved by the organizational members working within this environment" (p. 132).

It is also worth noting the ethical guidelines enacted by the advertising industry. Advertising practitioners engage in acts of social responsibility (Rotzoll, Hall, & Haefner, 1996; also see *Journal of Advertising* 36(2)), they can articulate the ethical problems of advertising (Drumwright & Murphy, 2004; Hunt & Chonko, 1987), and practitioners have suggested that an industry-wide moral deliberation is in order (Crain, 2010). Suggestions for industry-wide and cross-industry ethics will be presented shortly under future implications.

Current Trends in Persuasion and Ethical Implications

The advertising and public relations industries are undergoing significant transformations under the umbrella of two major trends: integrated marketing communication (IMC) and the rise of new media communication channels. Both of these trends have ethical implications for communication practitioners.

Integrated Marketing Communications and Ethics

Integrated marketing communication (IMC) has been defined as the "practice of coordinating all brand communication messages" and "marketing mix decisions" (Moriarty, Mitchell, & Wells, 2015, p. 41). IMC requires sharing ethical responsibility across advertising, marketing, and public relations disciplines, roles, and practices. Furthermore, some of the foundational principles associated with IMC have ethical implications, which include the desire to build long-term relationships with customers, to deliver a consistent message often referred to as "speaking with one voice," and a commitment to listening or two-way communication (Luck & Moffatt, 2009; Moriarty, Mitchell, & Wells, 2015). Kliatchko (2009) stressed that for companies to have long-term relationships with customers, they must "exude credibility, trustworthiness, sincerity, transparency, responsibility, social responsiveness," and other virtues (p. 164).

The consequences of unethical behavior are potentially greater than for advertising alone since IMC also requires an expansion of the target audience or stakeholders beyond just customers. Scholars have pointed out marketing professionals' tendency to limit their stakeholder analysis to the concerns of customers, a condition Smith, Drumwright, and Gentile (2010) referred to as the "new marketing myopia." Therefore, these same scholars advocated for a broader conception of stakeholders, which may include the media, government officials, and employees (Smith et al., 2010). As further support for this approach, Grunig and Grunig (1998) found CEOs valued this broader view of both internal and external stakeholders, a perspective more consistent with public relations. For both public relations and advertising practitioners to be influential in the IMC domain, they also need to be perceived by senior management as strategic advisers rather than tacticians (Grunig & Grunig, 1998; Luck & Moffatt, 2009).

New Media Trends and Ethics

Advancements in technology have drastically altered the way that advertising and public relations practitioners engage with their audiences. Trends include targeted online advertising enabled by data mining (Danna & Gandy, 2002; Schumann, von Wangenheim, & Groene, 2014) and online tracking, mobile advertising targeting consumers through smartphones (Ferris, 2007), sponsored tweets, company blogs, and fan pages on social media sites (Bowen, 2013). Online tracking is used to predict likely purchase prospects for goods and services (Laczniak & Murphy, 2006). Online tracking and data mining involves collecting online information from forms, purchases, entry and exit points, search terms, and Internet service provider addresses to identify trends and segment customers (Danna & Gandy, 2002). Through data mining, advertisers can implement behavioral targeting by first gathering information on an individual consumer's online activity and then directing tailored advertising back to that very individual (Gilbert, 2008). From an ethical perspective, these practices raise issues of privacy and potential harm to the consumer. On the one hand, data mining allows marketers to customize information and make it more relevant for web users. On the other hand, it can also lead to price and marketing discrimination, as more valued customers are offered better deals (Danna & Gandy, 2002).

While the Federal Trade Commission (2013) has issued guidelines for digital advertising to increase transparency and promote open disclosure, scholars and industry leaders are just now beginning to develop ethical principles to guide persuasive communicators. Through an examination of recent case studies, Bowen (2013) identified a range of questionable practices, including fake blogs referred to as flogs, the use of Astroturf or front groups to hide the identity of sponsored communication, blurring of personal versus professional speech in social media communication, and celebrities not identifying that they were being paid to tweet about products or services. More recent cases in the news have included companies faking that their social media accounts have been hacked (Fiegerman, 2013), and a stunt that purposely misled Twitter users by making it appear employees were tweeting while drunk, a J. C. Penny tactic in the 2014 Super Bowl (Heine, 2014).

Scholars have recommended several approaches to improve consumer trust in persuasive communication and reduce the likelihood that more government regulations will be established (Schumann et al., 2014). Danna and Gandy (2002) suggested that advertisers and marketers notify consumers regarding how information collected about them will be used in determining what prices and service opportunities will be offered to them in the future. Ferris (2007) also discussed the need to have customers "opt-in" or out of mobile promotion messages to avoid being spammed. Bowen (2013) identified 15 ethical guidelines for social media communication, some of which included avoiding deception and secrecy, being transparent regarding paid endorsements, and clearly identifying personal speech versus communication on behalf of a client or organization.

Future Implications for Education, Research, and in Practice

Advertising and public relations share a history and future. Therefore it seems appropriate that the future of ethical practices in both advertising and public relations benefit from a crossroads of recommendations for practice, research, and education. Advertising and public relations practitioners can learn from one another based upon a shared experience with ethical issues. With the lines blurred regarding ethical responsibility (e.g., Bowen, 2008; Drumwright & Murphy, 2004; Murphy, 1998), and with the introduction of new problems due to advancements in media and technology, now is the time for a joint ethical initiative across public relations, advertising, and, even perhaps, marketing industries.

Moral exemplars provide important insights into the practices and recommendations of morally conscious individuals and organizations. Through the organizational process of socialization, professionals learn from one another. Learning ethical awareness and ethical decision making are no exception. Baker (2008) suggested the importance of ethical role models in advertising and public relations. For example, role models with virtues of humility, truth, transparency, respect, care, authenticity, equity, and social responsibility can navigate dilemmas and guide other practitioners on how to act (Baker, 2008). As discussed earlier, some senior-level practitioners act as an ethical conscience in public relations. In part, this is relative to their role as a spokesperson (Neill & Drumwright, 2012) and responsibilities of reputation management (Wilcox & Cameron, 2009). While advertising practitioners are not involved in crisis management practices, their reputation is nonetheless on the line.

Students of advertising, public relations, and integrated marketing communication can learn about ethical decision making by reading case studies on moral role models, who can serve at the individual or practitioner level, as well as the organizational level. Identifying ethical role models in advertising and public relations begins with the identification of moral seeing/talking agencies proposed by Drumwright and Murphy (2004). Moberg (2000) suggested that moral role models possess characteristics and face challenges with which others can identify. Moral behavior should be made observable through annual awards programs tied to core values (Neill, 2015), "employee-of-the-month" recognitions, and in internal communications such as newsletters so that others can learn (Moberg, 2000). By observing and mimicking action, employees learn virtuous behavior. An example of a moral seeing/talking agency is one with an espoused and enacted ethical code. For example, BBDO New York teaches and tests all new employees on its ethical code of conduct (D. Alligood, personal communication, February 3, 2013).

Holding companies might also act as organizational role models. Drumwright and Murphy (2009) suggested ethical problems have changed in intensity due to the demands placed on advertising agencies by global communication networks. These demands include greater profit and the need for acts of social responsibility. Social responsibility is the concern for a wider public interest and common good, not merely self-interest or profit (Baker & Martinson, 2001). The new demands of holding companies are also placed on public relations agencies since the four global communication networks hold advertising agencies, along with public relations agencies, media companies, and companies of related services all acting as "sister" companies. However, the agencies within these holding companies also compete with each other, adding another layer of potential conflicts of interests.

In practice, advertising and public relations agencies also can adopt the trend of employer branding and regularly promote their core values to potential and current employees and clients as a means of distinguishing themselves from competitors. Similar to what is happening in other corporations, they can routinely reinforce those values as part of routine communication to their employees. However, they should heed the warnings regarding aspirational versus core values (Lencioni, 2002) and choose to adopt values that are reflective of the reality of working at that agency.

While our recommendations call for research on moral exemplars, it should be noted that limited cases exist for moral exemplars in advertising (e.g., Drumwright & Murphy, 2004; Krueger, 1998; Schauster, 2013a). Future empirical research on advertising ethics can borrow from the topics of public relations research, such as ethically exemplar organizations (e.g., Bowen, 2004), ethics counsel (e.g., Bowen, 2008), and ethical conscience (e.g., Neill & Drumwright, 2012). While practices such as ethics counsel might occur in advertising, more empirical research is needed to identify the ways in which advertising practitioners communicate organizational and ethical values and how moral role models in advertising enhance ethical awareness.

References

4A's. (1924, June 7, 2011). Standards of practice of the 4A's. Retrieved April 17, 2013 from http://www.aaaa.org/about/association/Documents/AA110.pdf

Alvesson, M. (2002). *Understanding Organizational Culture*. Thousand Oaks: Sage.

Baker, S. (1999). Five baselines for justification in persuasion. *Journal of Mass Media Ethics*, 14, 69–81.

Baker, S. (2008). The model of the principled advocate and the pathological partisan: A virtue ethics construct of opposing archetypes of public relations and advertising practitioners. *Journal of Mass Media Ethics*, 23, 235–53.

Baker, S., & Martinson, D. (2001). The TARES test: Five principles of ethical persuasion. *Journal of Mass Media Ethics*, 16(2 & 3), 148–75.

Barney, R. D., & Black, J. (1994). Ethics and professional persuasive communications. *Public Relations Review*, 20(3), 233–48.

Bishop, F. P. (1949). *The Ethics of Advertising*. London: Robert Hale.

Bivins, T. (2004). *Mixed Media: Moral Distinctions in Advertising, Public Relations, and Journalism*. Mahwah, NJ: Lawrence Erlbaum Associates.

Bonifield, C., & Cole, C. (2007). Advertising to vulnerable segments. In G. J. Tellis & T. Ambler (Eds.) *The Handbook of Advertising* (pp. 430–44). London: Sage.

Bowen, S. A. (2004). Organizational factors encouraging ethical decision making: An exploration into the case of an exemplar. *Journal of Business Ethics*, 52, 311–24.

Bowen, S. A. (2008). A state of neglect: Public relations as 'corporate conscience' or ethics counsel. *Journal of Public Relations Research*, 20, 271–96.

Bowen, S. A. (2013). Using classic social media cases to distill ethical guidelines for digital engagement. *Journal of Mass Media Ethics*, 28, 119–33. doi: 10.1080/08900523.2013.793523

Bunderson, J. S. (2003). Team member functional background and involvement in management teams: Direct effects and the moderating role of power centralization. *The Academy of Management Journal*, 46(4), 458–71.

Cohen, D. V. (1993). Creating and maintaining ethical work climates: Anomie in the workplace and implications for managing change. *Business Ethics Quarterly*, 3(4), 343–58.

Crain, R. (2010). If ad industry doesn't have frank debate on ethics, it's doomed to repeat its mistakes. *Advertising Age*, 81(25), 26.

Cunningham, P. H. (1999). Ethics of advertising: Oxymoron or good business practice? In J. P. Jones (Ed.), *The Advertising Business*. Thousand Oaks, CA: Sage.

Danna, A., & Gandy, Jr., O. H. (2002). All that glitters is not gold: Digging beneath the surface of data mining. *Journal of Business Ethics*, 40, 373–86.

Donnelley, S. (1995). The art of moral ecology. *Ecosystem Health*, 1, 170–76.

Douglas, S. P., & Craig, C. S. (2007). Advertising across cultures. In G. J. Tellis & T. Ambler (Eds.), *The handbook of advertising* (pp. 416–29). London: Sage.

Drumwright, M. E. (2007). Advertising ethics: A multi-level theory approach. In G. J. Tellis & T. Ambler (Eds.) *The Sage Handbook of Advertising*. London: Sage.

Drumwright, M. E., & Murphy, P. E. (2004). How advertising practitioners view ethics: Moral muteness, moral myopia, and moral imagination. *Journal of Advertising*, 33, 7–24.

Drumwright, M. E., & Murphy, P. E. (2009). The current state of advertising ethics: Industry and academic perspectives. *Journal of Advertising*, 38(1), 83–107.

Dumenco, S. (2014). The Truth in Advertising Act of 2014: Can Congress really regulate Photoshopping? *Advertising Age*, 85(8), 42.

Federal Trade Commission (2013). .com Disclosures: How to make effective disclosures in digital advertising. Retrieved September 15, 2015 from: http://www.ftc.gov/sites/default/files/attachments/press-releases/ftc-staff-revises-online-advertising-disclosure-guidelines/130312dotcomdisclosures.pdf

Ferris, M. (2007). Insights on mobile advertising, promotion and research. *Journal of Advertising Research*, 47(1), 28–37. doi: 10.2501/S0021849907070043

Fiegerman, S. (2013). Chipotle faked its twitter hack. Mashable. Retrieved September 15, 2015 from: http://mashable.com/2013/07/24/chipotle-faked-twitter-hack/

Fitzpatrick, K., & Gauthier, C. (2001). Toward a professional responsibility theory of public relations ethics. *Journal of Mass Media Ethics*, 16, 193–212.

Fleming, J. H., & Asplund, J. (2007). Where employee engagement happens. *The Gallup Management Journal*. Retrieved September 15, 2015 from: http://businessjournal.gallup.com/content/102496/where-employee-engagement-happens.aspx

Gallicano, T. D., Cho, Y. Y., & Bivins, T. H. (2014). What do blog readers think? A survey to assess ghost blogging and commenting. *Research Journal of the Institute for Public Relations*, 2(1), 1–35.

Gilbert, F. (2008). Beacons, bugs, and pixel tags: Do you comply with the FTC behavioral marketing principles and foreign law requirements? *Journal of Internet Law*, 11(11), 3–10.

Grunig, J. E., & Grunig, L.A. (1998). The relationship between public relations and marketing in excellent organizations: evidence from the IABC study. *Journal of Marketing Communications*, 4, 141–62. doi: 10.1080/135272698345816

Hackley, C. E. (1999). The meanings of ethics in and of advertising. *Business Ethics: A European Review*, 8(1), 37–42.

Heine, C. (2014). JC Penney isn't drunk tweeting the Super Bowl—It's wearing mittens: Stunt causes buzz and goads Kia Motors and Doritos. *Ad Week*. Retrieved December 3, 2014 from http://www.adweek.com/news/technology/jc-penney-isnt-drunk-tweeting-super-bowl-its-wearing-mittens-155437

Huff, C., Barnard, L., & Frey, W. (2008). Good computing: A pedagogically focused model of virute in the practice of computing. *Journal of Information, Communication & Ethics in Society*, 6(3), 246–78.

Hunt, S. D., & Chonko, L. B. (1987). Ethical problems of advertising agency executives. *Journal of Advertising*, 16(4), 16–24.

Hyman, M. R., Tansey, R., & Clark, J. W. (1994). Research on advertising ethics: Past, present, and future. *Journal of Advertising*, 23(3), 5–15.

Jones, J. P. (1999). The culture of an advertising agency. In J. P. Jones (Ed.) *The Advertising Business*. Thousand Oaks, CA: Sage.

Keyton, J. (2005). *Communication & Organizational Culture: A to Understanding Work Experiences*. Thousand Oaks, CA: Sage.

Kliatchko, J. G. (2009). The primary of the consumer in IMC: Espousing a personalist view and ethical implications. *Journal of Marketing Communications*, 15, 157–77. doi: 10.1080/13527260902757621

Krueger, D. (1998). Ethics and values in advertising: Two case studies. *Business and Society Review*, 99(1), 53–65.

Laczniak, G. R., & Murphy, P. E. (2006). Marketing, consumers and technology: Perspectives for enhancing ethical transactions. *Business Ethics Quarterly*, 16(3), 313–21.

Lee, S. T., & Cheng, I. (2010). Assessing the TARES as an ethical model for antismoking ads. *Journal of Health Communication*, 15(1), 55–75.

Lee, S. T., & Nguyen, H. L. (2013). Explicating the moral responsibility of the advertiser: TARES as an ethical model for fast food advertising. *Journal of Mass Media Ethics*, 28(4), 225–40.

Lencioni, P. M. (2002). Make your values mean something. *Harvard Business Review*, July, 5–9. Retrieved Sept. 15, 2015 from https://hbr.org/2002/07/make-your-values-mean-something

Lloyd, S. (2002). Branding from the inside out. *BRW*, 24(10), 64–66.

Luck, E., & Moffatt, J. (2009). IMC: Has anything really changed? A new perspective on an old definition. *Journal of Marketing Communications*, 15(5), 311–325. doi: 10.1080/13527260802481256

Marvin, G. (2013). 73% of online publishers offer native advertising, just 10% Still sitting on the sidelines [eMarketer]. *Marketing Land*, July 22, 2013. Retrieved April 24, 2014 from http://marketingland.com/73-of-online-publishers-offer-native-advertising-just-10-still-sitting-on-the-sidelines-emarketer-52506

Marvin, G. (2014). Native advertising still befuddles marketers: 73 percent don't know what it is, just 9 percent budget for it. *Marketing Land*, April 8. Retrieved April 24, 2014 from http://marketingland.com/native-advertising-still-befuddles-marketers-73-percent-dont-know-just-9-percent-budget-79348

McBride, G. (1989). Ethical thought in public relations history: Seeking a relevant perspective. *Journal of Mass Media Ethics*, 4, 5–20.

Moberg, D. J. (2000). Role models and moral exemplars: How do employees acquire virtues by observing others? *Business Ethics Quarterly*, 10(3), 675–96.

Moriarty, S., Mitchell, N., & Wells, W. (2015). *Advertising & IMC principles & practice*. Upper Saddle, N.J.: Pearson Education.

Moroko, L., & Uncles, M. D. (2008). Characteristics of successful employer brands. *Journal of Brand Management*, 16(3), 160–75. doi:10.1057/bm.2008.4

Murphy, P. E. (1998). Ethics in advertising: Review, analysis, and suggestions. *Journal of Public Policy Marketing*, 17(2), 316–19.

Neff, J. (2010). Ad industry battles back against bad rep, forms ethics institute. *Advertising Age*, 81(23).

Neff, J. (2011). Ad industry's new ethics code takes on brand integration, social-media disclosure. *Advertising Age*. Retrieved September 15, 2015 from: http://adage.com/article/news/advertisers-agencies-ethics-code-review/149464/

Neill, M. S. (2012). Seat at the table(s): An examination of senior public relations practitioners' power and influence among multiple executive-level coalitions (doctoral dissertation). Retrieved September 15, 2015 from: http://repositories.lib.utexas.edu/bitstream/handle/2152/22093/neill-dissertation-20126.pdf?sequence=1

Neill, M. S. (2015, March). Public relations' collaborative role in ethics & values communication. Presented at the International Public Relations Research Conference, Miami, Florida.

Neill, M. S. (in press). Beyond the C-suite: Corporate communications' power & influence. *Journal of Communication Management*.

Neill, M. S., & Drumwright, M. E. (2012). PR professionals as organizational conscience. *Journal of Mass Media Ethics*, 27, 220–34.

O'Barr, W. M. (2006). The advertising profession in the public's eye. *Advertising & Society Review*, 7(1). Retrieved September 15, 2015 from https://muse.jhu.edu/journals/advertising_and_society_review/summary/v007/7.1unit05.html

O'Barr, W. M. (2007). Ethics & advertising. *Advertising & Society Review*, 8(3). Retrieved Oct. 15, 2015 from https://muse.jhu.edu/journals/advertising_and_society_review/v008/8.3unit13.html

O'Guinn, T., Allen, C., & Semenik, R. (2009). *Advertising and Integrated Brand Promotion* (5th ed.). Mason, Ohio: South-Western Cengage Learning.

O'Guinn, T. C. (2007). Advertising, Consumption and Welfare. In G. J. Tellis & T. Ambler (Eds.) *The Sage Handbook of Advertising*. London: Sage.

Paluszek, J. (1989). Public relations and ethical leadership. *Vital Speeches of the Day*, 55(24), 747–50.

Patterson, P., & Wilkins, L. (2008). *Media Ethics: Issues and Cases* (6th ed.). Boston: McGraw Hill.

Patterson, P., & Wilkins, L. (2011). *Media Ethics: Issues and Cases* (7th ed.). Boston: McGraw Hill.

Pollay, R. W. (1986). The distorted mirror: Reflections on the unintended consequences of advertising. *Journal of Marketing*, 50 (April), 18–36.

Preston, I. L. (2010). Interaction of law and ethics in matters of advertisers' responsibility for protecting consumers. *Journal of Consumer Affairs*, 44(1), 259–64.

Redmond, J., & Trager, R. (1998). *Balancing on the Wire: The Art of Managing Media Organizations*. Boulder, CO: Coursewise Publishing.

Richards, J. I., & Petty, R. D. (2007). Advertising Regulation. In G. J. Tellis & T. Ambler (Eds.) *The Handbook of Advertising* (pp. 383–97). London: Sage.

Rotzoll, K. B., Hall, S. R., & Haefner, J. E. (1996). *Advertising in Contemporary Society: Perspectives Toward Understanding* (3rd ed.). Urbana, IL: University of Illinois Press.

Ryan, M. (1987). Organizational constraints on corporate public relations practitioners. *Journalism Quarterly*, 64, 473–82.

Ryan, M., & Martinson, D. L. (1983) The PR officer as corporate conscience. *Public Relations Quarterly*, 28(2), 20–3.

Saks, A. M. (2006). Antecedents and consequences of employee engagement. *Journal of Managerial Psychology*, 21(7), 600–19.

Schauster, E. (2013a). *Enabled and Constrained: Culture, Ethics and Structuration in an Advertising Agency* (doctoral dissertation), University of Missouri, Columbia, MO.

Schauster, E. (in press). The relationship between organizational leaders and advertising ethics: An organizational ethnography. *Journal of Mass Media Ethics*.

Schein, E. H. (2010). *Organizational Culture and Leadership* (4th ed.). San Francisco, CA: Jossey-Bass.

Schumann, J. H., von Wangenheim, F., & Groene, N. (2014). Targeted online advertising: Using reciprocity appeals to increase acceptance among users of free web services. *Journal of Marketing*, 78, 59–75. doi: 10.1509/jm.11.0316

Smith, N. C, Drumwright, M. E., & Gentile, M. C. (2010). The new marketing myopia. *Journal of Public Policy & Marketing*, 29(1), 4–11. doi: 10.1509/jppm.29.1.4

Vidaver-Cohen, D. (1997). Moral imagination in organizational problem solving: An institutional perspective. *Business Ethics Quarterly*, 7(4), 1–26.

Welch, M. (2011). The evolution of the employee engagement concept: Communication implications. *Corporate Communications: An International Journal*, 16(4), 328–46.

Wilcox, D. L., & Cameron, G. T. (2009). *Public Relations Strategies and Tactics*. Glenview, IL: Pearson Education.

Wilcox, D. L., & Cameron, G. T. (2012). *Public Relations Strategies and Tactics*. Glenview, IL: Pearson Education.

Wilkie, W. L., & Moore, E. S. (2007). Advertising performance in a market system. In G. J. Tellis & T. Ambler (Eds.) *The Sage Handbook of Advertising*. London: Sage.

Section II

Criticisms of PR and Advertising Messages

5 Stereotyping in Advertising

We Are Not the People in Those Pictures

Thomas Bivins

CHAPTER SUMMARY

Critics have complained for many years about how advertising portrays women in stereotypical ways, usually as moms or sex objects. Considerable research has shown that these stereotypical portrayals have real consequences for women, particularly girls who compare themselves with idealized images. This chapter explores another aspect of gendered advertising and examines how men are stereotyped differently than in the past. Stereotypes of men as tough, competent, and in control emerged in films and television programs, as well as in advertising. In recent years, images of the manly man, hero, breadwinner, and outdoorsman have been displaced by images of men as bumbling husbands and dumb dads. The usually humorous portrayals of men, particularly in home settings, show them as confused, incompetent, and in need of rescue by a calm and reasonable mom. The chapter explains how these portrayals may affect our beliefs about ourselves and sounds the alarm about "dumbing down" American males.

Introduction

Are men addicted to pickup trucks, fast cars, football, beer, and sexy women who will do just about anything to be near them? Yes. Especially if you believe what advertising tells us—which is, "men are in control." On the other hand, can they cook dinner, do the laundry without mixing the colors, change a baby's diapers, take the kids to school, or have *real* emotional connection with anything not on the first list? No. Especially if you believe what advertising tells us—which is, "men are not in control." Are men confused by this mixed message? Probably. This shouldn't come as a surprise. Men aren't used to being confused over who they think they are. Women, however, have been getting these kinds of mixed messages through advertising at least since the dawn of the 20th century when picturing them as the second line of defense in World War I shifted to returning them to the hearth where they supposedly belonged. Men, however, have generally been viewed as the first line of defense and the king of the workplace, where they not only saved the world but also brought home the bacon.

The problem is, and has been for over a century, that we are not the people in those pictures. We are complex, often bewildered, beings searching for who we are in a world that is increasingly loud, crowded, and baffling. Walter Lippman was among the first to suggest that stereotypes were a way of shorthanding the complexities of modern life. He knew that most of us simply couldn't comprehend a world that we didn't understand firsthand. Life is either familiar or strange, and stereotyping helped make the strange familiar. The downside, of course, is that what we're not familiar with may eventually *become* the stereotype, and therein lies the problem.

> Lippmann's is a view of stereotypes as being inherently dangerous in that they side-step rational thought in favor of a shadowy illusion of life, leading the masses clinging to a culture they barely understand while rejecting out of hand that which is foreign to them.
>
> (Bivins, 2009, p. 207)

How many of us believe, even tangentially, that Mexicans are lazy, that Asians are math whizzes, that the Irish are drunks and brawlers, that African-Americans are natural athletes? What do those beliefs lead to? Too often they reinforce a privileged class and power structure that seeks to exclude the unfamiliar or alien. Less obvious, however, are such stereotypical beliefs that little boys are by nature scruffy and dirty, that little girls are neat and clean, that women are adept at domestic chores, and that men are not. It could be argued that these seemingly innocuous stereotypes are less problematic. But are they? Many of these beliefs aren't, in fact, based in advertising. They are the product of years of images often born of social biases and structures further perpetuated by the film industry, television programming, and other forms of media. However, as advertising began to mimic the creative techniques of other media, the stereotypes already generated by those other industries began to dominate in marketing as well. And as the techniques were adopted, new stereotypes began to emerge, either supporting those already in existence or created as an adjunct to those images. The girl left behind to tend the home front in the Hollywood version of World War II became the girl who kept on tending the home on television following the war. At the same time, advertising continued to dramatize a world of modern appliances designed to entice women back into their homes from the factories, which in real life had become their temporary quarters during the war.

Of course, advertisements are not films, but increasingly, thanks to the Internet, they are often abbreviated versions complete with characters, plots, and the inevitable stereotypes—which is not necessarily a bad thing. Advertisers have always been limited, by space, by time, by format. How do you sell diamonds, for example, without stereotyping both the giver and the receiver? Is it even possible for a wedding photographer to sell herself without the standard and stereotyped images of a traditional Western-cultural ceremony? And how in the world does one sell perfume, especially given what its product attributes are really about—a substitute for the weak, human pheromones that enhance sexual attraction. Stereotypes provide a shortcut to the sales pitch. We are presented with familiar images that set a recognizable context for that pitch. If we accept Lippmann's (1920) premise that stereotypes provide us with at least an abbreviated image of the unfamiliar, then using this technique, on the face of it, shouldn't be problematic. What is problematic, however, is that a stereotype, by definition, is incomplete. And repeated viewings of stereotypes can lead us to assume a truth that may not be true—mostly because differences in people are reduced to simplistic categorizations, sometimes negative, which then are served up as reality.

It's clear, both from what we see every day in the media and from the innumerable academic explorations of the topic, that stereotyping abounds. Although many have argued that advertising merely reflects the society and culture inside of which it is produced, the question of what parts of society, which of its cultures, and what values are chosen to be portrayed is a big one. No one element in society is free from stereotyping in some form. Minorities, when they appear at all, are often portrayed as "representative" rather than individually defined. What this means is that minorities tend to appear consistently as a bundle of standard components representing a type rather than an individual. For example, journalist Tina Ramirez, writing for the *Huffington Post*, notes that the ongoing image of the "curvy, sexy and sultry Latina denies many Latinas their cultural identification based on the their physical appearances and sexual attractiveness, alone" (Ramirez, 2013). She points specifically to actor Sofia Vergara's role in the TV sitcom *Modern Family*, which "fuels the stereotype that Hispanic women are sexy but also loud, crazy and spicy" (Nittie, n.d.). It's also undeniable that some societal groups appear only as stereotyped afterthoughts (the old, the very young, the poor). Probably more than any other demographic in our society, women have been the focus both of stereotyping and of discussions on the subject. However, in order to take a different tack, we'll address only one of the numerous possibilities here as an example of how stereotypes work and their potential affects. The lessons learned from this example should be applicable to all stereotypes, and the solutions are the same.

While much has been written about the gender stereotyping of women and girls, much less has been written about men, who have traditionally enjoyed a privileged position in society. But men are stereotyped, too. Because audiences, especially those for advertising, are typically classified by market segmentation (often by using demographic characteristics), there is a tendency to compress the subtleties of individuality into the most obvious attributes of the group. This may lead to a picture that is not only simple, but also can be misleading and, sometimes, offensive. In recent years, television has created a genre of men on numerous sitcoms who could only be classified as "the bumbling husband" type (Bivins, 2009, p. 198). Advertising, in turn, has mimicked this stereotype by picturing both boys and men as incapable of understanding the mysteries of laundry or cooking a family meal without purchasing it in a bucket or keeping themselves clean more than a few minutes at a time. Examples range from Homer Simpson to the title character on *Everybody Loves Raymond*. Author Chris Turner (2004), in his in-depth look at the Simpsons phenomenon, calls Homer "a big fat clown, a bumbling doofus, an all-but-universal dimwit." (Turner, p. 320) And Australian journalist Alison Cameron (2005) writes that the character of Ray Barone is just one of a number of television husbands portrayed as inept fathers and poor role models. She notes that "as soon as Ray walks in the front door he mysteriously loses any of the abilities that make him a success outside. He is a thoughtless husband and a poor father interested only in television, food and sex."

Of course, the tried and true image of men as macho, muscular, athletic, and in charge still exists, but in an increasingly gender-confused society, is the "dumb dad" the new normal for the male stereotype? As Marcellus (2013, p. 128) notes, "stereotypes are designed to limit and exclude those who do not fit narrow ideas of normalcy." Thus being a male may also mean not being capable of doing anything remotely domestic or being childlike and very definitely *not* in control.

According to Gornick (1979), "Advertisements depict for us not necessarily how we actually behave as men and women but how we *think* men and women behave" (p. vii). She suggests that this serves a social purpose in convincing us that the stereotype is what we eventually believe we are or ought to be. How then do men relate to their environment when that environment tells them they are hapless imbeciles? Part of the problem is that this stereotype is relatively new. As late as 2002, Rohlinger categorized the role of men in advertisements into nine categories: the hero, the outdoorsman, the family man/nurturer, the breadwinner, the man at work, the consumer, the urban man, the quiescent (quiet/calm) man, and the erotic man. Nowhere to be seen, just a few years ago, was the image of the bumbling husband or the dumb dad.

Fast-forward ten years. In 2012, *Philadelphia Magazine* journalist Christine Speer Lejeune (2012) described what she considered to be "the most irritating commercial on TV."

> The narrative arc revolves around a man dipping his feet and his kid's feet in glue, in an attempt to keep their socks from slipping down their legs. Eventually, Mom comes home, shakes her head at all of the manly idiocy happening in her home and saves the day by tossing her boys some new socks that stay up on their own. The whole thing is so, so stupid.

Lejeune was not happy. She continued by noting how "lucky" we all are because,

> there are a billion more commercials just like it. Like the one with the dudes who track mud in on the carpet and then lie about it, because they're clueless. Or the one about the dad who can't cook without destroying the

kitchen, because he's clueless. Or the one where the guy doesn't know the difference between yogurt and pie, because he's clueless.

She ended by wondering whether "boys are getting the message that our society simply *expects* less from them? That it's okay to be . . . clueless?"

Fairly recent research seems to back up her observations. Tsai and Shumow (2011) analyzed hours of television commercials over several networks to determine the roles of men as representatives of fatherhood and domesticity. They suggest that, "understanding how men are represented in advertising is imperative for understanding how marketers conceptualize contemporary gender roles and family dynamics, and how these representations impact male viewers' understanding of gender roles in the family" (p. 39). Their findings support the belief that men are indeed depicted in marginal roles, especially in a family context. For example:

- They are less likely to be shown performing domestic chores.
- They have a lower involvement with their children (most often depicted as mischievous playmates instead of caretakers) and without wifely guidance are shown as incompetent as caregivers.
- No men are shown with infants. Tsai and Shumow suggest that this is because childcare may be the most demanding domestic task. We will come back to this one.

Josh Lev (2012), writing for CNN about the "dumb old dad" stereotype, points out that the "image of the hapless dad has long roots in American pop culture." He cites research done on comics going back to the 1940s (LaRossa, 2000) showing fluctuating levels of fatherly incompetence over several decades. Not surprisingly, television has played a major role in depicting men as bumbling fools. Despite early television portrayals of fathers—especially in the 1950s and early '60s—as the mature breadwinner full of sage advice (*Father Knows Best, Leave It to Beaver*), that characterization began to change in the '70s and '80s with shows such as *The Cosby Show, Family Ties*, and *Growing Pains* and has changed even further in the last decade as the still moderately wise fathers of those shows were replaced by targets of ridicule and indifference. (Lev, 2012). Today, it's as likely as not that stereotypes of incompetent men will greet those of us who still watch TV—both in programs and their embedded advertisements. Two Australian journalists tell us that, "Dopey dads can be found in any ad for cleaning or cooking products that aim to make it easy for clueless men" (Midena & Davidson, 2011).

Courtney Kane (2005), writing for the *New York Times*, suggests that men, as presented in advertisements, are becoming the target of what she calls "gender sneer." The portrayals of men as bumbling husbands "began as a clever reversal of traditional gender roles in campaigns, prompted by the ire of women and feminist organizations over decades of ads using stereotyped imagery of an incompetent, bumbling housewife who needed to be told which coffee or cleanser to buy." She notes that, "in the campaigns . . . men act like buffoons, ogling cars and women; are likened to dogs, especially in beer and pizza ads; and bungle every possible household task." Canadian scholar Paul Nathanson (2001) points out that "negative imagery in advertising is part of negative imagery in popular culture in general. If you add up the way men are presented in popular culture, then it is a problem because the message is that that's what men are" (cited in Kane, 2005). Two theories can help us understand why this can and does happen.

Cultivation theory, originally proposed by George Gerbner in the 1970s, proposes that if we are repeatedly exposed to stereotypes over a period of time, we may eventually begin to accept them as reality. Gerbner and his students found that heavy television use led viewers to perceive the world as a mean and scary place and those perceptions did not accurately reflect the levels of crime and violence in their geographic locations (Gerbner, Mogan, Signorigell, & Shanahan, 2002). Similarly, it is likely that constant media bombardment replete with seemingly congruent stereotypes is bound to color the way we view ourselves and others.

For example, how many of us tend to think of women as nurturing within a family setting? Don't all those sitcoms and commercials reinforce that? Even the more recent incursion of the "working mother" into the mix fails to diminish the perceived role of wife and stay-at-home mom as being primary. Think of all the television dramas that, while showing the steadfast woman taking the morning commuter train into her new job, also remind us that her real responsibility is being left behind with the home and family she has abandoned. And even if she manages to straddle the two worlds of worker/nurturer, her life becomes somehow unmanageable and filled with recrimination. Oddly enough, the gender opposite is also true. If a man is removed from his stereotypical element, he becomes bumbling, sloppy, childlike, confused. And, in most cases, the wife then becomes the voice of reason and symbol of familial staunchness. Role reversal? Recursive advertising designed to turn stereotypes "on their ears?" (Sheehan, 2014, p. 81)

Maybe, and it's all usually played for laughs. As Kane (2005) points out, "most marketers presenting incompetent, silly male characters say their campaigns provide harmless comedic insight into the male mentality while also appealing to women." Bob Thompson, director of the Bleier Center for Television and Popular Culture at Syracuse University says that "comedy is about inversion—taking people who are in authority and control and making them the butt of jokes." So in a society "that has been so dominated by men . . . comedy is naturally going to play against that" (cited in Levs, 2012). However, if we view this sort of stereotype enough, it may eventually come to represent reality for us. At the very least, it may affect what we expect from men and women, marriage and home life—which is probably much more that bumbling husbands and frustrated wives.

This leads us to *expectancy theory*, which states that if we see the same stereotypes over and over, we will eventually expect that the people who are being stereotyped will be that way in real life. In fact, if we're part of the group being stereotyped, we may even begin to believe we either are or should become that version of reality. The problem is that if we don't see much other than the stereotype, we will be increasingly likely to believe the less complex, abbreviated version. According to advertising scholar Kim Sheehan (2014), with reference to, "if expectancy theory is valid, then the use of stereotypes hinders one's view of any individual as a complete person" (Sheehan, p. 81).

The actual effects stereotyping seen through the lens of these two theories are mitigated by the degree to which three variables are present (Sheehan, p. 76).

- *The range of stereotypes presented over time*—Although it may be true that portraying husbands as incapable of cooking a meal constitutes a stereotype, whether we tend to believe the stereotype is accurate may depend on how many other "types" we are exposed too. For example, if the helpless chef is only one of a number of stereotypes of young men we see consistently over time (e.g., as aspiring student, young professional, romantic partner, family member), then we will have a more complete picture of what constitutes a "young man."
- *The frequency of portrayals of individual stereotypes*—This links closely with the range of stereotypes because a single image not repeated consistently over time is not likely to become a stereotype. In order for that to happen, it must be repeated to the exclusion of other possible images, ultimately presenting a one-dimensional portrait of a type.
- *The valence of the stereotype*—Are the portrayals negative or positive? Although a positive stereotype is still a stereotype, it is less likely that the results of viewing the stereotype will be harmful. A negative stereotype consistently presented over time (frequency) without balancing, contrary, or compensating images can cause a negative image to be imbedded in the life view of those watching it. As Sheehan puts it:

> Seeing one single, consistent portrayal of a group of people can affect how we perceive all members of the stereotyped group, either while we are creating advertising messages or when we encounter members of the group in the real world.
>
> (2014, p. 75)

The evidence is mounting that supports the image of men as totally helpless in domestic venues and their related tasks outside of the traditionally stereotypical rolls as breadwinner and macho-child who never grew up. For example, we know that men can't tell one form of food from another, especially if it's good for them:

- A Yoplait yogurt commercial shows a man looking for something to snack on in the refrigerator while his wife talks on the kitchen phone. He thinks her references to delicious, dessert-like comestibles are somehow hidden behind rows of Yoplait yogurt. When she mentions that she's even lost weight while eating these "desserts," he seems literally stunned. She turns from her phone call to ask him what he's rummaging about for. His befuddled look ends the commercial.

- A similar approach is taken by a Fiber One ad in which the wise wife is advising her husband to eat more fiber, while he is searching the kitchen for "something good" to eat. Fiber, apparently, makes him "sad." He mistakes the fiber bar she is eating for a candy bar, reproves her, and, taking the bar from her hand, bites into it with a sigh of pleasure. She knowingly smiles and rolls her eyes.

Of course men can't possibly understand the mysteries of making a simple meal, but there are always alternatives that even they can handle:

- A commercial for Pizza Hut shows a mom and two female children exiting their car as the teenage daughter questions, with dismay, "Dad's making dinner?" The mom assures her that "It'll be fine," and, in a whisper, adds, "maybe." They enter the dining room to view a table replete with a huge spread from Pizza Hut, the now stunned but happy children, and the father who proudly announces, "Who's the man?" Of course, mom, again in a whisper, says, "I love you."
- A commercial for Kellogg's Eggo-brand waffles shows the husband arising at 6:30 a.m., assuring his wife that she can sleep in while he makes breakfast. He subsequently watches a little TV, putts golf balls into drinking glasses in the kitchen, tosses basketball wads of paper into vases, finally popping Eggo waffles into the toaster. Of course his family, including two young children, are thrilled—until his wife asks if he's made coffee. He suddenly realizes that he probably missed something obvious saying, "Of course," as he quickly exits the breakfast table to add the final touch to the illusion.

And let us not forget that men, ultimately, are just little boys:

- Discover Card tells us that women can handle finances but men not only can't pay the bills, they also can't even pick up a carton of milk. On the phone with a Discover Card representative, the wife complains that her husband's incompetence includes forgetting the groceries and instead bringing home a puppy. As she talks about his fiscal inadequacies, he is seen running down the stairs with the new puppy pleading for it to "hold it" until he can get outside. He is, she says to the Discover Card representative, "not off the hook."
- In a warning about incompetent men in a T-Mobile ad, a mother cautions against a prospective choice on her daughter's "Fav-5s" as a failure in school who "eats pencils." She admonishes her daughter to associate with "smart guys." The daughter sarcastically calls out her dad and "Uncle Joe"

as her mom's smart guy referents. They are seen through the window driving an ATV over a makeshift ramp in the backyard—of course, crashing. So much for smart choices in men. Women, alas, are simply stuck with what's available in the gene pool.

And as far as men are concerned, women are still a mystery, especially during their monthly "transformation." An ad campaign entitled, "Everything I Do Is Wrong," produced by the California Milk Processor Board shows "befuddled men holding cartons of milk as offerings for the better, angrier halves" (Polis, 2011). Among the headlines:

- "I'm sorry I listened to what you said and not what you meant."
- "We can both blame myself."
- "I'm sorry for the thing or things I did or didn't do."
- "I apologize for not reading between the right lines."
- "Let's agree to disagree with me."

The ads end with the statement, "Milk can help reduce the symptoms of PMS." The campaign drew the ire not only of women but also men and was hammered in the media. *The Huffington Post* noted,

Once a month, some women have this pesky thing called PMS that turns them into raging demons if their boyfriends dare look at them wrong, or even, as the campaign says, if their boyfriends don't read between the *right* lines. But, even an out of control female monster can now be placated, thanks to milk! Oh, glorious PMS-relieving milk! Both females and males should just take one giant calcium-enriched sigh of relief.

(Polis, 2011)

In this world, and in others created by advertising, men become virtual lap dogs, constantly craving attention through any means possible, all the while fearing retribution if they do something wrong. Unlike the bumbling husband in the Pizza Hut commercial who buys his wife's love with a purchased meal, the hapless men seeking love in De Beers diamond ads are urged to placate women in a much more expensive way. "Hey, what do you know, she thinks you're funny again," suggests one print ad containing an image of a diamond bracelet. Or, "Imagine how happy she will be with the same ring as her friends, only bigger." Of course women can be bought, and De Beers has been telling us how for nearly one hundred years. A television commercial from 20 years ago shows a couple walking through an Italian piazza. The man suddenly shouts very loudly, "I love this woman." The pigeons aren't the only ones disturbed. The woman tries desperately to calm his unwanted and embarrassing outburst, until, of course, he pulls out a pair of diamond earrings. She then breathlessly whispers, "I love this man." Apparently an honest, if loud, expression of love isn't enough. After all, another commercial tells us that a diamond can say what words alone cannot: If your bank account is big enough, you may find love.

Will men ever attain a sense of self that does not include being viewed as practically incompetent by the women in their lives? Maybe, but it will have to include a fast car or a big truck. A recent Dodge commercial presents us with a series of sad-faced men agreeing to "perform" for their women. "I will say yes when you want me to say yes," a monotone voice announces over a head shot of a young African-American man in sweats with a melancholy expression on his face. "I will be quiet when you don't want to hear me say no," the voice continues. "I will listen to your opinion of my friends," the same voice continues over a different, equally disconsolate face. "I will listen to your friends' opinion of my friends." After a litany of equally demeaning chores, including putting the lid down and separating the recycling, the self-claimed reward is in sight. And, no, it's not love this time; it's a Dodge Charger, which the ad tells us above the roar of the engine, is "Man's Last Stand."

How did this become a last stand? Isn't anyone noticing? British scholar Mary Hedderman (2012), in summing up her research into how males are portrayed on television in the United Kingdom, wonders "how negative portrayals of men as dimwits or sex objects can persist with barely a complaint filed, whilst the literature review and primary research indicate that if women were portrayed in the same way there would be a public outcry" (p. 1). Her research also shows that females in all age groups tested "expressed strong views regarding the portrayal of men as Lazy/Incompetent, perceiving such representations as unfair and demeaning to men." So who *is* complaining?

Do you remember that we were going to revisit the Tsai and Shumow suggestion that childcare, especially of infants, may be the most demanding domestic task? In fact, it's apparently so demanding that Kimberly-Clark decided to use dumb dads as a test group for their Huggies brand diapers. A series of ads were shot during a five-day period in which a group of dads, all in the same house, had to take care of their infant children. This was, in the words of the female voiceover in the commercial, "to prove that Huggies diapers and wipes can handle anything," even incompetent dads. Lisa Belkin (2012), writing for the *Huffington Post*, says that the "marketers at Kimberly-Clark . . . figured it was a combination that couldn't miss. It showed fathers parenting! It included adorable babies! It was light-hearted and fun, what with those poor hapless dads responsible for their *own* children for five whole days!"

The ads show dads watching sports on TV while their babies languish in dirty diapers, changing poo-filled diapers while holding their noses, and dealing with kitchen walls covered in splattered food, among other scenarios. Funny? Not to everyone. What they didn't take into account, Belkin says, was another trend—

> the one where the growing number of men who consider themselves involved, equal parents (according to the U.S. Census, one in three are their child's primary caregiver) are more than a little sensitive about being portrayed as the butt of an advertiser's joke.

Chris Routly, a father from Pennsylvania, was so angered he started a petition titled, "We're Dads, Huggies. Not Dummies." Here's what he said:

> Why is a dad on diaper duty an appropriate or meaningful test of the product in any way a mom using them is not? Why reduce dads to being little more than test dummy parents, putting diapers and wipes through a "worst-case scenario" crash course of misuse and abuse? Is that what HUGGIES thinks dads do? We leave our children in overflowing diapers because sports is more important to us? Really?
>
> (Levs, 2012)

In an interview given to CNN, Routly said he is concerned that men and boys "see the bumbling dad . . . and think that's what's expected of them. And it can lead girls and women to have low expectations for how their husbands will handle fatherhood." His petition garnered over 1300 signatures. Huggies reacted almost immediately, promising Routly that they would take the offensive ads down and replace them with images of dads caring for their toddlers. A singular victory? Not really.

Remember the ads with the PMS-averse men clinging to arms full of milk cartons? The outcry over that campaign was so ferocious, from both men and women, that it was shut down early, only weeks after it debuted. The microsite that was developed as part of the campaign noted that "regrettably, some people found our campaign about milk and PMS to be outrageous and misguided," adding that others "thought it funny and educational" (Elliott, 2011). According to an article in the *New York Times*, the advertising agency handling the campaign and executives at the California Milk Board "seemed taken aback at how quickly the complaints came in—many only a day or two after the campaign began—and how intense, even angry, the critics were." The article also notes:

> The reaction to the campaign, and the subsequent changes, are indicative of the pitfalls in the age of social media to producing ads that seek to be noticed by being daring, provocative or shocking.
>
> The ability of consumers to quickly gather on Web sites like Facebook and Twitter and share their opinions with potentially millions of other consumers, as well as the creators of the ad campaigns they dislike, means that it is becoming harder for marketers to walk that fine line between getting noticed and getting berated.
>
> (Elliot, 2011)

This is certainly a step in the right direction, but is this the answer to gender stereotypes? No. The answer is to not develop them in the first place. As Sheehan suggests, one of the best ways to defeat stubborn stereotypes is to present a range of images more fully representative of reality. The nature of advertising, and its success, is based in large part on its repeatability. Given this, there would seem to be enough leeway to expand on any portrayal of any group so that a rounded, not a flat, image is created (Sheehan, 2014, p. 82). Referencing the bumbling husband type that was already beginning to appear several years ago, Sheehan noted that, "as an advertising trend, this could be problematic if such images are not balanced with other images of men that show them as confident and capable in traditional homemaking situations" (p. 94). Likewise, if men are actually shown as being perfectly capable of *all* of the things that make them competent human beings, then we don't have stereotypes. We have real people who, amazingly, resemble us. And guess what, this applies to any group being stereotyped.

So we have seen that stereotypes abound and noted that they are not limited to only the "usual suspects." Although men have certainly been stereotyped in the past, not surprisingly there hasn't been much objection to being depicted as woman-chasing, truck-driving, beer-loving, sports addicts. What is surprising is how quickly that stereotype has been altered and how quickly that alteration has been objected to. As Alex Gibson (2008), in an essay for a British online site on contemporary feminism, notes:

> Feminism has taught women who are prepared to listen that their traditional gender roles needn't be upheld as a good thing, that to branch out from the way women are "supposed to be" is a way of marking yourself out as independent and intelligent. Men simply haven't got anything to raise their consciousness about this issue.

There are others, however, who don't see the dumb dad stereotype as an issue at all—at least not in the sense we have been dealing with it here. In fact, they view it as a reaffirmation of already existing gender roles. Former professor turned science editor, Kali Tal suggests, "advertising employs the 'Trope of the Stupid Man' in ways that affirm, rather than challenge sexist notions of women's work and women's place." She believes that women helping clueless men take on chores stereotypically assigned to women is itself part of a stereotype. The notion of "separate spheres" for men and women is deeply ingrained in most Western societies: women "rule" the household in daily domestic matters, and men rule women . . . and the world (Tal, 2012).

She suggests that we take a second look at the ads appearing to belittle men. What seems to be the penalty for being a dumb dad? None, she says, "aside from some rolled eyes, there's not only tolerance, but often fondness for the big lug." She asks that "the next time you see a stupid man in a commercial, pay attention to what he's being stupid about, and see if that reinforces sexist stereotypes or challenges them."

Ultimately, however, the question isn't really about whether men are experiencing negative stereotyping for the first time in advertising history. It's whether stereotypes as a whole affect our perceptions of ourselves and others—and the answer is yes, they do. The image of women in the 19th century, perpetuated in art, magazine illustration, and advertising, was the buxom, Rubenesque figure used to sell everything from soap to liqueur. The thinning of the American woman began in the 20th century and continues today, and it's been the result of a combination of media, from movies and television shows to advertising. Women and girls are bombarded with images of thin, sexual, and often powerless and passive versions of who they should be. Both cultivation theory and expectancy theory are at work here, and the overall effect is painfully evident. Who gets to decide who we are? Are men macho or are they helpless wimps? Advertising shows us both. Is that a mixed message? Yes. Do men finally share the same space as women? Possibly they do, at least to some extent. As MacKinnon (2003) says, "Perhaps it is not that women have gained a measure of equality in access to social and economic power. Perhaps, rather, men have joined women in some measure—in powerlessness" (p. 99). Does that make us all equal? Of course not. But to some extent it does. As Walter Lippmann (1920) suggested so many years ago, we are *all* slaves to the images in our heads, and those images are put there, for the most part, by the media. Or, as cultural studies scholar Sut Jhally (2014) puts it:

> We define ourselves at our deepest level through the reality of advertising. We have to reach a socially accepted understanding of gender identity in some way. It is not an option one can refuse. If we do not cope at this level then the evidence suggests that it is very difficult to cope at any level.

Raise your hand if you're willing to accept the version of you and others portrayed by advertising. If not, then do something about it.

References

Belkin, L. (2012). Huggies pulls ads after insulting dads. Huff Post Parents. Retrieved January 22, 2015 from http://www.huffingtonpost.com/lisa-belkin/huggies-pulls-diaper-ads_b_1339074.html

Bivins, T. (2009). *Mixed Media: Moral Distinctions in Advertising, Public Relations, and Journalism* (2nd ed.). New York: Routledge.

Cameron, A. (2005). Everybody loves lazy stereotyping of male roles. *Sydney Morning Herald*. Retrieved January 23, 2015 from http://www.smh.com.au/news/Opinion/Everybody-loves-lazy-stereotyping-of-male-roles/2005/04/10/1113071851393.html

Elliot, S. (2011). Under fire, PMS-related milk campaign shut down early. *The New York Times*, mediacoder blogs. Retrieved January 22, 2015 from http://mediadecoder.blogs.nytimes.com/2011/07/21/under-fire-pms-related-milk-campaign-shut-down-early/?_php=true&_type=blogs&_r=0

Gerbner, G., Gross, L., Mogan, M., Signorigell, N. & Shanahan, J. (2002). Growing up with television: Cultivation processes. In J. Bryant & D. Zillman (Eds.) *Media Effects: Advances in Theory and Research*. Mahwah, NJ: Lawrence Erlbaum, pp. 43–67.

Gibson, A. (2008). Why men should care about gender stereotypes. The F-Word: Contemporary UK Feminism. Retrieved January 22, 2015 from http://www.thefword.org.uk/features/2008/02/men_stereotypes

Gornick, V. (1979). Introduction. In E. Goffman (Ed.) *Gender Advertisements*. Cambridge: Harvard University Press.

Hedderman, M. (2012). Is the stereotypical portrayal of males in British television advertising changing the attitudes and behaviours of women in society towards men? *Women in Society*, 3, 1–19.

Jhally, S. (2014). What's wrong with a little objectification? Sut Jhally. Retrieved January 22, 2015 from http://www.sutjhally.com/articles/whatswrongwithalit/

Kane, C. (2005). Men are becoming the ad target of the gender sneer. *The New York Times* online. Retrieved January 22, 2015 from http://www.nytimes.com/2005/01/28/business/media/28adco.html?_r=0

LaRossa, R., Jaret, C., Gadgil, M., & Wynn, G. R. (2000). The changing culture of fatherhood in comic strip families: A six-decade analysis. *Journal of Marriage and the Family*, 62, 375–87.

Lejeune, C. S. (2012). How the media make men look stupid. *Philadelphia Magazine, News + Opinion*. Retrieved January 22, 2015 from http://www.phillymag.com/news/2012/07/18/empowering-women-work-belittling-men/

Levs, J. (2012). No more dumb old dad: Changing the bumbling father stereotype. CNN.com. Retrieved January 22, 2015 from http://www.cnn.com/2012/06/12/living/dumb-dad-stereotype

Lippmann, W. (1920). *Public Opinion.* New York: Harcourt, Brace and Company.

MacKinnon, K. (2003). *Representing Men: Maleness and Masculinity in the Media.* New York: Oxford University Press Inc.

Marcellus, J. (2013). What's the harm in advertising stereotypes? In C. J. Pardun (Ed.) *Advertising and Society: An Introduction* (2nd ed.). Malden, MA: Wiley Blackwell.

Midena, K., & Davidson, H. (2011). Stereotypes and clichés push real men from television. News.com. Retrieved January 22, 2015 from http://www.news.com.au/entertainment/stereotypes-and-cliches-push-real-men-from-television/story-e6frfmq9-1226185623377

Nathanson, P., & Young, K. (2001). *Spreading Misandry: The Teaching of Contempt for Men in Popular Culture.* Quebec: McGill-Queen's University Press.

Nittie, N. K. (n.d.). Five common Latino stereotypes in television and film. About News & Issues/Race Relations. Retrieved January 25, 2015 from http://racerelations.about.com/od/hollywood/a/Five-Common-Latino-Stereotypes-In-Television-And-Film.htm

Polis, C. (2011). Got PMS? Drink some milk, says sexist ad campaign. Huff Post Food. Retrieved January 22, 2015 from http://www.huffingtonpost.com/2011/07/12/pms-milk-sexist_n_896333.html

Ramirez, T. (2013). Sofia Vergara loves playing stereotypes. HuffPost Latino Voices. Retrieved January 25, 2015 from http://www.huffingtonpost.com/tanisha-l-ramirez/sofia-vergara-sex-symbol-stereotype_b_2812691.html

Sheehan, K. B. (2014). *Controversies in Contemporary Advertising* (2nd ed.). Los Angeles: Sage.

Tal, K. (2012). Selling stupid men: Advertising and the myth of the incompetent male. Hepshiba's Pad. The Daily Kos. Retrieved January 22, 2015 from http://www.dailykos.com/story/2012/08/14/1119939/-Selling-Stupid-Men-Advertising-and-the-Myth-of-the-Incompetent-Male#

Tsai, W.H.S., & Shumow, M. (2011). Representing fatherhood and male domesticity in American advertising. *Interdisciplinary Journal of Research in Business.* 1(8), 38–48.

Turner, C. (2004). *Planet Simpson: How a Cartoon Masterpiece Defined a Generation.* Cambridge: Da Capo Press.

6 The Advertising Milieu and Beauty Advertising

Katherine Frith

CHAPTER SUMMARY

Standards of human beauty change with the times and vary in different cultures. Nevertheless, those standards have real consequences as people who are considered to be more attractive tend to be more financially and socially successful. Advertising has frequently been criticized for creating idealized images of beauty, images that are largely impossible for normal women to achieve. However, advertising is only a part of the larger media environment that surrounds us and defines what counts as attractive. In the United States and other Western cultures in particular, children are bombarded with visuals that "teach" them that certain types of looks are desirable. This process begins at a very young age as children watch television and online programming, including advertising messages. The beauty industries, media, and advertising contribute to expectations and stereotypes of beauty.

Introduction

Most advertisers use stereotypes to relay their messages. A magazine reader flips past the ads in an instant; a TV viewer sees the commercial for 30 seconds, so there is no time for character development. An advertiser will use a model who symbolizes the best "type of person" for their product so that the viewer can "make sense" of the message in a few seconds. Thus beautiful smiling women use cosmetics, strong handsome men drive sporty cars. Advertisers stereotype, but advertising is just one part of a much larger cultural media milieu that stereotypes men, women, and children and invites them to participate in modern consumer culture.

In this chapter, I review the literature on advertising and gender stereotyping and look at how this stereotyping starts with the very young and continues through a lifetime. Finally, I will argue that the stereotypical messages about gender are carried by media and advertising but have been fostered, for over a century, by the much larger beauty and entertainment industries.

Stereotyping Starts Young—The Smaller Milieu

The world of children's television is a gender-stratified world. Studies suggest that children's television is primarily a male world (Signorielli, 1993; Barcus, 1983) and that there are more male characters depicted than female in children's entertainment. Most animated product representatives such as Tony the Tiger and Captain Crunch are predominately male (Pierce and McBride, 1999). Also in children's commercials, the male characters carry the action while female characters offer support. Toy companies reinforce this gender bias by creating action-oriented products for boys (cars, guns, and action figures) and passive types of playthings for girls (dress-up dolls, pink ponies, and soft animals).

Advertisers further reinforce these stereotypes in the colors, settings, and behavior of each gender in the commercials (Frith & Mueller, 2010). The male characters in boy-oriented commercials wear dark-colored clothing and are filmed against bright primary-colored backgrounds (dark green, blue, and gray). Commercials aimed at girls use pastel colors, such as pink or white. Girls wear lighter-colored clothing. Boys are often filmed outside, while commercials aimed at girls are filmed in bedroom-style sets or in playrooms (Seiter, 1995).

In TV commercials, boys run, shout, ride bikes, compete with each other, and take risks. Commercials aimed at boys have frequent cuts and many close-ups (Seiter, 1995). In commercials aimed at girls, the camera techniques create a soft, warm, fuzzy feeling. Girls play quietly in their pastel bedrooms or watch boys in more active play. Seiter (1995) noted that when boys are shown playing with their toys, they are generally aggressive, even violent—crashing cars or aggressively competing with action figures. Girls, on the other hand, are shown playing quietly and gently. For girls a toy is a playmate; for boys a toy is a plaything.

Advertising does not operate in a cultural vacuum but is part of a larger milieu that shapes the development of young girls' identities. According to Markey & Markey (2012), "The media are a source of developmental information for adolescents and young adults, providing daily, omnipresent messages about gender, attractiveness, and ideal body shapes and sizes" (p.1). The messages to young people start very early. In Disney movies, heroines such as Cinderella, Rapunzel, and Goldilocks are blonde and blue eyed, while Cinderella's evil stepsisters have dark hair. Wicked witches and stepmothers are often dark or red haired, and, of course, Cinderella has a slim waist that would be unachievable for most children. Gaston, in *Beauty and the Beast*, is an example of the type of male images offered to young boys. Strong, muscular, and brash, he is admired in his community as "the greatest hunter in the whole world."

Disney has built an empire that surrounds most children growing up in the United States. There are movies featuring beautiful princesses, princess figurines, matching clothing for birthdays, holidays at Disney Resorts, and so on. The little princes and princesses are surrounded by gender messages that

Figure 6.1 Disney's Cinderella
Source: Photo by Esther Thorson.

support certain stereotypes. Advertising is part of this milieu, but the culture of gender stereotypes extends far beyond the advertising world.

Other large contributors to stereotypical images for children are the associated toys and figurines. Disney figurines, popular toys for little girls, use the same basic body image as Cinderella or the Barbie doll. Barbie, created by Mattel, has mirrored dominant U.S. beauty ideals for nearly half a century. One of the most common criticisms of Barbie is that she promotes an unrealistic idea of body image for young women. A standard Barbie doll is 11.5 inches tall, which on a 1/6 scale would equate to about a 5'9" tall woman. Barbie's vital statistics have thus been estimated at 36" chest, 18" waist, and 33" hips. At 5'9" and weighing 110 pounds, Barbie would have a BMI of 16.24 and fit the weight criteria for anorexia. According to research by the University Central Hospital of Helsinki, Finland, she would lack the 17 to 22% body fat required for a woman to menstruate. Mattel has said that the original waist of the Barbie doll was made small because the waistbands of her clothes, along with the snaps and zippers, would add bulk to her figure. However, after scathing criticism from feminists, in 1997, Mattel expanded her waist a bit (Etcoff, 2000).

Teenage Girls and Advertising

As girls grow into their teens, the media continue to play a significant role in the development of identity. In fact, much research has been done on images in the media and self-image in adolescents. One criticism is that advertisements

Figure 6.2 2015 Barbie dolls with the "improved" waist
Source: Photo by Esther Thorson.

present young girls with unrealistic beauty norms. Most advertisements that appear in magazines have been extensively retouched to remove even the slightest flaw. Techniques such as retouching led Lakoff and Scherr (1984) to accuse advertisers of creating a "cult of unrealizable beauty" (p. 290).

In a 2013 interview with *Teen Vogue's* advertising director, Lizet Martinez, Martinez states that the magazine is aimed at "trendsetting girls who know there's only one authentic source for emerging beauty" (Style Cognoscente, 2013). Aside from the print magazine, *Teen Vogue* has a strong online presence, apps, and is on social media such as Snapchat, Instagram, and Twitter.

Critics contend that the uniformly thin, perfectly proportioned models contribute to unhappiness with their own bodies among young girls and thus undermine self-confidence and reinforce problems such as eating disorders (Freedman, 1986). In addition, Walsh-Childers (1999) notes that advertising photographers often focus on women's breasts, regardless of the product category. She contends that the idea that sexy equals big breasts has created

Figure 6.3 Teen issue of *Vogue*

feelings of inferiority in young girls, so that "plastic surgeons report that they now see girls as young as 14 seeking surgery to enlarge their breasts" (p. 82). Yet one might argue that the content of the magazines is also highly retouched and that the ads do not stand alone. Fashion spreads, product "news," as well as the advertisements all present perfect images where all flaws and fat have been removed.

Interestingly, research in child development has shown that self-perceptions of physical attractiveness become markedly different between male and female adolescents (Martin & Gentry, 1997) as children grow up. Researchers have noted that self-perceptions of physical attractiveness appear to decline systematically over time in girls but not in boys (Hartner, 1993; Block & Robins, 1993). Boys tend to view their bodies as "process" and have a stronger view of themselves as holistic, while adolescent girls pay attention to individual body parts (Brown, Cash, & Mikulka, 1990). Advertisers contribute to this "body-as-object" focus for female adolescents by using difficult to attain standards of physical attractiveness in ads. An analysis of *Seventeen*, a magazine aimed at adolescent females, found that over a 20-year period from 1970 to 1990 models had become significantly thinner (Guillen & Barr, 1994).

The images we see in the media are never true to life. Photoshop allows companies to promote unobtainable beauty by simply airbrushing out imperfections in the models and digitally enhancing certain body parts. In practically every page in a women's magazine, women are shown the illusion of a perfect body that is thought to be achievable, but in reality it is not. In just one issue of *Vogue*, Pascal Dangin (artistic retoucher for *Vogue*) willingly admitted to changing some 144 pictures in the magazine (Orbach, 2011, p. 392). These included both advertisements and fashion spreads.

The ideal of beauty is ingrained in children from a very young age. Disney toys and movies, Barbie dolls, and yes, advertising all teach young girls what is considered "beautiful" and what is not. Girls begin to understand at a young age that thin and sexy is what they should be when they grow up (Hellmich, 2006). Many girls refuse to join in sports in fear of "bulking up." Thus media messages about beauty aimed at young girls may be taking away the possibility for some girls of growing up to their full potential (Kilbourne, 1999).

The number of magazines aimed at teen and preteen girls worldwide has been growing. These teen magazines are aimed at girls aged 12–16 years old (Wykes & Gunter, 2005, p. 90). Many are teen versions of women's magazines and reinforce the same unattainable beauty ideals as shown to women.

The content of these teen magazines is related to fashion, how to improve your looks, and how to attract boys. Featured in most of the magazines are advertisements for fashion, beauty products, hair removal, and deodorant (Wykes & Gunter, 2005, p. 90). A study done at Brigham and Women's Hospital in Boston discovered that the more girls and women read magazines the more likely they were to diet and feel the magazine had influenced their ideal body shape (Kilbourne, 1999). In addition, 70% of college women admitted to feeling bad about themselves after they read a woman's magazine (Kilbourne, 1999).

Marsha Richins (1991) studied attitudes and behaviors of college students exposed to advertisements and found that after viewing beautiful models, subjects rated average women as less attractive. In other words, images of highly attractive individuals can cause viewers to rate the attractiveness of more ordinary others lower than they would otherwise. In addition, she found that exposure to highly attractive images negatively affected the subjects' feelings about their own appearance. As the author notes, "while one may argue that temporary dissatisfaction is beneficial if it stimulates consumers to buy products that improve their appearance . . . it is difficult to argue that such is the case here" (p. 83). She points out that the repeated exposure to idealized images may have a cumulative effect on self-feelings.

The Beauty Industry–The Larger Milieu

Sociologists tell us that beauty is a universal part of human experience: "it provokes pleasure, rivets attention and impels actions that ensure the survival of the species" (Etcoff, 2000, p. 24). The conventions of beauty are not innate but rather socialized. They are taught to us by our culture and supported by the media and advertising. Backman and Adams (1991) describe the myth of beauty and illustrate how women are, from a young age, taught to prize relationships with men who they presumably attract with their beauty. Thus the idea that a woman's personal happiness or unhappiness is brought about by her beauty or lack of it is inculcated in women at a very early age.

It can be argued that beauty is a currency in every society. Researchers (Hunter, 2002; De Casanova, 2004) note that smooth skin, thick hair, and a symmetrical body have value in most cultures. For a woman, personal beauty is arguably the most important quality she can possess (Robinson & Ward, 1995). Beauty is a physical form that grants social acceptance as well as personal satisfaction.

In dollars and cents, beauty has a price. In the United States, people spend more money on personal care and beauty products than on reading materials, on education, or on social services (Etcoff, 2000). Worldwide, cosmetics and toiletries are a multibillion-dollar industry. Among the world's richest countries, consumers in France and Japan spend over $230 per capita annually on beauty products, while American and Germans spent $173 and $164 respectively. In Brazil (where there more Avon ladies than members of the army) people spend $100 per capita, while Indians spent less than $4 (Jones, 2012).

Feminist writers have regularly blamed advertising and the media for encouraging an obsession with physical perfection. Advertising has been criticized for trapping women in an endless spiral of hope, self-consciousness, and self-hatred (Jones, 2012). Naomi Wolf (1992) notes, "Beauty is a currency system like the gold standard. Like any economy, it is determined by politics, and in the modern age in the West it is the last, best belief system that keeps male dominance intact" (p. 12). Etcoff (2000) argues that beauty is a 'convenient fiction' used by multibillion-dollar industries to create images of beauty that they peddle to the female masses.

In the 21st century, global advertising and global media have helped build the worldwide beauty industry to what it is today. The images put forth by beauty companies and their agencies are, for the most part, controlled by a relatively small number of large, mainly Western corporations. In the following section, I will trace the history of the global beauty industry, explore the research on the value of beauty, and discuss how advertising fosters the ideal of beauty as power in our culture.

Beauty and Power

Beauty conveys real social and economic advantages (Etcoff, 2000). Women cultivate beauty and use the beauty industries to maximize the power their beauty brings. People spend billions of dollars on cosmetics and plastic surgery for a reason: these industries cater to a world where looking good has survival value. Etcoff (2000) cites some examples in her book, *Survival of the Prettiest*. In one study, an attractive and an unattractive woman approach a phone booth and ask the occupant, "Did I leave my dime there?" (There is, in fact, a dime in the phone booth). Eighty-seven percent of the people return the dime to the good-looking woman, but only 64% of the people return the dime to the unattractive woman. In another study, sets of college applications were left in a Detroit airport. On each set was a note from the daughter asking her father to mail them for her, making it appear that the father had accidentally left them behind in the airport. Each set of identical applications had a different photo attached. In the end, people were much more likely to mail the applications to the colleges when the picture of the applicant was an attractive young girl (Etcoff, 2000).

Unlike racism or sexism, "lookism" or beauty prejudice operates at a largely unconscious level. Numerous studies show that attractive people are more likely to succeed in the work world. They are more likely to earn more, persuade others of their opinion, and move ahead more quickly. They tend to have more self-confidence and are less likely to worry about negative opinions than unattractive people are. Generally speaking, attractive people are more likely to think that they are in control of their lives and are more likely to be assertive (Etcoff, 2000).

In one psychological study, people were asked to participate in an interview with a psychologist. During the interview, the psychologist was interrupted by a phone call, and she excused herself for 10 minutes. Researchers found that attractive people waited 3 minutes and 20 seconds on average before demanding attention. Less attractive people waited an average of nine minutes before asking what had happened to the psychologist. There was no difference in how the two groups rated their own assertiveness, but attractive people evidently felt more entitled to better treatment (Etcoff, 2000).

Beauty is an advantage in all realms of life. And it does bring power. While it does not approach racism or sexism in magnitude, "lookism" as Etcoff

(2000) calls it, is a form of discrimination. Good-looking men are more likely to be hired at a higher salary and to be promoted faster than unattractive men are. Good-looking women, like good-looking men, are also more likely to be hired and to receive higher salaries. This is particularly true in Asian cultures where photos are attached to a CV. Thus photo retouching is a huge industry in countries such as China and Korea where millions of college students graduate each year and getting a job is easier for attractive women. Ironically, while researchers have found that good looks helped a woman to be hired for a clerical position, they worked against her moving into a managerial job. Thus Etcoff notes that the economics of being female are never particularly advantageous. An attractive woman may be criticized as "too feminine" to do a high-powered job, likely to be sexually harassed by male coworkers who see her as very sexy, and discriminated against by female coworkers who envy her beauty (Etcoff, 2000).

Nonetheless, women worldwide spend billions each year on cosmetics and beauty procedures in an effort to be more attractive, and while it is debatable whether this pays off in terms of workplace economics, there is evidence that attractive women in both developed and traditional societies are better able to find husbands who can provide economic security.

In 1990, psychologist David Buss interviewed over 10,000 people between the ages of 14 and 70 from 37 countries around the world. Physical attractiveness and good looks showed up on the top-ten list of important and desirable qualities. In fact, in non-Western and non-North American countries, people placed more importance on the looks of their mates than did the Westerners (Etcoff, 2000). Buss found that men valued physical attractiveness and good looks in a partner more than women did in 34 of 37 countries he studied (In India, Poland, and Sweden there was no difference).

The Rise of the Global Beauty Industry

While women have used paints and potions to enhance their beauty for centuries, it was only in the 20th century that multinational corporations and their advertising agencies began to capitalize on women's interest in beauty and attractiveness for profit. In this section of the chapter, we look at the history and growth of the global beauty industry and how this growth has resulted in the spread of megabrands that have disseminated beauty ideals throughout the world.

Today, a large proportion of the beauty products sold worldwide are produced by a handful of multinational corporations. The 10 biggest beauty companies collectively account for over 50% of all sales of beauty products throughout the world. Two countries, France and the United States, have led the world in branding beauty. In fact, L'Oréal (France) and Procter & Gamble (United States) now account for over one-fifth of total world sales of all beauty products (Jones, 2012).

Two of the largest and oldest beauty giants, Lever Brothers (Unilever) and Procter & Gamble, had humble beginnings. Both companies began in the soap business with Procter & Gamble introducing the first branded soap, Ivory, in

Table 6.1 The world's 10 largest beauty companies

Company	Nationality	Total Beauty Revenues[a] ($)	Revenues Outside Home Region (%)
Procter & Gamble	U.S.	26,000	56
L'Oréal	France	24,089	55
Unilever	U.K./Neth	16,762	68
Colgate-Palmolive	U.S.	9,658	81
Estee Lauder	U.S.	7,911	59
Avon	U.S.	7,604	77
Beiersdorf	Germany	7,547	31
Johnson & Johnson	U.S.	7,200	49
Shiseido	Japan	7,011	20
Kao	Japan	6,267	15

Adapted from Jones, 2012, p. 372

the late 1800s. Lifebuoy and Lux soap were the Lever beauty brands (today Unilever owns the Dove soap brand, so it has continued over the years to appeal to women with its branded soaps). In the early 1900s, Lever invented the term "B.O." for body odor and used it in its advertising to remind women that what most intrigued a man was a woman's smell not her smile.

The second stage of the growth of the beauty industry began around the 1920s when Hollywood first started to have a major impact on women's self-perceptions. Prior to the era of "Hollywood Stars," beauty products such as "pancake makeup" were reserved for the stage. However, in the early 1900s, figurers such as Max Faktorowicz, the son of a Polish rabbi, immigrated to the United States. He moved to Los Angeles and opened a store in the city's theatrical district selling his new and improved "pancake makeup" to stars in the budding movie industry. He created thinner greasepaint for motion picture use, and his greasepaint cream and lipsticks became a hit with Hollywood movie stars and later the general public—and the Max Factor brand was born (today owned by Procter & Gamble). These new "make-ups" could hide imperfections and enhance a woman's natural beauty, and thus in the early 1920s, makeup began to take precedence in advertising over claims for cleanliness as the signifier of beauty.

It was also in the early 1902s that women entrepreneurs entered the beauty business. Two women in particular have come to be known for their beauty brands that have lasted for nearly a century: Helena Rubinstein and Elizabeth Arden. Both used the salon route to create their brands. Rubinstein, born in Poland later immigrated to Australia and then to the United States. She established a substantial business with beauty salons in Europe, Australia, and the United States.

The importance of media in creating and perpetuating norms about beauty and attractiveness cannot be underestimated (Frith, Shaw, & Cheng, 2005).

Stice and Shaw (1994) argue that a sociocultural female ideal is communicated to women, with mass media being "one of the strongest transmitters of this pressure" (p. 289). While magazine and billboard posters were the main types of advertising in the early 1900s, the advent of commercial advertising on radio provided a hugely important new medium for American beauty companies (Peiss, 1998). In fact, with the help of radio advertising during the 1950s, the American beauty market boomed. The social importance of smelling and looking clean was being promoted through ads to become a part of the American cultural psyche.

Procter & Gamble became one of the largest advertisers on American radio airways after the company invented the "soap opera" a genre that became popular on the radio in the 1920s. These early radio soap operas, which became a central aspect of P & G marketing campaigns, were broadcast in weekday, daytime slots when most listeners were predominantly female (Jones, 2012).

During the 1940s and '50s television transmission became available. In Europe, governments often controlled broadcasting and permitted little or no advertising. But this was not the case in the United States. Television's impact on the beauty industry has been profound. Early on, the United States became a major source of television programming for other countries, with programs dubbed or subtitled into local languages. Thus Hollywood celebrities became global beauty icons. The choice of television stars presented on U.S.-based shows was highly selective. For example, African-American actors were rarely seen on television before 1960. Non-whites generally were strictly limited on the kind of roles that they could play in Hollywood movies.

Television became especially important in turning beauty pageants into international media events. It started with the Miss America pageant and was followed by the British-based Miss World contest launched in 1951. Not to be topped, the United States introduced a Miss Universe pageant in 1952. These pageants were televised in many countries and widely watched.

Around the world, spectacles such as these set expectations and defined aspirations. The Western beauty ideals favored in theses pageants reflected and reinforced the ideal of pale skin and wide Western eyes. Scandinavian women were the first winners of the Miss World and Miss Universe contests. The early winners of Miss World included six Europeans and three pale-skinned contestants from Venezuela, Egypt, and South Africa. The winners of Miss Universe were also overwhelmingly pale-skinned contestants from the United States, Europe, or Latin America (Jones, 2012).

Television greatly expanded the advertising budgets of beauty companies. By the 1960s, American cosmetics companies were spending an average of 15% of their total sales revenue on advertising. The underlying message of all this advertising was, and continues to be, that every woman "has a responsibility to herself, as well as to those around her, to take control of her appearance and be beautiful" (Jones, 2012, p. 102).

Hollywood celebrities and models in advertising in fashion magazines such as *Vogue, Cosmopolitan,* and *Good Housekeeping* greatly contributed to the

Figure 6.4 Magazine cover featuring Miss America 1949

diffusion of Western, and especially American, ideals of lifestyle, fashion, and beauty.

Beyond Advertising: From Makeup to Makeovers

As we have seen, advertising is a primary medium for messages about beauty, but today advertising has been joined by TV reality shows that feature makeovers, weight loss, and surgical techniques deemed necessary for a woman to attain her full beauty. These shows have brought the beauty competition among women to frenzied heights and add a whole new level to the discussion on beauty persuasion and ethics.

The media tell women that through beauty surgery and beauty technologies a woman, regardless of age, can stay looking young forever. Cosmetic surgery is no longer just for movie celebrities. In the United States, 70% of cosmetic surgery patients earn less than $50,000 per year and 30% earn below $25,000. Most of the surgeries performed in the United States each year are done on Caucasian women in their 30s, 40s, and 50s. The American Society of Plastic Surgeons, which collects statistics on cosmetic surgery, claimed a 966% increase in cosmetic surgery procedures between 1992 and 2007, with a 68% increase between 2000 and 2007 alone. The vast majority, 91%, of these patients are women (Marwick, 2010). People of color represent only about 20% of cosmetic surgery patients (Etcoff, 2000). Breast augmentation, tummy tucks, and facelifts represent nearly half of all the cosmetic surgeries done in the United States.

Reality television shows such as *The Swan* and *Extreme Makeover* as well as the drama *Nip Tuck* have been extremely popular in the United States and have moved the beauty debate away from beauty products and beauty pageants to medical services. Marwick (2010) argues that shows like *The Swan* are examples of "body culture media—a genre of popular culture which positions work on the body as a morally correct solution to personal problems" (p. 252).

While plastic surgery has grown exponentially in the United States, America does not top the list of nations where cosmetic surgery is most popular. The country with the most cosmetic surgeries per capita is South Korea (Davies & Han, 2011). People in South Korea undergo invasive plastic surgery at a rate that is 1.8 times higher than people in the United States (Davies & Han, 2011). And the most popular Korean facial cosmetic surgery operation is double eyelid surgery to create an upper eyelid crease (which makes Asian eyes look more like Western eyes). The picture in Figure 6.5 of the candidates for Miss Korea in 2013 shows that through cosmetic surgery the women in the contest have managed to attain a "look" that is remarkably similar.

Conclusion

What are the ethical dimensions of all this beauty advertising? Traditionally, advertising has been singled out as a mostly evil activity that causes women to purchase products that, at worst, are inimical to their own well-being and at best only produce temporary improvements to their looks. Plus, big beauty corporations have been criticized for doing all this manipulative beauty advertising in the name of huge profits.

Beauty advertising presents viewers with images of beautiful models who appear to be perfect in every way. Through lighting, photography, makeup, and retouching with Photoshop, the models in beauty ads are so perfect that their beauty has been criticized as actually being "unattainable" for the average woman.

Figure 6.5 Candidates for Miss Korea 2013

Source: http://www.huffingtonpost.com/2013/25/miss-korea-contestants-2013-photos_n_3157026.
html

So is this an ethical dilemma for women consumers? Are women being duped by companies and made to believe that by purchasing beauty products they will become more beautiful? Yes and no.

Yes, if one believes that media present the truth, then of course we must conclude that advertising "lies," because most ads embellish the truth. In the case of beauty advertising, those images have been altered so extensively that the models appear to be perfect in every way. The women in the ads are no longer "real" people.

No, however, if we believe that most adults understand that media, and advertising, present actors who are showing a perfect face to the viewer. And in the case of beauty advertising, doesn't the viewer want to see perfection? For centuries we have been attracted to artists who have painted and sculpted their visions of perfect beauty. We visit museums to see these visions of perfect beauty. We read poetry that describes beauty. Etcoff argues that, "The idea that carnal beauty is visible evidence of spiritual beauty can be traced back at least as far as Plato . . ." (2000:40).

And as we have seen, beauty stereotypes are not just practiced by advertising, they are ubiquitous in media and socially learned through constant reinforcement of gender roles in our culture. Advertising conforms, for the most part, to cultural expectations. Research by cognitive psychologists such as Etcoff (2000) has given us much to ponder. If, as she suggests, that beauty is a "fungible asset" that conveys real social and economic advantages to women, then we cannot so much say that advertising stereotypes "manipulate" women into buying products that enhance their beauty. Rather, we must say that women in most cultures "cultivate beauty" and use the beauty industries to maximize the power their beauty brings. So women use the images of beautiful women models in ads to educate themselves about beauty and beauty products. The beauty industries cater to a world where "looking good" has survival value.

Of course, the reality is that the models in beauty advertising actually have pimples, wrinkles, and all the other things that normal women have, but the imperfections have been removed with makeup or retouching so the models appear perfect in the ads. The ethical question is are advertisers giving us what you want to see or are they manipulating us? What do you think?

References

Backman, C. B., & Adams, M. C. (1991). Self-perceived physical attractiveness, self-esteem, race, and gender. *Sociological Focus*, 24(4), 283–90.

Barcus, F. E. (1983). *Images of Life on Children's TV*. New York: Praeger.

Block, J., & Robins, R. W. (1993). A longitudinal study of consistency and change in self-esteem from early adolescence to early adulthood. *Child Development*, 64, 909–23.

Brown, T. A., Cash, T. F., & Mikulka, P. J. (1990). Attitudinal body-image assessment: Factor analysis of the Body Self Relations Questionnaire. *Journal of Personality Assessment*, 55, 135–44.

Davies, G., & Han, G.S. (2011). Korean cosmetic surgery and digital publicity: Beauty by Korean design, *Media International Australia*, 141, (Nov 2011), 146–56.

Etcoff, N. L. (2000). *Survival of the Prettiest: The Science of Beauty*. New York: Anchor Books.

Freedman, R. (1986). *Beauty Bound*. Lexington, MA: D.C. Heath.

Frith, K. T., & Mueller, B. (2010). *Advertising and Societies: Global Issues*. NY: Peter Lang.

Frith, K. T., Shaw, P., & Cheng, H. (2005). The construction of beauty: A cross-cultural analysis of women's magazine advertisements, *Journal of Communication*, 55(1), 56–70.

Guillen, E. O., & Barr, S. I. (1994). Nutrition, dieting, and fitness messages in a magazine for adolescent women, 1970–1990. *Journal of Adolescent Health*, 15(6), 464–72.

Hellmich, N. (2006). Do thin models warp girls' body image? *USA Today*. Retrieved August 24, 2012 from http://www.usatoday.com/news/health/2006-09-25-thin-models_x.htm

Hunter, M. L. (2002). If you light you're alright: Light skin color as social capital for women of color. *Gender & Society* 16(2), 175–93.

Jones, G. (2012). *Beauty Imagined: A History of the Global Beauty Industry.* NY : Oxford University Press.

Kilbourne, J. (1999). *Deadly Persuasion: Why Women and Girls must Fight the Addictive Power of Advertising.* New York: Free Press.

Lakoff, R. T., & Scherr, R. L. (1984). *Face Value. The Politics of Beauty.* Boston: Routledge & Kegan Paul.

Markey, C., & Markey, P. (2012). Emerging adults' responses to a media presentation of idealized female beauty: An examination of cosmetic surgery in reality television. *Psychology of Popular Media Culture*, (April 2012), 1–11.

Martin, M. C., & Gentry, J. W. (1997). Stuck in the model trap: The effects of beautiful models in ads on female pre-adolescents and adolescents. *Journal of Advertising*, 26(2), 19–33.

Marwick, A. (2010). There's a beautiful girl under all of this: Performing hegemonic femininity in reality television. *Critical Studies in Media Communication*, 27(3), 251–66.

Orbach, S. (2011). Losing bodies. *Social Research*, 78(2), 387–94.

Peiss, K. (1998). *Hope in a Jar: The Making of America's Beauty Culture.* NY: Metropolitan Books.

Pierce, K., & Mc Bride, M. (1999). Aunt Jemima isn't keeping up with the Energizer Bunny: Stereotypes of animated spokes-characters in advertising. *Sex Roles*, 40(11/12), 959–68.

Richins, M. (1991). Social comparison and the idealized images of advertising. *Journal of Consumer Research*, 18, 71–83.

Robinson, T. L., & Ward, J. V. (1995). African American adolescents and skin color. *Journal of Black Psychology*, 21(3), 256–74.

Seiter, E. (1995). *Sold Separately: Parents and Children in Consumer Culture.* New Brunswick, NJ: Rutgers.

Signorielli, N. (1993). Television, the portrayal of women, and children's attitudes. In Berry, Gordon L. (Ed.) *Children and Television: Images in a Changing Sociocultural World.* Thousand Oaks, CA: Sage.

Stice, E., & Shaw, H. (1994). The adverse effects of the media portrayed this ideal on women, and linkages to bulimic symptomology. *Journal of Social and Clinical Psychology*, 13(3), 288–308.

Style Cognoscente (2013). Interview with ad director of *Teen Vogue*, July 7. Retrieved June 29, 2015 from https://www.youtube.com/watch?v=L4bpsMVwpWo

Walsh-Childers, K. (1999). Women as sex partners. In Paul Martin Lester (Ed.) *Pictures That Injure: Pictorial Stereotypes in the Media.* Westport, CT: Praeger.

Wolf, N. (1992). *The Beauty Myth: How Images of Beauty Are Used Against Women.* New York: Perennial.

Wykes, M., & Gunter, B. (2005). *The Media and Body Image.* London: Sage.

7 What Do People Really Think About Commercials That Stereotype Women or Glamorize Dangerous Behavior?

Margaret Duffy and Esther Thorson

CHAPTER SUMMARY

Advertising is routinely described as unethical, trivial, untruthful, and exploitative. Ethicists and regulators have used many approaches to understand advertising's effects on various populations and which messages and strategies should be classified as ethical or unethical. This chapter reports results of a qualitative study investigating how people describe advertising in three different categories: sexualized ads, ads showing dangerous behaviors, and public service announcements promoting prosocial behaviors. We find that people interpret advertising meanings and appropriateness in very different ways and suggest that a more nuanced understanding of advertising ethics can emerge from a "mutualist" approach to meaning making. Instead of assessing ad messages from a rules-based standpoint, we ask the question "how do ads mean" as individuals interpret the persuasive messages they see.

Introduction

A crucial issue in understanding advertising ethics involves the differing perceptions people may have of an advertisement's content. When viewing the same ad, one person may see it as exciting and energizing, while another finds it irresponsible and dangerous. What one person finds seductive and interesting, another sees as gross and disgusting. For many years, considerable research has focused on advertising ethics and raised concerns that certain types of advertising have potentially harmful effects. This includes ads that stereotype women, minorities, or the elderly; those that show unsafe behaviors in using a product; those that are in bad taste; those aimed at vulnerable populations; and those that promote products considered to be dangerous, such as alcohol. Regulators, such as the Federal Trade Commission (FTC), review and rule on complaints related to advertising content, and advertising content is regularly criticized for ethical breaches.

This chapter is based on a study that gathered qualitative data about people's responses to ads identified as ethically problematic based on guidelines and conventions established by advertising ethics critics and the FTC (Institute for Advertising Ethics, 2010). We analyzed people's responses to the ads using social constructionist, rhetorical, and dramatistic theoretical lenses. There was total sample of 210 participants, with 69 responding to the dangerous category, 65 to the sexual category and 76 to the public service announcements (PSAs).

Literature Review

As individuals view an ad, they experience both positive and negative reactions (Ham, 2010). For example, a person may like a commercial that's entertaining or dislike it because she finds it boring or unrealistic. He or she may also respond to an ad based on content that is linked to ethical considerations, such as showing potentially offensive content, dangerous behaviors, or stereotypes.

Most of the research related to advertising ethics asks respondents about their perceptions of advertising and ethics. For example, Tinkham and Lariscy (1994) asked people to rate political ads on a scale that included the choices ethical/unethical. They found that ethical judgments predict people's evaluations of ads (p. 55). Schauster (2013) conducted an ethnography and interviews at a midsize advertising agency and found that employees believed that ethical behaviors were rooted in the virtuous characters of the employees themselves and especially the founders and leaders of the firm. Drumwright and Murphy (2009) investigated perceptions of ad ethics by practitioners and academics. They also examined advertising textbooks and called for additional deliberation, particularly in light of changes in technology and globalization of marketing.

In a nationwide online survey of 1,045 advertising students conducted by Fullerton, Kendrick, and McKinnon (2013), 9 out of 10 participants agreed that working for a company with high ethical standards is an important factor. At the same time, students acknowledged the overall perception of the field as unethical by most Americans and only one-fourth of the participants thought that advertising is ethical. The study also found several inconsistencies between students' attitudes and behavioral intentions. For example, assessing subjective roles or peer behavior might have an impact on students' behavior: If the questionable behavior, such as altering pictures, is what "everyone in advertising does," they might be more likely to do it (p. 44).

In their discussion of ethical dimensions of advertising, Lee and Nguyen (2013) contrasted two approaches to ethical thought and advertising: teleological ethics addressing consequences and effects of actions or, in this case, advertising and "deontological ethics" that looks rather at "intrinsic moral worth instead of its outcome alone" (p. 227). The authors adopted a deontological lens to look at the ethics of fast food advertising using Baker's and Martinson's (2001) TARES (Truthfulness of the message, Authenticity of the persuader, Respect for the persuadee, Equity of the appeal, and Social Responsibility for the common good) framework that established ethical principles of persuasive messages. Lee's and Nguyen's (2013) content analysis of 380 television and print fast food ads showed that few of them followed the five TARES principles and that the ads targeting children and teenagers had lower message ethicality than ads targeting adults. All of these studies, while useful and important, rely on asking individuals specifically about their reactions to ethical issues or beliefs about advertising. Thus issues of social desirability or even simply their awareness of a study's focus may affect subjects' responses. Social desirability means that even in an anonymous study, people will want to present themselves as being ethical or having other positive characteristics. Other studies, such as the TARES research cited earlier, apply rules and principles ethicists and philosophers developed without consulting audiences' worldviews.

Advertising, Rhetoric, and Social Constructionism

Social constructionism is rooted in theories of Symbolic Interactionism and draws on the work of Schutz (1962) and Mead (1934) among others. It holds that human beings create social reality through their interactions and discourses with others. Similarly, Berger and Luckman (1966) argued that language and symbols create symbolic realities that we must respond to as objective realities. Hackley (1999) suggests that social constructionism can provide us with a greater understanding of advertising ethics. Further, he posits that advertisers cocreate meanings with audiences in a highly complex process. Following Still and Good (1992), Hackley proposes that a "mutualist" theory of meaning making is useful. This meaning making will vary from audience to audience and individual to individual. Hackley (1998) writes that "social constructionist qualitative research allows [a] sense of constructed meaning to be acknowledged in the research" (p. 1).

Social constructionism focuses attention on people's everyday interactions and their social practices (Andrews, 2012). It assumes, as Gergen argued, that people understand their world through the media, "social artifacts," and the values that permeate that society (Gergen, 1994, p. 267). Of course, many interactions today are mediated, rather than face-to-face. Yet through media, advertisers and people are cocreating meanings, including those that relate to ethical judgments. Hirschman and Thompson (1997) used a grounded theoretical approach and argued that as people view advertisements as well as other media products, they interpret meanings based on their individual frames of reference that may or may not be the meanings intended by the ads' creators. Similarly, McCracken (1986) suggests that the typical research model of information processing in assessing consumers' responses to advertising doesn't account for the "cultural context of consumption" (p. 123). He argues that consumers do not simply absorb an advertisement's meaning but instead are active in creating its meanings. We suggest that this meaning making extends to consumers' interpretation of the ethical dimensions of an ad.

Rhetoric and Symbolic Convergence Theory

Rhetoric was famously described by Aristotle as discovering the available means of persuasion. As Foss (2009) points out, rhetoric, rather than being fanciful or high-flown language, in this case refers to human beings' use of symbols to communicate and persuade as well as creating our social reality: "Every symbolic choice we make results in seeing the world one way rather than another" (p. 4). In the process of interpreting a rhetorical artifact, we choose to define or label it in many ways. Those interpretations will frequently include judgments about advertising messages, spokespersons, and visuals that have ethical implications. Ads, then, are rhetoric, presenting messages and situations aimed at achieving certain goals. People's interpretations of the meanings of ads are rhetorical artifacts as well and reveal their understandings of the products, the goals of the advertiser, and the ethical components of an ad *from their points of view*.

Theoretical Approach and Methodology

In interpreting statements of respondents, we replicated and expanded categories of responses based on the interpretive strategies developed by Hirschman and Thompson (1997), and those categories are detailed in this section. In that study, the authors used grounded theory methods, including "grounded reading," allowing researchers to discern patterns as they analyzed data rather than developing hypotheses ahead of the analysis (Hirschman & Thompson, p. 146).

We are further guided by a Symbolic Convergence Theory (SCT) and its associated method of Fantasy Theme Analysis (FTA). SCT is a dramatistic theory that shows how people interpret media messages in terms of characters, settings, and action. It suggests that we understand the world through dramatic elements or stories. Dramas and stories in our usage do not refer to television shows, theater productions, or films. Instead, they have to do with how people explain their interpretations of events and media messages to others and to themselves. For instance, in an ad showing good friends enjoying beers at their favorite watering hole, the advertiser is seeking to connect its brands with the values of camaraderie and fun. Some viewers will like the ad's cheerful and friendly dialog and images of fellowship. Others may see it as dangerous and misleading, downplaying the negative effects of alcohol. Of course, most people don't study the ads they see, but FTA allows the critic to pull out and examine the underlying stories and the values embedded in those stories. As well, people's responses to dramas in advertisements offer insights into their values and beliefs and thus can show their responses to ethical issues.

Ernest Bormann created this approach, and it posits that human beings create social reality through symbols and communication identified as fantasy themes (Bormann, Cragan, & Shields, 2003). A fantasy theme is not a psychological phenomenon, but it is a technical term defined as "the creative and imaginative shared interpretation of reality" (Bormann, 1985, p. 130). Character themes involve interpretations of actors' personal qualities and motivations and some portray those actors as heroes or villains or bit players (Foss, 2009). Setting themes describe where the characters are situated and the features of the setting. Finally, action themes emphasize the behaviors and activities of the characters. Fantasy types are discovered as the researcher finds recurring themes in rhetorical artifacts and are more abstract summaries of the researchers' findings.

Many scholars have applied this theoretical approach to many different media and rhetorical artifacts. Benoit (2001) analyzed political cartoons relating to the Clinton-Lewinsky scandal and the impeachment hearings that followed. Page, Duffy, and Perrault (2014) studied social media memes in the presidential election, assessing their persuasive power. McKewon (2012) explored the media strategies of right-wing think tanks in Australia in denying scientific evidence for anthropogenic climate change. Another study applied SCT to e-mailed visual jokes among a group of acquaintances (Duffy, Page, & Young, 2011). Vasquez (1993) offered suggestions as to how SCT could be applied to improve effectiveness of advertising and public relations messages.

Fantasy themes and types comprise larger dramas that provide insights into the symbolic realities of people, known in FTA as "rhetorical visions." These worldviews or rhetorical visions often carry what Bormann called "master analogues" of three different types. The righteous master analogue involves judgments about right and wrong, proper behavior, and superiority or inferiority. The pragmatic master analogue emphasizes practicality, efficiency, and expedience. The social analogue emphasizes relationships, experiences, and empathy (Bormann, 1972).

For purposes of understanding people's ethical interpretations of advertising, it is useful to consider the relationship between fantasy themes and bases for argumentation. Foss (2009) suggests that when persuaders are constructing arguments for and against certain issues, they begin with certain assumptions based on shared fantasy themes (p. 99). She offers the example that scientists develop arguments based on systematic and replicable observations, while lawyers develop arguments based on past decisions and case law. Arguments built based on fantasy themes about ads perceived as disgusting and even pornographic will likely be different from those built on fantasy themes of attraction and seduction, even for people viewing the exact same ad.

In conducting the research for this study, we sought to provide a viewing experience that was similar to people's everyday commercial viewing and did not alert the viewers to the subject of ethics. As you certainly know from your own experience, you tend to watch most programming, especially advertisements, with casual interest rather than analytically. Advertising is seen by many as trivial, intrusive, and annoying.

We wished to learn whether viewers who saw ads showing reckless driving, for example, would apply adjectives such as "harmful," "violent," "controversial," or "silly." Similarly, would viewers seeing ads with strong sexual content apply negative adjectives or statements? Finally, would they apply different adjectives for the PSAs and spots with more benign content? Thus we developed the following research questions:

RQ1: How will respondents describe sexualized ads and will they be seen as unacceptable or inappropriate?

RQ1a: What fantasy themes emerge in the comments? What rhetorical vision emerges from those themes?

RQ2: How will respondents describe ads showing dangerous or reckless behaviors and will they be seen as unacceptable or inappropriate?

RQ2a: What fantasy themes emerge in the comments? What rhetorical vision emerges from those themes?

RQ3: Will respondents identify PSAs as portraying positive messages and portrayals?

RQ3a: What fantasy themes emerge in the comments? What rhetorical vision emerges from those themes?

RQ4: How do social constructionism, mutualism, and rhetorical visions connect to advertising ethics?

Method

We selected three types of ads that have distinct ethical implications based on the literature: One category had content that would likely be found ethically questionable by regulators and critics because of sexual content; another was selected because it could be ethically questionable because the ads show dangerous behaviors or activities; and the final category was public service announcements (PSAs), thought to be prosocial in nature and thus less likely to be evaluated as unethical. PSAs offer messages encouraging people to eat more healthfully, avoid drinking and driving, quit smoking, stop domestic abuse, and so on.

We randomly assigned participants to one of the three groups. After being exposed to an ad, the participants were asked to answer an open-ended question: *Please write at least two sentences to describe thoughts and feelings that you had when you were watching the ad.* This methodology is based on cognitive interviewing, a technique often applied as pretesting for survey research (Blair & Brick, 1999). However, instead of asking for verbal, in-person responses, we asked respondents to fill in a text box using Qualtrics research software, an online survey tool.

The study requested open-ended responses to ads that were subsequently coded by the three coders. Following Mayring (2000), a qualitative content analysis (based on inductive and grounded theory) begins with a research question, proceeds to category definition, formulates inductive categories, and ends in interpretation of results. Coding followed the eight steps suggested by Tesch (1990): 1) careful initial reading and note taking, 2) evaluating the underlying meaning of individual artifacts, 3) listing and clustering topics that emerge, 4) reviewing lists and rechecking the data, 5) developing an organizational scheme for emerging data, 6) create codes/associated abbreviations, 7) gather and categorize data for each topic, and 8) review and recode if required. Artifacts were reviewed by two coders and all categories achieved intercoder reliability of 90% or higher.

Such an approach is called "iterative" in that data coding and analysis are usually done at the same time, thus referring back to each other and refining the findings. This process reduced the data to domains relating to subjects' responses:

1 = Descriptive or neutral

> *The respondent did not express an opinion or simply described the ad.*

2 = Deconstructing/Rejecting

    a. Rejecting because of realism. *The respondent expressed rejection and dislike because the ad was unrealistic.*

    b. Stupid/ridiculous. *The respondent expressed rejection and dislike because the ad was silly, stupid, or lame.*

    c. Sexual. *The respondent expressed rejection and dislike because the ad was overly sexual.*

    d. Dangerous. *The respondent expressed rejection and dislike because the ad showed dangerous behaviors.*

3 = Positive/Connect *The respondent expressed liking for the ad based on one or more elements that were preferred.*

4 = Positive/Aspiration/Identify. *The respondent expressed liking for the ad and an interest in doing something similar or being part of the action in the ad.*

5 = Attempt at analyzing ad. *The respondent attempted to explain or analyze the ad or the goals of its creators.*

After categorizing the responses as described earlier, the authors identified fantasy themes from three ads, one from each set of dangerous, sexualized, and PSA ads, and analyzed them further. As discussed earlier, four different commercials for each category were seen by participants. The first category was sexualized ads: A Carl's Jr. spot featuring celebrity Kim Kardashian eating a salad in bed and in a bubble bath, a Radio Shack ad with singer Robin Thicke for Beats Pills, and an ad for Pot Noodles in which a young man fantasizes about a sexy woman. The second category was dangerous behavior: A Mountain Dew ad showing a young man and what appears to be a wrecking ball on a collision course, a Reebok ad showing young men bungee jumping from a bridge, a Samsonite luggage ad showing a man doing stunts on a high wire with a suitcase in each hand, and a Levi's ad showing a young man who lassos a car and rides the "wild" car as if in a rodeo competition. The third category was PSAs: An ad showing the effects of alcohol on driving ability, an anti-bullying spot, a commercial against domestic abuse, and an ad warning against unsafe sex. We analyzed responses to three of the ads, one of them in the sexual category, one in the dangerous behavior category, and one in the PSA category.

Findings

Sexual Category

In this category, respondents saw four ads. The first was for Carl's Jr., a quick service restaurant chain and featured celebrity Kim Kardashian. The second was a Radio Shack ad featuring singer Robin Thicke singing and dancing provocatively with scantily clad women. The Beats product is a speaker designed so as to have clear sexual connotations. The third spot is for Pot Noodles, a hot snack food. A young man is seen on a bus eating the product and is approached by a sexy young woman who aggressively comes on to him, starts dancing, and then begins to remove her clothes. The woman then turns into an unattractive man, and the protagonist is repelled by the image. The final spot was for Perrier, in which celebrity dancer Dita Von Teese seductively pours Perrier on herself while removing her clothing. See figures 7.4, 7.5 and 7.6 for a summary of the findings.

For the purpose of this article, we limit our analysis to one ad for each of the categories. The summarized results for ads in each category may be found in Figures 7.4–7.6. In the sexual category, we examine the Carl's Jr. ad. In the spot, available at http://www.youtube.com/watch?v=J11qUjHiGhs, a woman is shown in an upscale setting eating a salad on a luxurious bed and later in a bubble bath. Her voice-over (VO) is as follows: "I'm such a neat freak. Everything has to be clean, crisp, and tasty. And while the best things in life are messy, it's fun to get clean." The next VO is male saying: "Who says salads can't be hot? The new cranberry apple walnut chicken salad. One of the premium salads at Carl's Jr."

Distinct communities of meaning appeared in the textual responses. Of 65 responses, 27 were Deconstructing/Rejecting/Sexual, 13 were Positive/Aspiration/Identify, and 7 Deconstructing/Rejecting/Stupid. The negative responders were clearly offended by the sexual content. The negative respondents applied adjectives that would relate to inappropriate and unethical sexiness in the spot without being prompted or cued to questions of ethics. Those whose were coded as neutral often did not see a reasonable link between the ad's message and its sexual nature. It should be noted, however, that some of the negativity expressed was linked to the celebrity featured in the ad.

Comments representative of the negative reaction follow:

[The ad] is drenched in sexism and idiocy.

[The ad is] gross and overly sexual.

This is a hooker waiting for her john in a hotel room.

This ad is gross and overly sexual. The ad was rather tacky and too pornish.

I wondered what the brand was shown on the white bag in the background. Then I was disgusted with the sexual sell for a salad.

The Positive/Aspiration/Identify comments included:

Very attractive celebrity, sexually appealing.

The lady promoting the ad is very sexy. She is drawing attention away from the salad.

Kim Kardashian is pretty. I like carl's [sic] jr.

In the Carl's Jr. ad, the emphasis was consistently on character themes for those interpreting the ad both negatively and positively. In FTA, nonhumans can also be featured in character themes. Thus respondents described characteristics of the celebrity, Kim Kardashian, the advertiser, and the ad as if they were characters. The primary fantasy themes that emerged were:

- Celebrity as a prostitute.
- Respondent as outraged, disgusted, offended.
- Ad as disgusting, pornographic, sexist.
- Celebrity as beautiful, sexy, and attractive.

Analysis of the Carl's Jr. ad revealed that a majority of the respondents did find it objectionable. Repeated fantasy themes coalesced into several fantasy types, stock scenarios that define the social reality of respondents. Three primary fantasy types emerged:

- Celebrity/main character as a prostitute.
- Ad is disgusting, pornographic, and sexist.
- Celebrity/main character as beautiful, sexy, and attractive.

Thus two distinct rhetorical visions are seen in responses of viewers to this ad. The world view of the majority, expressed in the first two fantasy types, is one of embattled people facing an onslaught of degradation and sexism, which should be halted. The celebrity and the character embody the worst of commercial culture and violate proper norms: *Oversexualized ads degrade women and society* could summarize that viewpoint and rhetorical vision. This rhetorical vision's master analogue is clearly righteous, identifying what is good and bad.

The other fantasy themes create a much different rhetorical vision, one that sees interest and opportunity in the sexiness and beauty of the spokesperson. In these respondents' worlds, it is reasonable and right to sell salads with sex. Thus the fantasy themes from these responses coalesced into the following fantasy types:

> *The sexual appeal is enticing and interesting.*
> *The model's beauty and sex appeal adds to the salad's appeal.*

The rhetorical vision of this group is *sex and beauty are good aspects of life and make life interesting*. In this case, we see a master analogue that is social, focused on relationships, experiences, and connections. From an ethical standpoint, it is clear that these people are interacting with advertising in an entirely different way from the previous group. Moreover, the results from the other three ads in this category revealed sharply divided interpretations.

Similarly, in the Beats Pill ad, the celebrity himself and people's perception of him influenced their reception of the spot. Of the 65 respondents, 24 found the

Beats ad Deconstructing/Rejecting/Sex, 14 were neutral, 10 were Deconstructing/Rejecting/Stupid, and 9 were Positive/Aspiration/Identity.

Pot Noodles results were distributed differently with 14 in the category of Positive/Aspiration/Identity, 13 Deconstructing/Rejecting/Sex, 11 Deconstructing/Rejecting/Stupid, and 8 Deconstructing/Rejecting/Unrealistic. The Perrier ad results showed 22 Deconstructing/Rejecting/Sex, 18 Neutral, and 9 Deconstructing/Rejecting/Stupid.

Dangerous Category—Diet Mountain Dew

The four ads in this category were Diet Mountain Dew, which we analyze in detail, Reebok Bungee Jumping, Samsonite High Wire, Levi's Runway Car. The Reebok video shows two men about to bungee jump from a high bridge with rocky rapids below. One pumps up his sneakers so they fit better. The other has a competitor's shoe. Both have bungee cords fastened around their ankles. The action ends with the Reebok-wearer dangling from the bungee cord, while only the shoes of the other man are shown at the end of the cord, so presumably he has fallen on the rocks. The tagline is "Fits a little better than your ordinary athletic shoe." Samsonite's ad featured three tightrope walkers doing daring high wire acts with Samsonite suitcases in each hand. The ads end with the suitcases falling to the ground, unharmed. The Levi's action-packed ad is full of dangerous stunts and shows a dusty, runaway car lassoed by a young man. The man is first dragged through the streets, then pulls himself on top of the car, and rides it like a rodeo bull ultimately subduing it.

Mountain Dew

In the ad, available at https://www.youtube.com/watch?v=bJySiRuMLXw, a young man is hoisted up to a crane wearing a helmet and goggles and dressed like a stunt man. Directly across from him, a large balloon with the Mountain Dew logo is suspended from another crane. The man and balloon are released simultaneously, and the man collides with the balloon, which explodes, spilling what is presumably Mountain Dew on the watchers below. After the stunt, a group of young men who celebrate with Mountain Dew greet him as a hero. At the beginning of the video the message "Real stunt coordinated by professionals" is superimposed on the screen. The logo on the ball is prominently displayed reading "Sugar free Mountain Dew. Get Energised [sic]." At the close of the spot, a VO of a youthful male voice says "Great tasting sugar free from Mountain Dew. The energizing taste of awesome."

Once again, distinct communities of meaning emerged. Of the 69 total, 19 comments were Positive/Aspiration/Identify, 16 were Deconstructing/Rejecting/Stupid, 10 were Deconstructing/Rejecting/Dangerous, and 10 were Positive/Connect.

Positive comments included:

I thought it was a funny and awesome video. I felt energized watching it.

I was excited to see what happened. It was really energetic.

The ad is fun and makes you smile. It makes you want to have fun with your friends.

The positive comments revealed a successful effort on the part of the advertiser to communicate the brand's exciting and energizing characteristics.

Negative "danger" comments included the following:

I was worried about the man's safety. I was confused by what they were trying to sell. I know it was Mountain Dew, but why crash a man into a ball of Dew. Stupid.

I thought this was totally irresponsible on many different levels. It perpetuates the notion that when you are young you are indestructible, and we both know that is not the case.

I thought it was stupid. The guy could have been killed or hurt if something went wrong. And it was a waste of a product.

Six of the comments used variations on the terms "energized" and "excited." Much of the negative commentary had to do with safety issues and the dangerous situation portrayed in the ad. Interestingly, many of the negative comments referred to the behavior as stupid, dumb, silly, or lame. In fact, 12 of the negative statements included those terms. Does "stupid" refer to an ethical judgment of the ad's content or is it a reaction to the stunt in an ad as silly or pointless? This is unclear. However, it *is* clear that respondents were sharply divided in their interpretations of the ad.

Fantasy themes found in the Positive/Connect category center around action themes. Respondents felt excited, entertained, and energized. In the Positive/Aspiration category, action themes emerged as well:

The ad is refreshing and energetic. Makes me feel like I can do this.

I am actually drinking a Diet Mountain Dew while I was watching so it made me think of that and I also thought about how cool it would be to do something like that.

How much fun and exciting it would be.

Daring and dangerous. I felt like taking a risk.

In the Deconstructing/Rejecting categories, action themes emerged again, but they were the obverse.

The ad was a little stupid; nobody is going to jump off a crane for Mountain Dew.

I thought this was totally irresponsible on many different levels. It perpetuates the notion that when you are young you are indestructible and we both know that's not the case.

I thought it was stupid. The guy could have been killed or hurt if something went wrong.

From these fantasy themes and interpretations of the ad, we derived two fantasy types.

The risks I observe energize and excite me.

Risk-taking is unnecessarily dangerous and a foolish decision.

Two distinct rhetorical visions emerged. *Celebrate risk* is the rhetorical vision of the positive group. In the rhetorical world of this group, risk is not only acceptable but should be welcomed. The celebrate risk respondents detected nothing problematic about the spot but instead found it life enhancing. Those respondents saw themselves as identifying with and connecting with the stuntman in the commercial. This is a rhetorical vision with a social master analogue signifying empathy, relationships, and shared excitement.

Conversely, those responding negatively are part of a rhetorical vision that perceives the world as a place full of dangers that individuals can potentially avoid with intelligence and good judgment. Those who portray or undertake unnecessary risks potentially put others at risk, and the advertiser would be considered guilty of an ethical breach by airing the ad. Their rhetorical vision could be distilled to *unnecessary risks endanger people.* The master analogue for this vision would again be righteous with the observers making strong judgments about the actions seen in the ad.

For the other ads in the danger category, the numerical results were similar to the Mountain Dew ad. Results for Reebok were very positive with 31 as Positive/Aspiration/Identify, 13 Deconstructing/Rejecting/Danger, and 12 Neutral. Samsonite came in at 35 Positive/Aspiration/Identify, 10 Deconstructing/Rejecting/Stupid, and 8 Positive/Connect. Levi's results showed 16 Neutral, 16 Positive/Aspiration/Identify, and 13 Positive/Connect.

PSA Category

We expected significantly different outcomes from the PSAs and were not disappointed. However, each of the ads had different messages and tones and again we saw greatly different interpretations from different people. The four commercials we used were a PSA warning about drinking and driving, a PSA about domestic abuse, a PSA encouraging condom use, and an anti-bullying spot.

"Brain Drain," available at http://www.youtube.com/watch?v=4ezYSxTqM2o, portrays men in a bar enjoying beers, conversation, and shooting pool. The setting is warm, exuding friendliness and good cheer. The spot dramatizes alcohol's effect on the brain and resulting impairment by showing the men's brains "lighting up" as they drink. As they continue to drink, parts of their brains visually shut down (the lights go out), and the VO lists the various impairments the drinkers are experiencing. The VO closes saying:

> This becomes a serious danger when you drive. You can still change gears, but what's missing are those higher skills that handle things like emergencies. Most nights, you'll get home. But if something goes wrong, you're gone.

The spot ends with a car crash and the final visual shows the driver's brain "light" flickering to black. The video and VO have a tone of scientific concern and an unemotional and calm delivery. Of 76 respondents, Positive/Aspiration/ Identification scored 46, Positive Connect scored 17, with the remaining scores in the single digits.

Typical comments on Brain Drain were as follows:

> *I thought the ad was clever and used scientific information to make the case against drunk driving.*

> *I thought it was educational without being preachy.*

> *Not a very pleasant ad. Truthful, but not very pleasant.*

Examining "Brain Drain" from the standpoint of FTA, the respondents identified with the action depicted in the PSA. The plotline visually portraying a drinker's brain as lighting up and then fading resulted in a fantasy theme rooted in realism, education, learning, and information, according to the comments.

> *I like the way you get information about the effects of alcohol. It makes you think about the things we do while we drink.*

> *I thought the ad was clever and used scientific information to make the case against drunk driving. I liked the graphic representations of the brains on alcohol in the commercial.*

Respondents expressed both connection to and understanding of the PSA's message and also indicated that they might modify their drinking behaviors or continue avoidance of such behaviors. The responses came together in a fantasy type of "Drinking and driving risks are real and serious," and "I, too, could be a victim if I make poor decisions about drinking and driving." The rhetorical vision is *the danger is real* and it carries a righteous master analogue. The behaviors of drinking and driving cross a moral boundary and also form the bases for an argument on acceptable and unacceptable behaviors.

The condom use PSA "Places for Women" begins with a strong tone of seduction where two attractive people are in the early stages of a sexual encounter. As it begins to appear that the act will commence, the action stops and a label appears over the man's underwear stating, "Cathy Mills and 34 other people were here." Of the 76 respondents, Positive/Aspiration/Identification scored 40, Deconstructing/Rejecting/Sexual scored 13, while Neutral scored 9. While the response was strongly positive, the sexual nature of the ad was a negative for some. The PSA "Tea Party" showed only the feet of two children, a boy and a girl, each wearing oversize adult shoes. The conversation escalates into a shouting argument, china rattles, and the boy shouts at the girl that she can't do anything right. Again, Positive/Aspiration/Identification scored 40, Neutral scored 18, Positive/Connect scored 9. But 5 respondents identified the ad as Deconstructing/Rejecting/Sexual.

The PSA "Stop Bullying" portrays a middle or high school girl at school who receives a cruel taunt in a text from another girl calling her "an ugly bitch." The video then shows a spreading bloodstain on the bullied girl's wrist, and she falls to the floor amid screams. The screen reads "Words have consequences," and the following frame says, "19,000 bullied students attempt to commit suicide each year." Positive/Aspiration/Identification scored 40, Neutral scored 8, Positive/Aspiration/Identify scored 6. Positive/Connect scored 3.

Discussion

As individuals experience an advertising video, some viewers will identify with some characters and situations shown, while others will reject them. In engaging or rejecting, the viewer is also accepting or rejecting the values embedded in the drama that is shown in the video. The results of this study reveal that individuals watching advertisements occupy different social realities and rhetorical worlds. This goes beyond simplistic findings that some individuals like a given ad and others do not. Instead, they are watching commercials from completely different social realities, thus drawing significantly different conclusions and making much different ethical judgments. As suggested by Hackley (1999) and Still and Good (1992), individuals make meaning from the advertising content—often meanings that the advertiser may not have intended.

RQ1 and RQ1a asked if people interpret ads with strong sexual content as ethically problematic. Analysis revealed that a significant group of respondents to the "Carl's Jr." found the ad to be offensive in several different ways. Such ads would likely be identified as tasteless or offensive by regulators receiving complaints about the spot. Nevertheless, other individuals found the ad enticing, interesting, and attention getting. The scores in the categories, the fantasy types, and the rhetorical visions revealed very different worldviews. The contrasting rhetorical visions were *sex and beauty are good aspects of life and make life interesting* and *oversexualized ads degrade women and society.*

RQ2 and RQ2a two asked whether respondents would see dangerous ads as ethically problematic. As in the results from the sexualized content, respondents expressed sharply different views. The negative respondents expressed concern at an action creating unnecessary danger, while the positive respondents celebrated the energy and excitement of the stunt. The contrasting rhetorical visions were *celebrate risk* and *unnecessary risks endanger people.*

RQ3 and RQ3a asked how the respondents would view PSAs as presenting prosocial messages. As expected, the scores, the fantasy themes, and the rhetorical vision elicited very similar and positive responses: The rhetorical vision is *the danger is real* and it carries a righteous master analogue. This reinforces decades of research on the first-person effect wherein people are motivated to endorse noncommercial and prosocial concepts and to agree with their messages.

These stark differences in perceptions suggest that researchers and ethicists should reconsider how we study and talk about advertising ethics. Hackley (1999) observes that ethics advertising regulation is usually reactive to public complaints. Thus the beliefs and standards of those offended by certain content can emerge as the moral standards for practice. Instead, he proposes that "a cultivated sensitivity to the complexity and subtlety of various . . . forms of discourse seems a precondition for emancipatory forms of ethical regulation" (p. 41).

Lasch (1978) and many other critics label advertising as inherently morally bankrupt. Pollay (1986) summarizes many of the criticisms that we still hear today, particularly focusing on advertising's presumed negative impacts on social behaviors, saying it serves to increase materialism, selfishness, and cynicism. Following Hackley, we argue that such assumptions ignore the concept that those criticisms are themselves socially constructed. We suggest a broader and more inclusive view of ethical judgments that respects human agency, questions the paternalistic attitudes of regulators and critics, and acknowledges individual meaning making in responding to advertising and other communication.

As discussed earlier, most ethics studies ask people's reactions to the ethics of advertising rather than observing people's responses in more naturalistic settings. In addition, many advertising critics apply top-down standards and rules, such as the TARES test, Kantian deontological ethics, or standards developed by regulators usually in reaction to the complaints of some individuals or groups. Our argument in this chapter is that individuals are creating their own meanings and interpretations of an ad's content based on their own frames of reference and worldviews. They are doing this in the context of the larger cultural milieu. Hackley (1999) writes: "The thesis that meaning is constructed jointly and through discourse and through social interaction has radical implications for ethics" (p. 38). The social worlds individuals inhabit profoundly affect the values they hold and their assessments of what may be moral and right. Instead, a more nuanced understanding of the complexity of human communication including even a 30-second spot can enhance ethical judgments. Hackley writes:

> It seems odd to formulate normative ethical rules from within one frame of social life designed to guide behavior in another. How can advertising regulation make sense to consumers if regulators don't know how consumers make sense?

(p. 41)

Ethicists frequently argue that some advertisements will have negative effects on audiences who may have been encouraged to emulate dangerous behavior or who will internalize stereotypes. This is too simplistic and authoritarian. Advertisements, like any human symbolic representation from a news story to a novel to a children's book, may be interpreted in different ways. *Huckleberry Finn* has been banned from school reading lists because of some people's beliefs that it stereotypes African-Americans (CBS News, 2011). The Dr. Seuss book *Yertle the Turtle* has been criticized as having disguised messages that could incite unrest and rebellion (Eugenios, 2012). We could offer many other examples of linguistic and symbolic creations that are perceived differently by different people.

Historian Michael Schudson writes that "people's needs have never been natural but always cultural, always social, always defined relative to the standards of their society" (1984). This preliminary study shows a marked bifurcation in responses to ads with ethically questionable content and raises questions about the differing social worlds people inhabit. This analysis does not simply reveal that people have different points of view.

Figure 7.1 Carl's Jr. commercial

Figure 7.2 Diet Mountain Dew commercial

Figure 7.3 PSA about drinking and driving

References

Andrews, T. (2012). What is social constructionism? *Grounded Theory Review: An International Journal*, 14(1). Retrieved September 15, 2015 from http://ground edtheoryreview.com/2012/06/01/what-is-social-constructionism/

Benoit, W., Klyukovski, A., McHale, J., & Airne, D. (2001). A fantasy theme analysis of political cartoons on the Clinton-Lewinsky-Starr affair. *Critical Studies in Media Communication*, 18(4), 377–94.

Berger, P., & Luckman, T. (1966). *The Social Construction of Reality*. Garden City, NY: Doubleday.

Blair, J., & Brick, P. D. Methods for analysis of cognitive interviews. American Statistical Association. Retrieved September 15, 2015 from https://www.amstat.org/sections/srms/proceedings/y2010/Files/307865_59514.pdf

Bormann, E. (1972). Fantasy and rhetorical vision: The rhetorical criticism of social reality. *Quarterly Journal of Speech*, 58, 396–407.

Bormann, E. (1985). Symbolic convergence theory: A communication formulation. *Journal of Communication*, 35(4), 128–38.

Bormann, E., Cragan, J., & Shields, Donald. (2003). Defending symbolic convergence theory from an imaginary Gunn. *Quarterly Journal of Speech*, 89, 366–72.

CBS (2011). Huckleberry Finn and the N-word debate. *CBS News*, June 12. Retrieved March 18, 2015 from http://www.cbsnews.com/news/huckleberry-finn-and-the-n-word-debate/

Drumwright, M.E., & Murphy, P.E. (2009). The current state of advertising ethics: Industry and Academic Perspectives. *Journal of Advertising*, 38(1), pp. 83–107.

Duffy, M., Page, J., & Young, R. (2011). Obama as anti-American: Visual folklore in right-wing forwarded emails and construction of conservative social identity. *Journal of American Folklore*, 125(496), 177–203.

Eugenios, J. (2012). Dr. Seuss story accused of having a political agenda, barred from classroom. *Today Books*, April 26. Retrieved March 18, 2015 from http://www.today.com/id/47193483/ns/today-today_books/t/dr-seuss-story-accused-having-political-agenda-barred-classroom/#.VQmlZcY4i1A

Foss, S. (2009). *Rhetorical Criticism*. Prospect Heights, IL: Waveland Press.

Fullerton, J. A., Kendrick, A., & McKinnon, L. M. (2013). Advertising ethics: Student attitudes and behavioral intent. *Journalism and Mass Communication Educator* (68(1), Retrieved September 15, 2015 from https://www.questia.com/library/journal/1P3-2923955471/advertising-ethics-student-attitudes-and-behavioral

Gergen, K. J. (1994). *Toward Transformation of Social Knowledge* (2nd edition). Thousand Oaks, CA: Sage.

Hackley, C. E. (1998). Social constructionism and research in marketing and advertising. *Qualitative Market Research: An International Journal*, 1(3), 125–31.

Hackley, C.H. (1999). The meanings of ethics in and of advertising. *Business Ethics* 8(1), 37–42.

Ham, C. D. (2010). *Dual processes in persuasion inference: responses to user-generated advertising* (doctoral dissertation), University of Missouri, Columbia, MO.

Hirschman, E.C., & Thompson, C.J. (1997). Why media matters: Toward a richer understanding of consumers' relationships with advertising and mass media. *Journal of Advertising*, 16(1), 43–60.

Institute of Advertising Ethics (2010). Retrieved from the Reynolds Journalism Institute, October 16, 2014. Available at: http://www.rjionline.org/institute-for-advertising-ethics

Lasch, C. (1978). *The Culture of Narcissism: American Life in an Age of Diminishing Expectations*. New York: Norton.

Lee, S. T., & Nguyen, H. L. (2013). Explicating the moral responsibility of the advertiser: TARES as an ethical model for fast food advertising. *Journal of Mass Media Ethics*, 28(4), 225–40.

Mayring, P. (2000). Qualitative content analysis. *Forum: Qualitative Social Research,* 1(2), p. 1–8.

McCracken, Grant (1986), "Culture and Consumption: A Theoretical Account of the Structure and Movement of the Cultural Meaning of Consumer Goods," *Journal of Consumer Research,* 13 (June), 71–84.

McCracken, G. (1987). Advertising: Meaning or information. *Advances in Consumer Research,* 14, 121–24.

McKewon, E. (2012). Talking points ammo: The use of neoliberal think tank fantasy themes to delegitimise [sic] scientific knowledge of climate change in Australian newspapers. *Journalism Studies,* 13(2), 277–97.

Mead, G. H. (1934). *Mind, Self and Society.* Chicago: University of Chicago Press.

Page, J.T., Duffy, M., & Perrault, G. (2014). Sticking It to Obamacare: A Rhetorical Analysis of Affordable Care Act Advertising in Social Media. Conference paper presented at Association for Education in Journalism and Mass Communication, Montreal.

Pollay, R. W. (1986). The distorted mirror: Reflections on the unintended consequences of advertising. *Journal of Marketing,* April, 897–914.

Schauster, E. (2013). Enabled and constrained: The structuration of advertising ethics. Dissertation, University of Missouri, School of Journalism.

Schudson, M. (1984). *Advertising, the Uneasy Persuasion.* New York: Basic Books.

Schutz, A. (1962). *Collected Papers, Volume I.* The Hague: Nijhoff.

Still, A. W., & Good, J. M. (1992). Mutualism in the human sciences: Towards the implementation of a theory. *Journal of the Theory of Social Behaviour,* 22, 105–28.

Tesch, R. (1990). *Qualitative Research: Analysis Types and Software Tools.* New York: Routledge.

Tinkham, S. F., & Weaver-Lariscy (1994). Ethical judgments of political television commercials as predictors of attitude toward the ad. *Journal of Advertising,* 23(3), 43–57.

Vasquez, G. M. (1993). A homo narrans paradigm for public relations: Combining symbolic convergence theory with Grunig's situational theory. *Journal of Public Relations Research,* 5(3), 201–16.

	A	B	C	D
1	Sexy ad　　　　_Attutude	Sexy ad　　_Attitude	Sexy ad　　　_Attutude	Sexy ad　　　_Attutude
2	number reviewed = 65	number reviewed = 65	number reviewed = 65	number reviewed = 65
3	Totals			
4	1=4	1=14	1=6	1=18
5	2a= 3	2a=1	2a=8	2a=4
6	2b =7	2b=10	2b=11	2b=9
7	2c=27	2c=24	2c=13	2c=22
8	2d =0	2d=0	2d=0	2d=0
9	3= 4	3=2	3=14	3=3
10	4= 13	4=9	4=10	4=7
11	5=7	5=5	5=3	5=2
12				

Figure 7.4 Distribution of categories of response for sexual commercials

	PSA ads (Brain Drain)_Attutude	PSA ads (Condom use ad)_Attutude	PSA ads (Stop Bullying)_Attutude	PSA ads (Domestic Abuse)_Attutude
1				
2	number reviewed = 76	number reviewed = 76	number reviewed = 76	number reviewed = 75
3				
4	1 = 7	1 = 9	1 = 8	1 = 18
5	2a = 2	2a = 2	2a = 3	2a = 1
6	2b = 1	2b = 3	2b = 3	2b = 2
7	2c = 3	2c = 13	2c = 9	2c = 5
8	2d = 0	2d = 0	2d = 0	2d = 0
9	3 = 17	3 = 6	3 = 3	3 = 9
10	4 = 46	4 = 40	4 = 50	4 = 40
11	5 = 0	5 = 3	5 = 0	5 = 0
12				
13				

Figure 7.5 Distribution of categories of response for PSA commercials

	Dangerous ads (Mountain Dew)_Attutude	Dangerous ads (Reebook)_Attutude	Dangerous ads(Samsonite)_Attutude	Dangerous ads(Levis)_Attutude
1				
2	number reviewed = 69	number reviewed = 69	number reviewed = 69	number reviewed = 68
3				
4	1=7	1 = 12	1 = 2	1 = 16
5	2a=5	2a = 3	2a = 6	2a = 9
6	2b=16	2b = 3	2b = 10	2b = 10
7	2c= 0	2c = 2	2c = 0	2c = 0
8	2d=10	2d = 13	2d = 6	2d = 2
9	3=10	3 = 4	3 = 8	3 = 13
10	4=19	4 = 31	4 = 35	4= 16
11	5= 2	5 = 1	5 = 2	5 = 2
12				

Figure 7.6 Distribution of categories of response for dangerous commercials

8   Negative Political Advertisements

A Primer From the Academic Literature With an Ethical Marketing Commentary

T. J. Weber and Gene R. Laczniak

CHAPTER SUMMARY

You've no doubt seen many ads that attack a candidate for his or her character or actions. Such ads are often very dark, loaded with innuendo, and unfairly and inaccurately make claims and charges. These are negative political advertisements (NPAs), and they are a growing phenomenon in U.S. elections at almost every level. Citizens United (2010) and McCutcheon (2014) were Supreme Court rulings that, for the first time, allowed corporations and wealthy donors to make almost unlimited and often anonymous contributions to candidates. The court ruled that corporations and unions should be seen as "persons" entitled to First Amendment rights of free speech and that money could be considered a form of expression. This decision brought millions of additional dollars to campaigns, much of it funding NPAs. This chapter explores the potential consequences of NPAs, including eroding trust in government, the possibility of suppressing voter turnout, discouraging political discussions among citizens, preventing qualified candidates from entering politics, and giving corporations unprecedented power to influence elections. While political speech is and should be unfettered, political marketers should not only do what is permissible under the law, they should apply ethical standards to their work with campaigns.

Introduction

In the 2014 congressional election, Republicans increased their control in the House of Representatives and regained a majority in the U.S. Senate in what many characterized as a rebuke of President Obama. The various political campaigns across the country, including various state governor contests, were expected to be among the most partisan and negative in the history of the U.S. Republic (*The Economist*, 2012). Reality showed that prediction to be accurate, as $1 billion was spent on political campaign advertising (USA Today Editorial Board, 2014). Much of the bitter acrimony took the form of negative political advertising (NPAs), ads that essentially tear down the character or the ideas of the opposing candidate rather than address what the sponsoring candidate might proactively do. This state of affairs is a far cry from an idealized form of elections based on citizens' weighing of candidate platforms, achievements, and articulations as discussed in American civics books (Carr, Bernstein, Murphy, & Danielson, 1971). More ominous still is that negative advertising that is often unfair, inaccurate, or offensive is predicted to grow exponentially in future elections.

The purpose of this chapter is twofold: First, to provide some basic information drawn from the academic literature about the nature and scope of negative political advertising and, second, to offer some brief commentary about how the growth in NPAs might be both ethically troubling and socially problematic for the democratic process. Based on our ethical analysis, we point out some ethical weaknesses of NPAs but also reinforce the belief that political speech must remain largely unfettered. The negative political campaign, as a prominent and enduring feature of American elections, seems upon us. Scholars interested in the ethics of persuasion should understand its essence so that they might be better prepared and motivated to push forward with greater clarity the boundaries of empirical knowledge concerning NPAs.

Two other qualifiers about our commentary should be noted at this time. This chapter is not intended to constitute a literature review of NPAs, although it draws on that corpus of information to support many of the observations made. As identified in the paper title, this essay is more of a primer for those interested in the ethics of persuasion but who may be less familiar with the burgeoning sector of negative political advertising. For a more comprehensive and analytical literature review of NPAs, we suggest Lau, Sigelman, Heldman, and Babbitt (1999), Lau, Sigelman, and Rovner (2007), and Weber (2014). Also, political advertising is part of a larger and long-standing literature on the broader topics of political propaganda and persuasion (see, for example, Sears & Kosterman, 1994). Second, the focus of this essay is exclusively on the election system in the United States because of its unique environment with regard to the funding and execution of its political campaigns.

Rudyard Kipling, the 19th century British writer and Nobel Prize in Literature winner was, early in his career, a journalist in India. He once poetically remarked concerning his reportage: "I've always had six house servants; they've taught me all I knew. Their names are *What* and *When* and *Where* and *How* and *Why* and *Who*."

Consistent with Kipling, we structure our sampling of the selected literature concerning NPAs along these basic lines of inquiry, providing a primer concerning negative political advertising. We then offer some ethical analysis based upon the espoused normative ethics of professional marketers.

What Is Negative Political Advertising?

At the outset, we should offer a definition of negative political advertising (NPA). Hughes (2003) did an exhaustive analysis of papers dealing with NPA with a focus on Australian elections and pointed out the lack of formal NPA definitions in the published research. He also demarcated the different types of negative ads analyzed in various studies. Hughes rightly pointed out that there could be significant differences in the type of negativity used. For example, some negative ads were purely attacks on the character of the targeted candidate, while others were more comparative—distinguishing the issue positions of the one candidate with the disparaged and presumably inferior proposals of the other. Some ads were sponsored by a candidate, others by a third party interested in the election outcome. Taking all of this into account, Hughes (2003) offered a definition of NPA that had considerable scope, and we endorse it, with minor modification, due to its thoughtfulness and the flexibility it affords.

Negative political advertising is defined as *advertising that targets the attacked candidate's weakness in issues or image and/or that highlights the opposing candidate's strengths in these areas by sending a negatively framed message.*

(Adapted from Hughes, 2003; p.165)

Why are NPAs an Increasingly Important Issue?

There are at least two ways to answer this question. One has to do with the way the political spending environment has shifted in the United States. The second focuses on possible social outcomes driven by the increased usage of NPAs. We begin with a discussion of a major impetus for increased political negativity with one of its manifestations being more frequent negative political advertising.

Citizens United 2010: Pouring Fuel on the Partisan Fire

With the five to four U.S. Supreme Court decision in the Citizens United case of 2010, political campaign spending by organizations was deemed to be a form of free speech protected by the First Amendment. This ruling legalized unlimited and anonymous campaign spending, not only by citizens but also by corporations, unions, and special interest groups. (Citizen's United *v.* FEC, 2010). The rationale for the decision was that corporations and organizations were "persons" entitled to political speech, and their monetary expenditure on messaging was a mechanism to exercise that voice. This decision also allowed the formation of so-called super political action committees (i.e., Super PACs) that could channel huge amounts of money into the political campaign marketing without making public the source of its funds or its donors, so long as there was no overt coordination with a candidate's political campaign.

With this ruling, campaign spending for negative political ads and the quantity of such ads increased dramatically. In addition, as a percentage of total ad spending, NPAs increased substantially. Outlays via independent expenditures (also referred to as "IEs") increased to nearly a billion dollars in 2012, reaching $946 million. That is six times the amount spent for the 2008 elections and thirteen times higher than the 2004 campaign (Public Citizen, 2012a). Disturbingly, in 2012, one-third of all donations given to Super PACs came from just 10 donors (Public Citizen, 2012a), suggesting that the democratic playing field was no longer level for every citizen.

Here is what President Barack Obama said in his State of the Union address on January 27, 2010, about that Supreme Court decision:

> With all due deference to the separation of powers, last week the Supreme Court reversed a century of law that I believe will open the floodgates for special interests, including foreign corporations, to spend without limit in our elections. I don't think American elections should be bankrolled by America's most powerful interests, or worse, by foreign entities. They should be decided by the American people.

Such accelerated spending is not in itself problematic. An increase in campaign monies spent educating voters about issues of public policy being debated would potentially improve government and citizen involvement. However, these post Citizens United funds were often allocated to NPAs, many did not disclose the source of the funds, and almost $500 million was spent attacking specific candidates in the 2012 election.

According to the Wesleyan Media Project (Presidential Ads, 2012), negative ads increased to a 70% share of political advertisements during the 2012 presidential campaign; this was a 61% increase from just four years earlier in the 2008 presidential campaign. Without a doubt, this development represents a remarkable shift from past elections. Given an environment of unregulated and permissive anonymous campaign financing, the situation is unlikely to change. In April of 2014, in the U.S. Supreme Court's McCutcheon ruling and another tight five to four, further restrictions on campaign spending limits by wealthy individuals were loosened, allowing single donors to spend up to $3.5 million per election cycle (Strangler, 2014).

The Rise of Political Gridlock

A second reason for concern about the growth in negative political advertising has to do with its perceived correlation with a fierce political partisanship— i.e., the unwillingness among Republicans and Democrats to compromise, leading to frustration by the general public that the American political system is broken.

After years of partisan gridlock, a U.S. national credit downgrade, and the failure of legislators to complete the simplest legislative procedures, a survey by Public Policy Polling (2013) found the U.S. Congress was less popular than lice, root canals, and Genghis Khan. Congressional approval slipped down to an aggregate average of 15%, with disapproval reaching a historical high at 79% during 2013 (RealClearPolitics, 2013). This dismal approval rate of Congress is prefaced by nearly half a decade of the majority of Americans describing the United States as being "on the wrong track." Both of these averages are notable lows in the history of U.S. public opinion polling (RealClearPolitics, 2013).

Trust in governmental leadership and general support for political parties as a whole is eroding (Forgette & Jonathan, 2006). This is troublesome, to say the least, but it should also not be surprising. The ineffectiveness of Congress and massive and growing amounts of negative advertising are likely linked to the legislative body's increasingly partisan rhetoric and resulting negative perceptions of it by citizens. By some measures, the most recent Congress, the 112th, was the least effective in 65 years (Terkel, 2013), the most partisan ever (Poole & Hare, 2013), and its membership ran more negative advertising than any other U.S. Congress in history (Franklin-Fowler & Ridnout, 2012).

How Else Do NPAs Affect the Political and Social Milieu?

Most commentators attribute the Citizen's United decision as fueling NPAs and helping to create a climate of uncompromising partisanship. But the climate of negativity in politics has other realities that should be recognized. This includes the long-standing phenomenon of attack campaigns in the United States, the effects of NPAs on voter turnout, the erosion of trust in government, and potential fundamental changes in the role of individual citizens.

A Long Tradition of Political Warfare

First, attack campaigns have a long history in American politics. For example, in 1828, Andrew Jackson's fitness for the presidency was publicly questioned because his wife may have been an adulteress (National First Ladies Library, 2013). Abraham Lincoln, one of America's most revered presidents, was depicted in political cartoons of his time as a moron and an ape (Strother, 1863). However, many of these attacks were limited to local or regional newspapers. The era of mass media changed all that and multiplied the potential damage from negative attacks.

While negativity has always had a place in U.S. politics, most scholars and critics agree the preferred modern form of attack—negative political advertisements or NPAs—started in 1964 with President Lyndon B. Johnson's "Daisy" commercial. The "Daisy" ad immediately generated debate, criticism, and analysis concerning the efficacy and ethics of this type of political persuasion. The ad is described in a 2011 *New York Times* article revisiting the growth of NPAs and its genesis in the so-called "Daisy Ad Revolution":

> your attention is captured by the image of a young girl in a field counting petals as she pulls them off of a daisy, endearingly stumbling as she goes from one to ten. By the time she gets to nine, an ominous countdown booms in; as it reaches zero the camera freezes and pulls in on the girl's eye, suddenly cutting to a mushroom cloud explosion and President

Lyndon Johnson shouting about the high stakes of nuclear war. You have just witnessed the most revolutionary television ad in history during its first and last broadcast.

(Storey, 2011)

While the TV ad ran only once, it did not simply play on TV like an ad for a new Cadillac or a six-pack of beer; instead, it struck an emotional chord with voters already uneasy with the tough talk of the Republican candidate. The ad did not even mention the opposing candidate, Sen. Barry Goldwater (R, AZ) and it was not a desperate political ploy by an incumbent (Johnson) barely clinging to elected office. Johnson was already on track for a landslide victory. However, it signaled that U.S. campaigning had embarked on a slippery slope of NPA political campaigns and was a transitional moment for both U.S. culture and, arguably, the U.S. democratic process.

Since the "Daisy" ad, spending on negative advertisements has risen each year (Fowler & Ridout, 2013). Notable examples of NPAs in presidential campaigns include "The Convention Ad" run by Richard Nixon in 1968, the "Harry and Louise" ad run against Bill Clinton in 1993, the "Black Baby" robocalls against John McCain in 2000, and the "Swift Boat" ads against John Kerry in 2004.[1] With the billions of dollars spent on negativity, it is an imperative for our democracy that we question why so much negativity has arisen and what effects it may have from a marketing standpoint.

Negative Political Campaigns Drive Away Voters

Second, a very common criticism of negative political advertising is that it may suppress voter turnout (Lau et al., 2007). The logic chain goes something like this: NPAs → voter cynicism → reduced voter participation. This topic was thrust into the forefront with the publication of Ansolabehere and Iyengar's 1995 book, *Going Negative: How Political Advertisements Shrink and Polarize the Electorate*. These authors' assertions that NPAs reduce election turnout were the first of many similar studies. In fact, in the next five years of the 20th century there were as many published articles on negative political advertisements as the first 95 years.

The subsequent research studies inspired by Ansolabehere & Iyengar (1995) were wide-ranging. Additional research found that negative political ads actually increase voter turnout (Wattenberg & Brians, 1999; Brooks, 2006; Freedman & Goldstein, 1999). Other researchers found that the impacts of NPAs were multifaceted and variable and messages that were highly negative and uncivil were powerful for some individuals (Fridkin & Kenney, 2011). Ansolabehere and Iyengar reintroduced their theory with new evidence that appeared to confirm their earlier findings (1999). Well over a decade after the landmark book, little empirical agreement exists on the question of whether negative political advertising enhances or suppresses voter turnout. Thus one of the most commonly articulated fears regarding NPAs is as yet unsubstantiated.

Erosion of Trust in Government

Third, while uncertainty about effects of NPAs on voter turnout remains, NPAs may, nevertheless, be problematic from a social and political process standpoint. Lau et al.'s (2007) excellent meta-analysis of negative political campaigns suggests other possible dysfunctions. There is preliminary evidence that negative political contests, often characterized by NPAs, may erode the public's sense of controlling their own destiny, a concept known as political efficacy in the research literature. Further, some argue NPAs play a part in decreasing trust in government (Dardis, Shen, & Edwards, 2008). Ironically, most literature also finds that NPAs lower voters' liking for both the target of the attack and the attacker (Lau et al., 2007; Hitchon & Chang, 1995; Hitchon, Chang, & Harris, 1997; Kahn & Geer, 1994; Kaid & Boyston, 1987).

Finally, the evolution of NPA ad strategies and the license given by the Citizens United decision allowing corporations a much greater voice in elections raises the question of whether the role of individual citizens in U.S. elections has been changed for the long term. For many years, corporations have been adept in influencing legislation that furthers their interests through lobbying. With the ability to inject additional cash into campaigns, corporations now have more power in supporting individuals seen to be favorable to their interests.

Corporate Political Activism

The importance of positive interactions with Congress and government agencies has been established as a key factor in corporate success, especially when expanding internationally (Li, Peng, & Macauley, 2013). It has also been documented that corporate political activity, including the sponsorship of NPAs, is a complex calculation made to further the economic interests of a corporation. It has been found to have a positive correlation with profitability (Lux, Crook, & Woehr, 2011).

However, little research on corporate political activism has been done since the Citizens United (2010) decision. That ruling represents a visible shift from the status quo (companies spending for economically self-interested goals) toward a new age of companies spending on all types of issues, ranging from pro-gay rights (e.g., Starbucks) to anti-contraception (e.g., Hobby Lobby). In a few short years, corporate activism has spread to being highly prevalent and visible beyond company-focused economic issues.

This creates a potential for NPA usage to backfire when corporations are known to be funding political campaigns, especially negative ones, which violate the priorities and concerns of their customer base. For instance, Weber and Joireman (2015) find that corporate political activism aimed toward ideological goals reduces positive consumer perceptions of the spending corporation. Several politically active businesses were criticized when their political views became public. For example, both Target and Chick-Fil-A supported platforms and candidates that were opposed to gay marriage, resulting in prominent criticism in social media and threatened consumer boycotts. By investigating how NPAs affect the consumer brand perceptions of politically active corporations, academics can help society better understand the financial and brand equity related risks involved with the increased corporate funding of political activism.

To sum up, some negativity in political campaigns has been around from the beginning and the hypothesis that NPAs reduces voter participation has not been definitively supported. However, there are indications that other problematic factors might be at work, such as reduced citizen trust in government and the injection of increased corporate power into U.S. elections. Consider how the current climate of political negativity and pervasive attack ads (discussed earlier) differs from the ideal role attributed to political campaigns in civics textbooks as taught in secondary school:

> The ideal function of political parties in a democracy include informing the public about urgent problems, clarifying alternative courses, and offering choices among the solutions as well as candidates to execute those solutions . . . the political campaign should be the a prime area for the performance of these tasks.
>
> (Carr et al., 1971, p. 173)

When Do Political and Marketing Consultants Recommend NPAs Be Used?

Each political campaign is complex, unique, and dynamic. The conventional wisdom among consultants is that negativity must be responded to by the target of the attack (Roddy & Garamone, 1988). Clearly the intended purpose of most negative political advertisements is directed at shifting media attention and voter sympathy toward a more favorable comparison for the attacking candidate versus the attacked candidate (Geer, 2012). Thus once a negative cycle begins, it has its own vicious momentum as response begets reply. In the 2012 presidential election alone, nearly $900 million was spent by the two major party candidates just on television advertising, much of it negative (Mad Money, 2012).

Considering the many marketing and advertising professionals required to plan, create, and place these ads, the relative lack of published marketing research about NPAs is somewhat puzzling. For instance, in the years between Bill Clinton's election in 1994 and Barack Obama's re-election in 2012, there were only about two dozen articles published on political marketing in major marketing journals. One can surmise that much of the existing analysis of particular NPA dominated campaigns is unpublished and proprietary and likely closely guarded by candidates and campaigns.

Among the studies published in marketing journals, many focused on whether NPAs affected citizens' liking of the attacker and target candidates (Robideaux, 2004; Phillips, Urbany, & Reynolds, 2008; Pinkleton, 1997; Jasperson & Fan,

2002). As suggested earlier, assuming the attacked candidate responds, NPAs seem to lower the voters' positive affect for *both* candidates. Some examples of published research in marketing/advertising literature provides some context about the findings scholars in the field have investigated.

- Less credible and unfair attacks have the capacity to reduce the effectiveness of utilizing NPAs (Tinkham & Weaver-Lariscy, 1994; Lariscy & Tinkham, 1999);
- There are similarities in the use of negativity in consumer marketing and political marketing (James & Hensel, 1991; Egan, 1999);
- The efficacy of NPAs placed in newspapers may be offset by the information present in other newspaper articles (Faber, Tims, & Schmitt, 1993);
- The mix of positive and negative ads used in a political campaign influences the effectiveness of NPAs (O'Cass, 2002).

Overall, much like the research in the political science and communication literatures, the focus of NPA research within marketing and advertising has been varied and broad with very little firmly established about the effects of NPAs on voter behavior, especially when considering the massive spending on NPAs that has occurred.

Where Are NPAs Mostly Likely to Be Used in Election Campaigns?

Despite the surge of NPAs, little investigation has been done to identify the inherent causes of negativity in campaigns in general. However, research has found insights into what causes negativity. In primary campaigns, it has been established that the type of race, as well as the timing within the race, can predict negative expenditures and tactics (Peterson & Djupe, 2005). It also appears that in primary contests, negativity is directly related to the quality of candidates (quality defined as the candidates previously holding elected office), whether there is an incumbent, and the timing within the campaign period (Peterson & Djupe, 2005). Races featuring incumbents, perhaps because office holders have a documented voting record, also engender greater negativity. Candidates are also more likely to attack at the beginning and end of primary campaigns (Peterson & Djupe, 2005).

Another relevant study examined the negativity involved in 730 House and Senate campaign websites between 2002–06 (Druckman, Kifer, & Parkin, 2010). It differed from most studies in that it analyzed data from less visible House elections, which often have more NPAs in print format. This research was also unusual because it looked at campaign websites, which allow for increased information content compared to time-limited NPAs usually in 30-second television ads. The study found a number of effects, including an increased likelihood for challengers to use NPAs, as well as greater negativity likely to occur from the party not in power during midterm elections. In addition, the study found more negativity in highly competitive races. The investigators also found that the overall proportion of negative messages increased from 38% of ads in 2002 to 57% in 2006 (Druckman, Kifer, & Parkin, 2010).

Besides establishing that negative political advertising has become the norm in election campaigns, it appears that a playbook is being formulated as to when "going negative" seems to be most advantageous for the office seeker. However, this does not address the question of whether NPAs and other manifestations of political campaign negativity are good for democracy.

Who Should Pay Attention to the NPA Explosion?

The answer to the header question is "everyone" because there are political and societal risks in the growth of NPAs. In the next section, we address two additional risks of pervasive NPAs in the U.S. election system.

The Negative Electorate

With NPAs rapidly increasing and opinion polls showing that American's political views are part of their social identity, it is possible that citizens are changing the way they debate and discuss politics, absorbing greater negativity from the political environment around them (Pinkleton, Austin, Zhou, Willoughby, & Reiser, 2012). There is some case evidence to suggest things may be shaping up this way. For instance, Wisconsin has become a classic "purple" state with 46% of the populous entrenched in the conservative camp and 46% holding mostly progressive views. Recent state elections have been fought over the 8% that is truly "undecided" due to their extended deliberations or chronic apathy. In the bitter and NPA-rich 2012 Wisconsin gubernatorial recall election of Tea Party favorite Gov. Scott Walker (R), about one-third of voters reported ceasing communication with someone they knew because of a "conflict" related to the divisive recall election (Marquette University Law School Poll, 2012). In other words, negative political campaigns may fuel ever-greater voter partisanship, leading to the likelihood of more NPAs in an unfortunate vicious cycle.

A Barrier to Good Candidates

It is also possible that the negativity inherent in modern campaigning could have the potential to keep highly qualified candidates from running for office because the threat of negativity against them and their families deterred them in pursuing an elective office. The decision to run for office has been described in the research literature as a cost-benefit decision made by the potential candidate, where the benefits of running must outweigh the costs (Fox & Lawless, 2005). It has also been established that these cost-benefit decisions typically center on the perceived electability of the candidate and her political experience, as well as other general factors that discourage running, such as belonging to a class or minority group that has typically been underrepresented in elected office (Fox & Lawless, 2005). Considering this evaluative framework, and the intuitive classification of attack ads as a cost variable affecting the decision to seek office, it is reasonable to hypothesize that increased NPAs in the electoral system have made qualified potential candidates less likely to run. Furthermore, with minority ethno-racial status already being identified as a deterrent for running, the threat of NPAs could have a disproportionate deterrent effect on minority candidates' decisions to seek office.

Reduced Political Efficacy and Speech for Citizens

Nichols and McChesney (2013) note that the interests of corporations and those of wealthy donors are often different from those of individual citizens. Both seek lower taxes for the wealthy and often support privatization of government programs in pursuit of new profit-making opportunities. Moreover, small donors will have less and influence over candidates who are elected. This leads not only to the possibility that citizens will perceive that they have little political efficacy, but they will in fact have little efficacy to change the course of government policy.

Citizens may also have reduced their discussions about alternative political platforms because of high levels of negativity and feelings of increased tensions among neighbors and friends. The many NPAs may also lead citizens to ignore genuine policy issues and instead focus on the nature of the attacks and counterattacks of the candidates.

A Brief Commentary Drawn From Marketing Ethics

Political speech, and by extension political advertising, is highly unrestricted in the United States. School children sometimes are asked to memorize the language of the First Amendment to the U.S. Constitution: "Congress shall make no law . . . abridging the freedom of speech, or the press; or the right of the people peaceably to assemble." Unbounded political information is enshrined in American culture. As the Supreme Court, in New York Times versus Sullivan (1964) noted by invoking First Amendment considerations, political speech should be "uninhibited, robust and wide open." The unmistakable implication is that political statements are a sacrosanct form of marketing communications, far more unfettered than commercial speech involving products or services (Laczniak & Caywood, 1987). The reality is that if one wishes, in person or via negative advertising, to call some politician a "cheating scoundrel," the threshold for "evidence" that is required to support that postulation is almost nil.

Examples of legal NPAs characterized by innuendo, false information, and dubious allegations are rife. Consider these descriptions of three TV ads from the 2012 national election campaign (USA Today Editorial Board, 2012).

- In a national ad sponsored by a Democratic party affiliated PAC, a TV commercial voice-over berates then vice presidential candidate Paul

Ryan's proposal to replace traditional Medicare with private insurance health vouchers. As a man in the ad (symbolizing Ryan) pushes an elderly woman (representing seniors) along a park path, and as the "evidence" is given against Ryan's plan, the woman begins to struggle to get free, but she (or hopefully a dummy replacement) is pushed off a cliff.

- In the Connecticut Senate campaign, Republican Linda McMahon accuses her Democratic opponent of voting to raise taxes while he was "raking in $1 million in salary" from the federal government. In fact, her opponent had earned that total amount during his *over* six years of service in the U.S. Congress, drawing upon his regulated salary of about $175,000 per annum. This allegation of a "too rich to trust" legislator came from Ms. McMahon, whose stock portfolio from her family's professional wrestling empire was worth at least $400 million.

- In a Colorado U.S. House of Representatives race, candidate Joe Coors (R) accused Representative Ed Perlmutter (D) of "gaming the system" by working in Congress while his wife collected $140,000 as a Washington lobbyist. In reality, the congressman was divorced from this woman before he went to Washington and separated from her long before that.

These misleading NPAs, like hundreds of similar ads, are protected by freedom of speech. While some regulatory restrictions on negative political ads are proposed from time to time, their enactment stands as unlikely due to First Amendment protections. Fortunately, independent organizations such as Politi-Fact have emerged, which fact-check and rate for truthfulness various political campaign statements, but such analyses typically appear once in the newspapers while the NPAs in question continue to run many times during an election cycle.

To sum up, prohibition or regulation of NPAs should not be anticipated, while, at the same time, the political problems fueled by NPAs (e.g., loss of trust in government, partisanship to the point of gridlock) continue unabated. Given this reality, should doing nothing about the current political environment be the default option? Hopefully not.

This is where perspectives drawn from marketing ethics can play a role. Ethical codes do not have the force of law. But the normative standards of behavior professed by members of the marketing and advertising community should count for something (Laczniak & Murphy, 2006; Shaver, 2003). For those who care about professional ethics, there are a few clear considerations that ought to guide their moral compass when creating, planning, and implementing political marketing campaigns, especially ones that include negative attack ads.

For instance, the second general norm of the American Marketing Association's (2008 revision) *Statement of Ethics* reads in part: "Foster trust in the marketing system. This means striving for good faith and fair dealing so as to contribute to the efficacy of the exchange process as well avoiding deception." Since "norms" are an expected standard of conduct to be maintained by professional practitioners, this would seem to place a moral obligation upon experts in marketing to advise their political clients about the detrimental primary and secondary consequences of attack advertising. A primary effect of NPAs, especially those containing unfair innuendo, such as the examples discussed earlier, is that they could mislead voters. Such deceptions, while perhaps shielded by First Amendment protections, seem far more serious than marketing tricks that tout dubious consumer products, such as miracle cleaners, quick-diet products, or self-help books. A secondary consequence of NPAs is that they erode the general trust that the receivers of advertising have about the credibility and veracity of the marketing system and its practitioners, a clear violation of the second norm.

The third norm of the AMA statement (2008) asks marketers to "embrace ethical values" that will enhance "confidence in the integrity of the marketing system." Included here are values such as honesty, responsibility, fairness and transparency. Some of the points used to describe these values in a marketing/ advertising context would certainly prove challenging for many creators of negative political campaigns and their supporting NPAs. These include ethical aspirations for the marketing professional such as:

- Strive to be truthful in all situations and at all times.
- Acknowledge the social obligations to stakeholders that come with increased marketing and economic power.
- Reject manipulations and sales tactics that harm consumer trust.
- Strive to communicate clearly with all constituencies.

Reflection on these guides to ethical marketing, endorsed by the largest association of marketing practitioners in the world, *ought to* give ethical pause to marketing consultants and advertising professionals when formulating negative political advertisements, especially ones that disparage opponents with cloudy accusations.

Similarly, the American Association of Advertising Agencies (AAAA), going back as far as the early 1980s, has asked its member firms to observe "the highest standards of fairness and morality" when representing political clients. This includes not using quotes from politicians out of context; avoiding the disparagement of another candidate's race, creed, or ethnic background; not indulging in the misleading or deceptive use of a politician's photo, film clips, or sound bites, as well as refraining from making any accusation too late in the campaign for the opposing candidate to answer (Dougherty, 1984). The Institute for Advertising Ethics, a partner of the American Advertising Federation and the Missouri School of Journalism, offers similar guidelines and an educational program for agency and corporate professionals, students, and faculty. Institute for Advertising Ethics Principle 2 refers in individuals' personal responsibility in their work: "Advertising, public relations, and all marketing communications professionals have an obligation to exercise the highest personal ethics in the creation and dissemination of commercial information to consumers" (Institute for Advertising Ethics, 2011).

Cynics will reply with skepticism to such idealistic self-control and will venture forms of the following rebuttal:

- Attacking opposing candidate ideas, qualifications, or actions is a standard feature of political campaigning;
- Voters desire to know every possible negative attribute of those whom they are entrusting with public power;
- NPAs are legal;
- Typically all parties in an election will make "negative" accusations and not doing so may put the candidate who disavows NPAs at great disadvantage;
- Voters should be given credit for being smart enough to figure out what the truth really is.

The solution to this clash of viewpoints—ethical responsibility versus increasing political negativity—one where negativity is clearly winning the day, lies in the moral courage by political marketers, as well as in an enhanced transparency of the political process via the efforts of the media and academic researchers.

Moral Courage by Political Marketers and Their Clients

As the earlier comments concerning professional marketing ethics make clear, just because something is legal and strategically utilitarian does not mean that it ought *to be* done. Ethical marketing consultants and advertising agencies have an abiding moral responsibility to caution against negativity in political campaigns, especially the use of NPAs, due to the probable dysfunctions these approaches inflict on the social system. Professional marketers are expected, according to the ethical norms they endorse (AMA Statement on Ethics), to be "courageous and proactive" in the fulfillment of all promises explicitly and implicitly made to all their stakeholders. In a political marketing context, such stakeholders would include voters and the community, as well as their client politicians.

Opposing candidates in an election might voluntarily agree to a set of mutually agreed upon neutral judges who would screen, preview, and/or review all ads that they run in a particular campaign according to standards such as the ones described earlier (Caywood & Laczniak, 1985). This approach could allow the "judges" to suggest changes to negative ads that might be deemed unfair or misleading to the reasonable voter.

Enhanced Transparency of the Political Process via Tracking and Research

Simply stated, since moral courage alone is unlikely to foster major change, the debate about the merits of NPAs might be best advanced by greater discussion and investigation of their roles in the U.S. elections system. Journalists who document the day-to-day tactics of specific political campaigns and research academics interested in the big picture aspects of persuasion models can rekindle a thoughtful societal discussion by shining greater light on the factors surrounding pervasive negative political advertising.

Here is an overview of the issues that must be kept in the forefront of public consciousness and political debate:

The media should track the amount of negativity in political campaigns. They should strive to uncover what groups are sponsoring NPAs if they originate with other than the candidate. The media should hold campaigns responsible for inaccurate or untruthful charges and use their power to publicize false negatives that could shape the election. While vigorous political debate is essential, transparency of ad sponsorship should be encouraged in order to unmask conflicts of interests. Problematic here is the reality that the for-profit media depend on the revenue generated by selling political advertising, including NPAs.

Academic researchers interested in political persuasion should develop measures of various antecedents and consequences of negative political advertising. Multiple and longitudinal studies are required to establish how NPAs affect voter turnout, under what conditions attack ads are most effective, and whether NPAs kindle voter cynicism and increased partisanship. Similarly, research studies should establish the conditions that might impel particularly negative campaigns. Finally, trained ethicists should weigh in more vigorously on the tactics that underlie NPAs (Laczniak & Murphy, 1993). For example, it might be strongly argued that:

- To make dubious allegations in NPAs for the purpose of furthering a political campaign results in voters being used merely as a means to an end and constitutes a violation of philosopher Immanuel Kant's formulation of what he called categorical imperatives. One of those imperatives was the principle that we should never exploit people to accomplish our own ends (Black & Roberts, 2011). If voters are deceived and manipulated by ads, they are being exploited and thus are being deprived of their freedom and autonomy as human beings.
- Questionable attacks on the personal character of an opposing candidate in an NPA are an ethical violation of classical virtue ethics and its inherent values of fairness and honesty. Virtue ethics, a much-discussed concept originating with Aristotle, involves concerns with our nature as human beings. Lambeth (1986) said that virtues are "those traits of character or personhood that help one live up to or live out the principles of an ethical system (p. 54).
- Powerful political voices made possible by the amount of money one wealthy person or organization is able to spend should not cancel out the opinion of the many who cannot afford to sponsor counteradvertising. This also would be a violation of Kant's categorical imperatives.

Perhaps the final word in our discussion of negative political advertising should go to the late David Ogilvy, considered by many to be one of the most respected practitioners in the history of advertising. Ogilvy never allowed his iconic advertising agency to take on the accounts of political candidates or parties. As he presciently wrote many years ago:

> In a period when television commercials are often the decisive factor in deciding who shall be the next President of the United States, dishonest advertising is as evil as stuffing the ballot box. Perhaps the advertising people who have allowed their talents to be prostituted for this villainy are too naïve to understand the complexity of the issue.
>
> (Ogilvy, 1983, p. 213)

Note

1. The convention ad showed the Democratic candidate juxtaposed with scenes of strife, war, and worried citizens and closed with the message "This time, vote like your whole world depended on it."

   "Harry and Louise" was a campaign funded by insurance companies showing a fictional middle-aged couple who were worried about President Clinton's proposed health-care reforms. Sen. John McCain was the target of robocalls in a smear campaign during the 2000 South Carolina presidential primary insinuating that McCain had an illegitimate black child. In fact, he and his wife had adopted a child from Bangladesh. The "Swift Boat" campaign was a series of ads and interviews financed by a major Republican donor that sought to portray Democratic candidate John Kerry as having lied about his service in Vietnam.

References

American Marketing Association (2008). Statement on ethics, as reprinted by permission. In P. E. Murphy, G. R. Laczniak, & A. Prothero (Eds.) *Ethics in Marketing* (pp. 12–14). London: Routledge, 2012.

Ansolabehere, Stephen, & Shanto Iyengar. (1995). Going Negative: How Political Advertisements Shrink and Polarize the Electorate. New York: Free Press.

Black, J., & Roberts, C. (2011). *Doing Ethics in Media: Theories and Practical Application.* New York: Routledge.

Brooks, D. J. (2006). The resilient voter: Moving toward closure in the debate over negative campaigning and turnout. *Journal of Politics*, 68(3), 684–96.

Carr, R. K., Bernstein, M. H., Murphy, W. F., & Danielson, M. N. (1971). *American Democracy* (6th edition). New York: Holt, Rinehart and Winston, Inc.

Caywood, C. L., & Laczniak, G. R. (1985). Unethical political advertising: Considerations for policy and evaluation. In M. J. Houston & R. J. Lutz (Eds.) *Marketing Communications—Theory and Research.* (pp. 37–41). Chicago: American Marketing Association.

Citizens United v. Federal Election Commission, No. 08–205 (U.S. January 21, 2010). Retrieved January 25, 2015 from http://www.supremecourtus.gov/opinions/09pdf/08-205.pdf

Dardis, F. E., Shen, F., & Edwards, H. H. (2008). Effects of negative political advertising on individuals' cynicism and self-efficacy: The impact of ad type and message exposures. *Mass Communications & Society*, 11, 24–42.

Dougherty, P. H. (1984). Advertising: mixing ethics and politics. *The New York Times*, July 11, 1984, 133, 37.

Druckman, J.N.K., Martin J., & Parkin, M. (2010). Timeless strategy meets new medium: Going negative on congressional campaign web sites, 2002–2006. *Political Communication*, 27(1), 88–103.

Druckman, J. N., Kifer, M. J., & Parkin, M. (2007). The technological development of Congressional web sites: H and why candidates use web innovations. *Social Science Computer Review*, 25(4), 425–42.

Egan, J. (1999). Political marketing: Lessons from the mainstream. *Journal of Marketing Management*, 15(6), 495–503.

Faber, R. J., Tims, A. R., & Schmitt, K. G. (1993). Negative political advertising and voting intent: The role of involvement and alternative information sources. *Journal of Advertising*, 22, 67–76.

Forgette, R., & Jonathan, S. M. (2006). High-conflict television news and public opinion. *Political Research Quarterly*, 59(3), 447–56. Retrieved January 25, 2015 from http://search.proquest.com/docview/215334466?accountid=100

Fowler, E. F., & Ridout, T. N. (2013). Negative, angry, and ubiquitous: Political advertising in 2012. *The Forum*, 10(4), 51–61.

Fowler-Franklin, E., & Ridout, T. N. (2012). Negative, angry, and ubiquitous: Political advertising in 2012. *The Forum: A Journal of Applied Research in Contemporary Politics*, (10)4, 51–61.

Fox, R. L., & Lawless, J. L. (2005). To run or not to run for office: Explaining nascent political ambition. *American Journal of Political Science*, 49, 642–59. doi: 10.1111/j.1540–5907.2005.00147.x

Freedman, P., & Goldstein, K. (1999). Measuring media exposure and the effects of negative campaign ads. *American Journal of Political Science*, 1189–1208.

Fridkin, K. L., & Kenney, P. (2011). Variability in Citizens' reactions to different types of negative campaigns. *American Journal of Political Science*, 307–25. Retrieved September 15, 2014 from http://onlinelibrary.wiley.com/doi/10.1111/ajps.2011.55.issue-2/issuetoc

Geer, J. G. (2012). The news media and the rise of negativity in presidential campaigns. *PS: Political Science & Politics*, 45(03), 422–27.

Hitchon, J. C., & Chang, C. (1995). Effects of gender schematic processing on the reception of political commercials for men and women candidates. *Communication Research*, 22 (August), 430–58.

Hitchon, J. C., Chang, C., & Harris, R. (1997). Should women emote? Perceptual bias and opinion change in response to political ads for candidates of different genders. *Political Communication*, 14 (January), 49–69.

Hughes, A. (2003), Defining Negative Political Advertising: Definition, Features and Tactics ANZMAC 2003. Conference Proceedings Adelaide, (1–3 December), 163–71.

Institute for Advertising Ethics (2011). Institute for Advertising Ethics – Resolution. *Donald W. Reynolds Journalism Institute*. Retrieved October 15, 2015, from: http://www.rjionline.org/news/institute-advertising-ethics-resolution

James, K. E., & Hensel, P. J. (1991). Negative advertising: The malicious strain of comparative advertising. *Journal of Advertising*, 20(2), 53–69.

Jasperson, A. E., & Fan, D. P. (2002). An aggregate examination of the backlash effect in political advertising: The case of the 1996 US Senate race in Minnesota. *Journal of Advertising*, 1–12.

Kahn, K. F., & Geer, J. G. (1994). Creating impressions: An experimental investigation of political advertising on television. *Political Behavior*, 16(1), 93–116.

Kaid, L. L., & Boydston, J. (1987). An experimental study of the effectiveness of negative political advertisements. *Communication Quarterly*, 35(2), 193–201.

Kipling, R. (1913). The Kipling Society. I keep six honest serving men. Retrieved September 15, 2015 from http://www.kiplingsociety.co.uk/poems_serving.htm

Laczniak, G. R., & Caywood, C. L. (1987). The case for and against televised political advertising: Implications for research and public policy. *Journal of Public Policy & Marketing*, (6), 16–32.

Laczniak, G. R., & Murphy, P. E (1993). *Ethical Marketing Decisions*. Boston: Allyn & Bacon.

Laczniak, G. R., & Murphy, P. E. (2006). Normative perspectives for ethical and socially responsible marketing. *Journal of Macromarketing*, 26(2), 154–77.

Lambeth, E. G. (1986). *Committed Journalism: An ethic for the profession.* Bloomington, IN: Indiana University Press.

Lariscy, R.A.W., & Tinkham, S. F. (1999). The sleeper effect and negative political advertising. *Journal of Advertising*, 28(4), 13–30.

Lau, R. R., Sigelman, L., Heldman, C., & Babbitt, P. (1999). The effects of negative political advertisements: A meta-analytic assessment. *American Political Science Review*, 851–75.

Lau, R. R., Sigelman, L., & Rovner, I. B. (2007). The effects of negative political campaigns: A meta-analytic reassessment. *Journal of Politics*, 69(4), 1176–1209.

Li, Y., Peng, M. W., & Macaulay, C. D. (2013). Market–political ambidexterity during institutional transitions. *Strategic Organization*, 11(2), 205–13.

Lux, S., Crook, T. R., & Woehr, D. J. (2011). Mixing business with politics: A meta-analysis of the antecedents and outcomes of corporate political activity. *Journal of Management*, 37(1), 223–47.

Mad Money: TV ads in the 2012 presidential campaign (2012). *Washington Post.* Retrieved January 25, 2015 from http://www.washingtonpost.com/wp-srv/special/politics/track-presidential-campaign-ads-2012/

Marquette University Law School Poll. (2012). Marquette Law School poll finds Walker leads Barrett in Wisconsin recall. Retrieved January 25, 2015 from: https://law.marquette.edu/poll/2012/05/30/marquette-law-school-poll-finds-walker-leads-barrett-in-wisconsin-recall/

National First Ladies Library. (2013). Rachel Jackson juvenile/educational biography. Retrieved January 25, 2015 from: http://www.firstladies.org/curriculum/educational-biography.aspx?biography=7*New York Times Co. v. Sullivan*, 376 U.S. 254 (1964).

New York Times vs. Sullivan (1964). Legal Information Institute, Cornell University College of Law. Retrieved September 17, 2015 from https://www.law.cornell.edu/supremecourt/text/376/254

Nichols, J., & McChesney, R. W. (2013). Dollarocracy. *The Nation*, September 30. Retrieved January 25, 2015 from http://www.thenation.com/article/176140/dollarocracy

Obama, B. (2010). Remarks by the President in State of the Union. Retrieved Sept. 15, 1015 from https://www.whitehouse.gov/the-press-office/remarks-president-state-union-address

O'Cass, A. (2002). Political advertising believability and information source value during elections. *Journal of Advertising*, 31(1), 63–74.

Ogilvy, D. (1983). *Ogilvy on Advertising*. New York: Vintage Books.

Peterson, D., & Djupe, P. (2005). When primary campaigns go negative: The determinants of campaign negativity. *Political Research Quarterly*, 58(1) (March 2005), 45–54.

Phillips, J. M., Urbany, J. E., & Reynolds, T. J. (2008). Confirmation and the effects of valenced political advertising: a field experiment. *Journal of Consumer Research*, 34(6), 794–806.

Pinkleton, B. (1997). The effects of negative comparative political advertising on candidate evaluations and advertising evaluations: An exploration. *Journal of Advertising*, 26 (Spring), 19–29.

Pinkleton, B. E., Austin, E. W., Zhou, Y., Willoughby, J. A., & Reiser, M. (2012). Perceptions of news media, external efficacy, and public affairs apathy in political decision making and disaffection. *Journalism & Mass Communications Quarterly*, 89(1), 23–39.

Poole, K., & Hare, C. (2013). An update on political polarization through the 112th Congress. Retrieved January 25, 2015 from: http://voteview.com/blog/?p=726

Public Citizen. (2012a). Citizens United fuels negative spending. Retrieved January 25, 2015 from http://www.citizen.org/documents/outside-groups-fuel-negative-spending-in-2012-race-report.pdf

Public Policy Polling. (2013). Congress somewhere below cockroaches, traffic jams, and Nickelback in Americans' esteem. Retrieved January 25, 2015 from http://www.publicpolicypolling.com/main/2013/01/congress-somewhere-below-cockroaches-traffic-jams-and-nickleback-in-americans-esteem.html

RealClearPolitics (2013). Congressional job approval. Retrieved September 15, 2015 from http://www.realclearpolitics.com/epolls/other/congressional_job_approval-903.html

Robideaux, D. R. (2004). "A longitudinal examination of negative political advertising and advertisement attitudes: a North American example." *Journal of Marketing Communications*, 10(3), 213–224.

Roddy, B. L., & Garramone, G. M. (1988). Appeals and strategies of negative political advertising. *Journal of Broadcasting & Electronic Media*, 32(4), 415–27.

Sears, D. O., & Kosterman, R. (1994). Mass media and political persuasion. In S. Shavitt & T. C. Brock (Eds.) *Persuasion* (251–78). Boston: Allyn & Bacon.

Shaver, D. (2003). Toward an analytical structure for evaluating the ethical content of decisions by advertising professionals. *Journal of Business Ethics*, 48(3), 291–300.

Stangler, C. (2014). Oligarchy Enshrined. *In These Times*, May 19. Retrieved January 25, 2015 from http://inthesetimes.com/article/16662/oligarchy_enshrined

Storey, W. (2011). Revisiting the Daisy ad revolution. *The Caucus*. Retrieved January 25, 2015 from: http://thecaucus.blogs.nytimes.com/2011/10/24/revisiting-the-daisy-ad-revolution/

Strother, D. H. (1863). Un-named political cartoon. *Abraham Lincoln's Classroom*. Retrieved January 25, 2015 from http://www.abrahamlincolnsclassroom.org/Cartoon_Corner/index3.asp?ID=456& TypeID=5

Terkel, A. (2013). 112th Congress set to become most unproductive since 1940s. Huffington Post. Retrieved January 25, 2015 from http://www.huffingtonpost.com/2012/12/28/congress-unproductive_n_2371387.html

Tinkham, S. F., & Weaver-Lariscy, R. A. (1994). Ethical judgments of political television commercials as predictors of attitude toward the ad. *Journal of Advertising*, 23(3), 43–57.

USA Today Editorial Board. (2012). The 5 worst political ads. *USA Today*, Nov. 1. Retrieved January 25, 2015 from http://www.usatoday.com/story/opinion/2012/11/01/political-ads-election-vote/1675611/

USA Today Editorial Board (2014). The 5 worst political ads of 2014. *USA Today*, Oct 17. Retrieved January 25, 2015 from http://www.usatoday.com/story/opinion/2014/10/16/midterm-elections-2014-republican-democratic-editorials-debates/17380271/

Wattenberg, M. P., & Brians, C. L. (1999). Negative campaign advertising: Demobilizer or mobilizer? *American Political Science Review*, 93(4), 891–99.

Weber, T. J. (2014). Negative political advertisements (NPAs): Literature review, methodology analysis and agenda for future research. *Washington State University: Working Paper Series*, 1–41.

Weber, T. J., & Joireman, J. (2015). Politicized purchases: The citizen consumer, the polarized firm, and the paradox of corporate political activism. *Washington State University: Working Paper Series*, 1–22.

Presidential Ads 70% Negative in 2012, Up from 9% in 2008. (2012). Wesleyan Media Project, May 2. Retrieved January 25, 2015 from http://mediaproject.wesleyan.edu/2012/05/02/jump-in-negativity/#more-1729

9   Puffing the Claim

Jef Richards

CHAPTER SUMMARY

When you watch an ad that claims a brand's basketball shoes will let you fly, do you then have the expectation that the shoes will literally allow you to fly if you wear them? If a pizza company claims that its pizza is the best in the world, is the company being deceptive? These are examples of "puffing" or "puffery," a term that refers to exaggerated claims in advertisements. Courts and critics have tried for decades to draw distinctions between claims that are deceptive and those that are puffery. Most reasonable people, it's argued, aren't deceived by such puffery and advertisers' intentions are not to create a false belief in people's minds. Claims based on opinions (the best pizza in the world!) are seen as different from those making "objective" claims (our smartphone has a 16-megapixel camera!). See if you agree with the Better Living *decision that puffing is defined as exaggerations or claims about a product's quality that can't be precisely determined to be true or false—but are not in themselves deceptive. At some point, exaggeration may, however, become deception, and this is the area in which ethicists, legal experts, consumers, and consumer protection agencies often disagree.*

Introduction

Did you ever ask yourself what makes Wonder Bread a wonder? Is it somehow different and better than other breads? And who crowned Budweiser the King of Beers? Did it receive this award over all other beers? And exactly how, and when, did Wheaties become the Breakfast of Champions? Does that mean champions in all sports, champions in business, or what? We have all seen these slogans and other advertising claims suggesting one brand of product is somehow special, as opposed to its more mundane competitors. This sort of ad language is commonly termed "puffery."

In simple terms, "puffery" is exaggeration. As the term implies, it is about inflating (or adding air to) a claim or statement. This explains the title of the most thorough book on the topic, *The Great American Blow-Up: Puffery in Advertising and Selling* (Preston, 1975). It also frequently appears in verb form: to puff.

A Little History

The word "puffery" is used a lot in describing advertising. It is a word that can be traced back, at least, to the 18th century. *Merriam-Webster* dictionary (Merriam-Webster.com 2014), defining the term as "exaggerated commendation especially for promotional purposes," lists the first known use as 1782. However, it appears to have roots going back at least a bit further. Indeed, a play from late 1779, "The Critic," has a principal figure who is a playwright and charlatan named Mr. Puff. And the term can even be found as early as 1731 in a story about an election in Bagdad, referring to the "the Bumbast and Puffery of Councellor Glib" (Alexander the Coppersmith, 1731).

The earliest known book dedicated to the topic of advertising made puffery its centerpiece (Anonymous, 1856). The book's introduction announces, "We intend to devote a few pages to tracing the progress of the Art of Puffing during the last forty years, and shall then proceed to consider its condition at the present time." It then provides a typology of puffs (e.g., the Puff Ostentatious, the Puff Infantile, the Puff Interjectional, the Puff Mendacious, etc.). By this, it illustrates the fact that some puffery is stated explicitly (e.g., "the *best* beer") while some is a bit more obliquely expressed (e.g., "Oh, how very comfortable, *exclaims everyone.*").

And while the word "puffery" might be only a few hundred years old, most certainly the concept of selling a product, service, or idea with a spicing of exaggeration reaches back millennia. Of course, advertising with this spice continues to be used with abandon today. It is a reality and, we could argue, advertising without puffery would lack flavor. From a policy perspective, the only real question is how much puffery is acceptable. At some point exaggeration wanders across the line into deception, which is both legally and ethically reprehensible.

The "Puffery is Deceptive" Position

Ivan Preston, quite literally, wrote the (aforementioned) book on puffery (Preston, 1975). A social scientist with no formal legal training, Preston took on the challenge of researching legal cases and tracing the law back more than seven centuries, resulting in a masterful treatment of this topic, which previously had not received much scholarly consideration. Looking at how the law of puffery evolved from a legal environment that seemed to embrace untruthful claims by sellers, Preston built an argument that is compelling even after all those centuries, "Puffery lies to you and it deceives you, but the law says it doesn't" (1975, p. 3).

Preston shows how the law slowly evolved to put limits on the types of lies sellers could tell. False claims about *factual* aspects of a product or service, he explains, are no longer legally permissible. Puffery is not about facts, it is about opinions. Preston explains, "By legal definition, puffery is advertising or other sales representations which praise the item to be sold with subjective opinions, superlatives, or exaggerations, vaguely and generally, stating no specific facts" (p. 17).

His logic is that legal authorities, including the Federal Trade Commission (FTC)—the principal U.S. regulator of advertising—operate from the assumption that reasonable people automatically discount sellers' opinions, so they will not be deceived by such. The heart of Preston's argument is that while advertisers might be prohibited from explicitly lying about the factual product attributes, their opinions still *imply* facts (1975, p. 121), and those typically are false facts (p. 24).

Preston builds a strong and convincing case that the law has erected a legal safe harbor, or loophole (see also Preston, 1998), around puffery that gives advertisers carte blanche to deceive consumers without fear of legal retribution. If a claim is stated as an *opinion* rather than a *fact*, and it merely implies some form of factual superiority, sellers can mislead their customers with abandon. Puffery, Preston concludes, is deceptive and should be regulated, and he shows a number of examples where claims were declared to be puffs and yet must, by deductive logic, be conveying deceptive information to consumers.

He explains that it is a small remnant of a time when sellers were subject to almost no regulation whatsoever. Over the centuries, he shows, more and more regulations have been introduced to protect consumers and businesses. Puffery, he opines, is the one remaining technique by which sellers can deceive without penalty.

His argument has led to a long stream of researchers citing and repeating that argument (e.g., Oliver, 1979; Vanden Bergh, Bruce, & Reid, 1980; Rotfeld & Rotzoll, 1981; Russo, Metcalf, & Stephens, 1981; Aditya, 2001), and several have attempted to empirically test Preston's proposition that consumers are misled by puffed claims (e.g., Kamins & Marks, 1987; Patti, 1995; Haan & Berkey, 2002; Gao & Scorpio, 2011; Amyx & Amyx, 2011). Ironically many, if not most, of those empirical studies appear to run counter to Preston's allegation. Of course, that doesn't mean he is wrong, because it is possible the claims they tested were not the ones that are misleading or the methods simply are not sufficient to detect the deceptiveness.

There is, however, another interpretation of the facts that runs counter to Preston's allegation. It is one detailed a quarter century ago (Richards, 1990), but I will try to further explain it here.

An Alternative Viewpoint

Preston's argument, stated simply, is this: If (1) X is puffery and (2) X actually deceives people, then (3) puffery is deceptive. That's a statement of logic, which is the essence of Preston's approach to the topic.

In testing that proposition, most researchers have looked at #2, asking whether X deceives. Does, for example, "King of Beer" mislead people about the superiority of Budweiser? If not, then it would seem that not all puffery is deceptive. But another question to ask is regarding #1, whether X really is puffery. This depends, of course, on the definition of "puffery."

The FTC or the courts have never declared most of the questionable claims listed by Preston "puffery", but they do seem to fit the characterization of "subjective opinions, superlatives, or exaggerations." Preston does, of course, cite some examples where a legal authority has declared a claim to be puffery, and he explains how they must imply facts that are not true and so they must be deceptive. But the alternative view suggests that if any of these claims are deceptive, they are being erroneously labeled "puffery."

At the heart of this argument is the reality that there is more than one definition of puffery. Preston, indeed, traces his way through a variety of such definitional approaches. As noted earlier, the definition on which he seems to rely is:

> Puffery is advertising or other sales representations which praise the item to be sold with subjective opinions, superlatives, or exaggerations, vaguely and generally, stating no specific facts.
>
> (Preston, 1975, p. 17)

That definition appears to be his own, gleaned from a reading of hundreds of years of cases and other materials. Most of the definitions he presents, though, are far less complete.

Many of the quotes he finds from legal authorities are simpler, focusing on the hyperbolic nature of the claims in question. For example, he cites FTC Commissioner Humphreys as referring to puffing as merely "exaggeration" (p. 177) and Sen. Burton Wheeler as calling it "exaggerated opinions" (p. 179). He also points to examples where courts refer to exaggeration of a product's value, e.g., "the assertion of the defendant that it was worth more than its real value" (p. 125), as examples of puffery. These are similar to the *Merriam-Webster* definition, mentioned earlier.

But other definitions he notes focus less on the "exaggeration" of the claim and more on the "opinion" aspect. He cites William Prosser, an expert on tort law, who defined it this way:

> Puffing ... is considered to be offered and understood as an expression of the seller's opinion only ... An opinion may take the form of a statement of quality, of more or less indefinite content ... The 'puffing' rule amounts to a seller's privilege to lie his head off, so long as he says nothing specific, on the theory that no reasonable man would believe him, or that no reasonable man would be influenced by such talk.
>
> (p. 303)

And one court decision he cites says, "Puffing refers, generally, to an expression of opinion not made as a representation of fact" (p. 304).

Yet other citations look at the seller's intent. In one case he quotes the FTC as saying, "We are of the opinion that [these claims] are nothing more than a form of 'puffing' not calculated to deceive" (p. 179), thereby implying that the seller's intentions are part of what distinguishes a puff from a non-puff. He cites the FTC in another case drawing similar boundaries on puffery by declaring, "Statements made for the purpose of deceiving prospective purchasers and particularly those designed to consummate the sale of products by fright cannot properly be characterized as mere 'puffery'" (p. 183).

And he notes that the FTC even has had trouble with the actual definition. In the Fairyfoot Products case in 1935, the FTC admitted having some challenge delineating what is or is not a puff, stating, "Just where lies the line between 'puffing,' which is not unlawful and unwarranted, and misleading misrepresentations in advertising, is often very difficult of ascertainment" (p. 178).

Of all these definitions, Preston's is the most extensive and precise, although he sidesteps the issue of seller intent in both his definition and his discussion. But his definition is not the law; it is his interpretation of the law.

Not long ago an article about puffery by a lawyer and a law student used this definition: "Publicity or acclaim that is full of undue or exaggerated praise" (Gurnani & Talati, 2008). This definition also turns on exaggeration without mention of opinion or intent. A few years before that, another lawyer defined it this way: " 'Puffery' consists of promotional claims that no one out of diapers takes literally" (Boudreaux, 1995). So his definition focuses on consumer *belief*. Obviously, these legally trained experts interpret the law somewhat differently from Preston, while during that same period of time, another lawyer cited Preston as the source of the definition he used: "Puffery, broadly defined, refers to supposedly nonfactual representations, such as statements of opinion or value" (Goretzke, 2003).

There is no single legally established, or legally adopted, definition. And without such a single standard, the law of puffery will continue to be vague and unsatisfactory. These little differences in wording and emphasis might seem trivial, but they can mean wholly contradictory outcomes for lawsuits.

Two legal decisions do stand out as more precisely carving out the niche that is puffery than most of these others. One is the *Colgate-Palmolive* (1961) case, where the FTC said:

> "Puffing" is considered to be offered and understood as an expression of the seller's opinion only, which is to be discounted by the buyer, and on which no reasonable man would rely.

This, too, seems to turn on the concept of consumer belief and makes it clear that it is what the *reasonable* person believes that is important.

But an even more specific definition is found in *Better Living, Inc.* (1957),[1] where the Commission explained:

> Puffing, as we understand it, is a term frequently used to denote the exaggerations reasonably to be expected of a seller as to the degree of quality of his product, the truth or falsity of which cannot be precisely determined.

This includes most of the elements of the other definitions, all in a single definition. And it goes an important step farther by defining what constitutes "opinion": a claim that cannot be proved either true or false. This is a legal definition that seems to encompass the others.

The only element from previous definitions not included here is seller intent, but that makes sense because the FTC has never been concerned with a seller's intent. After all, consumers can be deceived and injured by that deception even if the seller had no intent to deceive, such as if a seller poorly phrases a claim in an advertisement. The FTC is concerned only with preventing such injury, regardless of what was intended.

If we pick apart this definition, it has two elements. First, it includes "exaggerations reasonably to be expected." If reasonable consumers expect such exaggerations, they will not believe the claims and therefore will not be deceived by them. Second, the "truth or falsity of which cannot be precisely determined" means that they are not demonstrably false, and deception cannot occur without the claims conveying untrue information.

Put simply, any claim fitting this definition of puffery cannot be capable of deception. Advertising deception requires *creating a false belief* in the mind of the consumer. By this definition a puff is not false, nor will it be believed. Puffery and deception are mutually exclusive categories. So if we accept this as the best, most precise, *legal* definition of puffery, Preston is wrong.

This argument is bolstered by the "Cigarette Rule" published by the FTC in 1964:

> The traditional broad scope of permissible "puffing" has been narrowed to include only expressions that the consumer clearly understands to be pure sales rhetoric on which he should not rely in deciding whether to purchase the seller's product. The test, thus, is not whether a representation is intended as a statement of fact or one of opinion, but whether it is likely to mislead the consumer.
>
> (FTC, 1964)

If it is deceptive, it is not puffery. Preston may be correct that many claims others have called "puffery" are actually deceptive, but it is not that puffs are deceptive, it is that those claims have been mislabeled. Admittedly, these are FTC definitions, and FTC decisions are not binding on the courts. But because the FTC is seen as the authority on advertising deception, the courts generally look to it for guidance on such things.

As noted earlier, this is the basic argument made about 25 years ago. So the question remains whether any major change has occurred in the law of puffery since that time. Because puffery is a defense raised in many contexts beyond just FTC actions, there are far too many cases across that time span to discuss, but a few of the more recent ones are worth analyzing to see whether Preston's concerns about the legal treatment of puffery are valid today.

Recent Puffery Cases

Pizza Hut v. Papa John's (2000)

Without question the most notable puffery case in the past two and a half decades—if not the most notable ever—is *Pizza Hut v. Papa John's*, in which the largest pizza chain in the United States sued the third largest over its slogan, "Better Ingredients, Better Pizza." This was not an FTC case but rather a trademark case under the Lanham Act,[2] because that slogan was protected as a trademark.

Pizza Hut contested the slogan as conveying a false statement of fact. Papa John's had begun using the slogan and ran a series of ads aimed at showing its pizza was better than Pizza Hut's. Papa John's claimed taste tests proved consumers liked its pizza best, which was not contested. But other ads claimed that it used clear-filtered water in its dough and "fresh-pack" sauce, while its competitors use "whatever comes out of the tap" and "remanufactured" sauce.

A jury found that Papa John's sauce and dough claims were likely to deceive consumers. Although Pizza Hut did not contest the specific water and "remanufactured" claims made by Papa John's, no credible evidence had proved a quantifiable difference in the resulting sauces and dough, as the ads had implied. The District Court found that the slogan alone was puffery and not deceptive, but when it was combined with the deceptive ads, the slogan "became tainted" and could no longer be characterized as puffery. That decision was appealed.

The Circuit Court of Appeals noted that, "Bald assertions of superiority or general statements of opinion cannot form the basis of Lanham Act liability," but that "specific and measurable claim, capable of being proved false or of being reasonably interpreted as a statement of objective fact." This, alone, fits a large part of that Better Living definition.

The court went on to define puffing as "advertising that is not deceptive for no one would rely on its exaggerated claims" under one federal court's approach and "exaggerated advertising, blustering and boasting upon which no reasonable buyer would rely and is not actionable under 43(a)" under another's, and "puffing has been described by most courts as involving outrageous generalized statements, not making specific claims, that are so exaggerated as to preclude reliance by consumers" under yet another's. It also looked at some expert's definitions.

The court went on to parse the Papa John's slogan, yet found that both "Better Ingredients" and "Better Pizza" were general statements of opinion not subject to scientific quantification and therefore were puffery, nor could it find that combining the two phrases changed anything.

The court then looked at whether the subsequent advertisements "tainted" the meaning of the slogan, as declared by the District Court. It agreed that the ads were misleading—by implication, though factually true—and agreed that the ads added specific details to the meaning of the slogan, thereby making the slogan misleading. However, there was no evidence that consumers would *rely* on those misleading details, i.e., no proof they were "material" (important) misrepresentations.

This case illustrates the problem in finding a universally adopted definition of puffery. After reviewing a variety of definitions, the court ended up deriving its decision based mainly on the opinion versus fact distinction.

And, contrary to Preston's earlier argument that puffery decisions were leading to consumers being deceived, this court's principal concern seemed to be the potential for deception. The puffing nature of the slogan did not stop the court from looking for deceptive effects. Also contrary to Preston's (1975, e.g., p. 92) allegations about legal authorities ignoring implications, this court distinguished between the isolated slogan and what it *implied* when juxtaposed with the sauce and dough claims.

Following that case, the Domino's pizza chain took aim at both Pizza Hut and Papa John's by running commercials declaring, "Our pizza tastes better and that's not puffery, that's proven" (Edwards, 2010). In that ad, for the viewing audience, Domino's provided yet a version of the puffery definition that actually mirrored the court's approach: "An exaggerated statement based on opinion. Not fact."

Time Warner Cable v. DirecTV (2007)

Time Warner sued DirecTV (again, under the Lanham Act) over the latter's advertising claiming its high definition (HD) service was superior to Time Warner's, alleging the ads were false. DirecTV defended its actions, saying that the claims were only puffery.

One of the advertisements featured Jessica Simpson, an attractive blonde celebrity depicting her role of Daisy Duke in *The Dukes of Hazzard* movie. Part of her lines included:

> Hey, 253 straight days at the gym to get this body and you're not gonna watch me on DIRECTV HD? You're just not gonna get the best picture out of some fancy big screen TV without DIRECTV. It's broadcast in 1080i. I totally don't know what that means, but I want it.

A narrator added, "For picture quality that beats cable, you've got to get DIRECTV."

Another ad featured William Shatner, the actor who played James T. Kirk in the original Star Trek television series, reprising that role. Referring to DirectTV HD, one of his lines was, "With what Starfleet just ponied up for this big screen TV, settling for cable would be illogical." The commercial ended with a narrator adding, "For picture quality that beats cable, you've got to get DIRECTV." A revised version later changed that narration to state, "For an HD picture that can't be beat, get DIRECTV."

Ads also appeared on the Internet. These ads indicated that for best picture quality, "Source Matters." The ads also offered, "Find out why DIRECTV's picture beats cable." Other ads showed a side-by-side comparison with DIRECTV HD picture quality on one side and "OTHER TV" on the other side. The "other TV" turned out to be non-HD cable.

The truth was that DirecTV HD and Time Warner Cable's HD services had equivalent picture quality, as far as the evidence showed. So the District Court supported Time Warner, deciding the claims were literally false.

An appeals court noted that under the Lanham Act, two different legal theories could be pursued to prove advertising deceptive: (1) literal falsity or (2) implied falsity. Time Warner, it declared, chose the first. While the commercials and Internet ads were likely to be literally false, said the court, the District Court erred in rejecting DirecTV's puffery defense, at least with regard to the Internet ads.

The court cites one definition of puffery as, "subjective claims about products, which cannot be proven either true or false," and one that says:

> Puffery is an exaggeration or overstatement expressed in broad, vague, and commendatory language. "Such sales talk, or puffing, as it is commonly called, is considered to be offered and understood as an expression of the seller's opinion only, which is to be discounted as such by the buyer . . . The 'puffing' rule amounts to a seller's privilege to lie his head off, so long as he says nothing specific."

It also includes a few others, including, "an exaggerated, blustering, and boasting statement upon which no reasonable buyer would be justified in relying."

The court decided that the Internet side-by-side ads were indeed puffery, because the "other TV" images were so blurry and distorted—"not even remotely realistic"—that no reasonable consumer would rely on the claims. As such, the court found that the District Court had exceeded its authority, so the case was affirmed in part, vacated in part, and remanded to the District Court. In essence, it was sent back for reconsideration, but the parties dropped the case at that point.

Again, this case brings a variety of definitions into the court's deliberation, with no single definition standing out. And, like the Pizza Hut case, this one looks at the real impact on consumers and the potential for them being deceived. The District Court rejected the puffery defense altogether, while the appeals court looked at it very carefully before deciding that it would apply to at least part of the decision. Neither allowed the wholesale defense Preston suggested as being the norm.

United States v. McGraw-Hill (2013)

Puffery is a factor in more than just advertising cases, but legal decisions in any area can influence those in another. So non-advertising interpretations of puffery are just as relevant as those in advertising cases. This case was about credit rating manipulation by McGraw-Hill subsidiary, Standard & Poors (S&P). A corporation's credit ratings evaluate whether the corporation will be able to repay debts it has incurred. It is a key measure for financial professionals in recommending stocks to investors and thus the ratings are crucial for a corporation's profitability. The ratings agencies are paid by investment banks that sell securities (corporate stocks and bonds) thus introducing the potential for conflicts of interest.

S&P had a reputation for reliable and credible ratings, with codes of conduct to manage any potential conflicts of interest. However, the government charged S&P with confirming ratings that did not accurately reflect the true credit risks, knowing that some high-risk, residential, mortgage-backed securities were about to be downgraded. S&P, as a result, was charged with criminal fraud for the ratings and related assurances the company gave to investors. S&P argued, however, that its statements consisted of no more than puffery.

The court in this case found that defense disturbing:

> Defendants lead off with a proposition that is deeply and unavoidably troubling when you take a moment to consider its implications. They claim that, out of all the public statements that S&P made to investors, issuers, regulators, and legislators regarding the company's procedures for providing objective, data-based credit ratings that were unaffected by potential conflicts of interest, not one statement should have been relied upon by investors, issuers, regulators, or legislators who needed to be able to count on objective, data-based credit ratings.

They acknowledged that a "general, subjective claim about a product is non-actionable puffery." It also cited another definition: "[a] statement is considered puffery if the claim is extremely unlikely to induce consumer reliance."

The court determined that S&P's claims (including incorporated in its internal policies) did not constitute a "general, subjective claim" about the company's avoidance of conflict of interests. Those claims included statements like, "the fact that Rating Services receives a fee from the issuer must not be a factor in the decision to rate an issuer or in the analysis and the rating opinion." Throughout its policies it used phrases like "must not" and "shall," but the court found those were not general subjective claims about a vague future, they were specific promises.

S&P argued no reasonable investor would have relied on its claims. The court found it incongruous for S&P to, in effect, defend itself by asserting that its ratings were of no value. As a result, S&P's defense was rejected.

Once again a court was faced with multiple definitions. The decision here was made principally on opinion-fact distinction found in the previous cases. And, like those other cases, this court was concerned with the likelihood of the audience being misled.

In re Tropicana Products (2013)

Finally, a little different take on puffery can be found in the decisions of the National Advertising Division (NAD) of the Council of Better Business

Bureaus. The NAD is part of the primary *self*-regulatory system for the advertising industry in the United States.

In this case, Campbell Soup Company—which makes V8 V-Fusion beverages—complained to the NAD that Tropicana deceptively claimed that its Tropicana Farmstand product was the "world's best fruit and vegetable juice." The key issue for the NAD was whether or not that claim constituted puffery. This is an interesting example because Preston (1975, pp. 22–24) specifically notes "best" as being a term of puffery that can be deceptive.

In this case, the NAD notes:

> If the use of the superlative is vague and fanciful and suggests no objective measure of superiority, then the claim is likely to be puffery. If, on the other hand, adjectives such as 'best' or 'greatest' are accompanied by specific attributes which are likely to suggest that product is comparatively 'better' in some recognizable or measurable way, the defense of 'puffery' is unlikely to prevail.

The NAD looked at the total context of the ad's voice-over, "If you want the world's best fruit and vegetable juice, look in the cooler," which was accompanied by images of non-refrigerated juice products falling on the floor. In the end, the NAD declared that the claim was puffery, apparently deciding that the tumbling competitor products in the ad did not rise to the level of the specifics needed to convert "world's best" into something more than puffery.

Although this decision upheld a defense of puffery, unlike the cases noted earlier, it is clear from the NAD's statement that it did not apply a blanket rule that assumes "best" is always puffery. Indeed, it is clear that the decision was largely in accord with Preston's own thinking, that terms like "best" might well be deceptive in many cases.

Conclusion

Advertising deception occurs in the consumer's head. Whether an ad claim is literally true or false can be irrelevant if that claim is *implying* something more than its explicit wording. And it is seldom that an ad claim occurs in isolation. It generally is surrounded by other claims or text, and often by visual imagery. Even the content of the media vehicle in which it is placed can potentially modify the meaning of a claim. This is what can make it difficult for any judge or jury to determine whether a claim truly is puffery. The lack of a single, unified, definition of puffery only makes this task more onerous.

Ivan Preston highlighted deficiencies in the treatment of puffery as a defense to charges of deceptive advertising. He might well have been accurate about the way it was being handled by regulators at the time he wrote his book, but it is clear that in the recent cases examined, regulatory and self-regulatory authorities are keenly aware of the potential for a so-called puffery claim to actually be deceptive. Perhaps his call to arms contributed to this current level of awareness.

But a continuing problem is the lack of an agreed-upon definition of puffery. All of the definitions touch upon some accepted aspect of the concept, but most of them cover only a part of it. And as the courts seem to unearth multiple definitions when confronting a puffery case, their decisions do not seem to follow any one definition in a methodical, step-by-step approach (e.g., "this claim meets the first part of the definition but not the second"). Instead, they glean the basic idea (e.g., fact vs. opinion) and then base their decision roughly on that idea.

The clearest, most complete, and most specific definition still seems to be the one from *Better Living, Inc.* (1957). If the FTC, the courts, and the NAD were all to use that definition, consistently, puffery would cease to be a confusing aspect and potential loophole in the law of advertising.

Notes

1. In the *Better Living* case (1957), a Wisconsin appliance store was accused of advertising washing machines at a low price with the major motivation of encouraging people to come to the store and then purchase more expensive sets.
2. The Lanham Act of 1946 established rules about trademark infringement and false advertising. It protects owners of trademarks from others who may intentionally or unintentionally use a mark that is similar to a registered mark or confuses consumers.

References

Aditya, R. N. (2001). The psychology of deception in marketing: A conceptual framework for research and practice. *Psychology & Marketing*, 18(7), 735–61.

Alexander the Coppersmith (1731). *Milk for Babes, Meat for Strong Men, and Wine for Petitioners*. Farmington Hills, MI: Thomson Gale (2003).

Amyx, D., & Amyx, K. (2011). Sex and puffery in advertising: An absolutely sensational and sexually provocative experiment. *International Business and Management*, 2(1), 1–10.

Anonymous (1856). *A.B. Has Returned; or, The Romance of Advertising*. London: W. Kent and Co., Paternoster Row.

Better Living, Inc. 54 F.T.C. 648 (1957).

Boudreaux, D. J. (1995). "Puffery" in advertising. *The Free Market*, 13(9). Retrieved Sept. 15, 2015 from https://mises.org/library/puffery-advertising.

Colgate-Palmolive, 59 F.T.C. 1452 (1961).

Edwards, J. (2010). The 10-year-old court ruling that explains Dominos' obscure new Ad. CBS Interactive, Feb. 12. Retrieved September 15, 2015 from http://www.cbsnews.com/news/the-10-year-old-court-ruling-that-explains-dominos-obscure-new-ad/.

Federal Trade Commission (1964). Statement of Basis and Purpose of the Cigarette Rule. *Federal Register*, 29 (July 2), 8324.

Gao, Z., & Scorpio, E. A. (2011). Does puffery deceive? An empirical investigation. *Journal of Consumer Policy*, 34(2), 249–64.

Goretzke, C. (2003). The resurgence of caveat emptor: Puffery undermines the proconsumer trend in Wisconsin's misrepresentation doctrine. *Wisconsin Law Review*, 2003, 171–223.

Gurnani, A. K., & Talati, A. R. (2008). Food and drug law institute, *Update Magazine*, 6, 42–5.

Haan, P., & Berkey, C. (2002). A study of the believability of the forms of puffery. *Journal of Marketing Communications*, 8(4), 243–56.

In re Tropicana Products (2013). NAD determines Tropicana ad is puffery following Campbell challenge. Press release of the Advertising Self-Regulatory Council, July 30.

Kamins, M. A., & Marks, L. J. (1987). Advertising puffery: The impact of using two-sided claims on product attitude and purchase intention. *Journal of Advertising*, 16(4), 6–15.

Merriam-Webster.com (2014). http://www.merriam-webster.com (August 11, 2014).

Oliver, R. L. (1979). An interpretation of the attitudinal and behavioral effects of puffery. *Journal of Consumer Affairs*, 13, 8–27.

Patti, C. H. (1995). Advertising claim styles: An assessment of relative effectiveness. *Journal of Promotion Management*, 2(3–4), 121–40.

Pizza Hut v. Papa John's, 227 F.3d 489 (5th Cir. 2000).

Preston, I. L. (1975). *The Great American Blow-Up: Puffery in Advertising and Selling.* Madison, WI: University of Wisconsin Press.

Preston, I. L. (1998). Puffery and other "loophole" claims: How the "law's don't ask, don't tell" policy condones fraudulent falsity in advertising. *Journal of Law and Commerce*, 18, 49–114.

Richards, J. I. (1990). A "new and improved" view of puffery. *Journal of Public Policy and Marketing*, 9, 73–84.

Rotfeld, H. J., & Rotzoll, K. B. (1981). Puffery vs. fact claims—Really different? *Current Issues & Research in Advertising*, 1981, 85–103.

Russo, J. E., Metcalf, B. L., & Stephens, D. (1981). Identifying misleading advertising. *Journal of Consumer Research*, 8, 119–31.

Time Warner Cable v. DirecTV, 497 F.3d 144 (2d Cir., Aug. 9, 2007).

United States v. McGraw-Hill, 2013 U.S. Dist. LEXIS 99961 (C.D. Cal., Jul 16, 2013).

Vanden B., Bruce, G., & Reid, L. N. (1980). Effects of product puffery on response to print advertisements. *Current Issues & Research in Advertising*, 1980, 123–34.

10 Online Behavioral Advertising and the Ethics of Privacy

Heather Shoenberger

CHAPTER SUMMARY

Several years ago, a writer for Ad Age, *the advertising industry's major trade publication, wrote about "the pants that stalked him around the web." The writer, Michael Learmonth (2010), searched for some shorts online and that's when he said the "weirdness began." Just the act of browsing resulted in Criteo (an advertising retargeting firm) serving him display ads for shorts available at Zappos—everywhere he went online. Most of us have had similar experiences and some of us wonder just how companies are gathering this information and how they are using it. Most of us are guilty of thoughtlessly clicking "Agree" when a website asks us to agree to their terms of service that also outline how the site will use and potentially share and sell our data. However, as this chapter explains, increasingly sophisticated technology poses real threats to individuals' privacy. These threats can include employers or criminals using your personal information to deny you a job or steal your identity. The chapter examines online behavioral advertising (OBA), the benefits it offers to consumers who want advertising relevant to themselves as well as the ethical challenges the practice offers.*

Introduction

It's a common experience to go to a favorite website, such as your local news source or Amazon, and find ads showing products you have recently looked at or get a list of suggestions for movies, books, clothing, or cars you have recently looked at online. It is clear that your online activity has been recorded and now it is being used to push advertising through via a process known as "online behavioral advertising" or OBA. This type of advertising is enabled by tracking an individual's online activities, analyzing the data collected, and then using those analyses to deliver advertising reflective of that knowledge about an individual (Self-Regulatory Principles For Online Behavioral Advertising, 2009). Netflix provides an example of a learning algorithm (also called machine learning) that you may find familiar. Analysts apply algorithms based on the types of movies selected and the rating each watched program receives allowing Netflix to offer suggestions similar to the content recently viewed (Greenfield, 2014). Experts predict that by 2015, online behavioral advertising will make up nearly one-third of all advertising expenditure online (Lunden, 2015).

In fact, every time you go online to search for a restaurant, let a friend know about your date last night via social media, or tweet a political opinion that information is being collected by any number of organizations and compiled into a rich dataset all about YOU. This information can be sold or acquired by the U.S. government, and it's worth a great deal of money. The focus in this chapter is on information about you that is used by advertisers to sell you products and services, which is also the raw material from which online behavioral advertising is created.

Online behavioral advertising is important to advertisers because of the strong finding that personally relevant advertisements based on previous browsing history are preferred by consumers to advertisements that are randomly placed (Berger, 2011). Research by Berger (2011) also demonstrates that college students *and* adults prefer receiving online advertising that is relevant to their own interests rather than advertising delivered in some random way. This research offers convincing empirical evidence that consumers prefer personally relevant messages to those that are not personally relevant (see also Liberman & Chaiken, 1996; Claypool, Mackie, Garcia-Marques, Mcintosh, & Udall, 2004; Campbell & Wright, 2008). Reinforcing the scholarly research are findings by advertisers that OBA is 22% more effective than traditional advertisements, representing major benefits for both advertisers and online consumers (Kee, 2007).

In spite of evidence for its effectiveness, there are ethical issues about online behavioral advertising that concern the privacy of those who are tracked. The controversy centers on what privacy means in today's society and the ethical challenges of making sure consumers understand how they may unwittingly lose control of it. To help us understand why the concept of privacy is an important but complicated one, and how it relates to ethics, this chapter first turns to a short overview of how privacy has come to be defined in Western cultures and then the ethical challenges of privacy. After providing this background, it will be possible to have a better-informed discussion about the ethics of online behavioral advertising.

Privacy

There is a lot of disagreement about what privacy is and how it relates to us. Distilled from the famous Warren and Brandeis (1890) law review, the first to mention a potential right to privacy that had not been included in the Constitution or the Bill of Rights, was the idea that a citizen has the right to "be left alone." It wasn't until 1965 in the case of *Griswold v. Connecticut* that the court suggested that citizens of the United States had a constitutional right to privacy found within the Amendments. The case involved the dissemination of birth control to married couples, and it was found that this was within the realm of their marital privacy. The judges noted that "zones of privacy" existed under what were eloquently named "penumbras" or shaded regions.

As noted earlier, the right to privacy is not a right guaranteed in the U.S. Constitution, although the Fourth Amendment to the Constitution guarantees this:

> The right of the people to be secure in their persons, houses, papers, and effects, against unreasonable searches and seizures, shall not be violated, and no warrants shall issue, but upon probable cause, supported by oath or affirmation, and particularly describing the place to be searched, and the persons or things.

This sounds as if people have a right to privacy within the confines of their own home. In fact, Moor (1990) refers to the home as a "private situation" where there are legal and moral barriers to entry or observation by others. But even private situations must be balanced against other ethical concerns: public safety and security, national security, prevention of crime, protection of health, and the protection of the rights and freedoms of others. Any of these reasons might be offered by those who claim a right to infringing on the private situation of the home.

Warren and Brandeis (1890) also spoke of concern about the potential for surveillance from the government with the advent of new technologies. They noted that what was once whispered behind closed doors would one day be available as public knowledge or easy to listen to by the prying ear. Their concerns seem to echo those of consumer advocates today who worry that information people put online and the behavior that is tracked may allow others to infer their identities and eventually lead to profiles of an individual that invade his/her privacy. Online profiles may have errors leading to minor consequences for a person, such as price discrimination, and major consequences, such as employment discrimination (Turow, Feldman, & Meltzer, 2005; Marcoux, 2012; Podesta, Pritzker, Moniz, Holdren, & Zients, 2014; Turow, Feldman, & Meltzer, 2005).

For example, a person's profile might include sexual preferences, health conditions, or financial information, such as one's bank balance or credit card number. If a person does not want information like this to be known, then this information can be considered to be in a zone of "private situation," according to Moor (1990). When someone else gains such information, such information, an individual can suffer harmful outcomes such as identity theft, embarrassment, or even loss of a job. But similar to the case of the home as a private zone, societal needs can be used to justify legitimate infringement on the privacy of that information. For example, if an individual has a highly communicable disease like Ebola, public health agencies may claim a right to know and act on that fact. If the person has a collection of child pornography, then legal authorities may infringe on privacy for the sake of law enforcement. "Private situation," is therefore a useful way to think about the relationship between a person and his or her own information.

Ethicists on Privacy

How do ethicists think about privacy? The philosopher Kant (2002) argued that every human has a value that must be respected. This means all individuals have a right to choose for themselves. These rights can be either negative or positive. Negative rights include owning property that others may not access, the right not to be killed or harmed, and the right of privacy, that is "owning" a zone that others may not observe. Positive rights, on the other hand, are those such as health and education, which obligate others to fulfill them.

Another philosopher, John Rawls (2009), referred to the "common good," meaning that certain "goods" should be equally provided to everyone. Examples of the common good are public safety, a functioning legal and political system, and an unpolluted environment. Situational privacy can be justified as part of this concept of common good. Rawls, however, also talked about "justice"; that is, the concept that individuals should be treated the same and each should be treated fairly. If a person is harmed, a legal remedy must be made available.

The current conceptualization of privacy in the OBA context by the Federal Trade Commission (FTC), the government agency charged with regulating advertising, is rooted in the concept of control over one's data, much like the control one can exert over her own home. It is intended to offer a meaningful choice of how one decides to wield that control. Because privacy is a culturally created concept (Solove, 2006), regulators often interpret it as control because it is more tangible than the multiple meanings the word privacy can evoke. It allows for the option of choice, an important tenet for ethicists for whom the right to choose is foundational (Kant, 2002). There are many other ethical theories that have implications for privacy issues, but as can be seen, the question of information privacy, as applied to advertisers and others collecting information from our "situational privacy zones," is certainly of ethical concern. When consumers fail to protect their information or pay attention to what happens to it, this becomes an ethical issue (Joinson, Reips, Buchanan, & Schofield, 2010; Metzger, 2007). With this brief background about the ethics of privacy in mind, we return to concerns about online behavioral advertising.

Online Behavioral Advertising

As suggested in our discussion of privacy and ethical concerns, a delicate balance between advertiser interests, consumer interests, and control over personal information must be struck carefully. Consumers may receive benefits from online behavioral advertising, such as free e-mail and access to large amounts of free online content. At the same time, however, they may be unaware of the vast amount of information gathered in receiving such services. In many cases, people do not pay attention to the notices and information provided about how their data are being gathered and how they may be used in targeting them. The services offered to consumers come at a cost to those who provide them. How personal information is collected, how it is used, and the consumer's knowledge about what's going on are all crucial to the ethical concerns of OBA.

We discuss two main types of online behavioral advertising here. The most common, and least concerning to ethicists, the FTC, and consumer advocates, is first-party advertising. When an Internet user visits a website such as Amazon.com, cookies (small data files) are generated, and they allow the site to save information about the users' preferences. Based on these cookies, the site is able to recommend products sold within that site and store usernames and passwords, as well as maintain virtual shopping carts (Sableman, Shoenberger, & Thorson, 2013). The FTC, attempting to view a situation through the eyes of the consumer, concluded that this type of consumer data tracking is acceptable, because consumers are likely to expect a site to offer a shopping cart and potentially receive suggestions based on what they've put in that cart as they browse the site.

Third-party online behavioral advertising is more complex and problematic. It involves a website's sharing of a consumer's browsing activities not only within its website but also with unrelated sites. These unrelated sites, often advertising networks, collect information from thousands of others, aggregate those data, and then use the information to deliver targeted advertising to many websites and individual visits. This allows for an advertisement to pop up on a different webpage when the consumer clicks on that item on another website at an earlier time. For the consumer, following the trail of consumer clickstream data via the cookies involved in collecting that data is a significant challenge with third-party advertising. The FTC and Congress have shown some interest in potentially regulating this type of advertising (Sableman et al., 2013).

Ethical Issues Arising From OBA

In thinking about the ethics of OBA, as we saw in our discussion of privacy and the ethics of privacy, one must constantly keep in the mind the balance between the advertisers' interests and right to disseminate information about products and services and the interests consumers may have in maintaining control over their personal data. Responsible decisions about how to advertise in ways that are truthful, fair, and transparent are the foundation of ethical advertising ("Principles and Practices for Advertising Ethics," 2014). Principle six, derived from the Institute for Advertising Ethics guidelines is the most relevant to online behavioral advertising. That principle states:

> *Advertisers should never compromise consumer's personal privacy in marketing communications, and their choices as to whether to participate in providing their information should be transparent and easily made.*
>
> (p. 8)

The ethical issues would be mitigated if consumers' online behavioral data were collected with their explicit permission and if this involved a meaningful

choice made by the consumer. However, the situation in reality is more complicated. In the following paragraphs, we discuss advertiser interests in OBA and
some of the common issues with consumers' perceptions of online behavioral
advertising. In addition, we cover consumers' level of understanding of online
behavioral advertising and their understanding of consent to terms of agreement allowing data collection.

Advertiser Interests in Online Behavioral Advertising

Advertising professionals believe OBA is integral to both the industry and consumers because it can offer relevant promotions and thus send messages that
are more likely to be positively received (Nyilasy & Reid, 2009). A recent
White House report entitled "Big Data: Seizing Opportunities, Preserving Values" makes it clear that this type of advertising activity is beneficial to the flow
of commerce and the integrity of the marketplace (Podesta, 2014).

Online Behavioral Advertising and Consumer Preferences

Research on the value of OBA for consumers shows some inconsistencies.
Some research shows that consumers prefer relevant to irrelevant advertising. High levels of personal relevance have been shown to increase positive
attitudes toward advertising, while the opposite was found true of low levels of personal relevance (Liberman & Chaiken, 1996). Another study (Claypool, Mackie, Garcia-Marques, Mcintosh, & Udall, 2004) demonstrated that
participants shown relevant messages had increased positive feelings about
the messages. However, as each message was repeated, attitudes toward the
repeated messages decreased when participants received messages that were
not personally relevant The result of this body of research was a consensus
that consumers preferred personally relevant messages to those that were not
personally relevant (Campbell & Wright, 2008).

In contrast, some studies reported consumers say they do not want "tailored
advertising" and that OBA violates their privacy expectations and thus OBA
should be curtailed or strictly regulated (McDonald & Cranor, 2010; Turow,
King, Hoofnagle, Bleakley, & Hennessy, 2009). It should be noted, however,
that in these last studies, many of the items used to derive the studies' conclusions
were based on abstractions. For example, some of the questions included in the
Turow et al. (2009) and many replicated in the McDonald and Cranor (2010)
study were written in a seemingly slanted way: "Consumers have lost all control
over how personal information is collected and used by companies" and "Are
there ways cookies do not help you?" (Sableman, Shoenberger, & Thorson, 2013,
p. 102). Furthermore, many of the questions used did not address what the studies claimed to be asking; namely, do consumers like relevant advertising versus
irrelevant advertising in the online context? The ethical issue becomes, then, not
whether consumers prefer advertisements relevant to their interests but at what
cost they are willing to receive them and whether they understand those costs.

Privacy in the Online Data Collection Context

While consumers have been willing to give up personal information that would have previously been considered private in return for a perceived benefit (Sheehan & Hoy, 2000), the issues surrounding online behavioral advertising are more profound. Although information is presumably stripped of personally identifiable information, advertisers can draw important inferences about the consumer. For example, a device's geolocation capability may pinpoint consumers' locale, and their purchase behaviors may indicate interests and life situations they wish to remain private. For example, Target is able to data mine the behavior of a consumer to the point of sending coupons for baby diapers when it becomes likely a consumer is pregnant. One infamous situation required a careful public relations response as the customer was a teenager and her father, enraged that Target would send baby diaper coupons to his teen daughter, learned she was pregnant because of the Target promotions (Hill, 2012). Consumers may be contributing information about themselves beyond their brick and mortar shopping lives. They may be unaware of digitally based information about them that may or may not be true. (Podesta, 2014). For example, Spokeo is a company that specializes in "people finding." This is the compilation of information on where people live, their home's value, and their professions, among other pieces of information. A consumer sued Spokeo alleging that the company posted false information about him and kept him from obtaining employment (Ramasastry, 2014). The consumer noted that the recent U.S. Court of Appeals decision that allows his lawsuit against Spokeo to begin is an important step toward "consumers' ability to control their own information and their own digital identities" (Ramasastry, 2014). As of this writing, there has not yet been a ruling on the case

In our discussion of privacy, we have established the notion of a zone of situational privacy applicable to private information. Perhaps a harder question involves people's expectations about the boundaries of that situational privacy. There is no consensus on the definition of expectation of privacy. Solove writes that the concept of privacy "suffers from 'an embarrassment of meanings'" (2006, p. 478). On the one hand, the concept of expectation of privacy is "too vague . . . to guide adjudication and lawmaking" (p. 478) and on the other, its "amorphous and socially contingent nature has led scholars to avoid specific definitions, instead suggesting characteristics of the concept" (Malphurs, 2009, p. 75). Regulators can attempt to build boundaries protecting violations of privacy but first privacy boundaries have to be established by a culture and within the context specific to online behavioral advertising.

As we have seen in other areas of this book (Chapters 15 and 16), when a persuasive tool such as OBA presents ethical contradictions and ambiguities, there are several ways that society can deal with it. First, government can create regulations about the activity. Or second, as advertisers would prefer, advertiser organizations can develop guidance in the form of self-regulation. We look at both alternatives next.

Government Regulation

In the case of *Griswold v. Connecticut* (1965), the Supreme Court noted that zones of privacy existed under what was termed penumbras. However, the aggregation of online clickstream data has not been clearly covered within these shadows, and OBA has been left largely free from of legal remedies. As of this writing, the FTC has shown concern over third-party, cookie-based behavioral advertising across unaffiliated websites and suggests that such advertising should be subject to either government regulation or robust self-regulation (Staff FTC, 2010).

Other agencies, however, have introduced new privacy initiatives. The FTC expanded its examination beyond behavioral advertising to a more sweeping look at the area of data collection, transfer, and use (Sableman et al., 2013). Some of the current proposed congressional bills would significantly change the requirements on use and disclosure of information about individuals. Some of their provisions would require businesses to adopt privacy policies and disclose their privacy practices whenever collecting personal information, except for information collected and used solely as part of a particular business transaction.

Other proposals would give consumers the ability to prevent businesses from transferring information about them to unrelated companies unless they opted in to such transfers. Such proposals may restrict the private sales of business lists of customers or prospective customers for marketing purposes unless customers specifically allowed it. Still other proposals would impose very stringent requirements on collection and use of particular kinds of data, including medical, financial, and location data. Finally, some proposed regulations would target privacy practices in the mobile telephone and mobile app area (Sableman et al., 2013). In the wake of several high-profile data breaches, President Barack Obama released two proposed data privacy and security bills in an effort to combat the ever-growing need for security in the digital context (Bohoroquez & Felz, 2015).

In May 2014, the White House published a paper broadly examining online data collection and the analyses of that data (Podesta, 2014). The report, spurred by Edward Snowden's leaked information involving the National Security Agency's surveillance activities, encompassed not only the technologies used by the intelligence community but also those employed by industry. Especially chilling to the advertising industry was the report's focus on "learning algorithms" used to serve online advertisements to consumers based on their online browsing activities and used to predict purchase behaviors. The report noted that these algorithms could be used not just to serve relevant advertisements but also to discriminate based on imperfect inferences drawn from the analyses of consumer data (Sanger & Lohr, 2014). The issue of consumer data collection online for purposes spanning industry and government use is contentious and worthy of discussion.

Recommendations made by the White House in the realm of big data regulation included the passing of national data breach legislation to benefit consumers and businesses, increased transparency about how consumer data is used (especially in the realm of third-party advertising and strengthening tools allowing consumers to opt out of online tracking (Podesta, 2014).

Self-Regulation

In an effort to forestall FTC regulations, the advertising industry has worked to provide logos on advertisements generated through the use of consumer online behavioral data. This effort was based on the FTC's notice that consumer control over data is a feature of privacy (Sheehan & Hoy, 2000). Four advertising industry groups (American Association of Advertising Agencies, Association of National Advertisers, Interactive Advertising Bureau, and Direct Marketing Association), together with the U.S. Council of Better Business Bureaus, have put together principles for industry self-regulation of third-party online behavioral advertising. Based on an opt-out model where consumers must actively refuse online behavioral advertising services, the principles suggest that consumers be notified of third-party behavioral advertising practices through either icons located in advertising or by icons placed on webpages containing behavioral ads. A special trademark (a small "i" and triangle design) was created as the "Advertising Option Icon," to identify behavioral ads and allow users to click on them for more information and choices (Sableman et al., 2013). The icons, when clicked, offer information about how to opt out of targeted advertising services and how the advertisements were generated. For example, if the icon is clicked, the consumer goes to a website displaying items recently viewed on a particular website. There is a link to read the privacy policy of the ad aggregator. The aggregator under investigation for the purpose of this chapter was Criteo, a company that describes itself as providing personalized performance advertising, in other words, OBA (Criteo, 2015). There are instructions on how to opt out of a particular brand's OBA and instructions on how to opt out of OBA temporarily or entirely.

Warning labels have been used to allow consumers the chance to make informed decisions about purchase and usage of products, an activity considered inseparable from a free-market system (Cox III, Wogalter, Stokes, & Tipton Murff, 1997). However, the studies on the effectiveness of warning labels have shown inconsistent outcomes (Cox III et al., 1997). The issue with privacy seals is that consumers have often misinterpreted them as safety seals rather an opportunities to gather additional information (LaRose & Rifon, 2007). The mere presence of a privacy policy easily visible on a website may be enough to increase consumer trust in a site regardless of the content of the policy (Pan & Zinkhan, 2006). This ignores the problem that most people don't bother to read policies. In fact, some have called on the FTC to regulate the icons to guarantee that the safety consumers assume the seal offers aligns with the actual safety provided by the seal (Turow, Hoofnagle, Mulligan, Good, & Grossklags, 2007).

The Digital Advertising Alliance's (DAA) use of the AdChoices icon on behaviorally targeted ads online has been shown to increase consumers' click through rate, the rate at which they click on an ad displayed to them via OBA placement. Over half of those surveyed said they would be more likely to click on an ad with the icon and some 73% said they were more comfortable with advertisements that followed the privacy policies of DAA's self-regulatory program (Bachman, 2013a). The Bachman article does not provide information on the number of people who actually read and understood the privacy policy offered by the DAA. However, according to a Zogby Analytics poll commissioned by the DAA, while privacy did remain a concern voiced by consumers, only 4% voiced concerns over targeted advertising, while 39% cited concerns about identity theft (Bachman, 2013a). Interestingly, Joseph Turow, whose own studies on the topic have been criticized for vague or leading items addressing OBA, criticized the Zogby study asserting that "the questions were designed to get the answer the DAA wanted" (Bachman, 2013a).

Commentary on the Ethics Involved in OBA

The goal of maintaining transparency, fairness, and truthfulness when collecting and using consumer online data is important to the success of the marketplace. This benefits consumers, who are able to exert meaningful control over their data, and businesses, which use the data to advance targeted advertising and more efficient marketing campaigns.

In the coming years, regulators and consumer privacy advocates will likely pay special attention to the collection and analysis of data collected about consumer activities online. Some previous safeguards such as notice and choice may be outdated since consumers frequently pay little attention to privacy icons (LaRose & Rifon, 2007; Pan & Zinkhan, 2006). In his report, Podesta noted that consumers almost always click on terms of service without reading them and of course, this places into question whether such a "safeguard" still gives consumers the ability to protect the privacy of their data online (Podesta et al., 2014).

The fact that consumers tend to ignore privacy icons or information about how to protect their information online is a blow to the notion that consumers should have control over their data online and maintain their privacy. It may be that consumers are less interested in exercising control but instead want to trust that their data are being used in ways they deem appropriate and that they have remedies to address perceived mishandling of data.

Institutional Trust

Trust in the institutions supporting data collection such as the advertising industry and the government may have resulted in minimal objections from consumers/citizens because they believe that their data will be kept secure by these responsible institutions. When data are misused or handled in ways citizens disapprove of, institutions should be held accountable. Ethicists such as Kant (2002) express the right of every human being to be respected and to have the right to choose. In this instance, the consumer should have the right to choose what data are being compiled and how he or she is being portrayed in the digital space. Rawls (2009) also would likely argue that such account-ability is important to serve the common good and ensure a functioning legal system, a system that cannot exist without the trust of its citizens.

Those storing and analyzing voluminous amounts of consumer data should work within an ethical framework and take care to be transparent in the collec-tion and use of the data and to maintain the integrity and safety of the data. The integrity of personal data is important in maintaining the integrity and respect of individual citizens who may unwittingly share personal data in the online context, unaware of the dangers that lurk in the digital space.

Data breaches and leaks of consumer data may result in the erosion of public trust in institutions such as the advertising industry and the government. Regu-lation must offer remedies for those injured by data breaches. Public trust in such institutions is integral to an efficiently functioning society, bolstering the common good (Freitag & Buhlmann, 2009; Rawls 2009).

It must be easy for consumers to correct information that is false or infer-ences derived from imperfect analysis. The ability to correct false information is entwined with the notion of institutional trust and also touches on fairness and human respect. If information collected about consumers' online activi-ties is in any way attached to personally identifiable information, consumers should have the ability to correct that information in the aggregator database.

The Future of Online Behavioral Advertising

Consumers must be given reasonable notice of personal data collection and use and the ability to make informed decisions on whether to opt out of data collection. Due to the lack of consumer attention paid to privacy seals, further research in this area is needed. Either privacy notices that catch con-sumers' attention and motivate them to fully understand the contents must be created or those using a privacy policy should abide by regulations guar-anteeing an agreed upon set of rules for data security and permissible uses (Turow et al., 2007).

This set of regulations would also benefit from empirical research on ele-ments of privacy in regard to online data, recognizing that all data are not equal in terms of sensitivity. It would be helpful to develop a taxonomy of the types of data consumers would like to control. Different types of information may be considered more important than others. For example, consumers may be more concerned about medical and financial information than they are about click-stream data being collected (Nowak & Phelps, 1992). Also, consumers may be less concerned about data analyzed by computer algorithms than they would be about people viewing their information.

As technologies grow in their power to gather, store, and analyze infor-mation, it's crucial that citizens and consumers become more aware of the potential for harm they may pose. As we develop strategies to deal with both online threats and opportunities, we see that the ethical guidelines provided by Kant and Rawls generations ago can still guide us in creating safeguards and policies.

Note

1. https://www.whitehouse.gov/the-press-office/2015/01/13/securing-cyberspace-president-obama-announces-new-cybersecurity-legislat
   http://www.criteo.com/

References

Bachman, K. (2013a). Users more likely to click on ads with AdChoices icon: DAA poll says it's good for brands. *AdWeek.* Retrieved September 15, 2015 from http://www.adweek.com/news/technology/users-more-likely-click-ads-adchoices-icon-153617.

Bachman, K (2013b). Poll: Targeted advertising is not the bogeyman: Nearly 70% like at least some tailored Internet ads. *AdWeek.* Retrieved September 14, 2015 from http://www.adweek.com/news/technology/poll-targeted-advertising-not-bogeyman-updated-148649.

Berger, D. D. (2011). Balancing consumer privacy with behavioral targeting. *Santa Clara Computer and High Technology Law Journal*, 27, 3.

Bohoroquez, F., & Felz, J. (2015). 2014 Mobile privacy and security trends and what to look for in 2015. *IMediaConnection.com.* Retrieved September 14, 2015 from http://blogs.imediaconnection.com/blog/2015/02/10/2014-mobile-privacy-and-security-trends-and-what-to-look-for-in-2015/

Campbell, D. E., & Wright, R. T. (2008). Shut-up I don't care: Understanding the role of relevance and interactivity on customer attitudes toward repetitive online advertising. *Journal of Electronic Commerce Research*, 9(1), 62–76.

Claypool, H. M., Mackie, D. M., Garcia-Marques, T., Mcintosh, A., & Udall, A. (2004). The effects of personal relevance and repetition on persuasive processing. *Social Cognition*, 22(3), 310–35.

Cox III, E. P., Wogalter, M. S., Sara, L. S., & Tipton Murff, E. J. (1997). Do product warnings increase safe behavior? A meta-analysis. *Journal of Public Policy & Marketing*, 16(2), 195–204.

Criteo (2015). Criteo eCommerce industry outlook 2015. Retrieved September 14, 2015 from http://www.criteo.com/resources/criteo-ecommerce-industry-outlook-2015/

Freitag, M., & Bühlmann, M. (2009). Crafting trust: The role of political institutions in a comparative perspective. *Comparative Political Studies*, 42(12), 1537–66.

Greenfield, R. (2014). Why the New York Times hired a biology researcher as its chief data scientist. *Fast Company.* Retrieved September 14, 2015 from http://www.fastcompany.com/3026162/most-creative-people/why-the-new-york-times-hired-a-biology-researcher-as-its-chief-data-sci.

Griswold v. Connecticut, 381 U.S. 479 (1965).

Hill, K. (2012). How Target found out a teen girl was pregnant before her father did. *Forbes.com.* Retrieved September 14, 2015 from http://www.forbes.com/fdc/welcome_mjx.shtml.

Joinson, A. N., Reips, U. D., Buchanan, T., & Schofield, C.B.P. (2010). Privacy, trust, and self-disclosure online. *Human–Computer Interaction*, 25(1), 1–24.

Kant, I. (2002). *Groundwork for the Metaphysics of Morals.* Yale University Press.

Kee, T. (2007). Revenue science finds BT ads 22% more effective. *Media Post.* Retrieved September 14, 2015 from http://www.mediapost.com/publications/article/67293/revenue-science-finds-bt-ads-22-more-effective.html?edition=.

LaRose, R., & Rifon, N. J. (2007). Promoting i-safety: effects of privacy warnings and privacy seals on risk assessment and online privacy behavior. *Journal of Consumer Affairs,* 41(1), 127–49.

Learmonth, M. (2010). The shorts that stalked me around the web. *AdAge,* August 2. Retrieved March 11, 2015 from http://adage.com/article/digitalnext/pants-stalked-web/145204/

Liberman, A., & Chaiken, S. (1996). The direct effect of personal relevance on attitudes. *Personality and Social Psychology Bulletin,* 22(3), 269–79.

Lunden, I. (2015). 2015 ad spend rises to $187B, digital inches closer to one third of it. *Techcrunch,* Jan. 20. Retrieved March 18, 2015 from http://techcrunch.com/2015/01/20/2015-ad-spend-rises-to-187b-digital-inches-closer-to-one-third-of-it/

Malphurs, R. (2009). Privacy in conflict: How implicit behavior norms inform expectations of privacy. *Kaleidoscope,* 8, 73-93.

Marcoux, A. M. (2012). Much ado about price discrimination. *Journal of Markets & Morality,* 9(1), 57–69.

McDonald, A.M., & Cranor, L. F. (2010, October). Americans' attitudes about Internet behavioral advertising practices. In *Proceedings of the 9th Annual ACM Workshop on Privacy in the Electronic Society* (pp. 63–72). Chicago: ACM.

Metzger, M. J. (2007). Communication privacy management in electronic commerce. *Journal of Computer-Mediated Communication,* 12(2), 335–61.

Moor, J. H. (1990). The ethics of privacy protection. *Library Trends,* 39(1–2), 69–82.

Nowak, G. J., & Phelps, J. (1992). Understanding privacy concerns. An assessment of consumers' information-related knowledge and beliefs. *Journal of Direct Marketing,* 6(4), 28–39.

Nyilasy, G., & Reid, L. N. (2009). Agency practitioner theories of how advertising works. *Journal of Advertising,* 38(3), 81–96.

Pan, Y., & Zinkhan, G. M. (2006). Exploring the impact of online privacy disclosures on consumer trust. *Journal of Retailing,* 82(4), 331–38.

Podesta, J., Pritzker, P., Moniz, E. J., Holdren, J., & Zients, J. (2014). Big data: Seizing opportunities. *Preserving Values, The White House,* 79, 1–79.

Principles and Practices for Adverting Ethics. (2014). *Institute for Advertising Ethics.* Retrieved September 14, 2015 from http://www.aaf.org/images/public/aaf_content/images/ad%20ethics/IAE_Principles_Practices.pdf.

Ramasastry, A. (2014). The Spokeo lawsuit and the perils of new people finder companies. *Justia.com.* Retrieved September 14, 2015 from https://verdict.justia.com/2014/02/11/spokeo-lawsuit-perils-new-people-finder-companies.

Rawls, J. (2009). *A Theory of Justice.* Cambridge, MA: Harvard University Press.

Sableman, M., Shoenberger, H., & Thorson, E. (August 2013). Consumer attitudes toward relevant online behavioral advertising: Crucial evidence in the data privacy debates. *Media Law Resource Center Bulletin,* 1, 84–99.

Sanger, D., & Lohr, S. (2014). Call for limits on web data of customers. *The New York Times.* Retrieved September 15, 2015 from http://www.nytimes.com/2014/05/02/us/white-house-report-calls-for-transparency-in-online-data-collection.html?_r=1.

Self-Regulatory principles for online behavioral advertising. (2009). *Federal Trade Commission.* Retrieved September 15, 2015 from www.ftc.gov/os/2009/02/P085400 behavadreport.pdf.

Sheehan, K. B., & Hoy, M. G. (2000). Dimensions of privacy concern among online consumers. *Journal of Public Policy & Marketing*, 19(1), 62–73.

Solove, D. J. (2006). A taxonomy of privacy. *University of Pennsylvania Law Review*, 477–564.

Staff, F.T.C. (2010). Protecting consumer privacy in an era of rapid change–A proposed framework for businesses and policymakers. *Journal of Privacy and Confidentiality*, 3(1), 5.

Turow, J., Feldman, L., & Meltzer, K. (2005). *Open to Exploitation: America's Shoppers Online and Offline*. Retrieved September 15, 2015 from http://repository.upenn.edu/asc_papers/35/

Turow, J., Hoofnagle, C. J., Mulligan, D. K., & Good, N. (2007). The Federal Trade Commission and Consumer Privacy in the Coming Decade, 3 ISJLP 723 (2007). Retrieved November 18, 2015 from http://scholarship.law.berkeley.edu/facpubs/935.

Turow, J., King, J., Hoofnagle, C. J., Bleakley, A., & Hennessy, M. (2009). Americans reject tailored advertising and three activities that enable it. Available at *SSRN 1478214*.

Warren, S. D., & Brandeis, L. D. (1890). The right to privacy. *Harvard Law Review*, 4(5), 193–220.

11 The Intersection of Culture and Advertising Ethics in a Global Marketplace

Carrie La Ferle

This chapter addresses the ethical complexities that arise when promotional messages developed for one culture are then translated to another. With so many corporations becoming multinationals, the questions about cultural differences in the ethics of persuasive messages are more important than ever. In fact, the ethics of persuading people about products and services is differently perceived in different countries and cultures. First, there is the question of whether ethics refers just to what is legal or if its meaning goes beyond legality. Next, there are questions about how fundamental values such as the relative importance of individuals compared with groups influence what is perceived to be ethically acceptable. The author argues that three important philosophical/ religious perspectives must also be taken into account (Western individualism, Confucian philosophy, and Islam). Finally, there is a discussion of if, out of all of these differences in belief and emphasis, some universal cultural ethics of advertising can be derived.

Introduction

As economies around the world become increasingly interdependent, marketing communication commentary focuses on the globalization of markets, brands, consumers, and media (de Mooij, 2014; Cateora & Graham, 2007; Levitt, 1983; Smith, 2011). Advances in communication technologies have broken down previous geographical barriers (Levitt, 1983), encouraging discussions of similarities and differences between cultures to flourish. Marketers are looking for common markets and audiences to benefit from economies of scale in both production and marketing communication.

As companies expand their global reach, it is imperative that cultural understanding is at the forefront of marketing and advertising decisions. Specifically, the environment within which people experience advertising differs greatly from country to country (Cateora & Graham, 2007). Often historical, geographical, political, economic, and demographic variations as well as maturity of the advertising industry are cited as key uncontrollable variables to assess for market viability and creating effective advertising (Cateora & Graham, 2007; de Mooij, 2014; Mueller, 2014).

Cultural expectations in relation to ethical advertising practices are often ignored but nevertheless can significantly influence the success or failure of a brand (Drumwright & Murphy, 2009; Hovland & Wolburg, 2010; Moon & Franke, 2000). This is particularly true when cultures differ greatly from each other, such as Asian cultures in comparison to Western or Muslim cultures. As China continues to take its place in the world market along with other strong non-Western countries, it is critical for multinational advertisers to have a clear understanding of business ethics from a variety of perspectives.

Accepted ethical practices in one country are often at odds with culturally accepted business and marketing practices in another. Gift giving between business associates is required to do business in some cultures, but for others it can raise ethical questions in relation to bribery (Donaldson, 1996). Nudity in ads is seen as offensive in most Muslim countries but has varying degrees of acceptability in others (Day, 1997). Unfortunately, ethical concerns in advertising tend to arise as a reaction to a complaint, and most advertising agencies have yet to incorporate ethics into their everyday practices or to see the profitability associated with ethical behavior (Drumwright & Murphy, 2009; Griffin & Morrison, 2008; Snyder, 2011). This is problematic because ethical practices are at the heart of garnering consumer trust along with offering quality products. As Wally Snyder (2011) has stated, "Companies that follow high ethical principles in their ads will 'do well by doing good.'" Advertising professionals need to consider ethical behavior and cultural knowledge as key ingredients to building successful brands in today's diverse marketplace.

The goal of this chapter is to encourage ethical sensitivity in global advertising. First, the chapter presents a discussion around ethics and the role of ethics in advertising. The author distinguishes between ethics and the law, and provides an overview of philosophies that influence ethical beliefs. She then elaborates on culture in terms of its pivotal influence on attitudes and behavior as they influence ethical decisions. Further, the chapter explores global values and cultural dimensions relevant to ethical decision making as means for assessing similarities and differences between countries. The chapter concludes with suggestions advertising practitioners can take toward implementing ethical practices in their everyday work, as well as ideas about building a global advertising community with shared ethical values.

What is Ethics in Advertising and Why Is This Behavior Important?

Ethics can be defined as "a set of prescriptive rules, principles, values, and virtues of character that inform and guide . . . the conduct of people toward each other and the conduct of people toward themselves" (Spence & Van Heekeren, 2005, p. 2). Using Cunningham's (1999, p. 500) definition, Drumwright and Murphy (2009) defined ethics as "what is right or good in the conduct of the advertising function. It is concerned with questions of what ought to be done, not just what legally must be done" (p. 83). Martinson (2001) distinguishes between ethics and law, stating that ethics is about "doing right" and "ought-ness" not just "obeying the law" which only sets minimal standards. He further suggests that ethical behavior in advertising is about providing truthfulness. Preston (2010) concurs that ethical behavior in advertising begins where the law ends and with an emphasis on being truthful and not self-serving.

Spence and Van Heekeren (2005) state that professionals follow ethical behavior if they perform the task they are meant to undertake for the pro-fession (role morality). Often in advertising practice, ethical behavior can be interpreted as doing what is necessary to make the client happy, even at the expense of ethical practices and societal benefits (Sheehan, 2014; Spence & Van Heekeren, 2005). If advertising objectifies women in an attempt to garner attention, advertisers may argue that they are morally fine within the profes-sion's role morality of providing well for the client while not breaking the law. However, Spence and Van Heekeren (2005) remind us that universal pub-lic morality takes precedent over role morality and "is said to be based on principles that apply universally to all human agents by virtue of their com-mon humanity" (p. 2). Role morality in advertising is therefore constrained by universal public morality, which requires that people are treated with dignity. Treating people as things to sell products violates human rights and would be deemed unethical.

From a Western perspective, one of advertising's main roles is to provide honest and truthful information for consumers to make decisions while giving advertisers the right to convey information about their products and in the pro-cess maintain a competitive marketplace (Hovland & Wolburg, 2010; Rotzoll, Haefner, & Hall, 1996). Beyond providing brand information, the social infor-mation conveyed is equally entrenched in advertising's role morality. There-fore, it should be within the industry's obligation to the public to treat people with dignity and fairness as well as providing honest and truthful information in the advertising created (Christians, Fackler, Richardson, Kreshel, & Woods, 2012; Pollay, 1986; Spence & Van Heekeren, 2005). Snyder (2011) has shown how consumers see real benefits from ethical behavior and will reward ethical advertisers with their business.

However, Drumwright and Murphy's (2009) research assessing advertising practitioners revealed that most professionals interviewed did not entertain ethical concerns in their work or the industry in general. The authors' attrib-uted the results to a lack of focus on ethical issues (moral myopia) and a lack of opportunity within the advertising environment to discuss ethical issues (moral muteness). From the previous discussion, several key problems arise for inter-national advertising ethics.

First, advertisers do not have a strong enough understanding of or apprecia-tion for ethical issues in advertising, nor the belief that ethical behavior can positively influence the client's bottom line (Beltramini, 2011; Frith & Muel-ler, 2010; Snyder, 2011). Second, although in the U.S. advertising industry an awareness and desire for ethical behavior does exist, differences in laws, politi-cal systems, and especially culture influence the specific principles and values that people use to decide between what is right and wrong in international business (Ferrell, Fraedrich, & Ferrell, 2013). With these issues in mind, the focus of the discussion will now turn to an overview of ethical issues specific to advertising followed by a discussion of culture and how individual moral philosophies can vary by culture. Both sections will lead to a more robust understanding of the intersection of culture and ethics in global advertising practices.

Ethical Issues in Advertising

Due in part to scandals in business and politics over the past decade from Lehman Brothers and AIG to Martha Stewart and Bernard Madoff (Keith, 2009), the issue of ethics has started to gain more interest across a wide range of organizations (Resick, Martin, Keating, Dickson, Swan, & Peng, 2011). Marketers have increasingly embraced corporate social responsibility practices to garner goodwill and build relationships with consumers (La Ferle, Kuber, & Edwards, 2013; Varadarajan & Menon, 1988). Business schools have started to add ethics into their curricula (Ferrell et al., 2013). The American Advertising Federation (AAF) has been developing the Institute for Advertising Ethics under the leadership of Wally Snyder (2011). Top industry executives and advertising academics have commented and published papers on the need for more ethical considerations in the advertising industry (Beltramini, 2011; Drumwright & Murphy, 2004; Preston, 2010; Snyder, 2011; Taylor & Rotfeld, 2009). Even the Vatican has been involved with the release of a report in 1997 by the Pontifical Council for Social Communications. The report focused on the ethics of advertising where advertising practitioners were challenged to uphold truthfulness, dignity, and social responsibility (Foley, 1997). This document has repeatedly been referenced over the years as highlighting areas for advertisers to continue to work on (Can Business Be Catholic, Zenit, 2008).

Ethical issues in global business tend to focus on risks, bribery, Internet security, and privacy, as well as more fundamental issues, such as human rights, health-care issues, labor, and compensation (Ferrell et al., 2013). Within advertising, ethical issues touch on similar areas of privacy and human rights, but there are also further specific concerns in regards to the images and messages conveyed to the masses. In a review of key ethical issues related to advertising, Drumwright (1993) cited a number of research studies and categorized them into those that were legally focused issues such as advertisers' rights and deceptive advertising and those more morally focused such as the social impact of advertising on society.

In the United States, researchers have undertaken numerous studies to assess consumer attitudes toward morally controversial practices in advertising (Drumwright & Murphy, 2009). Advertising that perpetuates stereotypes, promotes societally controversial product categories, such as alcohol, tobacco, and condoms, marginalizes groups of people or objectifies women as well as encourages consumption as the path to happiness are all areas of potential problems when it comes to ethics in advertising and the societal impact of advertising (Pollay, 1986; Sheehan, 2014; Spence & Van Heekeren, 2005). Typically these topics are considered "soft" issues in the United States and are not regulated by the Federal Trade Commission (FTC), which oversees "hard" issues, such as deceptive or misleading advertising. The main self-regulatory body in the United States, the National Advertising Division (NAD), also does not usually get involved in issues of taste and decency. However, this is not true of all countries, such as the United Kingdom and Canada, where regulators examine hard issues along with some soft issues.

While laws exist in most countries practicing advertising and common areas of advertising regulation can be found from nation to nation (Mueller, 2011), there are few international organizations overseeing advertising regulation (Frith & Mueller, 2010). The World Health Organization (WHO), the United Nations (UN), and the International Chamber of Commerce (ICC) are the most prominent. These organizations typically provide voluntary guidelines and do not have legal authority to mandate compliance among member countries. Nonetheless, the ICC does support self-regulatory efforts through a comprehensive set of guidelines that are currently in use across many countries.

The organization started in 1919 to encourage positive business environments with and between governments. From an initial representation of 5 countries to over 120 today, the ICC works to provide ethical standards and guidelines for businesses, including marketing and advertising practices around the world (www.iccwbo.org). According to the ICC website, the most recent code from 2011 is intended to help businesses demonstrate responsibility in advertising and marketing practices, enhance public confidence in the industry, maintain freedom of expression for marketers, and provide flexible solutions to minimize government regulation (www.codescenter.com).

While the guidelines are quite thorough and created with input from multiple countries and cultural backgrounds, they are voluntary and not legally binding. However, they do stress the importance of both hard and soft issues. Specifically, the code states that all practices should demonstrate respect for human dignity and standards of decency. This fact highlights the importance for advertisers to become versed in ethical issues, because the effectiveness of the guidelines depend first on the belief that ethics are important and second on being able to recognize the varied ethical issues in play, both within and across cultures. It is important for advertisers to understand cultural differences and similarities of ethical practices so as to better navigate the waters in international markets and potentially find common ground.

The use of stereotypes in advertisements is an example of a soft issue where ethical concerns often arise. A stereotype is a generalized way to categorize a group of people and is used in advertising to convey meaning quickly (Sheehan, 2014). Stereotypes can be unethical if the images conveyed degrade or diminish a specific gender, ethnic, racial, socioeconomic, religious, or other group, thereby disrespecting them and their right to human dignity (Donaldson, 1996; Spence & Van Heekeren, 2005). In the United States, some brands have used the image of a Chinese or Asian Indian consumer along with a strong accent to create humor with the intent to garner attention and enhance recall for the brand. Unfortunately, this type of ad exploits the different ethnic and racial groups by using inherent characteristics as a tool for humor to sell a product rather than respecting their value as humans. These types of ads also encourage an "us versus them" mindset in the United States when many Chinese people with accents are in fact American citizens. Spence and Van Heekeren (2005) support this point by suggesting that beyond violating individuals' rights, ads like this further work against society by maligning or misrepresenting the group to the detriment of society as a whole.

This type of advertising is not always recognized as unethical and is not limited to the United States, but cultural understanding is necessary to see where ads may cross the line of norms and be perceived as offensive. Historical events between China and Japan explain the tension and negative reaction by Chinese consumers to a series of ads by Toyota Japan. The ads showed lions and dragons, important symbols of strength in Chinese culture, as weak and being mocked. Chinese consumers were outraged and considered the ads offensive, disrespectful and hurtful (Peopledaily.com, 2003; Americansifu, 2013). Islamic leaders have raised concerns with several American companies such as Nike and Coke for offending religious Islamic beliefs. A Nike logo displayed an image that looked like the word "Allah" in Arabic script (Mueller, 2014). Allah means God in cultures practicing Islam, and typically references to anything related to God or religion for commercial purposes is forbidden (Mueller, 2014).

The *Journal of Advertising Research* published a special issue in 2011 devoted to ethics in advertising. Beltramini (2011) was the guest editor and provided three thought-provoking reasons why ethical problems still plague our industry. He suggested that these reasons included an inability to measure a one-to-one relationship between advertising and consumer behavior as well as a lack of ads being challenged, resulting in a status quo mentality. The third reason, seen as the largest problem, focused on what he perceived as a lack of desire to engage in ethical advertising practices. His hope was that the special issue would ignite real ethical action. However, Griffin and Morrison (2008) have argued that in order to engage in ethical behavior, one must first have an ethic of care. But to have an ethic of care one cannot have moral myopia but must be able to recognize potential ethical issues in advertising, such as those discussed to either avoid them or resolve them as they arise. This becomes even more problematic when advertising is undertaken outside one's native culture within which individual values and moral philosophies were first developed.

Culture and Ethics

Culture has been defined by Hofstede (1980) as the collective mental programming of a group of people. The impact of cultural orientation on behavior has been studied by researchers across multiple disciplines (Markus & Kitayama, 1991; Marsella, DeVos, & Hsu, 1985; Trafimow, Triandis, & Goto, 1991; Triandis, 1989). According to Markus and Kitayama (1991), the construction of self is influenced by the context within which it exists; self in turn then affects cognitions, motivations, and emotions. Ethical behavior and individual moral philosophies are therefore learned within the context of culture.

Advertising cannot be successful without understanding cultural context, including awareness of the culture's assumptions and beliefs about ethics. The beliefs, values, and customs of a culture influence how people engage in daily life, including consumer behavior processes and responses to advertising. National cultural orientations help in shaping individual values (Gudykunst, 1998; Gudykunst, Matsumoto, Ting-Toomy, Nishida, Kim, & Heyman, 1996). Therefore culture, as it shapes values, also influences consumer ethics.

Values are what Hofstede (1980) has called the core of culture. According to de Mooij (2014), a value is an enduring belief causing us to prefer one choice over another. Values are typically learned by the age of 10 and are quite stable (de Mooij, 2014). For these reasons, values are highly important for advertisers and marketers to understand to build brands and advertising messages that are personally relevant to consumers. However, values also drive ethical beliefs and can vary, if not in type, in order and strength, from one country to another (de Mooij, 2014).

Take for example a comparison of the top values among the United States, Belgium, and China. The majority of values for the Chinese are rooted in Confucian beliefs of obedience, harmony, and respect for others. In contrast, many of the top values for Belgium focus on safety and security, which de Mooij (2014) attributes to Belgium's high uncertainty avoidance or dislike for ambiguity and change. The United States' top values are heavily related to historical events and Hofstede's Individualism dimension with a focus on freedom, fairness, democracy, and equality (de Mooij, 2014).

International advertising requires advertisers to be culturally sensitive to their target audience when encoding advertising messages, because messages are being decoded by targets who may have very different values, life experiences, and perspectives (Cateora & Graham, 2007; de Mooij, 2014). De Mooij (2014) expands on this idea by suggesting that Western communication styles tend to be sender oriented. She argues that collectivistic cultures, especially those from East Asia, value communication with more of a dialogue, where having empathy and harmony with the receiver are critical to the communication process. Zhu (2009) suggests, for example, that the differences found in Chinese marketing and business communication styles such as being more circular, indirect, or ambiguous can be explained by Confucian ethics. Even ideas about advertising in Japan where building relationships through entertaining is the norm rather than hard-sell persuasion tactics (de Mooij, 2014) can be understood from this alternative ethical lens. Both point to the importance of understanding one's self-reference criterion (SRC), an unconscious reference to one's own values and culture in assessing situations, which can lead to cultural blindness and be responsible for ethical conflicts (Cateora & Graham, 2007; Ferrell et al., 2013).

Donaldson (1996) describes business ethics of the Japanese as being focused on loyalty to company, business networks, and nation, while Americans focus on liberty and rights with an emphasis on equality, fairness, and individual freedom. He goes on to highlight that Confucian and Buddhist traditions are not based on the notion of a right, which evolved for Europeans and Americans during the rise of democracy (Donaldson, 1996). This distinction can explain several different reactions to the same ethical conflicts and suggests the need to understand different world philosophies driving ethical beliefs. In contrast to Chinese moral philosophies rooted in Confucian ethics (Chan, 2008; Resick, Martin, Keating, Dickson, Kwan, & Peng, 2011; Zhu, 2009), Western cultures and business ethics textbooks often include references to moral philosophies and theories based on deontology, teleology, virtue ethics, and relativism (Ferrell et al., 2013). Awareness of these common Western philosophies is important not only to understand how ethical decisions are arrived at but also to contrast with decisions made, and why they were made, from other philosophies.

Western Philosophies in Business Ethics

Chan (2008) defines business ethics as "a discipline which explores the proper conduct of businesses and businesspeople" (p. 349). He goes on to argue that the study of business ethics tends to be Western-centric driven by Western-origin ethical theories and moral philosophers. Many of these theories function from a general premise of rules being absolute. The rules guide action as to what is ethical or not, even though the specific rule followed may differ for each theory. Teleological philosophies deal with the consequences of a behavior, while "deontological" philosophies are focused more on individual rights or absolute rules with no regard for the outcome (Ferrell et al., 2013; Spence & Heekeren, 2005). The action of accepting a bribe could be morally acceptable from a teleological perspective if the consequence is favorable and usually for the greatest number of people, but it would be considered unethical, regardless of the outcome, from a deontological viewpoint. In the former case, the rule followed was to achieve the best outcome for the greatest number of people regardless of how it was achieved. In the latter case, the rule followed was simply that bribery is not acceptable. In contrast, Confucian ethics is not as much about rules as it is a process of achieving social harmony by growing a person's moral character.

Another Western philosophy is moral relativism and is often discussed in relation to differences in cultural practices because it suggests there is no universal standard, as each culture has its own moral compass (Day, 1997). The problem with this theory is that it assumes any and all behavior is acceptable if it is accepted by a particular culture or subculture. Following this idea of "when in Rome, do as the Romans" may sound reasonable, but it does come with consequences. Most in the U.S. press do not allow practitioners to pay journalists to place favorable stories about clients in publications (Day, 2005). However, in some countries this practice is legal and ethical lines are not crossed. Currently, China is attempting to clean up this problem by arresting reporters/ editors who collect money for favorable stories (World Bulletin, 2014). The overall harm of the practice is that it undermines consumers' decision-making processes and therefore disrespects their human dignity. Consumers will attribute greater credibility to the so-called "journalist's" story than to the same information in an advertisement. Day (2005) further argues that participation by advertisers in this type of practice provides no incentive for regulatory sources to step in and change the practice, even though the outcome for society as a whole is negative.

As another example, Hong Kong allows preemption in media buying based on supply and demand. In this system, advertisers bid a price for a slot they want and the highest bidder wins (Lam, 2014). In some cases, an agency can bid for the space for a campaign with a negotiated rate, but right up until about an hour prior to the airtime, the station can sell the space to a higher paying client or demand more money from the original agency. While this practice is legal and considered ethical in Hong Kong, it is not legal or ethical in the United States. With a focus on human dignity, the practice harms the consumer, the agency, and the market system, as it undermines predictability and wastes money that will negatively influence consumers in the name of excessive profits for the media organizations. So while moral relativism allows for each culture to practice what it sees as acceptable, the concepts of universal public morality (Spence & Van Heekeren, 2005) and human dignity (Day, 1997) would suggest that these practices are ethically questionable because they violate the human dignity of treating people fairly and are also not in the best interest of society as a whole.

Ethical imperialism is at the other end of the continuum of Western philosophies, with an emphasis on people complying with the same cultural norms and ethics that they follow at home no matter where they are (Donaldson, 1996). Obviously this moral compass has its flaws, too, in that it ignores potential differences in cultural norms. As an example, comparative advertising is a form of advertising used quite extensively in the United States and by U.S. multinational companies overseas. However, comparative advertising is against the law in some countries, while in others it is not used because it is considered rude and unethical to stand out and say you are better than another (de Mooij, 2014; Mueller, 2011).

Virtue-based theories such as Aristotle's Golden Mean are different from other Western philosophies, as they focus on building one's character and in this sense share similarities with Confucian ethics (Christians et al., 2012; Day, 2005). Aristotle's theory of the 'golden mean' focuses on building a virtuous character over time through actions taken, as well as learning to avoid the extreme of any position. This theory is used in American advertising with the idea of content-neutral regulation where the time, the place, or the manner of the message is limited in some way as opposed to banning the speech completely (Trager & Dickerson, 1999). Day (1997) gives the example of the Federal Communications Commission's (FCC) regulation of indecency where they limit "indecent" content to hours outside of child viewing times.

It is important to have an understanding of Western philosophies, but they are not sufficient in the 21st century global economy in which China is a rising power and has become the second-largest economy in the world (Smith, 2011). As noted, many East Asian cultures such as Japan, South Korea, Taiwan, and Hong Kong along with China are rooted in Confucian philosophy (Chan, 2008: Hofstede & Bond, 1998), while Muslim countries are largely immersed in Islamic beliefs. Therefore we turn now to several other dimensions helpful in identifying, comparing, and assessing values and ethical beliefs across cultures. Our tools are Hofstede's cultural dimensions, along with Confucian ethics and the Islamic religion.

Hofstede's Cultural Dimensions and Ethics

Hofstede & Bond's (1998) model, which differentiates Individualism/Collectivism, Masculinity/Femininity, Power Distance, and Uncertainty Avoidance, is one of the most widely used in providing a framework explaining cultural differences among consumers (Albers-Miller & Gelb, 1996; de Mooij, 2014; Swaidan, 2012). The framework has been used to show differences in consumer behavior, advertising techniques, and consumer responses to advertising (Aaker & Maheswaran, 1997; de Mooij, 2014; Han & Shavitt, 1994; Matsumoto, 1989). It has further been used in studies focused on cultural differences in ethical beliefs, decision making, and behavior (Swaidan, 2012; Singhapakdi, Vitell, & Leelakulthanit, 1994).

Collectivism involves belief in group harmony and well-being of the group over the individual, where one's identity is tied to the group through loyalty, obligation, and dependence (Hofstede, 1980; Gudykunst, 1998; Mueller, 2011). The United States is the most individualistic country in the world, while many Asian and Latin Region countries are more collectivistic. This dimension influences aspects of the self (Singelis, 1994) and directly affects interpersonal relations (Markus & Kitayama, 1991).

Masculinity relates to competitive behavior and concepts of winning as well as a clear distinction between male and female roles. In contrast, cultures higher on femininity typically are the opposite, demonstrating preference for being humble and modest where relationships between people, and equality between male and female roles, are more common (de Mooij, 2014; Hofstede, 1980). Uncertainty avoidance is an index of how much comfort people have with ambiguous situations, while power distance involves how much a culture expects and/or accepts inequality between people (de Mooij, 2014; Hofstede, 1980).

Many studies have utilized one or more of Hofstede's (1980) cultural dimensions for classifying cultural behavior patterns and assessing ethical perceptions (Davis, Bernardi, & Bosco, 2012; Moon & Franke, 2000; Vitell,

Nwachukwu, & Barnes, 1993). Often the findings suggest ethical beliefs and behavior are stronger in cultures higher on collectivism and uncertainty avoidance, while lower in cultures characterized by power distance and masculinity (Moon & Franke, 2000; Getz & Volkema, 2001). In a study examining the role of culture on managerial ethics, Paul, Roy, and Mukhopadhyay (2006) showed how people low on collectivism and uncertainty avoidance but high on masculinity and power distance were less concerned with ethics in business than their counterparts.

Swaidan (2012) used Hofstede's dimensions on a sample of African-Americans to show the impact of culture on consumer ethics. The findings were similar to the previous study, revealing that unethical behavior is less acceptable for consumers higher on collectivism and uncertainty avoidance and lower on masculinity and power distance.

A fifth dimension, long-term versus short-term orientation was developed later in the context of Asian cultures and with Confucian undertones (Hofstede, 1991). Asian cultures tend to score relatively high on long-term orientation and have a greater appreciation for longer-term thinking, thrift, virtue, and pragmatism than short-term oriented countries such as the United States (de Mooij, 2014). Short-term cultures tend to focus more on truth than virtue and on religiously based issues of what individuals believe to be right and wrong (Moon & Franke, 2000). It is clear that these cultural dimensions can help to understand variations in culture and subsequent ethical beliefs and are a good starting point for advertisers as they enter various countries. It is also evident that several of these cultural differences are rooted in Confucian principles and not Western philosophies.

Confucian Ethics

As the Asian region continues to grow in importance, and especially with China forging its mark in the global marketplace, it becomes imperative for Western corporations to understand ethics from an Eastern perspective. Although it is debatable to pinpoint one influence on ethical philosophies of a country or region, as we have seen, researchers discuss Confucian ethics as a driving force within Chinese business and interpersonal relationships, as well as in other East Asian–region countries such as Korean and Japan (Chan, 2008; Zhu, 2009).

Hofstede and Bond (1998) explain that Confucianism is based on the teaching of Confucius, who provided values for everyday life based on observations of Chinese historical events. Confucius (551–479 BCE) believed a person was not necessarily born as good or bad but rather through learning virtuous habits, related to understanding one's responsibility to the community, ethical behavior was cultivated (Chong, 2007; Christians et. al, 2012). Confucian ethics places a high value on family, connections (*guanxi*), harmony, thrift, obligation, and interdependence, which are at the heart of today's Chinese culture and business practices (Chan, 2008; Zhu, 2009). Social harmony is the goal of Confucianism and is believed to be achieved by individuals knowing their dual roles as superior and subordinate, as well as the duties and obligations associated with each across five key relationships: ruler-subject, father-son, husband-wife, elder-younger brother, and friend-friend.

According to Hofstede and Bond's (1998) summary of Confucius beliefs, these unequal relationships between people create a stable society because each person knows his or her place in society, is held accountable, and depends on others to do the same for society to function well. In this type of an environment, if one does not fulfill his or her expected role, the well-being of the entire group is diminished, and people are motivated to avoid feeling this type of guilt, shame, and possible expulsion from the group (Chong, 2007; de Mooij, 2014). The importance of unequal relationships offers an understanding of the existence of hierarchical relationships in many Asian cultures and provides context for Hofstede's (1980) power distance dimension.

Confucian beliefs also suggest that the family is the prototype of all social organizations (Hofstede & Bond, 1998) and this helps to understand the widespread presence of collectivism among many Asian-region cultures, as well as the origin of "saving face." It is the idea that people are connected to family and have no individual identity outside of the group. An individual gains dignity and respect by fulfilling what is required for the group and maintaining face for all parties (Hofstede & Bond, 1998).

According to Triandis (1995), morality comes to an individual in a collective society from the welfare of the collective in-group, in contrast to following the rights of an individual as would be morally correct in an individualist culture. This difference in ethical behavior is used by Moon and Franke (2000) to suggest why American practitioners had less tolerance toward *fees for favors* than Korean practitioners, but Korean respondents listed kickbacks to clients as the second most common ethical concern in Korean advertising. The researchers attributed the findings to collectivistic thinking by Koreans who might not like to be asked to provide kickbacks by clients but found the practice more acceptable than their American counterparts and much more common. American practitioners did not even list kickbacks as an ethical issue facing them. The authors attributed the findings to the strong legal and ethical norms in the United States against bribery that are not as clear for Korean practitioners in a group reciprocity culture rooted in Confucian beliefs (Moon & Franke, 2000).

Other examples of Confucian teaching affecting behavior in business include Hofstede and Bond's (1998) work examining the economic success of Hong Kong, Taiwan, Japan, and South Korea. They uncovered a set of values that were common to each country, including persistence, hierarchical relationships, thrift, and having a sense of shame. They named this dimension, Confucian Dynamism and found it "strongly associated with economic growth over the period between 1965 and 1985 across all 22 countries, rich or poor, that were covered" (p. 16). Zhu (2009) was also able to show different reactions in business based on Confucian beliefs. He studied differences in reactions to a Chinese Expo invitation between a manager from China and one from New

Zealand. The Chinese manager found the invitation to be polite and appropriate, while the New Zealander thought it was unethical with hints of pressure and intimidation.

Moon and Franke (2000) used Hofstede's (1980) cultural dimensions to show cultural influences on reactions to ethical scenarios between South Korean and American advertising practitioners. In an example ethical scenario of hiring away an account executive to another agency, Moon and Franke (2000) found the Korean sample to be more negative. They attributed this to the Confucian beliefs related to collectivism, higher power distance, and high uncertainty avoidance, a context in which lack of loyalty to the group is unethical, as is encouraging others to avoid their duties to the in-group and to superiors.

Religion

Similar to the impact of Confucian teachings on East Asian cultures, religion can also have a strong impact on ethical behavior. As Bartels (1982) has noted, religion is equally as important as philosophic beliefs in determining social and business behavior. According to Mueller (2011), there are five major religions in the world: Buddhism, Christianity, Hinduism, Islam, and Shinto.

A variety of studies have used religion to examine reactions to advertising and ethical beliefs (Frith & Mueller, 2010; Saeed, Ahmed, & Mukhtar, 2001), with some countries such as Saudi Arabia, Iran, and Malaysia being unusually heavily influenced by religious teachings. This suggests that knowledge of Islamic beliefs shaping culture and ethical decisions is critical in today's global marketplace. Indeed, Muslim consumers make up 25% of the world's population and are a majority in more than 50 countries (Saeed et al., 2001).

In examining Egyptian consumers' attitudes toward ethical issues in advertising, Mostafa (2011) found that Muslims' attitudes toward ethical issues in advertising were not as positive as non-Muslims. The author outlined several of the rules regarding advertising based on the teachings of Islam as explanations for the more negative attitudes and those found in previous studies regarding Malaysia (Deng, Jivan, & Hassan, 1994). Specifically, Mostafa (2011) stated that sexual, emotional, fear, and pseudo-research appeals along with false testimonies and encouraging extravagance cannot be used in advertising under Islamic teaching. He goes on to explain that "to exploit the basic instinct of consumers with a view to gain profit" is unethical within Islamic beliefs (p. 54). This belief parallels the earlier discussion regarding some Western philosophies rooted in trying not to treat people as a means to an end along with Spence and Van Heekeren's (2005) concept of universal morality. Mostafa's (2011) findings also support Kotabe and Helsen's (1998) earlier research in 22 countries. They found Egyptians holding the most negative attitudes toward advertising and attributed this to the religious influence of Islamic law. Saeed et al. (2001) suggest "At the heart of Islamic marketing is the principle of value-maximization based on equity and justice for the wider welfare of the society" (p. 127). A common thread, therefore, across the various philosophies examined is the belief in the importance of considering the welfare of the society and upholding the dignity of the individual in business practices, which advertising is not seen as doing.

Ferrell et al. (2013) argue that while many differences exist across country values, the major religions share enough to suggest some global common values exist. Specifically, they suggest integrity, family and community unity, equality, honesty, fidelity, sharing, and unselfishness are desirable common values that transcend cultural differences. Similarly, ignorance, pride and egoism, selfish desires, lust, greed, adultery, theft, deceit, lying, murder, hypocrisy, slander, and addiction are listed as common undesirable values across the different religious groups (p. 278). With these similarities in mind, several researchers in the study of business ethics and advertising have tried to conceptualize common ethical beliefs across cultures to help formulate shared ethical values that would be globally consistent (Saeed et al., 2001; Day, 2005; Ferrell et al., 2013; Zhu, 2009). The goal is to help advertisers with global campaigns where common ground in ethical issues might transcend cultural differences.

Shared Ethical Values in Global Advertising

Day (2005) suggests that the world today, with the interdependent nature of countries, technology connecting people with content generated from outside national borders, as well as global problems in need of international solutions (e.g., threats to the environment), demands we search for a moral common ground. Ferrell et al. (2013) have also discussed the need for global business codes of ethics within the context of individual global corporations if they want to survive and thrive. Nationally and internationally the advertising industry and agencies within it would also benefit from guidelines for navigating ethical issues that influence the effects of advertising messages.

In the 21st century, we are seeing that Western philosophies traditionally dominant in business ethics and ethical models are being joined increasingly by powerful ideas from other regions, especially the Asian and Muslim countries. Advertisers cannot create effective ads and build relationships between brands and consumers in cultures different from their own without being aware of the cultures' values and attitudes toward ethics. Several articles have presented guidelines for working toward better ethical practices both in the home market and in foreign markets.

Day (1997) suggested that along with universally agreed upon 'hard' issues found in relation to the law, such as false advertising or exaggerated product claims, a universal standard for advertisers to follow covering both hard and soft issues is to have respect for consumers and their cultural norms in terms of human dignity considerations. Toward seeking ethical practices in advertisements, Griffin and Morrison (2008) suggest practitioners should ask themselves if the advertising is responsible and, further, to take into account potential consequences of the messages on society and/or to look for opportunities to effect positive social change with the messages. Donaldson (1996) recognizes the impact of culture in global business practices and provides help in suggesting we should distinguish between practices that are simply different versus those that are just wrong. To make this delineation, he recommends corporations should be guided by the following three principles: 1) respect for core human values, 2) respect for local traditions, and 3) a belief that context matters such as would be the case in a situation between a developing versus a developed nation (Donaldson, 1996). While Donaldson's (1996) article focused on how business corporations could respect basic rights, certainly his core ideas could be applied to the practice of advertising.

Specifically, Donaldson (1996) suggests that despite the variety of ideas across theologians and philosophers worldwide, and differences between Western and non-Western cultural and religious traditions, there is an *overlapping consensus*, as Rawls would argue, converging at "shared attitudes about what it means to be human" (p. 311). He defines this idea as having 1) respect for human dignity where people are not treated as tools or as a means to end, 2) respect for basic rights such as to health, education, safety, and an adequate standard of living, and 3) good citizenship where companies support societal institutions (Donaldson, 1996, p. 311).

Applying Donaldson's (1996) focus to advertising, it is argued here that a focus on respect for human dignity and good citizenship fit well in striving for a common ground in global ethics that transcend cultural differences. These concepts are shared with many other belief systems from Western philosophies, to Confucius teachings and Islamic laws, to also being acknowledged within the International Chamber of Commerce guidelines used at least in part across 120 countries.

Within an advertising context, the concept of human dignity means consumers should be valued as people first and not as a means to an end. Therefore, providing false or misleading information simply to sell a product at the expense of treating someone with dignity would be unethical and would not benefit the greater good of society. Issues related to fair representation in advertising such as size of models, accents of a group used to create humor, or questionable images based on ethnicity, gender, age, and religious symbols or objectification and marginalization of a group would also be considered as treating people as means to an end to convey a message about a product. But how can we actually implement these ideas in agencies across the globe?

Wally Snyder (2011) has provided some important guidelines for agencies today to be proactive in their approach toward ethics. He states that 1) advertising employees need to proactively discuss potential ethical consequences of ad claims and images, 2) certain devices such as stereotypes should be avoided, 3) concepts should be tested with focus groups to uncover ethical issues before a campaign runs, 4) case studies should be reviewed with similar products or claims, and 5) clients should provide their own ethical guidelines to agencies. In the end though, it is up to each individual, agency, and the industry as a whole to be motivated to engage in ethical behavior.

Conclusions

Multinational marketers and global advertising agencies will be more success-ful with an understanding of the varied cultural influences affecting ethical issues in the markets they enter. Specifically, ethical concerns, ethical decision-making styles, and consumer ethics are all influenced by culture and need to be researched in order to avoid many potential problems. This is particularly true to help avoid the creation of offensive advertisements. Cultural knowledge about ethical issues is not only beneficial for Western companies and agency practitioners as they work globally, but also for non-Western companies want-ing to do business overseas. Industry-specific and even agency-specific ethical codes of conduct and guidelines need to be created to help agency practitioners navigate ethical waters in cultures different from their own.

The difficulty in today's world is understanding that ethical behavior in advertising matters, agreeing on what constitutes upholding the dignity of a person within an advertising context, and ensuring that many different cultural perspectives are incorporated in the assessment. It is hoped that the chapter has helped to provide issues to consider in advertising ethics across cultures. Advertisers first need to understand that advertisements do more than sell products. They also convey dominant ideological beliefs, social norms, and cultural values, which all demand responsibility in using the tool (Frith, 1998; Pollay, 1986). Therefore, a shift in defining advertising's professional role morality (Spence & Van Heekeren, 2005) from only servicing clients and the market with information to also treating the audience with respect and human dignity is required (Day, 1997; Donaldson, 1996). In making this shift, the gap between values of advertising professionals' role morality and universal public morality decreases and the potential for more laudable ethical practices in advertising rises. Similarly, it is critical for advertisers to believe the trend that consumers value ethical behavior and advertisers' doing good, whereby consumers will reward ethical companies with their business more than other brands (Snyder, 2011).

As recognition of the need to respect consumers becomes a universal norm, a rise in appreciation for ethical practices should ensue with a desire to better understand the impact of culture on ethical beliefs. Zhu (2009) sug-gests that moral principles or philosophies can include both Western and Eastern beliefs, such as Confucian ethics and virtue ethics. Zhu (2009) and Chan (2008) both stress the importance to integrate Confucian ethics into today's business ethics. Others would argue for the inclusion of Islamic teachings, such as the concept of value-maximization for the benefit of the wider society, along with an appreciation that consumers will reward this behavior (Saeed et al., 2001).

By reviewing the various dimensions, philosophies, and ethical principles, advertising professionals can be better prepared to recognize ethical issues in order to create effective advertising campaigns in a culturally diverse global marketplace.

References

Aaker, J., & Maheswaran, D. (1997). The effect of cultural orientation on persuasion. *Journal of Consumer Research*, 24(3), 315–29.

Albers-Miller, N. D., & Gelb, B. D (1996). Business advertising appeals as a mirror of cultural dimensions: A Study of eleven countries. *Journal of Advertising*, 25(4), 57–70.

Americansifu. (2013). Business to consumer marketing in China: Nike & Toyota and the power of symbols: Part 2. Retrieved July 10, 2014 from http://americansifu. wordpress.com/ 2013/03/02/business-to-consumer-marketing-in-china-nike-toyota-and-the-power-of-symbols-part-2/

Bartels, R. (1982). National culture-business relations: United States and Japan contrasted. *Management International Review*, 22(2), 4–12.

Beltramini, R. (2011). From platitudes to principles: An advertising ethics call to action. *Journal of Advertising Research*, 51(30), 475–76.

Can Business Be Catholic? (2008) Interview with Michael Naughton. Zenit.Com. Retrieved October 14, 2015 from http://www.zenit.org/en/articles/can-business-be-catholic

Cateora, P., & Graham, J. (2007). *International Marketing* (13th edition). New York, NY: McGraw-Hill.

Chan, G. (2008). The relevance and value of Confucianism in contemporary business ethics. *Journal of Business Ethics*, 77, 347–60.

Chong, Kim-Chong. (2007) *Early Confucian Ethics*. Chicago, IL: Open Court.

Christians, C., Fackler, M., Richardson, K., Kreshel, P., & Woods, R. (2012). *Media Ethics: Cases and Moral Reasoning*. Glenview, IL: Pearson Education.

Cunningham, P. H. (1999). Ethics of advertising. In J. J. Jones (Ed.), The Advertising Business. London, Sage, 499–513.

Davis, J. D., Bernardi, R. A., & Bosco, S. M. (2012). Examining the use of Hofstede's uncertainty avoidance construct as a definition or brief comparison in ethics research. *International Business Research*, 5(9), 49–59.

Day, L. (1997). *Ethics in Media communications: Cases and Controversies*. Belmont, CA: Wadsworth Publishing.

de Mooij, M. (2014). *Global Marketing and Advertising: Understanding Cultural Paradoxes*. Thousand Oaks, CA: Sage Publications.

Deng, S., Jivan, S., & Hassan, M. (1994). Advertising Malaysia: A cultural perspective. *International Journal of Advertising*, 13, 153–66.

Donaldson, T. (1996). Values in tension: Ethics away from home. *Harvard Business Review*, September-October, 48–62.

Drumwright, M., & Murphy, P. (2004). How advertising practitioners view ethics: Moral Muteness, Moral Myopia, and Moral Imagination. *Journal of Advertising*, 33(summer), 7–24.

Drumwright, M., & Murphy, P. (2009). The current state of advertising ethics. *Journal of Advertising*, 38(1), 83–107.

Ferrell, O., Fraedrich, J., & Ferrell, L. (2013). *Business ethics*. Manson, OH: South-Western, Cengage Learning.

Foley, J. (1997). Pontification council for social communications: Ethics in advertising. Retrieved July 5, 2014 from http://www.vatican.va/roman_curia/ pontifical_councils/pccs/ documents/rc_pc_pccs_doc_22021997_ethics-in-ad_en.html#top

Frith, K. (1998). *Undressing the Ad: Reading Culture in the Ad*. New York, NY: Peter Lang Publishing.

Frith, K., & Mueller, B. (2010). *Advertising & Societies: Global Issues*. New York, NY: Peter Lang Publishing.

Getz, K., & Volkema, R. (2001). Culture, perceived corruption, and economics. *Business and Society*, 40(1), 7–30.

Griffin, W., & Morrison, D. (2008). Beyond obligation: Advertising's grand potential to do good. In Tom Reichert (Ed.) *Issues in American Advertising: Media, Society, and a Changing World* (2nd edition) (pp. 265–81). Hudson, NY: The Copy Workshop.

Gudykunst, W. (1998). *Bridging differences: Effective Intergroup Communication*. Thousand Oaks, CA: Sage Publication.

Gudykunst, W. B., Matsumoto, Y., Ting-Toomy, S., Nishida, T., Kim, K., & Heyman, S. (1996). The influence of individualism-collectivism, self construals, and individual values on communication styles across cultures. *Human Communication Research*, 22, 510–43.

Han, S., & Shavitt, S. (1994). Persuasion and culture: Advertising appeals in individualistic and collectivist societies. *Journal of Experimental and Social Psychology*, 30, 326–50.

Hofstede, G. (1980). *Culture's Consequences: International Differences in Work-Related Values*. Beverly Hills, CA: Sage Publication.

Hofstede, G. (1991). *Culture and Organizations: Software of the Mind*. New York, NY: McGraw-Hill.

Hostede, G., & Bond, M. (1998). The Confucius connection: From cultural roots to economic growth. *Organizational Dynamics*, 16(4), 4–21.

Hovland, R., & Wolburg, J. (2010). *Advertising, Society, and Consumer Culture*. Armonk, NY: M.E. Sharpe.

Keith, T. (2009). Decade in review: Corporate scoundrels and scandals. *NPR.ORG*. Retrieved July 2, 2014 from http://www.npr.org/templates/story/story. php?story ID=122083807

Kotabe, M., & Helsen, K. (1998). *Global Marketing Management*. New York, NY: John Wiley and Sons.

LaFerle, C., Kuber, G., & Edwards, S. M. (2013). Factors impacting responses to cause-related marketing in India and the United States: Novelty, altruistic motives and company origin. *J. Business Research*, 66(3), 364–373.

Lam, A. (2014). TVB ad slots are so expensive during world cup. *Marketing Magazine*. Retrieved July 5, 2014 from http://www.marketing-interactive.com/why-tvb-ad-slots-so-expensive-world-cup/

Levitt, T. (1983). The globalization of markets. *Harvard Business Review*, 61(3), 91–102.

Markus, H., & Kitayama, S. (1991). Cultures and the self: Implications for cognition, emotion, and motivation. *Psychological Review*, 98(2), 224–53.

Marsella, A., DeVos, G., & Hsu, F. (1985). *Culture and Self*. London: Tavistock.

Martinson, D. (2001). Using commercial advertising to build an understanding of ethical behavior. *The Clearing House*, Jan/Feb, 131–35.

Matsumota, D. (1989). Cultural influences on the perception of emotion. *Journal of Cross-Cultural Psychology*, 20(1), 92–105.

Moon, Y., & Franke, G. (2000). Cultural influences on agency practitioners' ethical perceptions: A comparison of Korea and the US. *Journal of Advertising*, 29(1), 51–65.

Mostafa, M. (2011). An investigation of Egyptian consumers' attitudes toward ethical issues in advertising. *Journal of Promotion Management*, 17, 42–60.

Mueller, B. (2011). *Dynamics of International Advertising*. New York, NY: Peter Lang Publishing.

Mueller, B. (2014). *Dynamics of International Advertising*. New York, NY: Peter Lang Publishing.

Paul, P., Roy, A., & Mukhopadhyay, K. (2006). The impact of cultural values on marketing ethical norms: A study in India and the United States. *Journal of International Marketing*, 14(4), 28–56.

Peopledaily.com (2003). Controversial Japan ads draw Chinese anger. Retrieved September 15, 2015 from http://www.chinadaily.com.cn/english/doc/2004-12/22/content_402391.htm

Pollay, R. W.(1986). The distorted mirror: Reflections of the unintended consequences of advertising. *Journal of Marketing*, 50(2), 18–36.

Preston, I. (2010). Interaction of law and ethics in matters of advertisers' responsibility for protecting consumers. *The Journal of Consumer Affairs*, 44(1), 259–64.

Resick, C., Martin, G., Keating, M., Dickson, M., Kwan, H., & Peng, C. (2011). What ethical leadership means to me: Asian, American, and European perspectives. *Journal of Business Ethics*, 101, 435–57.

Rotzoll, K., Haefner, J., & Hall, S. (1996). *Advertising in Contemporary Society: Perspectives Toward Understanding*. Chicago, IL: The University of Illinois Press.

Saeed, M., Ahmed, Z., & Mukhtar, S. (2001). International marketing ethics from an Islamic perspective: A value-maximization approach. *Journal of Business Ethics*, 32(2), 127–42.

Sheehan, K. (2014). *Controversies in Contemporary Advertising*. Thousand Oaks, CA: Sage Publications.

Singelis, T. (1994). The measure of independent and interdependent self-construals. *Personality and Social Psychology Bulletin*, 20(5), 580–91.

Singhapakdi, A., Vitell, S., & Leelakulthanit, O. (1994). A cross-cultural study of moral philosophies, ethical perceptions and judgments: A comparison of American and Thai marketers. *International Marketing Review*, 11(6), 65–78.

Smith, W. (2011). *The Changing World of International Advertising*. Dubuque, IA: Kendall Hunt Publishing.

Snyder, W. (2011). Making the case for enhanced advertising ethics. *Journal of Advertising Research*, 51(3), 377–483.

Spence, E., & Van Heekeren, B. (2005). *Advertising Ethics*. Upper Saddle River, NJ: Pearson Prentice Hall.

Swaidan, Z. (2012). Culture and consumer ethics. *Journal of Business Ethics*, 108, 201–13.

Taylor, C., & Rotfeld, H. (2009). The advertising regulation and self-regulation issues ripped from the headlines with (sometimes missed) opportunities for disciplined multidisciplinary research. *Journal of Advertising*, 38(4), 5–14.

Trafimow, D., Triandis, H., & Goto, S. (1991). Some tests and distinction between the private self and the collective self. *Journal of Personal and Social Psychology*, 60(5), 649–55.

Trager, R., & Dickerson, D. (1999). *Freedom of the Expression in the 21st Century*. Thousand Oaks, CA: Pine Forge Press.

Triandis, H. (1989). The self and social behavior in differing cultural contexts. *Psychology Review*, 96, 506–20.

Triandis, H. (1995). *Individualism and Collectivism*. San Francisco: Westview Press.

Varadarajan, R., & Menon, A. (1988). Cause-related marketing: A coalignment of marketing strategy and corporate philanthropy. *Journal of Marketing*, 52(3), 58–74.

Vitell, S., Nwachukwu, S., & Barnes, J. (1993). The effects of culture on ethical decision-making: An application of Hofstede's typology. *Journal of Business Ethics*, 12(10), 753–60.

World Bulletin (2014). Chinese journalists arrested in fraud probe, September 4, 2014. Retrieved March 2015 from http://www.worldbulletin.net/middle-east/143738/chinese-journalists-arrested-in-fraud-probe.

Zhu, Y. (2009). Confucian ethics exhibited in the discourse of Chinese business and marketing communication. *Journal of Business and Marketing Communication*, 99, 517–28.

Section III
Special Topics

12   Ethical Challenges of Framing in Persuasive Communication, in Words and Pictures

Stephanie Geise and Renita Coleman

CHAPTER SUMMARY

A frame is a way of presenting an idea, an advertisement, a message, or a news event in a particular way by emphasizing certain aspects while downplaying others. The frames we select in communication, verbally or visually, change the meaning that audiences may take from messages (Entman, 1993). Sometimes communicators consciously select the frames to elicit the maximum persuasiveness or credibility. And sometimes communicators are unaware that in their choices of message strategies, they are inevitably affecting how audiences may respond. For example, a news story about parents who choose not to vaccinate their children may be framed in many ways. They might portray parents as irresponsible or silly or show them as courageously exerting their religious or political beliefs. A story may emphasize the role of experts such as physicians, quoting them as arguing that vaccines have been scientifically proven as safe and effective. A different story frame may blame parents or schools that don't insist on vaccinations for putting other children at risk. Frames are important because they serve to simplify complex ideas, and in the process of simplifying, they are persuasive, for good or for ill. In addition, the act of choosing which problems deserve our attention is an aspect of framing. Framing involves defining problems and their severity, and identifying what may be causing the problems. In assigning blame or responsibility for a problem, a normative element usually arises—what's the right thing to do? What's the best way to deal with it? This chapter discusses framing in health communication and dilemmas that communicators face in presenting messages that are both effective and ethical.

Introduction

Since the 1980s, a growing amount of research emerged within persuasive communication on the topic of framing (Barker, 2005; Smith & Petty, 1996). Studies of health communication, a subdomain of persuasion, have been particularly important in understanding framing effects (Keller & Lehmann, 2008; Salovey & Wegener, 2003; Yan, Dillard, & Shen, 2010). Because good framing strategies can be highly effective at achieving outcomes desired by persuasive communication, framing's popularity with researchers and practitioners has grown exponentially. However, in the drive to find the most effective ways to frame persuasive messages, the ethics of framing have largely been over-looked. The purpose of this chapter is to present ethically problematic frames, much as Semetko and Valkenburg (2000) did for frames in the news. We propose three of the frames found consistently in health communication and explain our argument for extending analysis of those frames to other areas of persuasion. This includes advertising, public relations, social marketing, and political communication. This essay is theoretical, based on literature, and we encourage empirical validation and expansions of our concepts.

Instead of a set of frames that apply strictly to health communication and another different set that apply to political communication, and so on for every type of content, a common set of ethical frames is necessary to help standard-ize the often idiosyncratic microframes found in research in order to allow for replication, to track frame developments over time, and to compare fram-ing similarities and differences between and among genres. From there, we can discover which of the ethically problematic frames are most prevalent in persuasive communication so that we may begin to search for more ethical alternatives.

Petty and Wegner (1998) define persuasion as "any instance in which an active attempt is made to change a person's mind," (p. 4). Persuasive com-munication of all types should meet certain moral standards, and this is espe-cially true of social marketing, as distinct from commercial marketing (Dahl, 2009). Persuasive communication to achieve a social good also aims to change beliefs, attitudes, opinions, values, behavior, and/or behavioral intentions (Seo, Dillard, & Shen, 2013; Atkin & Salmon, 2009). Such messages are generally held to higher ethical standards. Using persuasive strategies that are ethically questionable to achieve ethical goals is clearly problematic. For example, com-munication that perpetuates stereotypes, stigmatizes people, blames individu-als who may not be entirely in control of their situation, and causes feelings of guilt and emotional distress benefits no one. It is imperative that we find alternatives that respect all people while still achieving the benefits that adver-tising, public relations, and other persuasive communication have to offer.

A second purpose of this chapter is to encourage the inclusion of visual framing in the quest for more ethical research and practice. Compared to years of research on verbal messages, there is a relative dearth of framing knowledge about visual messages (Garcia-Retamero & Cokely, 2011; Rodriguez & Asoro, 2012). A growing number of communication studies have begun to focus on visuals, often relying on framing theory (Coleman, 2010).

Visuals have special potential to exert persuasion, and they make it easy for viewers to adopt the communicator's frames (Messaris & Abraham, 2001; Müller, 2007; Rose, 2012).It is also important to note that in most cases visual and verbal messages occur together and receivers process them simultane-ously. Thus it is not only artificial for research to view the visual channel of communication in isolation but such a narrow perspective can also result in an incomplete understanding of any communication (Coleman, 2010). Research, therefore, should acknowledge that visual and textual frames not only have mode-specific effects but also occur jointly in multimodal media settings, creating interconnected meanings for audiences (Geise & Baden, 2013). The ethically problematic frames outlined in this chapter apply equally to visual and verbal communication, but their uses and effects may be different.

The Importance of Ethical Framing

While considerable research has focused on the professionalization and optimization of framing strategies (Edwards, Elwyn, & Mulley, 2002, Hallahan, 1999; Keller & Lehmann, 2008; Pelletier & Sharp, 2008) and the measurements of its direct effects, ethical questions in media framing strategies are still widely overlooked. Strategic communication that aims to affect people's views or behavior obviously carries a multitude of ethical issues, especially dealing with topics that are integral to deeply held personal preferences and social values. Most, if not all, decisions that relate to the intention, design, execution, and evaluation of health communication, for example, are connected to ethical issues (Burdine, McLeroy, & Gottlieb, 1987). Following the idea that ethics is at the core of all communication aiming for social change, identifying and addressing ethical issues has become crucial, especially when communication takes place in changing media landscapes. This includes communication in multinational and multicultural settings, where commercial marketing strategies are widely incorporated and where new media channels are rapidly emerging (Guttman, 2003).

In this essay, we present a theoretical reflection on the ethical issues of framing strategies in persuasive communication, drawing especially from the literature on health campaigns. Our understanding of social and individual consequences of framing in persuasive communication cannot be complete if ethical issues are not addressed appropriately. Moreover, we believe that addressing ethical issues also helps to overcome the limitations of existing communication strategies and will help us meet future challenges.

Although persuasive communication strategies often appear to be the most efficient way to influence people to adopt intended health-related beliefs, attitudes, opinions, values, behavior, and/or behavioral intentions, they are clearly fraught with potential ethical issues (Faden, 1987; Guttman, 2003). These issues include privacy matters, such as gathering information about behaviors of targeted audience segments. This research may look at audiences' media usage patterns, levels of knowledge, and their socioeconomic status. Another factor involves who has the power to define positive health outcomes and who determines acceptable behaviors of individuals. Only recently has scientific discourse turned attention to explicit and implicit ethical issues of health communication messages and the potentially conflicting relationship between ethical communication and the need to attract attention and resonate with audiences (Bouman & Brown, 2010; Coleman & Hatley-Major, 2014; Guttman, 2003; Guttman & Salmon, 2004; Lee & Cheng, 2010). The social discourse on ethical issues in communication has led to the definition of ethical principles and obligations (e.g., Beauchamp & Childress, 2013; Coughlin, Soskolne, & Goodman, 2009; Seedhouse, 2009; Veatch, 1980, 1982, 1999; Witte, 1994).

Front and center is the tension between ethical imperatives and the need to change health-related behaviors. What might be the most effective strategy for increasing healthy behaviors could be ethically questionable. Framing strategies of health communication should result in the greatest benefits and contribute most to communicate information in a balanced, accurate, and truthful way to improve people's health. This includes the need to respect people's individuality, autonomy, and privacy and to ensure equity and fairness. In particular, a health-communication ethic should assure protection for individuals who are vulnerable or who have special needs.

Framing and Persuasion

Frames are defined as the "central organizing idea[s] or story line[s] that provides meaning to an unfolding strip of events" (Gamson & Modigliani, 1987, p. 143). Frames highlight certain aspects of reality and leave out others, affecting people's perception, interpretation, and evaluation of issues or events (Entman, 1993). Over the last few decades, research has shown that frames exert a relatively substantial influence on perceivers' beliefs, attitudes, and behaviors (Tewksbury & Scheufele, 2009). Because of this, framing also has been discussed as a persuasive strategy (Smith & Petty, 1996). While some framing scholars have explicated key differences between framing and persuasion (Nelson, Oxley, & Clawson, 1997; Tewksbury & Scheufele, 2009), especially in the context of health communication, the persuasive perspective on framing remains central (e.g. Yan, Dillard, & Shen, 2010).

Framing's Morality Function

Frames can be defined as highlighted interpretation patterns, structuring an issue in a certain way to meaningfully order and efficiently process information (Entman, Matthes, & Pellicano, 2009; Gamson & Modigliani, 1989; Gitlin, 1980; Reese, 2001, 2007; Tankard, 2001). According to Entman (1993, p. 52), frames are constituted by four dimensions: They 1) define problems by pointing out what is happening and the costs and benefits of it; 2) identify causal relations—that is, who or what creates the problem; 3) make moral judgments; and 4) propose solutions to the problems and assess their likely effects The morality function of frames is especially important. Studies of framing strategies involving moral judgments such as politics (Nelson, 1993), race (Gamson, 1992; 1995; McCants, 1990), individual rights (Nelson, Clawson, & Oxley, 1997), gender equality (Jenness, 1995; Williams & Williams, 1995), or the discrimination of various subgroups in postmodern society (Harper, 1994) have shown that the perception and interpretation of public issues, the solutions proposed, and sympathy for affected people or groups can be influenced dramatically according to how they are framed in the media. For example, sympathy for AIDS victims decreases when HIV is framed as a disease involving high-risk groups and resulting from risky practices (Goss & Adam-Smith, 1995). On that basis, communicators should be concerned whether their messages may be interpreted as blaming, victimizing, or offering moral evaluation of others. Rather than pointing fingers, a moral standard should be to protect people who are already in a weak position from further harm.

Three Ethical Frames

What follows are three ethically questionable frames consistently found in health communication and are proposed to be expanded to other types of persuasive communication. Four frames were originally examined in a study assessing the prevalence of the most common frames identified as ethically problematic in health communication (Coleman & Hatley-Major, 2014). Those were negative emotional appeals, individual responsibility, harm reduction, and stereotypical primes. For this essay on the frames found in all types of persuasive communication, we focus on three of those frames—negative emotional appeals, individual responsibility, and stereotypical primes. The harm reduction frame is unique to health communication rather than universal to all types of persuasive messages, so it is not included here. Harm reduction is based on the assumption that some unhealthy behaviors will occur and puts more emphasis on reducing harm than on eliminating it (Mattson, 2000). An example of a harm reduction frame would be a message encouraging teens to use condoms. Rather than attempting to prevent teens from engaging in sex, it seeks to prevent pregnancy and sexually transmitted diseases. Some object to harm reduction messages, saying it is unethical to implicitly condone immoral, illegal, or risky behavior. Literature reveals the harm reduction frame may occur in other persuasive communication but does not appear in topics other than health. Thus in the interest of parsimony, we concentrate on three ethical frames.

Negative Emotional Frame

In strategic message framing, research has examined tactics that use frames to achieve communication goals. A special focus has been put on comparing persuasive health messages framed to emphasize the benefits of adopting health-related behavior (gain frame) or the risks of not adopting it (loss frame) (e.g. Cho & Boster, 2008; O'Keefe & Jensen, 2008, 2009; Zhao et al., 2012). Much of the gain and loss framing research is done under the rubric of prospect theory, which describes the way that people choose between alternatives when risk is involved and the probability of a particular outcome is unknown (Kahneman & Tversky, 1984). Within the context of loss framing in particular is the role of specific emotions (Candel & de Vries, 2010; Dillard & Meijnders, 2002; Nabi, 2002; Cho & Boster, 2008; Shen & Dillard, 2007; van't Riet, Ruiter, Werrij, Candel, & de Vries, 2010). Fear especially exhibited a robust effect on persuasion (Mongeau, 2013), and higher levels of fear have been frequently linked to higher levels of perceived message effectiveness.

Fear appeals and loss framing are part of one of the four ethically problematic frames identified by Coleman and Hatley-Major (2014). The negative emotional appeals frame includes fear appeals and loss framing, as well as other types of frames, such as shocking messages and those likely to induce guilt or other negative emotions. Because of the negativity bias (Petty & Wegener, 1998), information such as this is especially effective at attracting and holding people's attention. The negativity bias suggests that people process negative information more carefully than positive information and rely on it more heavily when forming impressions and making decisions (Fiske, 1980; Kahneman & Tversky, 1979). Because positive information is expected as the norm, negative information stands out and attracts attention, making us think harder about what it might mean (Marcus, Neumann, & McKuen, 2000). Therefore, negative emotional appeals have a special ability to induce persuasive framing effects.

When well-intentioned message creators use fear appeals, shock tactics, or other negative emotional frames, the rationale for doing so may be that they must vie for attention by any means possible in an overcrowded message environment (Stephenson & Witte, 1998). But ethical challenges arise because such tactics can cause unnecessary fear or be unduly offensive (Sabogal, Oterso-Sabogal, Pasick, Jenkins, & Pérez-Stable, 1996). One example from Beaudoin's (2007) study of HIV campaigns is the message, "If you don't use condoms you may die" (p. 201). This represents a loss frame in that it highlights the negative consequences of not doing something and also is a fear appeal with the threat of death. These types of messages also have been criticized for their potential to stigmatize people by presenting negative portrayals of them and for their lack of accuracy when they overstate risks by misrepresenting statistics (Blakeslee, 1992; Covello, 1992). In one study of ethically questionable frames in health PSAs, the negative emotional frame was the second-most frequent, occurring in 48% of the PSAs in the study (Coleman & Hatley-Major, 2014).

Negative emotional appeals are also prevalent in contexts other than health. They abound in political communication as negative campaigning strategy, with examples such as the 1964 "Daisy Girl" commercial that showed a child counting while picking petals off a flower and in the background there was a nuclear missile countdown and launch. The juxtaposition struck fear in the hearts of some voters who voted against challenger Barry Goldwater and for the incumbent, President Lyndon Johnson. Another example is the infamous 1988 "Willie Horton" TV advertising spot about a convicted murderer who, after a furlough granted by the state's governor, raped and stabbed a young couple. This ad alarmed voters in 1988 and was criticized for its racist tone.

We note also that both of the TV commercials described earlier used primarily visual language to communicate a fear frame, while the words themselves were rather neutral. Research also has investigated the interaction of visual and verbal negative emotional frames. For example, based on the idea that visual images might buttress and intensify the persuasive effects of textual gain and loss framing, Seo, Dillard, and Shen (2013) proposed a visual amplification hypothesis and tested if the presence of a visual image increased the persuasive effects of textual message framing on the use of dental floss and sunscreen. Results showed partial support for visual amplification with regard to the impact of loss framing on fear: the presence of an image produced more fear in the loss-framed conditions.

Fear appeals have been shown to be effective in many persuasive communication contexts, including computer security (Johnston & Warkentin, 2010), safe driving (Goldenbeld, Twisk, & Houwing, 2008), mountain biking etiquette (Hendricks, Ramthun, & Chavez, 2001), earthquake preparedness (Mulilis & Duvall, 1995), and obeying laws (Van Erp, 2006), among others. Thus we feel confident that the negative emotional appeals frame should be included among those classified as ethically problematic for other forms of persuasive communication as well as health communication.

Individual Responsibility Frame

With this frame, individuals are blamed for their own health conditions or other problems, and the roles of society, government, or others are overlooked. It is well documented in the research of Iyengar & Kinder (1987) under the concept of framing as episodic or thematic. Iyengar (1991) showed that people tend to attribute responsibility to individuals when frames are episodic but to society when frames are thematic. This held true for multiple issues, including crime and terrorism, poverty, unemployment, and racial inequality (Iyengar, 1991). An episodic frame "takes the form of a case study" and "depicts concrete events that illustrate issues," while a thematic frame presents "collective or general evidence" (Iyengar, 1991, p. 14). People have a natural tendency to blame an individual person for a problem, in a phenomenon known as the fundamental attribution error, when a problem is framed with an episodic frame. However, they tend toward attributing responsibility to society or larger social instances when it is framed thematically (Iyengar, 1991). A comparative content analysis (Semetko & Valkenburg, 2000) showed that the attribution of responsibility frame was the most commonly used in the news, followed by frames of conflict, economic consequences, human interest, and morality. The individual responsibility frame has been identified as ethically questionable because of its predisposition to "blame the victim" and its downplaying of the role of social factors (Blane, 1995). This frame also does not acknowledge that people may not be in control of others. For example, the message

"Friends don't let friends drive drunk," does not take into account that it may not be possible to persuade inebriated people to comply. Another example is a message that says individuals can avoid obesity simply by exercising and eating right. As innocuous as such a message may seem, some people do not have access to healthy foods, may live in areas unsafe for outdoor exercise, and can't afford gym memberships. Blaming individuals is morally questionable under the ethical principle of causing no harm. It is unjust to cause people to suffer by thinking they are solely responsible when their actions alone may not cause a condition or phenomenon (Blane, 1995). For example, corporations aggressively market unhealthy foods, and government policies make it difficult for people just above the poverty level to afford health care or insurance. Nonetheless, many health messages are framed this way, implying that disease or disability result from poor lifestyle choices and that those who behave irresponsibly will be a burden to others (Guttman & Ressler, 2001). For example, a message that shows family members burdened with the care of a smoker with lung cancer invokes the individual responsibility frame. The frame does not acknowledge that nicotine is physiologically addictive and thus the behavior is not entirely within an individual's control. It carries connotations of weak character, raising tensions between the ethical principle of autonomy and public good. Some messages go so far as to suggest people should be held legally and morally accountable for certain behaviors. Despite these concerns, the individual responsibility frame is one of the most frequently occurring frames in health communication (Callahan & Jennings, 2002). In their study of health PSAs, Coleman and Hatley-Major (2014) found this to be the most frequent ethically problematic frame, occurring in 80% of the PSAs.

The ethically questionable individual responsibility frame has already been identified as one of the most prevalent in all news stories (Semetko & Valkenburg, 2000), as well as in health communication (Callahan & Jennings, 2002; Coleman & Hatley-Major, 2014). Thus it seems likely that this frame occurs frequently in other types of persuasive communication. Studies have examined individual responsibility in the context of natural disasters (Lalwani & Duval, 2000), behavior in organizations such as businesses and the military (Skerker, 2014; Zhang & Gowan, 2012), environmental issues such as climate change (Banks, 2013; Harris, 2012), disposal of electronic equipment (O'Connell, Hickey Besiou, Fitzpatrick, & Wassenhove, 2013), politics (Hobolt & Tilley, 2014; Payson, 2012), law (Boggero, 2013), human rights (Talsma, 2012), and economics (Duch & Stevenson, 2013), among many others. Again, we find ample evidence for including the individual responsibility frame in discussions of ethical frames in persuasive communication in many fields.

There is also evidence of visual framing of individual responsibility, although less so than for verbal frames. Coleman and Hatley-Major (2014) found that individual responsibility was found in the written and spoken mode significantly more often than in the visual channel—78% of the verbal portion of PSAs had this frame versus 9.5% of the visuals.

Stereotype Priming

The third category of ethically questionable frames is more accurately described as a prime than a frame. However, framing is related to priming in that it is a construct that describes the way information is presented so that it resonates with our preexisting ideas about something (Shoemaker & Reese, 1996) and "primes" us to think about it that way. We interpret the frames deployed in a message and that becomes the central effect of a frame (Scheufele & Tewksbury, 2007). Framing is an "applicability" effect, in that it makes connections between concepts so that audiences see them as related to each other. Priming is conceived of as an "accessibility" effect, relying on information in memory. Thus a persuasive message that uses a stereotypical message—presenting women as homemakers and mothers, for example—relies on priming audiences' preconceived ideas about women. Framing, on the other hand, attempts to create new connections between gender and some other idea. Thus messages that use words or pictures that activate our preconceived stereotypes, about race and gender, for example, are more precisely described as primes than frames. The other two categories in this study, individual responsibility and negative emotion, are more accurately described as frames because the messages are making connections—that individuals are responsible for climate change, for example. However, because accessibility and applicability jointly affect whether a certain concept will be activated (Price, Tewksbury, & Powers, 1997), these types of primes are included as one of the categories of ethically questionable framing devices.

Stereotyping primes are found in all kinds of persuasive communication other than health, most notably advertising. Research shows ongoing issues in advertising with stereotypes of gender and ethnicity (Rubie-Davies, Liu, & Lee, 2013; Zawisza & Cinnirella, 2010), as well as with age (Lee, Kim, & Han, 2006; Robinson, Gustafson, & Popovich, 2008). Gender stereotyping is also prevalent in political communication (Fridkin, Kenney, & Woodall, 2009). Visuals hold special potential to prime stereotypes (Fahmy, 2004) and create racial, gender, and age biases (Martindale, 1990; Rodgers & Thorson, 2000). For example, Abraham and Appiah (2006) have shown that African-Americans are negatively framed in the news through the accompanying images that communicate biases and stereotypes, which are not otherwise expressed in the written text (Abraham & Appiah, 2006; Messaris & Abraham, 2001). In addition, stereotyping is more pervasive in visual than in written communication (Messaris & Abraham, 2001). For example, perpetuating stereotypes of women as sex objects by showing a scantily clad woman is easier with visuals than it would be in text. In their study of health PSAs, Coleman and Hatley-Major (2014) found twice as many stereotyping primes in visuals as in textual messages. That held true for both gender and ethnicity stereotypes—26% of the visuals had gender stereotypes versus 11.5% of the text and 7% of the visuals had ethnic stereotypes versus 3% in words.

One new category of people who are increasingly being stereotyped is the obese. This is another area where stereotyping may occur more in visual messages than in textual ones. In one study, two-thirds of news photographs showed overweight people, and they were depicted in negative and stigmatizing ways (Heuer, McClure, & Puhl, 2011). Visual framing strategies included showing obese individuals with their heads cut out of photos, showing only their abdomens or lower bodies, eating or drinking, not fully clothed, not wearing professional clothing, and not exercising or playing sports significantly more often than non-overweight individuals (Heuer, McClure, & Puhl, 2011). In a controlled experiment, people who read a news story about obesity accompanied with a negatively stereotyped photograph showed higher levels of weight bias than did those who read the same news story about obesity paired with a non-stigmatizing photograph (McClure, Puhl, & Heuer, 2011).

Visual stereotypes of obesity also hold the potential to cause negative emotional responses, such as disgust and antipathy. Instead of visually portraying an obese person as an individual, stereotypical portrayals assign obese people to an epidemic subgroup, thus degrading and dehumanizing them instead of treating them as valued members of society deserving of medical help, empathy, and respect (Heuer, McClure, & Puhl, 2011, p. 10). Since most people cannot count on personal experience alone to know about health topics, they must rely on media information. How the media communicate and visually frame that information holds important implications for public perceptions of health-related issues.

Visual framing relies on visual metaphors, symbols, and typical visual representations, often resulting in the depiction and social reconstruction of visual stereotypes. From an ethical standpoint, this may cause a variety of undesired and unintended effects. Research on stereotypes in general has demonstrated that recipients will more readily recall information that corresponds with their preexisting stereotypes (Bodenhausen, 1990) and that the activation of stereotypes holds potential to stimulate negative attitudes and negative treatment toward members of the stereotyped group (Greenberg & Pyszczynski, 1985; Henderson-King & Nisbett, 1996). But these undesired effects may be even more dangerous if induced by visual stereotyping. Because of the logic of visuals and their "true-to-life" quality, people generally do not question the relationship between images and their meanings in messages (Messaris & Abraham, 2003).

Another strategy related to stereotyping is the practice of targeting or segmentation marketing techniques (Guttman & Salmon, 2004). The choice of which groups of people to target for a message carries ethical implications. Some groups may be hard to reach and are excluded, while others may be considered to have special needs and receive priority (Rothschild, 2001). These practical choices may also reflect preferential treatment or discrimination. Segmentation of this sort also raises ethical questions about messages that perpetuate stereotypes or stigmatize. For example, HIV prevention messages that target gay men could perpetuate the stereotype that all gays have unprotected sex. Other messages can prime stereotypes of culture and diversity, age, obesity, and other issues. For example, in some cultures, teenage motherhood is considered normal but not in others. An issue becomes a problem only if it is defined as such by the dominant groups in society (Guttman, 1997).

Processing of Visual Frames

Understanding the ethical frames and primes in visual images is especially important because of the way human brains process visual images. People are more likely to process images peripherally rather than centrally. That means that individuals tend to draw conclusions and react emotionally to an image without thinking much about it or questioning its meaning (Barry, 1997; Geise & Baden, 2013). Audiences are thus less likely to be aware of media framing through visuals (Messaris & Abraham, 2001; Rodriguez & Asoro, 2012). For communicators, critical reflection on the choice of frames is especially important when selecting visual frames and images primarily for promotional reasons based on the images' attractiveness, ability to attract attention or elicit surprise, or when the images bear little correspondence to the factual information behind the interpretation they imply.

Visual frames deploy images that come together to communicate an overall message. Gamson and Stuart (1992) argue that such frames offer "a number of different condensing symbols that suggest the core frame" of the issue (Gamson & Stuart, 1992, p. 60). Through visuals, people are able to quickly process details into frameworks relevant and to their understanding of the social world. Nonetheless, visuals are open to many interpretations, and different receivers decode them in many different ways. Visuals thus not only enhance people's interpretations of social phenomena, they also suggest which social interpretations should be favored above others (Coleman, 2010; Rodriguez & Dimitrova, 2011).

Intended and Unintended Effects and Ethical Issues

Persuasive communication of all forms can take a cue from health communication regarding intended and unintended effects and its ethical implications. Health communication purposely tries to develop and communicate arguments consistent with desired goals aiming to change a recipient's beliefs, attitudes, opinions, values, behavior, and/or behavioral intentions (Seo, Dillard, & Shen, 2013; Atkin & Salmon, 2009). Although the intention is to encourage social good rather than harm, health communication sometimes has unintended effects (Rogers, 1995). However, with few exceptions (Guttman & Salmon, 2004; Salmon & Atkin, 2003; Salmon & Murray-Johnson, 2001), framing in health communication has been underexamined with regard to the unintentional, negative effects on audiences.

The first step in successful health communication is developing clear, understandable messages (McGuire, 1989). Nevertheless, some of the most common unintended effects of health communication result from misleading or confusing messages. As Cho and Boster (2008) pointed out, health-related messages are often complicated. This complexity, along with inherent limitations of the communication process, makes media-based communication strategies particularly vulnerable to unintended effects (Slovic, 1987). As outlined earlier, visuals can be a helpful tool here (Edwards, Elwyn, & Mulley, 2002; Lipkus, 2007; Lipkus & Hollands, 1999). By depicting concrete persons, objects, or situations instead of abstract or hard to understand textual messages, visuals can increase understanding of complex issues.

However, the ethical standard of providing well-balanced und truthful information suggests that oversimplified, one-sided arguments should not be acceptable. This includes presenting scientific findings as definitive when they are actually only tentative (Guttman, 2003). Besides that, understanding an image is no trivial task. Oversimplified visual representations and examples hold the potential for misunderstandings, confusion, and misinformation. Due to the richness and ambiguity of meaning conveyed by pictures, visuals are open to multiple interpretations and are decoded in different ways by different receivers in different contexts (Rose, 2012; Mitchell, 1986).

In fact, reactance and boomerang effects have been repeatedly reported in the context of negative emotional appeals. For example, a strong fear appeal can result in defensive feelings and can backfire. These appeals are frequently seen in health communication and often presented as loss frames. These frames communicate that certain behaviors will result in negative consequences or missed opportunities. Considerable research shows greater impact for loss-framed messages aiming to motivate recipients to pay greater attention to the health-related information and to stimulate information-seeking behavior (Brader, 2006). However, Janis and Feshbach (1953) discovered that after exposure to fear appeals, recipients avoided thinking or further communicating about the addressed risks. Furthermore, research has reported that exposure to fear appeals may also result in an increase in drinking (Kleinot & Rogers, 1982), smoking (Rogers & Mewborn, 1976), and unsafe sexual behavior (Witte, 1992). Likewise, research about the effects of erotic stimuli in health communication shows that they increase attention to and retention of messages.

On the other hand, "vampire effects," advertisers call them, may occur when a too strong erotic visual is sucking up attention that would otherwise have been spent on the health-related message (Nudo, 2005). While the potential of erotic visual frames to shape health-related attitudes and behavior is less clear, visual framing strategies that operate with sexual appeals may also reinforce gender stereotypes and objectify depicted characters. Thus applying visual media framing strategies that communicate respect, acceptance, and support rather than perpetuating objectification, stigma, and shame are more appropriate and may be more effective in promoting social good.

Ethical Issues with Individual- and Societal-Level Effects

Although social change communication often seeks to encourage large-scale transformation, the focus often is on the micro level, where changes in individual attitudes, beliefs, thoughts, and actions are intended. Social change communication is embedded in social, political, and cultural contexts and thus may have both macro and micro effects (Reese, 2010). Health communication may change individual perceptions, but it is also part of the wider social formation of knowledge and attitudes in groups and societies. Unintended effects of negative stereotyping in the media are a good example of when messages aimed at changing individual behaviors have a wider social impact. When individuals adopt the intended media frames and carry certain stereotyped information to broader social contexts, they unintentionally become part of the social construction and reconstruction of stereotypes.

Communication on public issues intending changes in individuals may unintentionally also modify parts of a social system, its cultures, norms, and values in a direction that was not premeditated (Hornik, 2002).

Of course, unintended outcomes on a societal level are not necessarily negative: health communication or environmental communication, for example, can also positively empower social groups to disseminate intended messages. It can motivate scientists to further explore an issue, politicians to recruit support for addressing an issue, the industry to develop preventative or remedial goods and services, and the public to consider the topic as an important problem worth assigning sympathy and concern (Viswanath & Finnegan, 2002; Davis, 1995).

However, framing strategies that destructively label individuals or groups also may perpetuate negative visual stereotypes and stigmatization, causing significant social and political consequences that go beyond effects on individuals. Any stigmatization of a social group where responsibility for a health problem is attributed only to the individual and not to societal factors may not only affect the public's perception of this group, but it may also influence the agenda of policy makers (McCombs & Shaw, 1972). For example, when an environmental issue is widely perceived as caused by the individuals affected by it, it can be expected that solutions are likely to focus on the individuals' problematic behaviors. When the issue is perceived as caused by economic conditions, it is more likely that changes in government policies and business practices will be considered.

Likewise, ongoing exposure to health-related or environmental messages about risks may also cause an "epidemic of apprehension" (Thomas, 1983). This is an unreasonably high level of public concern accompanied by insecurity, eroding people's sense of well-being (Tenner, 1997). Such messages may lead to the perception that health or environmental risks "lurk in every aspect of daily life: the air we breathe, the water we drink, the food we eat, the homes we live in, the substance we touch, and the work we do" (Feinstein & Esdaile, 1987, p. 113).

Persuasive communication, even when it aims for social change, typically is not designed to reach a whole society. In most cases, it is created to target a specific group and meet that audience's needs and capabilities. For example, in the creation of messages for populations with low levels of visual literacy, the information needs to be adapted accordingly (Messaris, & Moriarty, 2005; Garcia-Retamero & Galesic, 2009; Peters et al., 2007). If audiences with dissimilar skills and visual experiences see certain specialized messages, audiences may react with irritation or confusion. Thus ethical issues of the effects of persuasive communication are often caused by misunderstanding and misinterpretation. Good visuals that are culturally sensitive can reduce the ambiguity of visual messages (Jenks, 1995).

The decision of which target group is "intended" and which is "unintended" addresses ethical issues because it may conflict with the ideal of equal and fair opportunity (Guttman & Salmon, 2004). Communicators, for example, may decide to exclude specific groups in their segmentation for various reasons. They may conclude that certain groups are too difficult or costly to reach. If they decide to focus on a special group that is favored above others, such as the wealthy, ethical concerns would involve issues of equity and fairness (Rothschild, 2001). If communication is focused on one specific group, this may leave the impression that the issues are only a problem for that group and this may cause indirect stereotyping effects. For example, if messages aiming to prevent sexual diseases are mainly targeted to African-American women, this target group segmentation could encourage a stereotype that African-American women tend to have unprotected sex or loose sexual relationships (Coleman & Hatley-Major, 2014).

Exposure to ethically questionable frames in the long run also may affect policy makers and motivate actions in the political sphere. In the long term, exposure to communication focusing on a specific risk, for example, can diminish the social relevance of that issue (Thomas, 1983; Tenner, 1997). This also may contribute to desensitizing the public rather than energizing a society to directly address problems. Kinnick and colleagues (1996) have argued that media coverage is interconnected with desensitization and emotional burnout about issues such as AIDS, child abuse, homelessness, and violent crime, thus causing "compassion fatigue."

Conclusion

Persuasive framing strategies inevitably involve a number of issues that must be addressed by communicators and designers in order to be ethical. Our theoretical reflection has focused on the distinctions among ethical framing strategies in health communication and other forms of persuasive communication. In our view, our proposed three ethically problematic frames should be incorporated in research and practice. Professionals in advertising, public relations, political communication, and other forms of persuasive communication should consider our simple, 12-point checklist of questions when creating any new message:

- Does this message create undue fear, negative emotions, or shock, cause feelings of guilt or emotional distress?

- Does this message stereotype any ethnic or racial group, gender, age, obese people, or other marginalized, discriminated against, or vulnerable populations?
- Does it stigmatize anyone?
- Does this message outright state or imply that individuals are solely responsible, overlooking the role of society, government, or corporations?
- Does it blame the victim and de-emphasize the role of social factors?
- Does it fail to acknowledge that people may not be in complete control of their situations or others?
- Does it overstate risks by misrepresenting statistics?
- Does it imply that those who behave a certain way will be a burden to others or should be held legally or morally accountable?
- Does it imply weakness of character?
- Does it respect people's individuality, autonomy, and privacy, ensure equity, objectivity, and fairness?
- Does it make allowance for those who are particularly vulnerable or who have special needs?

And, above all,

- Does it avoid doing harm?

By asking these 12 questions of every persuasive message created, communicators may begin to address some of the ethically questionable frames found in their messages. This should be done for both verbal and visual message modes.

For researchers, this chapter has several implications, the most important being that persuasive communication should broaden its perspective and better integrate theoretical and empirical findings from other interconnected research fields. In this case, health communication ethics and visual communication research have much to add to other forms of persuasive communication. Persuasive framing strategies sometimes are accompanied by dysfunctional effects that do not benefit society in the long run. A strong perspective focused on "the greater good" is not always ethically responsible. Following Coleman and Hatley-Major (2014, p. 102–103), in an attempt to promote good practices in one area, it is not ethical to cause harm in others.

Against that background, practitioners should be aware of the power of visual frames, their effects, and ethical questions that may be raised. Research reveals that persuasive messages are making use of stereotypic, negative emotion-inducing, and victim-blaming messages, both verbally and visually. This holds the potential to create or reinforce biases and to induce a misleading view of social reality. The fears of those who worry about the ethical messages in persuasive communication are not unfounded (Coleman & Hatley-Major, 2014).

An important recommendation is to sensitize, and sensitize again, and shift attention to alternatives. Framing strategies can also work with positive portrayals, and nonstigmatizing messages hold potential to attract attention, shape attitudes, and change behavior. In addition, it is not necessary for persuasive communication to eliminate all messages that contain these frames identified as sometimes ethically problematic but to better balance their use with frames that are more equitable. We recognize that occasionally the most effective messages for positive behavior changes will sometimes be ethically questionable. We acknowledge the tension between moral imperatives and the need to change undesirable or dangerous behaviors. We do not criticize the goals of social marketers who seek to improve conditions in society. However, we suggest that there are other outcomes, such as the reduction of stereotypes and promotion of social solutions in society that are worthy goals as well. The challenge is to balance the need to achieve both. We do not suggest that the ethical outcomes discussed here should take precedence but that other negative effects should be weighed alongside the benefits. For example, when it comes to portraying certain populations that are most affected by an issue, the goal is not to portray all groups equally but to portray the affected group in proportion to its representation in society. It would be unethical not to address the African-American population with AIDS messages in greater proportion given that this group is disproportionately affected by HIV/AIDS. However, aiming AIDS messages only at African-American is stigmatizing and perpetuates stereotypes. Another way to mitigate harm from ethically questionable message frames is to counteract and balance it with other messages framed more equitably. For example, for every message with an individual responsibility frame, create one that includes societal responsibility messages. This should not be too difficult, as most advertising is conducted in campaigns that feature more than one ad, commercial, or other message. It is more complex to consider ethical and behavioral outcomes at the same time but worth attempting in order to maximize the overall good in society.

References

Abraham, L., & Appiah, O. (2006). Framing news stories: The role of visual imagery in priming racial stereotypes. *Howard Journal of Communications*, 17(3), 1083–1203.

Atkin, C., & Salmon, C.T. (2009). Communication campaigns. In C.R. Berger, M.E. Roloff, & D.R. Roskos-Ewoldsen (Eds.) *The Handbook of Communication Science* (2nd edition) (pp. 419–436). Thousand Oaks, CA: Sage.

Banks, M. (2013). Individual responsibility for climate change. *The Southern Journal of Philosophy*, 51(1), 42–66.

Barker, D. C. (2005). Values, frames, and persuasion in presidential nomination campaigns. *Political Behavior*, 27, 375–94.

Barry, A. M. (1997). *Visual Intelligence: Perception, Image, and Manipulation in Visual Communication*. Albany, NY: SUNY Press.

Beauchamp, T.L., & Childress, J.F. (2013). Principles of Biomedical Ethics (7th edition). New York: Oxford University Press.

Beaudoin, C.E. (2007). HIV prevention in sub-Saharan Africa: A multilevel analysis of message frames and their social determinants. *Health Promotion International*, 22(3), 198–206.

Blakeslee, S. (1992, March 15). Faulty math heightens fears of breast cancer. *The New York Times*, p. 1.

Blane, D. (1995). Editorial: social determinants of health—socioeconomic status, social class, and ethnicity. *American Journal of Public Health*, 85, 903–05.

Bodenhausen, G. V. (1990). Stereotypes as judgmental heuristics: Evidence of circadian variations in discrimination. *Psychological Science*, 1(5), 319–22.

Boggero, G. (2013). Without (state) immunity, no (individual) responsibility. *Goettingen Journal of International Law*, 5(2), 375–98.

Bouman, M., & Brown, W. (2010). Ethical approaches to lifestyle campaigns. *Journal of Mass Media Ethics*, 25, 34–52.

Brader, T. (2006). *Campaigning for Hearts and Minds: How Emotional Appeals in Political Ads Work*. Chicago: University of Chicago Press.

Burdine, J. N., McLeroy, K. B., & Gottlieb, N. H. (1987). Ethical dilemmas in health promotion: An introduction. *Health Education Quarterly*, 14, 7–9.

Callahan, D., & Jennings, B. (2002). Ethics and public health: Forging a strong relationship. *American Journal of Public Health*, 92(2), 169–76.

Cho, H., & Boster, F. J. (2008). Effects of gain versus loss frame antidrug ads on adolescents. *Journal of Communication*, 58, 428–46.

Coleman, R. (2010). Framing the pictures in our heads: Exploring the framing and agenda-setting effects of visual images. In P. D'Angelo & J. A. Kuypers (Eds.) *Doing News Framing Analysis: Empirical and Theoretical Perspectives* (pp. 233–62). New York: Routledge.

Coleman, R., & Hatley-Major, L. (2014). Ethical health communication: A content analysis of predominant frames and primes in public service announcements. *Journal of Mass Media Ethics*, 29(2), 91–107.

Coughlin, S. S., Soskolne, C. L., & Goodman, K. W. (2009). *Case Studies in Public Health Ethics*. Washington, DC: American Public Health Association.

Covello, V. T. (1992). Risk communication: An emerging area of health communication research. In S. Deetz (Ed.) *Communication Yearbook* (pp. 359–73). New Brunswick, NJ: International Communication Association.

Dahl, S. (2010). CURRENT THEMES IN SOCIAL MARKETING research: text-mining the last five years. Social Marketing Quarterly, 16(2), 126-36.

Davis, J. J. (1995). The effects of message framing on response to environmental communications. *Journalism & Mass Communication Quarterly*, 72(2), 285–99.

Dillard, J. P., & Meijnders, A. (2002). Persuasion and the structure of affect. In J. P. Dillard & M. Pfau (Eds.) *The Persuasion Handbook: Developments in Theory and Practice* (pp. 309–27). Beverly Hills, CA: Sage.

Duch, R., & Stevenson, R. (2013). Voter perceptions of agenda power and attribution of responsibility for economic performance. *Electoral Studies*, 32(3), 512–16.

Edwards, A., Elwyn, G., & Mulley, A. (2002). Explaining risks: Turning numerical data into meaningful pictures. *British Medical Journal*, 324, 827–30.

Entman, R. M. (1993). Framing: Towards clarification of a fractured paradigm. *Journal of Communication*, 43(4), 51–58.

Entman, R. M., Matthes, J., & Pellicano, L. (2009). Framing politics in the news: Nature, sources and effects. In Thomas Hanitzsch & Karin Wahl-Jorgensen (Eds.) *Handbook of Journalism Studies*. (pp. 175–90). London: Routledge.

Faden, R. R. (1987). Ethical issues in government sponsored public health campaigns. *Health Education Quarterly*, 14, 227–37.

Fahmy, S. (2004). Picturing Afghan women: A content analysis of AP wire photographs during the Taliban regime and after the fall of the Taliban regime. *Gazette*, 66(2), 91–112.

Feinstein, A. R., & Esdaile, J. M. (1987). Incidence, prevalence, and evidence: Scientific problems in epidemiologic statistics for the occurrence of cancer. *The American Journal of Medicine*, 82(1), 113–23.

Fiske, S. T. (1980). Attention and weight in person perception: The impact of negative and extreme behavior. *Journal of Personality and Social Psychology*, 38(6), 889.

Fridkin, K. L., Kenney, R. J., Woodall, G. S. (2009). Bad for men; better for women: The impact of stereotypes during negative campaigns. Political Behavior, 31(1), 53–77.

Gamson, W. A. (1992). *Talking Politics*. New York: Cambridge University Press.

Gamson, W. A. (1995). Hiroshima, the holocaust, and the politics of exclusion. *American Sociological Review*, 60, 1–20.

Gamson, W. A., & Modigliani, A. (1987). The changing culture of affirmative action. In R. G. Braungart & M. M. Braungart (Eds.) *Research in Political Sociology* (pp. 137–77). Greenwich: JAI Press.

Gamson, W. A., & Modigliani, A. (1989). Media discourse and public opinion on nuclear power: A constructionist approach. *American Journal of Sociology*, 95(1), 1–37.

Gamson, W. A., & Stuart, D. (1992). Media discourse as a symbolic contest: The bomb in political cartoons. *Sociological Forum* 7(1), 55–86.

Garcia-Retamero, R., & Cokely, E. T. (2011). Effective communication of risks to young adults: Using message framing and visual aids to increase condom use and STD screening. *Journal of Experimental Psychology: Applied*, 17(3), 270.

Garcia-Retamero, R., & Galesic, M. (2009). Communicating treatment risk reduction to people with low numeracy skills: A cross-cultural comparison. *American Journal of Public Health*, 99(12), 2196–2202.

Geise, S., & Baden, C. (2013). Bilder rahmen. Ein integratives modell (multi-)modaler informationsverarbeitung im framing-prozess. In S. Geise & K. Lobinger (Eds.) *Visual Framing*. Perspektiven und herausforderungen der visuellen kommunikationsforschung. (pp. 143–75). Köln, Germany: von Halem.

Gitlin, T. (1980). *The Whole World is Watching: Mass Media in the Making and Unmaking of the New Left*. Berkeley, CA: University of California Press.

Goldenbeld, C., Twisk, D., & Houwing, S. (2008). Effects of persuasive communication and group discussions on acceptability of anti-speeding policies for male and female drivers. *Transportation Research* Part F, 11, 207–20.

Goss, D., & Adam-Smith, D. (1995). Framing differences: Sexuality, AIDS and organizations. In P. Aggleton, P. Dvies, & G. Hart (Eds.) *AIDS: Safety, Sexuality and Risk*. (pp. 68–89). London: Taylor & Francis.

Greenberg, J., & Pyszczynski, T. (1985). The effect of an overheard slur on evaluations of the target: How to spread a social disease. *Journal of Experimental Social Psychology*, 21, 61–72.

Guttman, N. (1997). Ethical dilemmas in health campaigns. *Health Communication*, 9, 155–90.

Guttman, N. (2003). Ethics in health communication interventions. In Thompson, T. L., A. Dorsey, K. I. Miller, & R. Parrott (Eds.) *Handbook of Health Communication* (pp. 657–58). New York, NY: Routledge.

Guttman, N., & Ressler, W. H. (2001). On being responsible: Ethical issues in appeals to personal responsibility in health campaigns. *Journal of Health Communication*, 6(2), 117–36.

Guttman, N., & Salmon, C. (2004). Guilt, fear, stigma and knowledge gaps: Ethical issues in public health communication interventions. *Bioethics*, 18, 531–52.

Hallahan, K. (1999). Seven models of framing: Implications for public relations. *Journal of Public Relations Research*, 11(3), 205–42.

Harper, P. B. (1994). *Framing the Margins. The Social Logic of Postmodern Culture.* New York: Oxford University Press.

Harris, P. G. (2012). Inviting people to climate parties: Differentiating national and individual responsibilities for mitigation. *Ethics, Policy & Environment*, 15(3), 309–13.

Henderson-King, E., & Nisbett, R. E. (1996). Anti-black prejudice as a function of exposure to the negative behavior of a single black person. *Journal of Personality and Social Psychology*, 71, 654–64.

Hendricks, W. W., Ramthun, R. H., & Chavez, D. J. (2001). The effects of persuasive message source and content on mountain bicyclists' adherence to trail etiquette guidelines. *Journal of Park and Recreation Administration*, 19(3), 38–61.

Heuer, C. A., McClure, K. J., & Puhl, R. M. (2011). Obesity stigma in online news: A visual content analysis. *Journal of Health Communication*, 16(9), 976–87.

Hobolt, S. B., & Tilley, J. (2013). Who's in charge? How voters attribute responsibility in the European Union. *Comparative Political Studies*, 47(6), 795–819.

Hornik, R. C. (2002). Public health communication: Making sense of contradictory evidence. In R. C. Hornik (Ed.) *Public Health Communication: Evidence for Behavior Change* (pp. 1–22). Mahwah, N.J.: Erlbaum.

Iyengar, S. (1991). *Is Anyone Responsible?: How Television Frames Political Issues.* Chicago: University of Chicago Press.

Iyengar, S., & Kinder, D. R. (1987). *News that Matters: Television and American Opinion.* Chicago: University of Chicago Press.

Janis, I. L., & Feshbach, S. (1953). Effects of fear-arousing communications. *The Journal of Abnormal and Social Psychology*, 48(1), 78–92.

Jenks, C. (1995). *Visual culture.* London: Routledge.

Jenness, V. (1995). Social movement growth, domain expansion and framing processes: The gay/lesbian movement and violence against gays and lesbians as a social problem. *Social Problems*, 42(1), 145–70.

Johnston, A. C., & Warkentin, M. (2010). Fear appeals and information security behaviors: An empirical study. *MIS quarterly*, 34(3), 549–66.

Kahneman, D., & Tversky, A. (1979). Prospect theory: An analysis of decision under risk. *Econometrica: Journal of the Econometric Society*, 263–91.

Kahneman, D., & Tversky, A. (1984). Choices, values, and frames. *American Psychologist*, 39(4), 341–50.

Keller, P. A., & Lehmann, D. R. (2008). Designing effective health communications: A meta-analysis. *Journal of Public Policy & Marketing*, 27(2), 117–30.

Kinnick, K. N., Krugman, D. M., & Cameron, G. T. (1996). Compassion fatigue: Communication and burnout toward social problems. *Journalism & Mass Communication Quarterly*, 73(3), 687–707.

Kleinot, M. C., & Rogers, R. W. (1982). Identifying effective components of alcohol misuse prevention programs. *Journal of Studies on Alcohol and Drugs*, 43(07), 802–11.

Lalwani, N., & Duval, T. S. (2000). The moderating effects of cognitive appraisal processes on self-attribution of responsibility. *Journal of Applied Social Psychology*, 30(11), 2233–45.

Lee, B., Kim, B.-C., & Han, S. (2006). The portrayal of older people in television advertisements: A cross-cultural content analysis of the United States and South Korea. *The International Journal of Aging and Human Development*, 63(4), 279–97.

Lee, S. T., & Cheng, I.-H. (2010). Assessing the TARES as an ethical model for anti-smoking ads. *Journal of Health Communication*, 15, 55–75.

Lipkus, I. M. (2007). Numeric, verbal, and visual formats of conveying health risks: Suggested best practices and future recommendations. *Medical Decision Making*, 27, 696–713.

Lipkus, I. M., & Hollands, J. G. (1999). The visual communication of risk, *JNCI Monographs*, (25), 149–63.

Marcus, G. E., Neuman, W. R., & MacKuen, M. (2000). *Affective Intelligence and Political judgment*. Chicago: The University of Chicago Press.

Martindale, C. (1990). Coverage of Black Americans in four major newspapers, 1950–1989. *Newspaper Research Journal*, 11(3), 96–112.

Mattson, M. (2000). Empowerment through agency-promoting dialogue: An explicit application of harm reduction theory to reframe HIV test counseling. *Journal of Health Communication*, 5(4), 333–47.

McCants, D. M. (1990). Changing perceptions of racial differences through effects of framing. *Dissertation Abstracts International*, 51(B-11), 5640.

McClure, K. J., Puhl, R. M., & Heuer, C. A. (2011). Obesity in the news: do photographic images of obese persons influence antifat attitudes? *Journal of Health Communication*, 16(4), 359–71.

McCombs, M. E., & Shaw, D. L. (1972). The agenda-setting function of mass media. *Public Opinion Quarterly*, 36(2), 176–87.

McGuire, W. J. (1989). Theoretical foundations of interventions. In R. E. Rice & C. K. Atkin (Eds.) *Public Communication Interventions* (pp. 43–65). Newbury Park: Sage.

Messaris, P., & Abraham, L. (2001). The role of images in framing news stories. In S. Reese, O. Gandy, & A. Grant (Eds.) *Framing Public Life* (pp. 215–26). Mahwah, N.J.: Erlbaum.

Messaris, P., & Moriarty, S. (2005). Visual literacy theory. In K. Smith, S. Moriarty, G. Barbatsis, & K. Kenney (Eds.) *Handbook of Visual Communication. Theory, Methods, and Media* (pp. 479–502). Mahwah, N.J.: Erlbaum.

Mitchell, W.J.T. (1986). *Iconology. Image, Text, Ideology*. Chicago: University of Chicago Press.

Mongeau, P. (2013). Fear appeals. In J. P. Dillard & L. J. Shen (Eds.) *The Persuasion Handbook: Developments in Theory and Practice* (pp. 184–99). Thousand Oaks, CA: Sage.

Mulilis, J. P., & Duval, T. S. (1995). Negative threat appeals and earthquake preparedness: A person-relative-to-event (PrE) model of coping with threat. *Journal of Applied Social Psychology*, 25(15), 1319–39.

Müller, M. G. (2007). What is visual communication? Past and future of an emerging field of communication research. *Studies in Communication Science*, 7(2), 7–34.

Nabi, R. L. (2002). Discrete emotions and persuasion. In J. P. Dillard & M. Pfau (Eds.) *The Persuasion Handbook* (pp. 289–308). Thousand Oaks, CA: Sage.

Nelson, T. E. (1993). Political harmonics: Issue framing and attitude expression. *Dissertation Abstracts International*, 53(B-11), 6041.

Nelson, T. E., Clawson, R. A., & Oxley, Z. M. (1997). Media framing of a civil liberties conflict and its effect on tolerance. *American Political Science Review*, 91(3), 567–83.

Nelson, T. E., Oxley, Z. M., & Clawson, R. A. (1997). Toward a psychology of framing effects. *Political Behavior*, 19(3), 221–46.

Nudo, T. (2005, October 17). Does sex really sell? *Adweek*.

O'Connell, M., Hickey, S., Besiou, M., Fitzpatrick, C., & Wassenhove, L.N. (2013). Feasibility of using radio frequency identification to facilitate individual producer responsibility for waste electrical and electronic equipment. *Journal of Industrial Ecology*, 17(2), 213–23.

O'Keefe, D.J., & Jensen, J.D. (2008). Do loss-framed persuasive messages engender greater message processing than do gain-framed messages? A meta-analytic review. *Communication Studies*, 59(1), 51–67.

O'Keefe, D.J., & Jensen, J.D. (2009). The relative persuasiveness of gain-framed and loss-framed messages for encouraging disease detection behaviors: A meta analytic review. *Journal of Communication*, 59(2), 296–316.

Payson, J. (2012). Individuals, institutions, and structures: Agents of political responsibilities. *Social Theory and Practice*, 38(4), 645–62.

Pelletier, L.G., & Sharp, E. (2008). Persuasive communication and pro-environmental behaviours: How message tailoring and message framing can improve the integration of behaviours through self-determined motivation. *Canadian Psychology*, 49(3), 210–17.

Peters, E., Hibbard, J.H., Slovic, P., & Dieckmann, N.F. (2007). Numeracy skill and the communication, comprehension, and use of risk and benefit information. *Health Affairs*, 26, 741–48.

Petty, R.E., & Wegener, D.T. (1998). Attitude change: Multiple roles for persuasion variables. In D.T. Gilbert (Ed.) *The Handbook of Social Psychology* (pp. 323–90). Boston: McGraw-Hill.

Price, V., Tewksbury, D., & Powers, E. (1997). Switching trains of thought: The impact of news frames on readers' cognitive responses. *Communication Research*, 24(5), 481–506.

Reese, S. (2001). Prolgue—Framing public life: A bridging model for media research. In S. Reese, O. Gandy, & A. Grant (Eds.), Framing Public life. *Perspectives on Media and our Understanding of the Social World* (pp. 7–31). Mahwah, N.J.: Erlbaum.

Reese, S. (2010). Finding frames in a web of culture: The case of the war on terror. In P. D'Angelo & J.A. Kuypers (Eds.) *Doing News Framing Analysis: Empirical and Theoretical Perspectives* (pp. 17–42). New York: Routledge.

Reese, S.D. (2007). The framing project: A bridging model for media research revisited. *Journal of Communication*, 57(1), 148–54.

Robinson, T., Gustafson, B., & Popovich, M. (2008). Perceptions of negative stereotypes of older people in magazine advertisements: Comparing the perceptions of older adults and college students. *Ageing and Society*, 28(2), 233–51.

Rodgers, S., & Thorson, E. (2000). "Fixing" stereotypes in news photos: A synergistic approach with the Los Angeles Times. *Visual Communication Quarterly*, 7(3), 189–92.

Rodriguez, L., & Asoro, R.L. (2012). Visual representations of genetic engineering and genetically modified organisms in the online media. *Visual Communication Quarterly*, 19(4), 232–45.

Rodriguez, L., & Dimitrova, D.V. (2011). The levels of visual framing. *Journal of Visual Literacy*, 30(1), 48–65.

Rogers, E.M. (1995). *Diffusion of Innovations*. New York: Free Press.

Rogers, R.W., & Mewborn, C.R. (1976). Fear appeals and attitude change: Effects of a threat's noxiousness, probability of occurrence, and the efficacy of coping responses. *Journal of Personality and Social Psychology*, 34(1), 54.

Rose, G. (2012). *Visual Methodologies. An Introduction to the Interpretation of Visual Materials* (3rd edition). London: Sage.

Rothschild, M. L. (2001). Ethical considerations in the use of marketing for the management of public health and social issues. In A. R. Andreasen (Ed.) *Ethics in Social Marketing* (pp. 39–69). Washington, D.C.: Georgetown University Press.

Rubie-Davies, C. M., Liu, S., & Lee, K.-C. K. (2013). Watching each other: Portrayals of gender and ethnicity in television advertisements. *The Journal of Social Psychology*, 153(2), 175–95.

Sabogal, F., Otero-Sabogal, E., Pasick, R., Jenkins, C., & Perez-Stable, E. (1996). Printed health education materials for diverse communities: Suggestions learned from the field. *Health Education Quarterly*, 23, S123–41.

Salmon, C., & Atkin, C. (2003). Using media campaigns for health promotion. In T. Thompson, A. Dorsey, K. Miller, & R. Parrott (Eds.) *Handbook of Health Communication* (pp. 449–72). Mahwah, N.J.: Erlbaum.

Salmon, C. T., & Murray-Johnson, L. (2001). Communication campaign effectiveness: Some critical distinctions. In R. Rice & C. K. Atkin (Eds.) *Public Communication Campaigns* (pp. 168–80). Thousand Oaks, CA: Sage.

Salovey, P., & Wegener, D. T. (2003). Communicating about health: Message framing, persuasion, and health behavior. In J. Suls & K. A. Wallston (Eds.) *Social Psychological Foundations of Health and Illness* (pp. 54–81). Malden, MA: Blackwell Publishing.

Scheufele, D. A., & Tewksbury, D. (2007). Framing, agenda setting, and priming: The evolution of three media effects models. *Journal of Communication*, 57(1), 9–20.

Seedhouse, D. (2009). *Ethics: The Heart of Health Care*. Chichester, MA: John Wiley & Sons.

Semetko, H. A., & Valkenburg, P. M. (2000). Framing European politics: A content analysis of press and television news. *Journal of Communication*, 50(2), 93–109.

Seo, K., Dillard, J. P., & Shen, F. (2013). The effects of message framing and visual image on persuasion. *Communication Quarterly*, 61(5), 564–83.

Shen, L., & Dillard, J. P. (2007). The influence of behavioral inhibition/approach systems and message framing on the processing of persuasive health messages. *Communication Research*, 34(4), 433–67.

Shoemaker, P., & Reese, S. (1996). Mediating the Message: *Theories of Influences on Mass Media Content*. White Plains, N.Y.: Longman.

Skerker, M. (2014). Seeking a variable standard of individual moral responsibility in organizations. *Ethical Theory and Moral Practice*, 17(2), 209–22.

Slovic, P. (1987). Perception of risk. *Science*, 236(4799), 280–85.

Smith, S. M., & Petty, R. E. (1996). Message framing and persuasion: A message processing analysis. *Personality and Social Psychology Bulletin*, 22(3), 257–68.

Stephenson, M. T., & Witte, K. (1998). Fear, threat, and perceptions of efficacy from frightening skin cancer messages. *Public Health Reviews*, 26, 147–74.

Talsma, L. (2012). UN human rights fact-finding: Establishing individual criminal responsibility. *Florida Journal of International Law*, 24, 383.

Tankard, J. W. (2001). The empirical approach to the study of media framing. In S. Reese, O. Gandy, & A. Grant (Eds.) *Framing Public Life: Perspectives on Media and our Understanding of the Social World* (pp. 95–106). Mahwah, NJ: Erlbaum.

Tenner, E. (1997). *Why Things Bite Back: Technology and the Revenge of Unintended Consequences*. New York: Vintage Books.

Tewksbury, D., & Scheufele, D. A. (2009). New framing theory and research. In J. Bryant (Ed.) *Media Effects* (3rd edition) (pp. 17–33). New York: Routledge.

Thomas, L. (1983). An epidemic of apprehension. *Discover*, 4, 78–80.

Van Erp, J. (2006). Words kill faster than bullets: Communication as an instrument to promote regulatory compliance. Paper presented at the annual meeting of the Law and Society Association.

van't Riet, J., Ruiter, R.A.C., Werrij, M.Q., Candel, M.J.J.M., & de Vries, H. (2010). Distinct pathways to persuasion: The role of affect in message-framing effects. *European Journal of Social Psychology*, 40(7), 1261–76.

Veatch, R. M. (1980). Voluntary risks to health: The ethical issues. *Journal of the American Medical Association*, 243, 50–5.

Veatch, R. M. (1982). Health promotion: Ethical considerations. In R. B. Taylor, J. R.

Veatch, R. M. (1999). The foundation of bioethics. *Bioethics*, 12, 206–17.

Viswanath, K., & Finnegan, J. R. (2002). Reflections on community health campaigns: Secular trends and the capacity to effect change. *Public health communication: Evidence for behavior change*, 289–313.

Williams, G. I., & Williams, R. H. (1995). All we want is equity: Rhetorical framing in the father's rights movement. In J. Best (Ed.) *Images of issues. Typification of Social Problems* (pp. 191–212). New York: Aldine de Gruyter.

Witte, K. (1992). Putting the fear back into fear appeals: The extended parallel process model. *Communications Monographs*, 59(4), 329–49.

Witte, K. (1994). Fear control and danger control: A test of the extended parallel process model (EPPM). *Communications Monographs*, 61(2), 113–34.

Yan, C., Dillard, J.P., & Shen, F. (2010). The effects of mood, message framing, and behavioral advocacy on persuasion. *Journal of Communication*, 60, 344–63.

Zawisza, M., & Cinnirella, M. (2010). What matters more—Breaking tradition or stereotype content? Envious and paternalistic gender stereotypes and advertising effectiveness. *Journal of Applied Social Psychology*, 40(7), 1767–97.

Zhang, L., & Gowan, M.A. (2012). Corporate social responsibility, applicants' individual traits, and organizational attraction: A person–organization fit perspective. *Journal of Business and Psychology*, 27(3), 345–62.

Zhao, X., Villagran, M.M., Kreps, G.L., & McHorney, C. (2012). Gain versus loss framing in adherence-promoting communication targeting patients with chronic diseases: The moderating effect of individual time perspective. *Health Communication*, 27(1), 75–85.

13 Seeing and Believing

Issues in Visual Persuasion Ethics

Margaret Duffy and Janis Page

CHAPTER SUMMARY

In an earlier chapter you learned how persuasion permeates all human interactions as we seek to accomplish our everyday goals, influence people to change their habits, buy a product, or even just watch the movie we prefer. Sometimes we're intentionally persuading people, while at other times we may be influencing without being consciously aware of it. Many people are concerned that visual images including video and other technologies may be extremely powerful persuaders with potentially unintended consequences. For instance, if a child sees a video showing potentially risky behaviors—perhaps even a cool trick on a trampoline—might she be persuaded to emulate that behavior? Are we more susceptible to images than text in advertising or promotion? Considerable research shows that visuals have the potential to produce more positive attitudes toward brands and help consumers visualize themselves enjoying the benefits of a product (MacInnis & Price, 1987). You have no doubt seen thousands of political advertisements, excerpts of speeches, and photos and cartoons of political candidates. Again, research shows that most of us respond with higher levels of emotion to how candidates look and sound rather than what they say. In an era of easy sharing of messages on social and other media, photos and video have become overwhelmingly popular. This chapter discusses how social media images, memes, and videos communicate through various apps and on various platforms.

Visual Images and Ethics

Scholars mark the mid-1990s as a turning point in the comparative influence of visual images over text. Theorist W.J.T. Mitchell announced that the "pictorial turn" had supplanted the "linguistic turn" in contemporary culture (1994, p. 15). Visual images, mass distributed primarily through video, had become a dominant breeding ground for values, attitudes, and ideas (Barry, 1997, p. 2). Furthermore, with the growth of digital technology and the Internet, the influence of visual communication continued to magnify and reverberate. Shift forward well into the 21st century and visual images—still, moving, self-created, co-created, or crafted by professionals—infiltrate and stimulate our waking lives on multiple devices. How this rich form of communication works in our mediated environment is the subject of this chapter. In particular, we'll discuss how visual imagery influences viewers through ethical and unethical means, both intentionally and unintentionally.

To better understand the power of the visual, we will consider the application of visual information and images in public communication, along with their ethical dimensions. While all messages are not intentionally persuasive, it's crucial to understand the rhetorical properties that distinguish pictures from words, as well as the contemporary visual cultural environment into which persuasive communication enters. Drawing from a rich body of literature, we'll survey visual theory to better understand how visuals create meaning.

We will then consider the ethical dimensions of visual images used purposefully to influence attitudes and behaviors. However, we should note that there are more similarities than differences within the various modes of contemporary communication, including in journalistic settings. For example, ethical issues surround the use of photo manipulation, whether on magazine covers or on the full-page ads inside, on pictorial depictions of criminals and victims in news stories, or in fashion marketing campaigns. They include visual representations that may stereotype in television programming or in public relations health campaigns.

The Influence of Visuals in Public Communication

Media ecologist Marshall McLuhan issued early warning of moving imagery's facility to immerse viewers in an "all-inclusive *nowness*" that would replace critical thinking (1964, p. 292). Images, more so than words, work instantly to carry a viewer into the depth of experience. There are various reasons why visuals can have more impact than their accompanying text: Readers perceive visuals as a whole or "gestalt" with emotional impact, readers who scan materials will see visuals when they won't read words, and readers remember visuals longer (Kienzler, 1997, p. 171). It is estimated that visual processing is only 10% ocular and 90% cognitive (Newton, 2005, p. 433). In other words, seeing through our eyes is simply opening doors to a spectrum of light, yet the processing of what we perceive is the work of our brains—interpreting, associating, imagining.

While Kienzler's concern focused on technical communication and document design, her belief that a good visual aid depends on both visual and textual elements is the basis of Paul Martin Lester's thesis in his widely quoted text, *Visual Communication: Images with Messages*: "The most powerful, meaningful, and culturally important messages are those that combine words and pictures equally and respectfully" (2014, p. xi). He advises us to consider the ethics of visual persuasion not only with images that stand alone but also in context of their interplay with words. However, as studies reveal, visual imagery often dominates to the point of minimizing the effect of accompanying words.

According to Gurri, Denny, and Harms (2010), "The wholesale transformation of the media information landscape during the last decade in fact represents the triumph of the image over the printed word" (pp. 101–9). Visual material is felt far more viscerally than text, and human beings are far less skilled at guarding their judgment against this style of persuasion (Lester, 2014). Today we face a deluge of visual communication yet as visuals are more accessible and as we intuitively accept them as informative or descriptive, the consequences can be significant if they misrepresent or distort.

Visual scholars suggest various ways to understand how visual communication constructs meaning. One way is through the lens of gestalt theory. According to gestalt (which means "unified whole"), elements are structured to create a whole through their relationships according to various principles, such as similarity or proximity. Zakia (2013, p. 260) explains, "what you experience when you look at a picture is quite different from what you would experience were you to look at each item in the picture separately." However, these gestalts don't work in isolation; they are coordinated through a simultaneous perceptual process into what Walter Lippmann called pictures in our heads. Barry writes, "they are stories, always implying more than their parts, always in process and actively seeking meaning" (1997, p. 69). One way they do this is through what Gibson called "affordances" (1986, pp. 127–43)—aspects the viewer finds potentially useful or harmful, and thus they become keys to understanding. Visual affordances function to signal meaning, just as a handle on a cup invites someone to pick up and hold a hot beverage and a computer mouse promises easy movement around a screen. An image may also be an affordance as it imposes meaning or capabilities to a user. Thus the process of reading images is a sense-making one, compelling a viewer to find what is salient—first to locate the trace of meaning and then to engage in completing the meaning. Through this interactive construction, meaning emerges for individuals and groups.

We know that readers of images derive meaning in various ways: drawing on memory, past experience, or cultural knowledge. Ambiguity in visual images creates tension, pulling viewers into solving the puzzle by playing a role in the ad or illustration. Viewers fill in the blanks, thus identifying more with the message and often creating more personalized meanings colored by one's needs, desires, knowledge, etc. This is an example of the gestalt of closure, writes Barry: "The perceptual tendency to complete the gestalt is what actively involves the viewer in the formation of the commercial message" (1997, p. 257). The long-running Absolut Vodka campaign ads, for example, purposefully leave a void that needs to be filled by the viewers' imaginations. Another way to understand visual syntax is through metaphoric propositions, a common device in advertising. A typical quarter-page ad in the *New York Times* is composed of minimal elements: the product, a logo, and an image from which it borrows qualities. For example, a gold ring with inset gemstones, the Cartier logo, and the face of a Jaguar cat, which associates the product and brand with qualities of boldness, sensuality, and elegance.

In another vein, Semiotic theory conceives of visual images as signs that carry meaning to some degree below the surface, also requiring that the viewer work to grasp it (Leiss, Kline, & Jhally, 1990, p. 201–2). However, this semiotic process, often a shortcut or heuristic, leads the viewer toward some messages encoded by the producer. Developed by Charles Sanders Pierce, semiotic theory identifies three classes of signs: the icon, the index, and the symbol. While the icon resembles the real (e.g., a picture of a ship), the index only suggests relationships to the real (e.g., fingerprints), and a symbol has abstract associations known through some perceived experiential connection or cultural knowledge (e.g., a red octagonal road sign means "stop").

Gurri, Denny, and Harms (2010) suggest there are four broad elements useful for analyzing visual persuasive imagery. These include 1) themes of nationalism, tradition, nostalgia, and authority; 2) master narratives rooted in cultural contexts, for example, the American Dream in the United States; 3) symbolic or structural cues, for example, gang tattoos or camera angles; and 4) measurements of audience resonance and effects. Beyond content, one should also consider form. When analyzing advertising, Hilligoss and Williams (2007) suggest we consider the context, how the elements combine, the typography, the colors, the angles, the placement—all visual grammar that interacts with existing social and political contexts to craft a particular meaning.

"In the broadest sense, everything packaged is designed," writes graphic designer, writer, and educator D. K. Holland in her article, "Deceit of Packaging" (Holland, 2008, p. 167). Packaging is defined as "the presentation of a person, product, or action in a particular way" (Oxford Dictionaries Online, 2015). That's what designers do, says Holland: design the visual expression of packages to be presented to the public. And there is power and responsibility in that role.

Ethics in Visual Communication

The relationship of ethics to visual rhetoric and communication is an intimate one. This relationship is tied to how visuals, either static or moving, make meaning. In her classic book, *Visual Intelligence: Perception, Image, and Manipulation in Visual Communication*, Barry explains the visual world is "an image created in the brain, formed by an integration of immediate multisensory information, prior experience, and cultural learning." (1997, p. 15).

There are good reasons to focus on the ethics of visuals, given how powerful they are in the communication process. An important perspective on ethics that may be applied to visual persuasion could begin with Johannesen's definition in *Ethics in Human Communication* (2002). He defines ethics as the grounds and principles for evaluating human behavior as right or wrong (p. 2) and summarizes various ethics scholars describing the ethical obligations of communicators. These responsibilities may emerge from a position or role earned or granted from commitments (pledges, promises, agreements) made, from established ethical principles, from relationships formed, or from consequences (effects, impacts) of their communication on others (p. 8). Thus, in line with Johannesen, we believe the moral character of organizational communication, including advertising and other persuasive communication, should be evaluated on the basis of these relevant obligations.

Visual communication scholars have grounded their ethical perspectives in many philosophies; among them are the ancient Greek philosophy of the golden rule and Mills's utilitarianism (Lester, 2014, pp. 138–43).[1] Lester suggests analyzing an image from an ethical perspective, which he defines as the "moral and ethical responsibilities that the producer, the subject, and the viewer of the work have and share" (p. 135). Ethics are compromised when certain missing elements cause the viewer to construct meaning in ways that are misleading or if people are harmed through certain depictions. For example, the producer of a public service announcement (PSA) warning about the risks of drunk driving might decide against using testimonials from the parents of a teen who lost his life. This decision would be grounded on the golden rule, which holds that people should be as human as possible and not harm others due to thoughtlessness. The creation and airing of the PSA might augment their grief. On the other hand, home advocacy campaigns must weigh the ethics of using disturbing photos of poor children against the likelihood that they will draw more attention and donations. An art director might base the decision to use such photos on utilitarianism, which ethically justifies actions based on the greater good they would serve.

In her chapter, "Visual Ethics Theory," in the *Handbook of Visual Communication* (2005), Newton calls visual ethics the soul of communication. She defines visual ethics as an ecological system of process and meaning—how visuals are made and received. Visual ethics involves "how images and imaging affect the ways we think, feel, behave, and create, use and interpret meaning, for good or for bad" (p. 433). Newton adds that visual ethics is "the appropriate use of imaging power in regard to self and others" (p. 434). Similarly, for creators of visual documents, Allen (1996) proposed a set of questions one should answer to determine if there are ethical concerns. They prompt the critic to ask if the product omits essential information, contains concealed arguments, presents any inaccuracies or ambiguities, and reflects personal and community values (pp. 102–3).

There is much critical scholarship on the ethical dimensions of persuasive visuals. A.A. Berger (2008) cautions the "image" industries to be ever mindful of responsibilities toward those who will see what is created and, in many cases, believe what they see (p. 37). Earlier scholarship (J. Berger, 1972) had suggested that the ideal spectator is always assumed to be a man, thus privileging male points of view and the male gaze. Goffman (1979/1988) identified codes of gender display in ads—women in positions of submission, lack of readiness, less serious expressions, sexualized clothing and hand positions—a visual arsenal of "gender propaganda" (Barry, 1997, p. 270) to perpetuate normalization of role behavior in society. Williamson argued that all advertising is an ideological process that is "invisible," insinuating identification with an imaginary relationship between a product and an emotion that seems natural (1987, p. 41). Visuals in advertising would likely carry even more ideological power.

Professional Codes of Ethics as Applied to Visual Communication

Professional organizations and firms frequently develop codes of ethics and codes of conduct for practitioners. In 2011, the American Advertising Federation (AAF) established an ethics code with eight guiding principles. Principle 5 advises advertisers to treat consumers fairly based on the nature of the audience to whom the ads are directed and the nature of the product or service advertised. The principle specifies media with visual advertising content: television, print, the Internet, DVDs, video games, and mobile phones. This may concern visual imagery targeted to specific demographic groups, children, or any vulnerable populations and ads concerning products such as alcohol, pharmaceuticals, and foods. It also may concern pictorial representations of the human body that involve violence, stereotypes, and pornography. Fashion brands Benneton and Abercrombie & Fitch have often used ethically questionable images; for example, the former involving human suffering and the latter teenage group sex and homoeroticism (Shaer, 2014).

The Public Relations Society of America (PRSA) (n.d.) has a statement of values that is intended to set the standard for the professional practice of public relations. The values are "fundamental beliefs that guide our behaviors and decision-making process . . . and are vital to the integrity of the profession as a whole." PRSA has a six-count code of ethics based on its values. It advances "honesty" and "fairness" in serving and representing clients to publics accurately and truthfully, and in fostering informed decision making with publics by revealing all information needed by those publics. While visual communication is not singled out in the code, whenever the practice of public relations employs pictorial imagery, ethical questions arise when images are crafted to mislead or negatively shape public opinion. Examples abound in political public relations. An infamous "photo op" devised by the George W. Bush administration featured the president prematurely announcing the end of the then two-month-old Iraq invasion in March 2003. A news conference was staged on the deck of the aircraft carrier USS Lincoln, with a prominent background banner reading "Mission Accomplished." Of course, the war was nowhere near over and continued on for years (Lester, 2014).

In its statement of ethics, the American Marketing Association (AMA) (n.d.) advocates doing no harm, fostering trust, and embracing the ethical values of honesty, responsibility, fairness, respect, transparency, and citizenship. As with PRSA, visual aspects are not singled out in the AMA statement of ethics. However, as marketing communication often has pictorial qualities, ethical considerations enter if visual images function coercively, deceptively, or ignore obligations to society. Children are particularly vulnerable to products tied in with movie, television, or cartoon characters.

Examples of Ethical Issues in Visual Persuasion

The explosion of digital media and the ability to create, manipulate, and widely disseminate visuals, vastly expands the potential influence and possible ethical issues related to visual persuasion. The following section offers three examples that illuminate some of the ethical issues in play. The first looks at a postgame interview of Richard Sherman, an NFL football player, with Fox Sports news reporter Erin Andrews. After Sherman made a game-winning play in a crucial playoff game, his intense and aggressive statements captured on video became worldwide news and explode across social media.

The second examines a presidential debate between President Barack Obama and former Massachusetts governor Mitt Romney. The debate was notable in that the terminology used by the two rivals sparked a remarkable series of images and Internet memes that were widely shared.

The third example considers advertising related to the Affordable Care Act (also known as the ACA or Obamacare) and analyzes the visual elements of both pro- and anti-ACA spots.

Richard Sherman

Sports celebrities in public dramas create substantial publicity that generates attention, conversation, imitation, and often vehement approval or rejection. In the field of sports public relations, the postgame interview is an opportunity provided by the organization to generate publicity and positive relationships with fans and the media. However, when aggression in the culture of professional football migrates to online discourse, the stage is set for possible ethical transgressions. In early 2014, the national media spotlight focused on NFL star cornerback Richard Sherman for what many reporters called a publicity stunt. Sherman had just executed a final dramatic play against a notorious rival, leading the Seattle Seahawks to win a championship game. The customary press interview immediately followed in which Fox Sports news reporter Erin Andrews briefly interviewed the animated and exultant player. In that quick televised exchange, Sherman, an African-American, provided an after-game performance quite consistent with his on-field playing, confrontational and competitive, yet also ratcheted up in volume and intensity carried over from his final play. The visuals of this scene were as arresting as the script, and the broadcast interview quickly moved from airing live to reverberating throughout social media. Almost immediately, football fans and sports commentators cast firm opinions online, predominantly critical of Sherman's "thug"-like behavior, a term connoting the N-word for many African-Americans.

As vitriolic rhetoric fueled the social media conversation, some participants took to meme generators to visually express their opinions via Twitter and in blogs—often depicting exaggerated, negative interpretations of both Sherman and Andrews. Using digital manipulation, the image-macros assigned the characters a range of deleterious qualities—distorting their facial features, superimposing faces of known villains from popular culture, and juxtaposing photos of notorious or pitiful celebrities and film/TV characters as points of comparison. Sherman was characterized as a brute or a bully, otherwise as a freak, with Andrews his victim in various stereotypical female roles. For example, one meme (Figure 13.1) places Sherman in the cult horror film *Alien*, playing the role of the horrifying extraterrestrial stalking the female protagonist Ripley (actress Sigourney Weaver), in this meme standing in for Andrews.

This particular meme circulated widely via Twitter and in "Top-10" lists of Sherman memes on sports and popular culture blogs, online magazines,

Figure 13.1 Alien meme

and other sites. It illustrates how visual images violate ethical dimensions to purposefully influence attitudes. As persuasive visual imagery, it asks us to understand its meaning through the symbolic cues of known popular culture references. Moving beyond the initial associations obvious to many viewers familiar with the film, the compositional juxtaposition of the two scenes functions as a visual metaphor. The Sherman/Andrews photo is the target of the construction, informed by a dark and terrifying Alien/Ripley photo as the source, lending all its horrific insinuations to the former, including violence, violation, and female subjugation.

As an example of compromised visual ethics, it illustrates how choices in images and imaging set in process a preferred reading of a meme, with missing or manipulated elements, causing viewers to construct meaning in ways that are misleading and potentially toxic. Michael McGee writes, "Culture, society, even our very identities are matters of representation" (1990, p. 27), and skewed representations can reinforce stereotypical gendered and racist viewpoints—especially due to the shared, collective behavior of the Internet.

Big Bird, Binders, and Bayonets

Beginning with the 2012 U.S. presidential election, candidates used new social media platforms for instant messaging with constituencies. Citizens, too, found direct avenues to not only respond but to set their own agendas. As in the Richard Sherman case, easily created and disseminated image-macros poured into the collective online dialogue. Their visual resonance colored the political discussion, dramatizing and demonizing candidates' images, statements, and blunders. After each of the three televised presidential debates between President Obama and Republican challenger Mitt Romney, social media responded. Political marketers for the two campaigns uploaded images to extend the debate. For example, in the first debate, Romney vowed to cut federal funding to PBS, adding a qualifying statement, "I like Big Bird." In response, Obama's Twitter feed posted a photo of a young multiracial child holding the sign, "My American Dream is to save Big Bird's job so kids can learn!" In the second debate, Romney defended his efforts for gender equality as governor of Massachusetts by stating, "I went to a number of women's groups and said, 'Can you help us find folks?' And they brought us whole binders full of women.'" In response to immediate social media ridicule, GOP committee chairman Reince Priebus tweeted an image attempting to flip the verbal metaphor: It pictured an opened binder with blank pages labeled, "Obama's second-term agenda." In the final presidential debate, Republican challenger Mitt Romney contended that the U.S. Navy now had fewer battleships than in 1916. President Obama responded,

> Well, Governor, we also have fewer horses and bayonets, because the nature of our military's changed. We have these things called aircraft

carriers, where planes land on them . . . And so the question is not a game of Battleship, where we're counting ships. It's what are our capabilities.

("Third Presidential Debate," 2012)

We feature this example to demonstrate the new reality for public relations and marketing professionals, given the utility the Internet offers citizen advocates and activists. Almost immediately, a "Horses and Bayonets" Tumblr featuring GIFs and images went live; a "Horses and Bayonets" Facebook page quickly collected more than three thousand likes (Stenovec, 2012); and the hashtag #horsesandbayonets became the number one trend on Twitter in the United States and third in the world (Judkis, 2012). The phrase became code for an uninformed and out of touch Romney, inspiring image-macros exposing the comically old-fashioned Republican. The memes quickly spread from laptops and smartphones and into broadcast, print news, and popular entertainment. Many of them poked fun at Romney's seemingly unknowing and outdated ideas. The social media news website Mashable carried one satirical image, a rudimentary mashup of illustrations and photos of Romney astride a horse, waving a bayonet, in a sea of battleships (Figure 13.2).

The meme's naïve composition frames Romney's narratives as incongruent and frivolous, illustrating the often crudely constructed visual "jokes" that circulate online. Without much context, background information, or invitation for deeper engagement, these memes function heuristically as intentional provocateurs of viral sharing. They share some of the same traits as traditional propaganda, for example, dehumanizing (or demonizing) the enemy and repetition. Romney is dehumanized by the visual propositions that his ideas are worthless. This denigration is amplified by repetitive caricatures that depict him as a simpleton and recurring visual cues that reinforce the narrative. While

Figure 13.2 Horses, bayonets, and battleships meme

citizen memes can either amplify or subvert candidates' messaging, in the final month before the 2012 presidential election, they demonized and trivialized Romney, which likely contributed to his brand disintegration.

Obamacare

There is no dearth of reportage and research on questionable ethics in U.S. political campaigning. Negative advertising has become prolific and effective, beginning with 1964's "The Daisy Girl" attack ad by Lyndon Johnson's campaign on opponent Barry Goldwater. Controversial, yet effective, negative advertising continued as almost a norm through future election seasons. With the anonymous funding of Super PACs, legalized in the 2010 Citizens United ruling, negative advertising is now even more evident for both political candidates and political issues. In fall 2013, Internet users were startled by video ads set in doctors' exam rooms that used suspenseful audio as well as body penetration imagery. The online ads sought to discourage participation in insurance exchanges mandated by the new Affordable Care Act (ACA) in the United States. One spot featured a young woman expecting a pelvic exam by a physician. Instead, a large, grotesque Uncle Sam figure ominously appears, holding the procedure's instrument, a speculum (Figure 13.3). On-screen printed wording cautioned viewers against signing up for "Obamacare"—as the ACA was coined—even though they would likely incur fines. Called "The Exam," the ad was created by the Koch brothers-funded PAC, Generation Opportunity, established primarily to influence college-age voters.

Besides employing dark humor and popular culture allusions to engage and influence its viewers, the ad also relies on propaganda techniques in its depictions of a "doctor visit," including appeals of fear and uncertainty as well

Figure 13.3 "The Exam" 1

as elements that confused, oversimplified, dictated, and led to cognitive dissonance. Propaganda is widely defined, from fooling an unsuspecting public through misleading information and emotional appeals to the more specific use of spoken, written, or pictorial representations to influence thought and action through debatable techniques (Lester, 2014). This ethically challenged ad transforms health care into a horror show where foolish participants are subjected to surveillance, loss of free will, humiliation, and molestation by a cruel and bullying government. Camera framing and angles communicated powerful and powerless positioning of the characters (Figure 13.4). Facial expressions ranged from detached and sneering looks on the medical staff to the distrustful, fearful, and foolish appearances of the patients.

Video is a powerful form of social media content. Videos tell stories that more easily connect with viewers and are often created with shareability in mind, as visual storytelling is an established way to encourage content sharing. Thus a video's virality in social media elevates the impact of its questionable ethics. Along with the Richard Sherman and Romney memes, this ad soared in popularity on the Internet. In the first 24 hours it went viral and was featured in over one hundred publications with most noting the ad's use of creepiness to garner attention. Within the first two weeks after uploading to YouTube, the video, combined with another Koch ad featuring a young man getting a proctologist's exam, accumulated more than three million hits combined. Data derived from Topsy, a social media listening tool, indicated that "The Exam" garnered more than one hundred thousand impressions on tweets linking to the video in less than two weeks.

In comparison, MNsure, the state of Minnesota's marketplace for health insurance, produced a pro-Obamacare ad, "Paul Goes Waterskiing," (Figure 13.5) released during the same time period as "The Exam." The MN ad received modest viewership, likely because it was a simply constructed animation telling a gently funny story. In it, the mythical hero Paul Bunyan comically

Figure 13.4 "The Exam" 2 (loud female scream heard)

Figure 13.5 "Paul Goes Waterskiing"

crashes into land while waterskiing. The culprit piloting the boat? His trusted companion, Babe, the blue ox. We find no ethical breaches in this video. While mild, and mildly amusing, it downplayed the role of government and high-lighted the benefits of helping oneself to avoid misfortune. With its folkloric references and naïve form, the ad relies on humor for its fear appeal. Minne-sotan viewers likely know the potential dangers for fans of outdoor sports. Yet even in familiar territory and with trusted companions, random and unexpected accidents can happen. Its cartoonish quality supports its playfully serious mes-sage that probably rang true with many viewers.

The Obamacare ad uses rhetorical techniques that are deliberately provoca-tive and humorous and likely to appeal to youthful audiences; however, the anti-Obamacare persuasive messages, while visually persuasive, are ethically challenged and portend negative health outcomes for the young people it targets.

The examples in this chapter sought to illustrate how visual persuasion can veer into unethical territory—in sports, politics, and issues of public policy. The introduction of the image-macro meme in the mid-2000s, and the subse-quent arrival of websites offering visual templates for meme generation, have allowed anyone to widely publicize and promote visual messages seeped in derogation and sarcasm, often violating ethical boundaries. Messner's Man-hood Formula in sports (2000) found that sports media certainly herald aggres-sion, violence, and "sports as war," yet citizen-created visual messages can condemn athletes for following these same norms and can also influence tradi-tional media outlets with their unethical messages. Political discourse in social media now uses quick-create visual rhetoric to demonize or trivialize legiti-mate candidates. And negative messaging has gained new potency in political campaign ads due to PAC money and visual strategies of deliberate outrage.

Concluding Thoughts

The examples provided in this chapter considered the visually persuasive elements in image-macro memes and negative political issue ads designed to attack and denigrate. Much has been written about the growing numbers and potential harmful effects of the latter, although research findings vary how much they may affect attitudes, beliefs, and behaviors. While our example dealt with political issue messaging and not campaign messaging, it was funded by a PAC. The percentage and amount of negative attack ads during political elections has increased sharply in the United States since 2012 due to independent groups formed with anonymous money, legitimized by the Citizens United ruling. Unencumbered by identification with candidate, party, or even funding source, they devote their resources primarily to negative attack ads (McChesney & Nichols, 2012). The visual rhetoric in these ads, constructed by both content and form, works to advance a skewed agenda. For example, Barbatsis (2005, p. 346) criticized "ambiguously 'transparent' film and video narrative(s)." She points to visual tricks in negative ads that use close-up shots of potent images to amplify the ad's message, e.g., foul water to suggest Dukakis's association with Boston Harbor pollution, featured in an attack ad during the 1988 U.S. presidential campaign. Research also shows that negative political ads have unintended but detrimental effects on the political system itself (Lau, Sigelman, & Rovner, 2007). In a meta-analytic assessment of relevant literature, the authors found that negative political ads lower feelings of political efficacy, trust in government, and possibly overall public mood. Beyond these damaging effects, the ads are also ethically questionable, as they use the format of video advertising to skirt libel laws the creators would face in print advertising (Hinerfeld, 1990).

Regarding image-macro memes, studies show that content plays a critical role in determining the virality of posts on social media. When a photograph accompanies a post on Twitter, it accelerates both the amount and speed of retweeting (Bruni, Francalanci, & Giacomazzi, 2012). In an earlier study, the authors found that negative tweets have a higher probability to be retweeted (Barbagallo, Bruni, Francalanci, & Giacomazzi, 2012). Emotionally charged visual images are central to this activity (Botha & Reyneke, 2013).

In this chapter, we raised the concern that visual images may be extremely powerful persuaders with potentially unintended consequences. Unquestionably, visual images are proliferating in video and other technologies with capacities to influence, deceive, and manipulate. Decades of research establish that visual imagery often supersedes the effects of accompanying verbiage for multiple reasons, including immediate emotional and or humor appeals, triggers of memory, accessible popular culture associations, sensory appeals, alluring visual puzzles, and more. We don't generally guard against the heuristic nature of visual imagery. Rather, the immediacy of our experience with visual material often triggers a visceral absorption of its propositions, skirting or blurring judgments on its believability, as well as obscuring any omissions.

Statements that may be identified as hyperbolic in print, for example, the messages carried in the Richard Sherman memes or the Creepy Uncle Sam videos, can reside in the ambiguity, humor, or interesting aspects of the visual, strongly suggesting meaning without really spelling it out. As creators and consumers of media messages that are increasingly visual in nature, it is crucial that we are aware of the potential for intentional and unintentional ethical breaches.

Note

1. Other chapters of this book offer explanations of various philosophies and theories of ethical behaviors. For useful and accessible explanations, see Black & Roberts (2011) *Doing Ethics in Media*.

References

Allen, N. (1996). Ethics and visual rhetorics: Seeing's not believing anymore. *Technical Communication Quarterly*, 5(1), 87–105.

American Advertising Federation (n.d.). Principles and practices for advertising ethics. Retrieved February 28, 2015 from http://aaftl.com/wp-content/uploads/2014/10/Principles-and-Practices-with-Commentary.pdf

American Marketing Association (n.d.). Statement of ethics. Retrieved February 28, 2015 from https://www.ama.org/AboutAMA/Pages/Statement-of-Ethics.aspx

Barbagallo, D., Bruni, L., Francalanci, C., & Giacomazzi, P. (2012). An empirical study on the relationship between sentiment and influence in the tourism domain. *Information and Communication Technologies in Tourism*, 506–16.

Barbatsis, G. (2005). Narrative theory. In K. L. Smith, S. Moriarty, K. R. Kenney, & G. Barbatsis (Eds.) *Handbook of Visual Communication: Theory, Methods, and Media* (pp. 329–50). New York: Routledge.

Barry, A. M. S. (1997). *Visual Intelligence: Perception, Image, and Manipulation in Visual Communication*. Albany, NY: State University of New York Press.

Berger, A. A. (2008). *Seeing Is Believing*. New York, NY: McGraw Hill.

Berger, J. (1972). *Ways of Seeing*. London: Penguin.

Black, J., & Roberts, C. (2011). *Doing Ethics in Media*. New York: Taylor and Francis.

Botha, E., & Reyneke, M. (2013). To share or not to share: The role of content and emotion in viral marketing. *Journal of Public Affairs*, 12(2), 160–71.

Bruni, L., Francalanci, C., & Giacomazzi, P. (2012). The role of multimedia content in determining the virality of social media information. *Information*, 3, 278–89.

Gibson, J. J. (1986). *The Ecological Approach to Visual Perception*. New York: Taylor & Francis.

Goffman, E. (1979/1988). *Gender Advertisements*. New York, NY: HarperCollins.

Gurri, M., Denny, C., & Harms, A. (2010). Our visual persuasion gap. *Parameters*, 40(1), 101–9.

Hilligoss, S., & S. Williams. (2007). Composition meets visual communication: New research questions. In H. McKee & D. N. DeVoss (Eds.) *Digital Writing Research: Technologies, Methodologies, and Ethical Issues*. New York: Hampton Press, 229–49.

Hinerfeld, D. S. (1990). How political ads subtract: It's not the negative ads that are perverting democracy, it's the deceptive ones. *Washington Monthly*, 22(4), 12–22.

Johannesen, R. L. (2002). *Ethics in Human Communication* (5th edition). Prospect Heights, IL: Waveland Press.

Jones, P., Hoffman, L., & Young, D. (2012). Online emotional appeals and political participation: The effect of candidate affect on mass behavior. *New Media and Society*, 15(7), 1132–50.

Judkis, M. (2012). Horses and bayonets meme saddles Romney. *The Washington Post* (Oct. 23). Retrieved November 19, 2015 from https://www.washingtonpost.com/ blogs/arts-post/post/romney-saddled-with-horses-and-bayonets-meme/2012/10/23/ 7c340d3c-1d14-11e2-b647-bb1668e64058_blog.html.

Kienzler, D. S. (1997). Visual ethics. *Journal of Business Communication*, 34(2), 171–87.

Lau, R. R., Sigelman, L., & Rovner, I. B. (2007). The effects of negative political campaigns: A meta-analytic reassessment. *Journal of Politics*, 69(4), 1176–1209.

Leiss, W., Kline S., & Jhally, S. (1990). *Social Communication in Advertising: Persons, Products and Images of Well-Being* (2nd edition). London: Routledge.

Lester, P.M. (2014). *Visual Communication: Images with Messages* (6th edition). Boston: Wadsworth.

MacInnes, D. J., & Price, L. L. (1987). The role of imagery in information processing: Review and extensions. *Journal of Consumer Research*, 13(4), 473–91.

McChesney, R., & Nichols, J. (2012). The bull market. *Monthly Review*, 63(11), 1–26. Retrieved October 15, 2015 from http://monthlyreview.org/2012/04/01/the-bull-market/#en41.

McGee, M.C. (1990). Text, context, and the fragmentation of contemporary culture. *Western Journal of Speech Communication*, 54, 278–9.

McLuhan, M. (1964). *Understanding Media: The Extensions of Man.* New York, NY: Signet.

Messner, M.A., Dunbar, M., & Hunt, D. (2000). The televised sports manhood formula. *Journal of Sport & Social Issues*, 24, 380–94.

Mitchell, W. J. T. (1994). *Picture Theory.* Chicago: University of Chicago Press.

Newton, J. (2005). Visual ethics theory. In K. L. Smith, S. Moriarty, K. R. Kenney, & G. Barbatsis (Eds.) *Handbook of Visual Communication: Theory, Methods, and Media* (pp. 429–44). New York: Routledge.

Oxford Dictionaries Online (2015). Packaging. Retrieved February 28, 2015 from http://www.oxforddictionaries.com/definition/american_english/packaging

Public Relations Society of America (PRSA) (n.d.). Member Code of Ethics. Retrieved February 28, 2015 from http://www.prsa.org/aboutprsa/ethics/codeenglish/#. U4OrIPldWSo

Shaer, M. (2014). Why Abercrombie is losing its shirt. *The New Yorker*. Retrieved February 9, 2015 from http://nymag.com/thecut/2014/02/why-abercrombie-is-losing-its-shirt.html

Stenovic, T. (2012, October 23). Obama's 'horses and bayonets' comment goes viral (VIDEO). Retrieved October 15, 2015 from http://www.huffingtonpost.com/2012/ 10/23/horses-and-bayonets-debate-obama-video_n_2004038.html

Third Presidential Debate: Full Transcript (2012, October 22). Retrieved February 15, 2015 from http://abcnews.go.com/Politics/OTUS/presidential-debate-full-transcript/ story?id=17538888&page=14#.UVYQnhzqnX4

Williamson, J. (1987). *Decoding Advertisements*. London: Marion Boyers.

Zakia, R. D. (2013). *Perception and Imaging: Photography—a New Way of Seeing.* New York: Focal Press.

14　Ethics Theory and Application in Public Relations, Advertising, and Health Communication

Seow Ting Lee

CHAPTER SUMMARY

Persuasion involves changing attitudes, beliefs, and behaviors and is often seen as controversial. This chapter explores ethical dimensions of persuasion in three major areas: public relations, advertising, and the growing field of health communication. These areas utilize persuasive tools in various ways and share many characteristics. However, they also are perceived differently by publics and often have different goals. Persuasion is a fundamental element of PR seeking to change attitudes and behaviors. Some argue that like lawyers, PR practitioners should be seen as advocates for clients and points of view and can function ethically in those roles. Further, because PR has different goals from journalism, it should not be evaluated along the same ethical guidelines. Moreover, most PR activities are protected by First Amendment rights. Advertising is also intrinsically persuasive and discussions of what constitutes truth in advertising are at the heart of critiques and government regulation. The Federal Trade Commission and other regulatory bodies monitor claims and insist that advertising not be deceptive and that its messages should be supported by evidence. Health communication has largely been exempted from ethical criticisms, primarily because the goals of such communication are perceived as emerging from good intentions, such as promoting health behaviors and preventing disease. However, even well-intentioned messages are aimed at changing attitudes and behaviors and may have unintended consequences. Thus health communication should receive the same scrutiny as any persuasive or informational campaigns or promotions.

Introduction

In the field of communication, persuasion is the focus of considerable controversy. As defined by Perloff (2010), persuasion is an attempt by an individual or a group of individuals to mold, alter, and reinforce the perception, cognition, affect, and behavior of another and is "the study of attitudes and how to change them" (p. 4). Many mass media messages, consciously or otherwise, persuade their audience to believe in something, or to believe in something enough to do something about it. Beauchamp and Childress (2001) argued that persuasion is about influencing others when a person "comes to believe in something through the merit of reasons another person advances" (p. 94). To Strauss (1991), to "persuade" does not mean simply to "induce" because "persuasion denotes a process of appealing, in some sense, to reason" (p. 335).

Despite its associations with reasoning and human rationality, persuasion is controversial to some because it may conflict with certain human values, including truth, autonomy, free will, and intent. Individuals who are misled or confused by persuaders may be seen as victims of persuasion. This may involve being presented with untruths or being deceived about the true state of an event, person, or issue. Such individuals may also experience a denial of autonomy in the sense that their control over their reasoning processes is being interfered with. The situation is considered more egregious if the persuasive message is motivated by the persuader's intent to mislead his or her audiences rather than without intent, as in the case of a genuinely inadvertent mistake then if the persuasive action were propelled by good intention that results unexpectedly in bad outcomes.

This chapter outlines some of the major ethical issues in persuasion ethics as applied to health communication, public relations, and advertising. While all of these areas of practice share many characteristics, they also have differences in goals, audiences, and expectations of ethical actions. The chapter in particular examines the TARES model of ethical analysis in health communication messages. To better understand persuasion in health communication, insights can be drawn from two allied subfields, public relations and advertising.

When asked about the ethical defensibility of persuasion, many communication professionals find it a difficult question. Persuasion is a crucial element of public relations, advertising, and health communication; and when mass media messages are vested with considerable power to change the attitudes and possibly the behaviors of large groups of people, it is compelling to investigate the standards of right and wrong for persuasion and to prescribe the rights and obligations of persuaders toward the to-be-persuaded that align with the notion of good to individuals, communities, and society at large. Considering ethics as a branch of philosophy and applied inquiry that addresses the moral correctness of an action or conduct of individuals or groups, it behooves us to first answer a fundamental question: What is ethical persuasion?

The literature on persuasion ethics in mass communication (e.g., Barney & Black, 1994; Edgett, 2002; Potter, 2010) tends to focus on public relations because public relations practitioners, by virtue of their job functions, are professional advocates who are tasked with using selective information to advance their clients' interests under an adversarial system in which debate and exchange of ideas underpin a large part of the democratic processes that characterize most contemporary communities—with the exceptions of North Korea and Cuba, two fully communist states still in existence today. Persuasion, with its liberal theoretical roots, aligns with the notions of freedom of media and of expression.

Persuasion has a fundamental role or an "intrinsic function" in public relations as is seen in explanations of persuasion in public relations textbooks (Pfau & Wan, 2006). The "goal of nearly all PR problem situations is to change attitudes and behaviors" (Robinson, 1969, p. x), irrespective of whether the solution lies in building stronger relations between an organization and its publics, in managing the effects of a crisis on an organization's reputation, or in changing a community's attitudes toward water conservation. Public relations organizations and professionals have made efforts to distance themselves from propaganda and other questionable forms of persuasive messages.

Two other communication disciplines that require practitioners to function as advocates are advertising and health communication. In a system based on competition, advertisers use advertisements in all forms and shapes to persuade individuals to make the decision to select and purchase certain goods and services over their competitors' offerings. In the realm of public health, health authorities, instead of relying on coercion through laws (such as laws aimed at disease quarantines or viral epidemics), use health messages not only to inform individuals of information expected to be relevant to them but also to persuade. Public health campaigns seek to persuade audiences to adopt particular beliefs or pursue courses of action to promote individual well-being, support public health, and prevent diseases.

The term persuasion often conjures images of salespersons, con artists, and victims, but there are other aspects to persuasion that are often neglected: the potential good outcomes of persuasion. Jaksa and Pritchard (1994) rightly observed that, "it cannot be seriously maintained that all persuasion is bad or undesirable" (p. 128). Persuasive communication is a powerful tool for social change and has been used to produce change for the better, be it in changing people's attitudes toward consumer rights, parenting, and toward treatment of women and minorities. Health communication campaigns have changed and are continuing to change people's attitudes toward smoking, exercise, nutrition and diet, vaccinations, and food safety in communities all over the world. Risk and crisis communications play essential roles not only in helping organizations recover from reputational damage but also in saving lives and property and in preventing future losses. In itself, persuasion is neither good nor bad, but it takes on the motives, values and aspirations of the persuader as well as the persuaded.

A Moral Confusion for Advocates

Because of its historical roots in journalism and press agentry, PR practices are often compared with journalistic practices. Rightly or not, the discourse about persuasion ethics in communication tends to pit public relations against journalism. According to Barney and Black (1994), among the first communication ethics scholars to investigate persuasion, a "moral confusion" arose when "public relations practitioners are torn between two distinct heritages: the objectivity ethic of the journalist, and the persuasion ethic of the advocate" (p. 233).

Journalism itself is arguably not free of persuasion. Journalists' intent to persuade may be less apparent or may have received less professional sanction, but journalists do possess an array of strategies to convince and persuade their audience, for example, through the particular use of facts and statistics, rhetorical questions, and emotive language. Within journalism, news editorials and opinion columns are structurally discrete for their persuasive intent as seen in the use of selective facts and figures to present particular opinions of a news organization or columnist. In fact, there is ample evidence, as seen in the substantial body of news framing research, to suggest that even hard news is not sacrosanct nor as free of persuasive intent and outcome as expected. The conflict regarding public relations versus journalism runs wide and deep in popular and academic discourses about public relations ethics. Public relations practitioners are vilified for their persuasive intent, but news framing by journalists, on the other hand, is accepted as an unconscious act shaped by work routines, social norms, and organizational culture (see Shoemaker & Reese 1996; Tuchman, 1978), thus absolving journalists of any moral responsibility for persuasion. However, a few scholars have questioned this assumption of journalistic guilelessness. For instance, Gamson (1989) noted the motives behind a journalist's framing of news may be unconscious as well as conscious and may involve intent.

Public Relations

Although journalism is not a focal point of this chapter, a comprehensive examination of persuasion ethics is incomplete without understanding that existing parameters of persuasion ethics that originated from journalism. Public relations' shared evolutionary parentage, imagined or otherwise, with journalism has continued to shackle public relations and impede its attainment of a legitimate advocacy purpose. Many public relations scholars (e.g., Bowen, 2009; Grunig & Grunig, 1992; Pfau & Wan, 2006) acknowledge that persuasion is a critical part of all public relations activities, and yet it is persuasion that poses the biggest ethical challenge for public relations.

Edward Bernays' (1923) vision of public relations as a "pleader to the public of a point of view" (p. 57) is firmly anchored in persuasion. Bernays believed that persuasion is necessary in society for shaping public opinion, because he viewed the public as fundamentally irrational. One of his favorite persuasive techniques was third-party authorities or paid experts to give credibility to the ideas or products to be sold. Grunig and Grunig (1992), who rejected the persuasive core of Bernays' model, offered four models of contemporary public relations practice that provide useful perspectives to dissect persuasion in public relations and concomitantly one of the fundamental building blocks in persuasion ethics: truth. In order to communicate, one has to be believed. Under J. E. Grunig and L.A. Grunig's models (public information and one-way asymmetrical), truth is used selectively to persuade. To tell the truth is to present facts that are in accordance with fact or reality.

Truth or factual accuracy is not a priority in Grunig's press agentry model, which relies on spin and is not above manufacturing news through pseudo-events to persuade.

For thousands of years, truth has been a central topic of discussion in philosophy. Plato discussed extensively the concept of truth in the "Allegory of the Cave." Truth telling is a complex concept, as truth and untruth may involve not only factual information but also omission of true facts. One can deceive another not only through intentional fabrication of facts but also through the intentional withholding of true facts. Even the concept of "true facts" can be problematic. Patterson and Wilkins (2007) discussed the changing view of truth over time. What were considered true facts invariably changed from the earliest perspective of truth based on memory or oral discourse to that later understood and accepted under Platonic, Medieval, Miltonic, Enlightenment, and Pragmatic views of truth. Under the Pragmatic perspective, for example, truth is relative.

The act of not telling the truth is widely acknowledged to be wrong but remains a systemic occurrence in human behavior. Truth may be a universal value, but at least a quarter of all human communication involves deception or a message knowingly transmitted by a sender to foster a false belief in the receiver (Buller & Burgoon, 1996; DePaulo, Kashy, Kirkendol, Wyer, & Epstein, 1996). Mieth (1997) observed that truth telling is a basic norm, but people often "invoke at one moment the norm of truthfulness and at the next moment, the right to lie, depending on circumstances and context" (p. 87). However, Bok (1978 argued that lying, regardless of benefits, always damages trust that is essential to a society's functioning.

The first three models of public relations exert pressures on public relations practitioners to change the publics' attitudes without negotiating a concomitant change in the organization, thus rendering persuasion problematic. According to Grunig (1989), the fourth model, two-way symmetrical, the model most likely to emerge from a participatory organizational culture, is the best way to mitigate pressures on public relations practitioners to transgress ethical boundaries of persuasion. They argue that persuasion based on two-way symmetrical communication is a win-win situation for publics and organizations. Other scholars including Pfau and Wan (2006) disagreed with this assertion, arguing that both asymmetrical and symmetrical approaches are needed depending on the circumstances. Persuasion, according to Wan and Pfau, "continues to be an essential function of contemporary public relations, especially in campaigns designed to establish, change, and/or reinforce an organization's commercial or social marketing efforts" (p. 102).

In reality, contemporary public relations practice has not come as far as anticipated with regard to the two-way symmetrical model. While academics and researchers seek a stronger professional identity and legitimacy amid the derisive taunts from some critics accusing them of being "spin doctors," the question of ethical defensibility of persuasion in public relations remains largely unanswered. Three decades ago, Barney and Black (1994) accurately diagnosed the problem of persuasion ethics in public relations, of which little seems to have changed since:

> The argument is that public relations entails dissemination of *selective truth* intended to persuade rather than merely to inform. Therefore, the reasoning goes, an objective moral theory cannot be spelled out for an industry whose express purpose is to overtly manipulate decisions of large numbers of people through the mass media, using tactics bordering on the deceptive. The logical conclusion, of course, is that public relations will need to change its very nature in order to claim a moral high ground.
>
> (p. 236).

Perhaps public relations need not change its very nature. Barney & Black (1994) offered a rationale role-defined argument for identifying a set of persuasive ethics for public relations. By specifying and outlining the positive contribution of public relations to a society, in other words in divorcing and setting apart public relations from its paternalistic older sibling journalism, new ethical boundaries can be established to help position public relations practitioners in a legitimate role as advocates and free public relations from the journalistic parameters of objectivity and truth that have been applied unquestioningly to public relations.

A similar argument was made by Deaver (1990) in his *Journal of Mass Media Ethics* article that explicated the concept of truth in communication. One of the first mass communication scholars to define truth, Deaver observed that "communication of all sorts is passed off as 'truth,' when in fact it is a collection of truth, half-truth and untruth" (p. 168). Deaver used four continua to explain truth and untruths: intent to be open and fully honest, intent to be honest but with selective use of information, use of untruths but with no intention to deceive, and conscious intent to deceive. Persuasive content such as advertising and public relations copy are characterized by intent to persuade by using selective information and the use of truth but not the whole truth. Deaver suggested that persuasion does not permit the telling of untruths but merely introduces the element of selectivity in communication, with the assumption that truth is still achievable in public relations. Based on Deaver's framework, public relations, advertising, and health communication fall into the category of persuasive messages. They can be ethical when selective information is used to persuade the audience without compromising truth telling.

In the United States, the selective and persuasive messages of the public relations practitioner are protected by law. What is legal is not always ethical—hence the seeming reluctance of the general public to endorse public relations work and accord it the professional legitimacy it deserves. In the American system, what Barney and Black called an adversarial system, it is widely accepted that more satisfaction and social good are achieved through "techniques of debate and advocacy than through calm, rational, objective discourse" (Barney & Black, 1994, p 238).

Others suggest that the public relations practitioner is akin to a lawyer in litigation (Barney & Black, 1994; Pfau & Wan, 2006). Barney and Black made a compelling case as to why public relations practitioners have a legitimate role in society, just as the lawyer in litigation who is an advocate for his or her client. In a trial system, even the most notorious criminal is entitled to a defense counsel. Under an adversarial system, adversaries present the most persuasive evidence to secure and make best use of available resources and generate the best decisions—not unlike in the days of Ancient Greece. The ancient Greeks viewed persuasion and rhetoric as critical ingredients for egalitarian structuring and functioning of a deliberative democracy. By allowing for free exchange of opinions and counterarguments, political consensus could be forged on the basis of persuasion and free choice. "To be political, to live in a polis, meant that everything was decided through words and persuasion and not through force and violence" (Arendt, 1958, p. 26–27).

Advertising

Similar to public relations, advertising also has persuasion as an intrinsic function. Like public relations practitioners, advertisers are advocates for their clients or companies. Advertising messages not only serve to inform and to remind consumers about goods and services but also to persuade consumers with the express goal of influencing them to purchase a particular good or service. The advertising industry uses a wide range of techniques to persuade its audiences, including emotional appeal, price appeal, snob appeal, testimonial, sex appeal, and technical jargon among others. Interest in advertising ethics has a long history. In one of the earliest books on the subject of advertising ethics, Bishop (1949) recorded a wide array of "moral indictments" of the persuasive sway held by advertisements that stimulated individuals' unworthy desires, misled consumers with exaggerations, untruths, and half-truths, and encouraged wanton consumerism—ethical issues that advertising continues to grapple with today.

Truth in advertising, as in the case of public relations, is an area of concern. In most societies, truth-in-advertising standards mandate that advertisers must have proof to support the express and implied claims made about products and services featured in advertisements. In the United States, under the U.S. Federal Trade Commission Act, advertising must be truthful, nondeceptive, and its claims must be supported by evidence. However, few cases actually escalate to the level of official complaints and meaningful actions and state enforcement because self-regulation by industry is still the prevailing mode of operation in advertising ethics. Cunningham (1999) rightly observed that advertising ethics is not only about "what is right or good in the conduct of the advertising function" but also "questions of what ought to be done, not just with what legally must be done" (p. 500). However, self-regulation practices by advertisers, facilitated through national advertising standards boards, remain fraught with missteps and mixed messages.

As a topic, advertising ethics has received considerable popular and academic attention, mostly in the form of philosophical debate or commentaries, but it has not received commensurate treatment as a research topic, as research in advertising ethics continues to be "thin and inconclusive in many important areas" (Drumwright & Murphy, 2009, p. 85). Although advertising ethics continues to be a mainstream topic in advertising literature, it is plagued by a lack of practitioner interest, lack of sound measures and frameworks, lack of relevant theories, and lack of academic interest (Drumwright & Murphy, 2009; Hyman, Tansey, & Clark, 1994).

Health Communication

Insights into persuasion in advertising and public relations illuminates health communication, one of the younger communication subfields. In health communication, the use of persuasive messages has complemented the information-only approach of letting information speak for itself so that individuals can make informed decisions about the best course of action for their health. There is strong support from scholars and clinicians for the use of persuasive messages in health communication. Worden, Flynn, Solomon, Secker-Walker, Badger, and Carpenter (1996) suggested that persuasive messages, rather than information, are more effective and may be the only approach to get results in some health contexts involving populations that are difficult to reach and are at risk.

Although health communication has developed over the last three decades into an important field of study and practice, little is understood about the ethicality of persuasive messages in promoting public health, disease prevention, and individuals' adoption of healthful behaviors. Historically, a significant body of the discourse about ethics in public health has focused on state coercion in public health interventions, but much less attention has been given to ethics analyses of health communication, although any form of persuasive communication aimed at changing people's attitudes and behaviors by touching on deeply held personal preferences and values—regardless of good intentions and benevolence—is bound to be ethically challenging.

Persuasion ethics has not received commensurate attention in health communication practice and scholarship for several reasons. As targeted, goal-driven, strategic communication that seeks to effect positive changes in people's lives by promoting health and preventing diseases, health communication efforts are widely accepted as benevolent endeavors grounded morally in noble, altruistic justifications and beneficent regard for others (Andreasen, 2001; Faden & Faden, 1978; Guttman, 1997, 2000; Guttman & Salmon, 2004; Kirklin, 2007a, 2007b; Kozlowski & O'Connor, 2003; Lee & Cheng, 2010; Lee, 2011; Salmon, 1989; Seedhouse, 2008, 2004). There is an implicit understanding that persuasion, as a purposeful attempt to bring about desired changes in individuals' health-related behaviors or attitudes through messages of awareness, instruction, and persuasion, is inherently and categorically moral, as it is a pursuit of a larger axiomatic good: individuals' and societies' well-being in health, a matter of fundamental import. As a result, "ethics is rarely thought to be an issue in standard health promotion work" (Seedhouse, 2004, p. 53). Not surprisingly, the literature in health communication rarely discusses ethics, and most of the limited discussion is based on debate or philosophical discussions.

Although public relations, advertising, and health communication share considerable common ground, health communication sets itself apart from the mass-communicated persuasive messages in public relations and advertising. Unlike in health communication, popular and academic discourses about advertising and public relations ethics are dominated by a negative perception as to the intention of the communicators. With regard to motives, persuasion in advertising and public relations is viewed as inherently manipulative in seeking to alter individuals' attitudes and behaviors, often to the detriment of their interests or well-being, with the goal of selling a product or service or of satisfying organizational goals at the expense of public interest (Jaksa & Pritchard, 1994). However, largely due to health communication's historical associations with public service, its lack of commercial motivations, and strong linkages with the activities of governmental agencies, international and charitable organizations, robust theory-practice linkages, as well as "a promise that scholarship, when applied to practice, can help individuals and groups with particular needs, or better society as a whole" (Guttman 2000, p. xii), health communication's values and motivations have invited little scrutiny. There is little discussion about persuasive health messages, although health communication, with its inherent goals to change people's attitudes or behaviors, is replete with ethical issues—of which issues pertaining to truth, autonomy, and free will remain areas of grave concern.

Utilitarianism and Kantian Ethics

Broadly speaking, ethical thought can be differentiated according to two broad approaches, teleological and deontological. The former focuses on the outcomes of an action, whereas the latter highlights the soundness of an action. The tensions between teleological and deontological ethics can be seen in the following example. In health communication, tools of persuasion that include untruths may be justified through teleological ethics, although such techniques will not hold up under deontological scrutiny. This is because the deontological approach suggests that some acts, such as telling the truth, are bound by duty and must be executed regardless of consequences. The teleological approach, which is consequentialist in emphasizing the outcome of an action, is often represented by utilitarianism, a theory proposed by English philosophers Jeremy Bentham and J. S. Mill that focuses on maximizing the greatest good for the greatest number of people within a society's limited resources. In utilitarianism, as a theory of normative ethics, the moral worth of an action is determined by the resulting consequences. Utilitarianism is an influential ethical approach in contemporary society and is intuitive for many people because of its cost-benefit articulation of ethics. For most individuals, to weigh the pros and cons of an action has become a conditioned reflex when considering what to do. Although utilitarianism is not without weaknesses, for most communication practitioners, utilitarianism is an appealing approach because it "poses a collectivist ethic" that is "useful when dealing with large publics" (Bowen, 2009, p. 166) by providing a focus on the consequences of communicators' actions. As a theory, when applied with care to avoid pitfalls, utilitarianism's direct link to consequences provides a reliable mechanism for assessing the impact of a communicator's persuasive messages and actions.

According to deontological ethics, however, an individual's actions should be guided by duty. Whether an action is good or bad is independent of the action's outcome. The deontological approach to ethics is best represented by Kantian ethics, a theory of normative ethics that focuses on the intrinsic good of an action rather than the action's outcomes. German philosopher Immanuel Kant offered the strongest objection to deception. In *Grounding for the Metaphysics of Morals: On a Supposed Right to Lie Because of Philanthropic Concerns*, Kant (1785/1981), who defined a lie as any intentional statement that is untrue, considered lying to be an affront to human dignity and mankind. Under Kantian ethics, telling the truth is a perfect duty, which always holds true compared to a lesser set of duties or what he called imperfect duties, such as giving to charity, which is a more accommodating duty.

According to Kant, human beings have duties to the moral law, which he conceptualized as categorical imperatives or human duties without exceptions. The first categorical imperative is grounded in universalism, in that an action, to be considered ethical, is one that can be applied to all people and situations without contradiction. The second categorical imperative focuses on autonomy and human dignity; an action, to be considered ethical, must treat people not as means to an end but as ends in themselves. In Kantian ethics, an autonomous individual is an unmanipulated individual. This categorical imperative demands that the action accords dignity and respect to the person or persons to which the action is being directed. An individual must also possess autonomy or free will in decision making. Another core concept in Kantian ethics is rationality. It assumes that any individual performing an ethical analysis of an action is making a decision based on the considerations that any rational person would use to arrive at the best decision possible. Finally, a third and lesser-known categorical imperative acknowledges the primacy of intention, or the underlying motivation of the individual, as an important determinant of ethicality. In Kantian ethics, goodwill is the purest motivation, because all other motivations can be easily corrupted by human desires and foibles.

Kantian ethics is not without problems, but it offers communication practitioners an alternative or, some may argue, a more robust approach to ethical decision making. This is based on concepts of fairness and a universal perspective often neglected in communicating with large groups of people and multiple publics. This is a particular concern in that an emphasis on message and strategic efficacy tends to tilt decision making in the favor of an outcome-oriented approach to ethics. The Kantian approach "allows the communicator to consider the perspectives of multiple publics and to understand the values they hold." It removes the bias toward what the organization and communicator desire from the decision-making process to achieve the right course of action based on moral principle "rather than cost or profit, self-interest, or expedience" (Bowen, 2009, p. 172).

In health communication, where the altruistic and benevolent motivations of health communicators seemingly overcompensate for the reliance on teleological ethics, health communication's overwhelming focus on consequences (beneficence and avoidance of harm) as the main determinant of a message's ethicality is debatable. Some scholars have questioned the teleological focus in health communication by suggesting that a message should be assessed also for its intrinsic moral worth rather than its outcome (e.g., Guttman, 1997; Kirby & Andreasen, 2001). Others (e.g., Baker & Martinson, 2001; Fagothey, 1976) focused on a message's relative ultimate outcome to distinguish it from the more immediate instrumental ends, such as improved fatality rates or reduction in smoking rates. The ultimate outcome of communication, including health communication, is open to debate and involves a number of complex variables, including human values, education, advocacy, and the freedom to make a voluntary choice.

An alternative perspective is communitarianism, which focuses on the importance of balancing the individual's rights with that of the community. Communitarianism emphasizes the importance of the community in shaping and defining individuals. Communitarianism, often contrasted with classical liberalism, offers a reorientation of Western personhood and has yet to establish itself fully in the field of media ethics, although a few scholars have attempted to apply communitarianism to ethics of persuasion. Bouman and Brown (2010), in rejecting utilitarian ethics in favor of a communitarian approach to lifestyle campaigns as a means to promote public health, offered a stakeholders' model. Communitarianism "calls for the recognition of the perspectives of all groups in the collaborative process" (p. 48). Under the stakeholders' model, the success of a lifestyle campaign can be determined by the quality of interaction and negotiation between and among groups of stakeholders in four areas: team quality, organization quality, process quality, and chain quality. Bouman and Brown observed "no one group can view the campaign process in isolation of other groups" (p. 48).

Although utilitarianism, Kantian ethics, and communitarianism are general theories of ethics, they are useful for helping communicators decide on what to do about a specific case of persuasion. Ralph Potter of the Harvard Divinity School developed the Potter Box (see Figure 14.1) as a tool for ethical decision making. The first quadrant of the Potter Box is *definition* (sizing up the circumstances). The second quadrant is *values* (asking ourselves what values motivate our decisions). The third quadrant is *principles* (applying ethical theories grounded in universal morality). The fourth and final quadrant is *loyalties* (identifying the stakeholders to whom we owe moral duty).

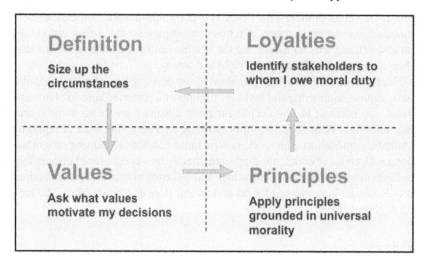

Figure 14.1 The Potter Box

Utilitarianism, Kantian ethics, and communitarianism, when applied within the Potter Box, function as fundamental cornerstones in the Potter Box. The Potter Box's third quadrant requires the individual to consider a wide range of general ethical principles, including Aristotle's Golden Mean, Rawls' Veil of Ignorance, and Ethics of Love/Agape[1]. Despite the Potter Box's quadrant structure, ethical theories do not function in isolation from the other elements. In the third quadrant, ethical theories or *principles* are related to *values*, the second quadrant. Values are our presuppositions about life and human nature. When conducting a Potter Box analysis, under *values*, one encounters the motivations behind his or her actions. When values compete, a dilemma arises. Put simplistically, an example would be the dilemma resulting from a clash between two values often found in many health communication situations: truth telling versus saving lives. Is it ethical to fabricate facts about smoking mortality to stop people from smoking? In a Potter Box analysis, when a health communicator considers whether or not to use false information in a particular campaign to persuade audiences to change their unhealthful behavior, he or she encounters the value of truth telling in quadrant 2. Truth telling would emerge again in the application of *theories* (quadrant 3), including Kantian principles that expressly reject lies since Kant's categorical imperatives are grounded in the concepts of universality, dignity, and respect for others.

Although the Potter Box was not created specifically for communicators, it is a valuable and comprehensive tool for ethical decision making, because it recognizes that ethical dilemmas emerge from conflicts and tensions that arise among values, ethics theories, loyalties—and understands the need for a clear problem definition or facts of the situation. As an ethical reasoning tool, the Potter Box stands out for its inclusiveness. Instead of propagating a particular ethical viewpoint or theory, the Potter Box allows for a more thorough deliberation and assessment, not only in terms of multiple ethical theories and values but also offers a lens for discerning the loyalties and stakeholder concerns that often cloud people's judgment of right and wrong.

The flaws of the Potter Box, in allowing the decision maker to use selective facts, values, arguments, and loyalties to support a preferred solution (Bowen, 2004), are inherent in any decision-making situation involving humans and their fallibility. Ethical decision tools such as the Potter Box must be a part of a holistic approach to ethics, where structured and formal training programs, along with codes of ethics, are supported directly by a congruence between formal initiatives and the personal values and informal norms that are embodied in individuals' inner sense of right and wrong (Lee & Cheng, 2011; McDonald & Nijhof, 1999).

TARES

One normative model of persuasive communication that unifies both deontological and teleological approaches to ethics is Baker and Martinson's (2001) TARES. The TARES framework is the first to explicate the notion of practitioner accountability toward the message receiver in persuasive communication as an expression of prima facie duties. The TARES, using truthfulness as a core value, establishes ethical boundaries for persuasive communications through a five-part test. The five interconnected principles in the normative model are: *Truthfulness* of the message, *Authenticity* of the persuader, *Respect* for the person being persuaded, *Equity* of the persuasive appeal, and *Social Responsibility* for the common good. According to Baker and Martinson, "Although professional persuasion is a means to an instrumental end, ethical persuasion must rest on or serve a deeper, morally based final (or relative) end" (p. 172). To pass the TARES test and be considered ethical, a persuasive message must fulfill all five principles.

In the TARES, *truthfulness* is a multifaceted concept. Veracity of the information presented in a persuasive message is only one dimension of truthfulness, as omission of information could still lead a message receiver to a false belief. Many ads communicate only part of the truth but not all omissions are deceptive. For deception to occur, there must exist the intent to deceive (Bok, 1978; Deaver, 1990, Elliot & Culver, 1992: Patterson & Wilkins, 2007). Many ads also contain exaggerations, or what is commonly known as fluff or puffery, but an exaggeration is not misleading unless there is intent to mislead. For example, Patterson and Wilkins (2007) discussed a Cheerios commercial that omitted the fact that other components of a heart-healthy lifestyle and that other breakfast cereals are equally healthful. However, the commercial does not lead the consumer to make false assumptions and bad choices. From the perspective of the TARES, the ad met the *Truthfulness* principle, although it communicated only part of the truth. Like commercials, health communication and social marketing messages are inherently time limited and often tightly constrained on content, thus restricting the amount of information that could be fully provided to audiences. This constraint, however, does not automatically imply a lack of truthfulness consistent with Deaver's (1990) definition of truth in communication. By operationalizing truth as a multifaceted ethical principle, the TARES extends beyond a simplistic notion of truth as "telling it all," and expands the ethical boundaries of persuasion through a recognition of selective truth.

Putting the TARES to the Test

The TARES received its first empirical testing when Lieber (2005) conducted an exploratory online survey of public relations practitioners. In a survey with 116 public relations practitioners, Lieber found that the TARES is better suited for a three-factor configuration based on civility, integrity, and credibility—factors that combine to classify someone as morally virtuous. The study also found that ethical considerations for the audience differ based on the practitioner's age, education, gender, and political ideology.

Two later published studies that applied the TARES are those of Lee and Cheng (2010) and Lee (2011). Using content analyses, these studies sought to empirically and directly test the TARES. Lee and Cheng (2010), the first study to operationalize the TARES to assess the ethicality of public health messages, focused on antismoking public service announcements. The study content analyzed 826 television ads from the U.S. Centers for Disease Control and Prevention's (CDC) Media Campaign Resource Center for *Truthfulness, Authenticity, Respect, Equity,* and *Social Responsibility,* the five elements of the TARES. Their operationalization of *Truthfulness* is multifaceted to take into consideration not only the veracity of the information presented but also the omission of information. Lee and Cheng used eight items to assess visual and verbal content for evidence of truth telling, exaggeration, omission of information, and intention to mislead or to deceive.

Authenticity was evaluated through two items specific to the message's sincerity and convincingness in asking whether there is a sincere need for this ad within the range of goods and services available and whether the reasons presented in the ad are equally convincing to the audience and to the persuader. *Respect* was assessed with two items that examined the persuader's demonstrations of respect toward the audience and of taking full, open, public, and personal responsibility for the persuasive message. *Equity* was evaluated through two items that assessed whether the audience must be unusually well informed and intelligent to understand the message of the ad and whether the ad takes advantage of human weakness by exploiting people's anxieties, fears, low self-esteem, etc. Lastly, *Social Responsibility* was assessed through five questions that asked about the ad's societal impacts in terms of change and improvement for society, benefits to some groups, harm to others, the level of trust the average person has for ads in general after viewing this ad, and the perceived interest of the persuader in improving human life and welfare through the use of the persuasive message.

The study found that overall the sample of antismoking ads scored high on ethicality. Lee and Cheng (2010) also drew a first link between message ethicality and message attributes (thematic frame, emotional appeal, source, and target audience). Ads that portrayed smoking as damaging to health and socially unacceptable scored lower in ethicality than ads that focused on tobacco industry manipulation, addiction, dangers of secondhand smoke, and cessation. Emotional appeals of anger and sadness were associated with higher ethicality than shame and humor appeals. Ads targeting teens/youth audiences scored lower on ethicality than ads targeting adult and general audiences. There were significant differences in ethicality based on source, as ads produced by the CDC ranked better in ethicality than ads produced by state tobacco agencies and health departments, tobacco companies, and the American Legacy Foundation.

Lee (2011), using the TARES framework, focused on truthfulness in persuasive health communication. Based on content analysis of 974 television antismoking ads from the CDC, the study sought to explicate truth in health communication through eight dimensions and explored the relationships among message truthfulness, message attributes, and audience characteristics. *Truthfulness* was measured based on eight items that assessed the visual and verbal content of antismoking television ads for elements of truth telling, exaggeration, omission of information, and intention to mislead or to deceive. Each message was coded based on verbal truth, visual truth, omission of information, misleading omission of information, verbal exaggeration, misleading verbal exaggeration, visual exaggeration, and misleading visual exaggeration.

For example, one ad stated that not smoking is an example of heart-healthy behavior. The ad omitted information that other components of a heart-healthy lifestyle such as exercise and low-fat diet and not smoking cigars or Turkish water pipes also met these heart-healthy requirements. However, the omitted information did not lead reasonable people into making false assumptions or bad choices. The study found the sample showed a high degree of truthfulness, but truthfulness was selectively associated with thematic frames, emotional appeals, source, age, social role and smoking status, and positive framing of consequences. For example, ads targeted at teens/youth and smokers were less truthful than ads targeting older age groups and nonsmokers. Ads with humor and fear appeals were also less truthful.

The third study, by Lee and Nguyen (2013), applied the TARES to examine the ethicality of fast-food ads in a departure from most research on fast-food advertising that adopted a cognitive-behavior, effects-based approach in examining the relationships between exposure to advertising and consumption. In moral terms, fast food—with its high calories and low nutritional value—is a questionable product in itself, irrespective of advertising messages. According to Lee and Nguyen, a

> deontological-ethical perspective, by focusing on the quality of the advertising message, shifts the focus from the product to a more measured

deliberation about the moral responsibility of fast food advertisers to repo-
sition them as moral agents who are accountable for their messages.

(p. 228)

The content analysis of 380 TV and print ads from McDonald's, KFC, Pizza
Hut, and Burger King found that few ads met the TARES expectations. Ads
for children and teenagers were lower in message ethicality than ads targeting
adults and general audiences, lending empirical support to the literature critical
of fast-food ads' insidious approach of targeting the young.

In the three studies applying the TARES, most troubling is the finding that
persuasive messages targeted at the young scored lower in message ethicality
than messages targeted at adults. One major limitation of the TARES is that
it does not address the ethical obligations of the receiver of the persuasive
message. Although the notion of a child as a rational individual does not pass
scrutiny, such a finding raises questions about the ethical responsibilities of
adult audiences in public relations, advertising, and health communication.
Some of the truisms dished out to audiences of persuasive messages include
being informed, keeping an open mind, being critical, and speaking up, but
such advice may not be meaningful without considering the communicative
contexts in which persuasion occurs and associated questions of information
access, human agency, and cultural values. Ethics is necessarily an expression
of both nature and culture. Although universal values exist, many of which
are encapsulated within the framework of the TARES, culture and context can
be influential in shaping audiences' ethical responses to persuasive messages.
Ethics also is perceptual. It is the perception of receivers of the persuasive message that helps define message ethicality. Insulated by denial and defensive-
ness, communicators may believe that their persuasive messages are ethical,
but if their audiences perceive that the messages are not ethical, a problem
exists and it demands resolution. In explicating the ethics of persuasion, one
area that deserves more attention is the ethical responsibilities of the message
receiver. With new ways of disseminating and sharing information, and more
opportunities for audience empowerment as well as audience marginalization
at the same time, the new media landscape presents unique challenges and
situations for all parties, not only the communicators but also audiences of
persuasive messages.

Note

1. The "Veil of Ignorance" is an approach to ethics that emphasizes fairness by eliminating biases and perceptions about the social position of individuals (Black & Roberts,
2011, p. 372). "Agape" emerges from Christian religious traditions and emphasizes
our human responsibility to love other human beings regardless of their characteristics and not to use people for one's own goals (Christians, Rotzler, & Fackler, 1991,
p. 20). Aristotle's "Principle of the Mean" suggests that ethical behavior may be
found between two extremes, and individuals who live their lives temperately and in
the Golden Mean will be successful and ethical (Christians et al., (1991), p. 12)

References

Andreasen, A. R. (2001). *Ethics in Social Marketing*. Washington DC: Georgetown University Press, 2001.

Arendt, H. (1958). *The Human Condition*. Chicago: University of Chicago Press.

Baker, S., & Martinson, D. L. (2001). The TARES test: Five principles for ethical persuasion. *Journal of Mass Media Ethics*, 16(2–3), 148–75.

Barney, R. D., & Black, J. (1994). Ethics and professional persuasive communications. *Public Relations Review*, 20(3), 233–48.

Beauchamp, T. L., & Childress, J. F. (2001). *Principles of Biomedical Ethics*. Oxford: Oxford University Press.

Bernays, E. L. (1923). *Crystallizing Public Opinion*. New York: Boni and Liveright.

Bishop, F. P. (1949). *The Ethics of Advertising*. New York: Hale, 1949.

Black, J. & Roberts, C. (2011). *Doing Ethics in Media: Theories and Practical Applications*. New York: Routledge.

Bok, S. (1978). *Lying: Moral Choice in Public and Private Life*. New York: Random House LLC, 1978.

Bouman, M. P., & Brown, W. J. (2010). Ethical approaches to lifestyle campaigns. *Journal of Mass Media Ethics*, 25(1), 34–52.

Bowen, S. A. (2004). Expansion of ethics as the tenth generic principle of public relations excellence: A Kantian theory and model for managing ethical issues. *Journal of Public Relations Research*, 16(1), 65–92.

Bowen, S. A. (2009). Foundations in moral philosophy for public relations ethics. In T. Horn-Hansen & B. Neff (Eds.) *Public Relations: From Theory to Practice*, (pp. 159–76). Boston: Allyn and Bacon Publishers.

Buller, D. B., & Burgoon, J. K. (1996). Interpersonal deception theory. *Communication Theory*, 6(3), 203–42.

Christians, C. G., Rotzell, K. B., & Fackler, M. (1991). *Media Ethics: Cases and Moral Reasoning*. New York: Longman.

Cunningham, P. H. (1999). Ethics of advertising. In J. J. Jones (ed.), *The Advertising Business*. London, Sage, 499–513.

Deaver, F. (1990). On defining truth. *Journal of Mass Media Ethics*, 5(3), 168–77.

DePaulo, B. M., Kashy, D. A., Kirdendol, S. E, Wyer, M. M., & Epstein, J. A. (1996). Lying in everyday life. *Journal of Personality and Social psychology*, 70(5), 979.

Drumwright, M. E., & Murphy, P. E. (2009). The current state of advertising ethics: Industry and academic perspectives. *Journal of Advertising*, 38(1), 83–108.

Edgett, R. (2002). Toward an ethical framework for advocacy in public relations. *Journal of Public Relations Research*, 14(1), 1–26.

Elliott, D., & Culver, C. (1992). Defining and analyzing journalistic deception. *Journal of Mass Media Ethics*, 7(2), 69–84.

Faden, R. R., & Faden, A. I. (1978). The ethics of health education as public health policy. *Health Education & Behavior*, 6(2), 180–97.

Fagothey, A. (1976). *Right and Reason: Ethics in Theory and Practice* (6th ed.). Saint Louis: Mosby.

Grunig, J. E. (1989). Public relations theory. *New Jersey*.

Grunig, J. E., & Grunig, L. A. (1992). Models of public relations and communication. In J. Grunig (Ed.) *Excellence in Public Relations and Communication Management* (pp. 285–326). New York: Routledge.

Guttman, N. (1997). Ethical dilemmas in health campaigns. *Health communication*, 9(2), 155–90.

Guttman, N. (2000). *Public Health Communication Interventions: Values and Ethical Dilemmas.* Thousand Oaks, CA: Sage Publications.

Guttman, N., & Salmon, C. T. (2004). Guilt, fear, stigma and knowledge gaps: Ethical issues in public health communication interventions. *Bioethics*, 18(6), 531–52.

Hyman, M. R., Tansey, R., & Clark, James W. (1994). Research on advertising ethics: Past, present, and future. *Journal of Advertising*, 23(3), 5–15.

Jaksa, J. A., & Pritchard, M. S. (1994). *Communication Ethics: Methods of Analysis.* Belmont, CA: Wadsworth.

Kant, I. (1785/1981). *Groundwork for the Metaphysics of Morals,* translated by JW Ellington. Indianapolis: Hackett.

Kirby, S. B., & Andreasen, A. R. (2001). Marketing ethics to social marketers: A segmented approach. In A. R. Andreasen (Ed.) *Ethics in social marketing* (pp. 128–43). Washington, DC: Georgetown University Press.

Kirklin, D. (2007a). Framing, truth telling and the problem with non-directive counseling. *Journal of Medical ethics,* 33(1), 58–62.

Kirklin, D (2007b). Truth telling, autonomy and the role of metaphor. *Journal of Medical Ethics*, 33(1), 11–14.

Kozlowski, L. T., & O'Connor, R. J. (2003). Apply federal research rules on deception to misleading health information: an example on smokeless tobacco and cigarettes. *Public Health Reports*, 118(3), 187.

Lee, S. T. (2011). Understanding Truth in Health Communication. *Journal of Mass Media Ethics*, 26(4), 263–82.

Lee, S. T., & Cheng, I.-H. (2010). Assessing the TARES as an ethical model for anti-smoking ads. *Journal of Health Communication*, 15(1), 55–75.

Lee, S. T., & Cheng, I.-H. (2011). Characteristics and dimensions of ethical leadership in public relations. *Journal of Public Relations Research*, 23(1), 46–74.

Lee, S. T., & Nguyen, H. L. (2013). Explicating the moral responsibility of the advertiser: The ethics of fast food advertising targeting children. *Journal of Mass Media Ethics*, 28(4), 225–40.

Lieber, P. S. (2005). Ethical considerations of public relations practitioners: An empirical analysis of the TARES test. *Journal of Mass Media Ethics*, 20(4), 288–304.

McDonald, G., & Nijhof, A. (1999). Beyond codes of ethics: An integrated framework for stimulating morally responsible behaviour in organisations. *Leadership and Organization Development Journal*, 20(3), 133–46.

Mieth, D. (1997). The basic norm of truthfulness. In C. G. Christians & M. Traber (Eds.) *Communication Ethics and Universal Values* (pp. 87–98). Thousand Oaks, CA: Sage.

Patterson, P., & Wilkins, L. (2007). *Media Ethics: Issues and Cases.* New York: McGraw-Hill.

Perloff, R. M. (2010). *The Dynamics of Persuasion: Communication and Attitudes in the Twenty-First Century.* New York: Routledge

Pfau, M., & Wan, H.-H. (2006). Persuasion: An intrinsic function of public relations. *Public Relations Theory II*, (2006), 101–36.

Porter, L. (2010). Communicating for the good of the state: A post-symmetrical polemic on persuasion in ethical public relations. *Public Relations Review*, 36(2), 127–33.

Robinson, E. J. (1969). *Public Relations and Survey Research.* New York: Appleton-Century Crofts.

Salmon, C. T. (1989). *Information Campaigns: Balancing Social Values and Social Change.* Newbury Park, CA: Sage.

Seedhouse, D. (2004). *Health Promotion: Philosophy, Prejudice and Practice.* New York: John Wiley & Sons.

Seedhouse, D. (2008). *Ethics: The Heart of Health Care*. New York: John Wiley & Sons.

Shoemaker, P.J., & Reese, S.D. (1996). *Mediating the Message*. White Plains, NY: Longman.

Strauss, D.A. (1991). Persuasion, autonomy, and freedom of expression. *Columbia Law Review*, 334–71.

Tuchman, G. (1978). *Making news: A Study in the Construction of Reality*. New York: Free Press.

Worden, J.K., Flynn, B.S., Solomon, L.J., Secker-Walker, R.H., Badger, G.J., & Carpenter, J.H. (1996). Using mass media to prevent cigarette smoking among adolescent girls. *Health Education & Behavior*, 23(4), 453–68.

15 Do the Right Thing

Advertising Law, Self-Regulation, and Ethics

Wally Snyder

CHAPTER SUMMARY

Most people are surprised to learn that for many years advertisers have made significant efforts to monitor and regulate their own practices. Advertisers are motivated toward self-regulation, both out of the desire to do the right thing for consumers as well as to forestall regulations that they might deem as overly stringent. At the same time, government regulators in the United States have kept a close eye on changing advertising content and platforms, particularly for target audiences that might be considered as vulnerable, such as children. At the heart of much regulation and self-regulation is the concept of truth in advertising and judging advertising messages for their accuracy and realistic portrayals of products' features and benefits. Another aspect of efforts at self-regulation includes the Institute for Advertising Ethics, a partnership between the American Advertising Federation, an industry trade group, and the Missouri School of Journalism. This chapter explores the legal requirements facing the advertising industry and the relationship between a strong self-regulatory program and the ethical responsibility professionals have "to do the right thing" for the consumer.

Introduction

According to business ethicist Gene Ahner, advertising is one of the six services considered critical in a global economy (Ahner, 2007). Advertising's importance to consumers both explains the government's powerful regulatory mandate and inspires the industry to practice enhanced professional ethics in self-regulatory efforts. This article first provides a description of the advertising regulatory requirements and processes; second, it shows how the industry's self-regulatory program complements government action; and third, it explains how enhanced business and personal ethics complement and inspire the self-regulatory mission.

Government Regulation of Advertising and PR

As suggested earlier, the federal government is highly involved in the regulation of advertising because of advertising's importance to the economy and consumers. The notion that truthful advertising benefits consumers emerged from federal court cases in the 1970s that struck down prohibitions by professional associations (particularly associations of doctors and dentists) against their members' advertising their services. The legal support for professional advertising was formally codified in 1976 in a Virginia Pharmacy Board case when the Supreme Court ruled that truthful advertising is protected under the First Amendment to the United States Constitution. Justice Blackmun, speaking for the majority of the court, stated that truthful commercial information is as important to the public as political speech (*Virginia Pharmacy Board v. Virginia Council* (1976)). Truthful advertising's importance was recognized and government regulation strengthened during the 1970s as Ralph Nader and other activists created the consumer protection movement. Nader spearheaded landmark consumer protections, including automobile safety standards and on-the-job safety laws, and put a spotlight on advertisers' claims (Auto safety, 1966).

The Federal Trade Commission (FTC) held in a landmark ruling in 1972 that companies must have a prior "reasonable basis" of fact for their advertising claims (Pfizer, Inc., 1972). It was up to the FTC to prove that the challenged claim had been made; that is, that the advertiser did, indeed, make a questionable assertion about a product or service. This legal requirement remains today.

The FTC responded to the consumer protection movement by strengthening its Bureau of Consumer Protection and expanding its advertising trade regulation mission. In 1971, the small division challenging advertising claims became the new Division of National Advertising and tripled its legal strength to over 30 attorneys who initiated national ad cases against companies and their advertising agencies.

In regulating commerce, the Commission follows very specific procedures to insure that its involvement will benefit consumers. This includes reviewing the scope of its orders and determining to investigate, including using its subpoena power to require advertisers to appear and testify in legal proceedings.

As part of its procedures, the Commission can approve its attorneys' recommendation to seek consent settlements remedying alleged deception and then approve these settlements as formal orders against the company (Part II Consent Orders). As part of this process, the legal staff can consult with the Commissioners. The FTC can also issue formal complaints, charging the respondent (defendant) with specific violations of the FTC law and assigning the case to an administrative law judge to hear the case and render a decision that can then be appealed by the respondent to the Commission (Part III Orders). The staff is not permitted to discuss these orders with the Commission until the formal hearing or if the case is voluntarily removed from litigation. The Commission's final order can be appealed by the respondent through the federal court system. Final FTC Orders (whether Part II or III) are enforced by federal district courts with money damages. For instance, if a judge finds that the advertiser made an untruthful claim, as prohibited by the FTC order, the judge may rule that the advertiser must pay fines.

The Federal Trade Commission is an independent government agency whose power to regulate is based on federal law with congressional oversight.

Section 5 of the FTC Act provides the agency with authority to prohibit "unfair and deceptive" acts or practices. Deception includes false claims, as well as claims that require disclosures so as to avoid misleading the consumer. This is known as "deception by half-truth." There are many examples of "half-truths" in advertising, such as health claims not fully supported by scientific evidence. Disclaimers in ads report limitations of product availability or performance and must be presented in a "clear and conspicuous" manner. For instance, a car ad may feature a sale price that's substantially below retail value. It may include a disclaimer that the price is only available for a limited number of vehicles or for a certain model.

A different kind of deception was seen in a 2014 case when the FTC charged home security company ADT with deceptive advertising that implied that paid endorsements from safety and technology experts were genuine independent reviews. The complaint alleged that ADT paid spokespeople to demonstrate and review the ADT Pulse product on NBC's *Today Show* and on 40 other television and radio programs nationwide, as well as on posted blogs and other online materials. ADT set up the interviews for the endorsers—often providing reporters and news anchors with suggested interview questions and background video—leaving the consumer to believe they were impartial, expert reviewers of the products.

Jessica Rich, director of the Bureau of Consumer Protection, stated, "It's hard for consumers to make good buying decisions when they think they're getting independent expert advice as part of an impartial news segment and have no way of knowing they are actually watching a sales pitch." She added, "When a paid endorser appears in a news or talk show segment with the host of that program, the relationship with the advertiser must be clearly disclosed" (FTC approves, 2014).

This case is part of a major legal and ethical problem of the blurring of the line between advertising on the one hand and editorial and entertainment on the other without adequate disclosure of the content as advertising. This is discussed in the Institute for Advertising Ethics Principles 3 and 4 (Institute for Ad Ethics, 2011). If consumers think they are reading or watching a news program that is actually paid advertising, they may well give the content more credibility. The FTC has shut down six fake news sites that the Commission charged were "designed to falsely appear as if they were legitimate news organizations, but were actually nothing more than advertisements deceptively enticing consumers to buy weight-loss products." The online sites had titles such as "New 6 News Alerts" and "Health 5 Beat Health News." The FTC received numerous complaints from consumers who paid $70 and $100 for weight-loss products after having been deceived by the fake news sites (FTC seeks, 2011).

The blurring of the line between paid content and editorial content has now become one of the biggest issues in the ad and regulatory world. The pros and cons of a major trend, called "native advertising," or "branded content," are being discussed as they grow in controversy and usage. E-Marketer

(Seventy-three percent, 2013) found that "nearly three quarters U.S. publishers offer online native advertising opportunities on their sites." *New York Times* advertising columnist Stuart Elliott (2013) defined native advertising as "digital pitches styled to look like the editorial content of the publication in which they run." The FTC held a hearing in late 2013, but as of this writing have not yet announced findings or recommendations. The associate director for Advertising Practices, Mary Engle, urged that paid content should have more prominent shading from the original content and that the disclosure as to ad content should be delivered "explicitly and unambiguously" (Winkler, 2014). The Internet Advertising Bureau (IAB) and Word of Mouth Marketing Association (WOMMA) also have issued disclosure guidelines.

Another example is a 2014 case in which the Federal Trade Commission prohibited Sony Computer Entertainment America from engaging in false and misleading claims, and the consent order required the company to provide refunds to consumers. The Commission charges that Sony "deceived consumers with false advertising claims about the 'game changing' technological features of its PlayStation Vita handheld gaming console." Sony agreed to provide notice via e-mail to consumers who were eligible for refunds. Bureau Director Jessica Rich stated, "The FTC will not hesitate to act on behalf of consumers when companies or advertisers make false product claims" (Sony Computer Entertainment, 2014).

Sony's advertising agency also joined in the investigation and agreed to a consent settlement that impacts marketing on social media, in this case Twitter. The Commission charged that Deutsch LA "Knew or should have known" the legal standard for ad agencies, that the advertisements it produced contained misleading claims about the console's capabilities. Also, the Commission alleged that Deutsch further "misled consumers by urging its employees to create awareness and excitement about the (product) on Twitter, without instructing employees to disclose their connection to the advertising agency or its then-client Sony." Under a separate consent order, the agency is barred from such conduct in the future (Sony Computer Entertainment, 2014). This case makes it clear that the Commission's Endorsement Guides, requiring disclosure of all material connections involving an endorsement, including payment and relationship to the advertiser, must be clearly and conspicuously disclosed in short-form ads as in traditional advertising.

The area of consumer privacy is a matter of increasing concern for consumers, activist groups, and regulators. The FTC, Federal Communications Commission (FCC), as well as the U.S. Congress are actively engaged in protecting consumer privacy and giving consumers a choice as to whether they want their data collected online. Behavioral advertising, also known as behavioral targeting, presents a great online opportunity for advertisers, yet it raises great concerns for consumers. Behavioral targeting allows advertising to often be more effective and economical as the ads go to consumers most likely to be interested in a particular product or service.

Ads are targeted to consumers via their computers according to the interests they express in online activities, such as search queries, ads they click on, information they share on social sites, and products they put in online shopping carts. The process presumably does not collect personally identifiable information (PII) but identifies the consumer's computer. Consumers can benefit by receiving commercial information on products and services with which they are interested. Yet consumers express worries about losing their privacy and feel they are not in control.

The FTC has held hearings and released staff reports and recommendations to bring transparency and give consumers control over their data use. The staff has recommended that consumers be allowed to choose whether they want their information collected with "Do Not Track." The Commission has not yet decided, but the industry has introduced a voluntary program providing consumers with the ability to learn what information is being collected and to choose to opt out immediately. However, many consumers appear to be unaware or unconcerned about tracking, and thus there is a need to continue educating consumers as to this practice.

In addition, the FTC is making sure companies keep their privacy promises to consumers. Under Section 5 of the FTC Act, the Commission has sued numerous companies that have violated consumers' privacy rights or misled consumers by failing to maintain security for sensitive consumer information. For instance, Google paid $22.5 million to settle FTC charges that it misrepresented privacy assurances to users of Apple's Safari Internet browser (Google will pay, 2012).

The FTC also has authority from Congress to protect children's online privacy under the Children's Online Privacy Protection Act (COPPA). Under the rule enacted by the FTC in 2013, companies cannot collect images, audio, or personal identifiers of children under 13 without obtaining parental consent. Companies also are liable if third parties operating on their sites collect those data without consent. The FCC also has been active in the area of privacy. In 2014, it required Verizon to pay a $7.4 million fine because the company failed to tell two million customers that they could opt out of having their personal information used for marketing purposes (Verizon to pay, 2014).

The Federal Trade Commission regulates children's advertising under its authority to prohibit deceptive acts or practices, including false claims and failure to make material disclosures. Children (defined as age 12 and under) are connected to products on TV, radio, print and online. This includes ads on cell phones, G-rated DVDs, and computer games and video games on company websites where the products are featured. A major legal and ethical issue relates to children's inexperience, immaturity, susceptibility to being unduly influenced, and lack of cognitive skills to evaluate the credibility of advertising. Children's understanding depends on the manner in which the ad is designed and disseminated. As will be seen in the next section of this chapter, the industry is highly involved in the self-regulation of children's advertising through the Children's Advertising Review Unit (CARU).

In 1978, the FTC staff conducted an industry-wide, trade regulation rulemaking proceeding into food advertising directed to children under the age of 12. The focus was on the negative impact on dental health from certain foods and beverages. That investigation, which was based on the Commission's unfairness authority, considered banning advertising directed to children. It was terminated when Congress withdrew the FTC authority for rulemaking on fairness issues. That authority has been reinstated with constitutional safeguards.

The FTC has been active regarding health claims directed at children. In 2010, the Commission entered into a consent order with the Kellogg Company that prohibits making claims about any health benefits of any food unless the claims are backed by scientific evidence and are not misleading. The agreed-to order resulted from claims made for Rice Krispies that the product "has been improved to include antioxidants and nutrients that your family needs to help them stay healthy" (FTC investigates, 2010).

While the FTC regulates over-the-counter drugs, the Food and Drug Administration has sole authority over prescription drug advertising. Direct-to-consumer (DTC) advertising of prescriptions was prohibited until the 1970s when it was first permitted in print and then later TV advertising. The FDA requires elaborate disclosures in all prescription drug advertising and the pharmaceutical industry has published a code on DTC advertising, which is available at www.phrma.org. The National Conference of State Legislatures website shows the laws and regulations of the many states governing DTC advertising (Marketing and direct-to-consumer advertising (DTCA) of pharmaceuticals, 2013).

Cigarette advertising has a long history of federal regulation, first by the FTC on a case-by-case basis and subsequently by the Food and Drug Administration. Congress requires the current health warnings on packaging and on print and online advertising. Congress also prohibited television advertising of cigarettes. The FDA also has been given legal authority to regulate the increasing advertising of e-cigarettes. The newly proposed rules go beyond truth, including warning users of nicotine addiction. The FDA prohibits the sale of these products to children.

The Advertising Industry's Self-Regulatory Mission

The advertising industry's self-regulation programming began in the 1970s when the federal government sharpened its focus on the industry and the Federal Trade Commission significantly increased its advertising regulation. Howard Bell, then president of the American Advertising Federation, led a major commitment of the AAF with the other two national advertising associations, the American Association of Advertising Agencies and the Association of National Advertising, to build a national program that is complementary to the federal regulation. Its mission was, and is, to conduct voluntary reviews of advertising and recommend appropriate changes to questionable advertising to reduce the need for formal government regulation. The program today is conducted by lawyers and other professionals and is administered by the Council of Better Business with active oversight of the three founding associations. The program is funded by contributions from the industry.

The National Advertising Division (NAD) and the Children's Advertising Review Unit (CARU) are the two self-regulation units responsible for independently monitoring and reviewing national advertising for truthfulness and accuracy. CARU is responsible for national ads primarily directed to children 12 years of age and under. These organizations review complaints from industry members and the public and initiate their own investigations into ad claims. The NAD and CARU may also call on outside experts.

After a complaint is made, the advertiser submits a written response to which the challenger files its response. After the advertiser files its response to the challenger, the NAD/CARU staff may meet with the parties to discuss the issues, and then staff will formulate its decision as to the truth and accuracy of the clams at issue. If it is determined that some or all of the advertising claims are not substantiated, the advertiser may either submit a notice that it will correspondingly modify its claims or that it will appeal the decision to the National Advertising Review Board (NARB), the self-regulation appellate body. All filings are required within specified time periods laid out in the policy and procedures for NAD, CARU, and NARB. The Advertising Self-Regulatory Council (ASRC) spearheads the industry's process of voluntary self-regulation and can be found at http://www.asrcreviews.org/about-us/.

The advertiser has an absolute or unqualified right to file an appeal to the NARB. The challenger may file a request for an appeal to the NAD/CARU decision, and it is up to the chairman of the NARB to determine whether to grant the challenger's appeal based on the likelihood of a review panel changing the decision of the NAD. During the process, the NARB chair may also be asked to determine if the appellants are raising new issues, new arguments, or introducing new evidence that should not be considered by the review panel. The NARB chair then appoints a panel of five qualified NARB members and designates the panel member who will serve as panel chair.

Upon a panel ruling affirming all or part of the NAD/CARU recommendations that the advertising be modified, the advertiser has the choice of complying with the changes or not. If it determines not to do so, the NAD/CARU may refer the file to the appropriate government agency for review.

At the conclusion of the self-regulation process, the NAD/CARU publishes the facts and findings as part of its case reports distributed throughout the year. This provides guidance to the industry, offering the conclusions and reasoning of the NAD. Each group also holds conferences to educate the industry as to recent trends and decisions. During 2014, the NAD reviewed over 80 challenges to advertising claims. The focus of the NAD has been on whether there is sufficient substantiation for claims made by advertisers and whether disclosures are clear and conspicuous.

The 2014 case involving Euro-Pro Operating claims for its Shark brand vacuum cleaners brought by a challenger illustrates the NAD investigative and self-regulation process. The challenged cases included the claim that Shark vacuum cleaners are "America's Most Recommended Vacuum Brand." Dyson challenged, and the NAD and NARB panel agreed that the "advertiser's evidence was insufficiently reliable or robust to provide a reasonable basis for the claim" (AD Reviews "Geomean" Evidence, 2014).

Dyson's substantiation rested upon aggregated consumer reviews from several marketing websites. NAD, while acknowledging that online comments and reviews by consumers are relevant, found several defects with the survey research. In most cases, the online reviews could not be verified as actual users or owners of the vacuum, verifications by the sites were not adequate to prevent unreliable and false reviews, and the data were not clear as to whether the newer models were adequately represented in the reviews utilized. The NAD conclusion, upheld by the NARB, was that the aggregated online review data relied upon by the advertiser did not represent American upright vacuum cleaner consumers (AD Reviews "Geomean" Evidence, 2014).

In another 2014 NAD case, which the NARB upheld, BP Lubricants USA was recommended to discontinue challenged "stronger" claims, made for the company's Castrol EDGE motor oil, that were based on a "torture test." NAD concluded that the claims made in television commercials and on its website, YouTube, and Facebook pages conveyed that its torture test results were relevant to consumer's normal driving conditions, when in fact the results did not support that superiority claim. ExxonMobil Corporation originally challenged the BP motor oil claims at the NAD. While not agreeing with the conclusion, BP noted that nevertheless it "respects the self-regulatory process and will take the panel's decision into consideration in future advertising" (NARB Panel Recommends, 2014).

As discussed previously, CARU actively monitors advertising directed to children under the age of 12 and addresses ads that are misleading and inappropriate. During 2014, CARU reviewed approximately 1500 television commercials and 1190 magazine ads and completed approximately 30 decisions. CARU also works with the Motion Picture Association of America to insure that promotions for PG-13 films are not advertised during children's programs.

CARU is a lead participant in the education and implementation of the Children's Online Privacy Protection Act (COPPA) administered by the FTC and discussed in the preceding section of this chapter. This includes clarifying a number of issues surrounding recent modifications of the Act by which the FTC prohibits collection of information from children online without parental consent.

CARU examines content on both TV and online websites designed for children to insure that the children understand the content advertised. This includes television ads that are structured like newscast segments. The concern, as in such ads directed to adults, is that the editorial format gives the ad a greater sense of objectivity and importance.

CARU investigated and recommended that IHOP modify its website to better disclose advertising within one of its online games. The game featured "The Lorax," a character from the Dr. Seuss book and movie. Directions for the game stated that winning "would bring you closer to saving Truffula Valley and treating yourself and the Lorax to a delicious Lorax's breakfast at IHOP." NAD concluded that this was an ad for IHOP "delicious breakfasts" CARU recommends IHOP, 2012).

In its monitoring program, CARU reviewed a television ad for Telebrands Saucer and concluded that the toy did perform the tricks and aerial movements depicted in the commercial. However, it recommended that the ads include an audio disclosure so that children would know the total cost of the toy, including shipping. The company agreed and implemented the audio disclosure for its broadcast ads (CARU finds Telebrands, 2014).

CARU has published complete guidelines for advertising to children under the age of 12 that includes core principles and specific areas of concern. The main principles that inform the guidelines focus on the limited knowledge and experience of children, hold that ads should not be deceptive or unfair and are adequately substantiated under terms applied by the Federal Trade Commission, should avoid content inappropriate for children, and should avoid social stereotyping. Disclosures should be understandable to children and use clear, age-appropriate language.

Areas of concern include using understandable disclosures for children, only using endorsements that are accurate and reflect actual experience, avoiding blurring advertising and editorial/program content, and prohibiting unsafe and inappropriate advertising to children. The last point includes avoiding the use of content that will frighten or provoke anxiety in children, such as violent depictions or encouraging inappropriate behavior.

The Advertising Self-Regulation Council also oversees another important children's advertising program, the Children's Food and Beverage Advertising Initiative. Under this voluntary program, 17 major food and beverage companies, including Burger King Corp., Kraft Foods Group Inc., Coca-Cola Co., General Mills Inc., and Hershey Co., adopted a set of uniform standards covering which foods should be advertised to children on child-directed television. The FTC has acknowledged the benefits of this initiative. The Children's Food and Beverage Initiative has a series of guidelines for advertising such products. It mandates that:

> All foods must meet limits on calories, saturated fat, trans fat, sodium and total sugars and must satisfy requirements for nutrition components to encourage (fruits, vegetables, non/low-fat dairy, whole grains or essential nutrients or some combination of these components. Advertising branded food to children in elementary schools is not allowed.
>
> (CBAI, 2015)

The ASRC also oversees development of voluntary principles to govern behavioral advertising. The guidelines were developed by the Digital Advertising Alliance, the Networking Advertising Initiative, the Direct Marketing Association, and other major trade associations and are enforced by the ASRC's

Online Internet-Based Advertising Accountability Program. The ASRC backs the industry's position that information collected for online advertising purposes cannot be used to make credit, employment, or other eligibility decisions and is gearing up to enforce the recent expansion of the behavioral advertising principles to the mobile space. The FTC has been willing to allow the industry to self-regulate before determining if formal action is necessary.

The Electronic Retailing Self-Regulation Program (ERSP) completed its tenth year in 2014 under ASRC oversight. In providing self-regulatory services for the direct response industry, ERSP investigates and modifies advertising claims, conducts conferences, and interacts with the government on direct marketing for a variety of products, such as dietary supplements and medical devices.

While this thicket of acronyms for various regulatory agencies and bodies may sound confusing, it's clear that both advertisers and the government take ethics seriously. Each of them focuses on different aspects of the business, and this also highlights the complexity of the advertising and public relations process. The next section discusses an important initiative that brings professionals and the academic world together to conduct research and broaden understanding of emerging issues in persuasion.

Practicing Enhanced Advertising and PR Ethics Complements and Supports Industry Self-Regulation

The Institute for Advertising Ethics (IAE) mandate includes encouraging and inspiring industry professionals to support and follow the industry's self-regulatory program, as well as the laws and regulations of our government. IAE Principle 7 states: "Advertisers should follow federal, state and local laws, and cooperate with industry self-regulatory programs for the resolution of advertising practices."

The IAE's website posts commentary and cases with links to the National Advertising Division (NAD) and Children's Advertising Review Unit (CARU). And the IAE Ad Ethics Certificate Program for advertising and PR professionals includes self-regulatory principles and cases (Ethics and Principles, AAF, 2015).

The mission of the Institute for Advertising Ethics is to "Build Awareness and the Practice of Enhanced Advertising Ethics." This mission is directed to the advertising and PR professionals responsible for the daily planning, managing, creating, and selling of commercial information online and offline. To accomplish the mission, a central question to be asked is *why* enhanced ad ethics should be practiced. Further efforts examine *what* current ethical dilemmas professionals are encountering and *how* we inspire our professionals to practice enhanced ethics.

As to why ad ethics is important, we can begin with business ethicist Gene Ahner's proposition that our business purpose "will eventually come to making some contribution to the general welfare of society. And that is what can inspire and motivate dedication to the core values of the company" (Ahner, 2007, p. 51).

The institute proposes that commercial information, including advertising and PR, has a very positive impact on the welfare of society. The core purpose of advertising and promotion is to provide consumers with commercial information on products and services in making purchase decisions. This includes the important areas of price and product innovation. If a business couldn't advertise a product or service, there would be little reason to improve it. Advertising also pays for much of the entertainment the public gets offline and, increasingly, online. Moreover, the First Amendment protects so-called commercial speech, as noted in the first section of this chapter. Thus advertising and public relations messages are important contributors to the free marketplace of ideas. That free marketplace of ideas is crucial to Western economic systems and democracy.

Teaching why advertising ethics is important is based on both a business case and a personal case. The business case is driven by the high importance our consumers place on ethics. Consumer research tells us that consumers rank "ethics" as central to a company's being seen as a "corporate good citizen" (The Importance of Being Ethical, 2000) In support, research conducted by four advertising student teams at the Missouri School of Journalism found that "honest advertising" is the main aspect as to whether a company is considered ethical. Eighty-nine percent ranked honest advertising as most important to ethics, followed by socially responsible at 80% and "environmentally friendly" at 59% (Institute for Advertising Ethics, 2011). The student research found that a majority of market professionals believed ethics was "very important" with the underlying reason given that ethics builds consumer trust.

Current and former advertising leaders agree with this conclusion. David Bell, chair emeritus, Inter-Public Group (IPG), stated at an American Academy of Advertising conference in 2012 that, "Trust is the currency of our Business and Ethics is the engine of Trust." Speaking at an AAF Conference in 2012, Rich Stoddert, president of Leo Burnett USA, cited founder Leo Burnett as stating, "Ethics is at the center of how we express a brand." This statement, as well as many others regarding advertising and ethics, is hanging on the walls of the Chicago office.

Building trust with consumers through enhanced ethics is very important, because consumers have online "information power" to learn when a company has not been honest and ethical with them. And they share this information—good and bad—daily with other consumers on YouTube, Facebook, and Twitter. Also, websites are available where consumers may share their opinions about the credibility of advertising, such as the EnviroMedia Website where consumers rate the credibility of green marketing claims (www.greenwashingindex.com).

The business case of building trust with consumers through enhanced ethics leads to the Institute for Advertising Ethics Principle 1: "Advertising, public relations, marketing communications, news and editorial all share a common objective of truth and high ethical standards in serving the public." This principle is based on the Journalist's Creed, written by Walter Williams, the first dean of the Missouri School of Journalism. Note that this principle equates the importance of advertising as equal to that of editorial. Both must be carried out with care and high ethics to benefit the public.

In his book *Business Ethics*, Ahner explains the need for an "Ethics of Compliance" and an "Ethics of Achievement" (2007, p. 84). He writes,

> An ethics of compliance basically forbids us from doing things while an ethics of achievement demands our engagement. A person or a business becomes moral not by 'not doing things' but by doing things rightly. An ethics of achievement calls out the best in us: have courage, be creative, find a way.
>
> (p. 90)

The personal case for ethics is based upon our internal feelings or we might say, what our heart dictates. Feelings are very personal and subjective and yet very powerful in determining our actions. Many ad professionals believe and practice the personal case for ad ethics. This began with the giants of advertising such as Leo Burnett who Rich Stoddert quoted at the 2012 AAF Conference: "Cling like wildcats to the only realities we can swear we have hold of—our own sacred and individual integrities."

The personal case for ad ethics brings us to Institute for Advertising Ethics Principle 2: "Advertising, public relations, and all marketing communications professionals have an obligation to exercise the highest personal ethics in the creation and dissemination of commercial information to consumers."

A guiding IAE principle is to "Do the Right Thing for Consumers." This builds on the legal regulation of advertising, our industry's self-regulation guides and cases, and in creating and maintaining ethical business relationships among clients and agencies, suppliers, media companies, and internally. Truth is the foundation upon which ethical ads are constructed. But ethics rises above being truthful and not misleading. Rich Stoddert, president of Leo Burnett USA, stated at a 2012 AAF Conference, "Laws are the boundaries; they don't tell you when you have gone over the boundary; they don't tell you what the right thing to do is."

This applies, for example, in product advertising to vulnerable groups, such as children, where in addition to being truthful, we need to treat the audience "fairly." As already discussed, the industry's Children's Advertising Review Council (CARU) follows several guidelines that rise above being truthful, including showing products being used safely, not promising to make children popular, protecting privacy, and not portraying or encouraging inappropriate or dangerous behavior, such as violence.

Advertising should treat consumers fairly based on the "nature" of the product or service. For example, the beer, distilled spirits, and wine industries limit advertising of their products to television programs with 70% adult audiences.

The rules put forward by the Food and Drug Administration for e-cigarettes also go beyond testing for claims of truthfulness and provide warnings to users of the dangers of nicotine addiction. As of this writing, it seems clear that the FDA also will prohibit sale of these products to children, and it would be unethical to advertise e-cigarettes to children or adolescents in a manner or medium that will draw their attention. Of course, online delivery of programming and advertising in digital and mobile platforms further complicates issues of protecting selected audiences from certain messages. Until the industry has better means of identifying online audiences, availability of some questionable content likely will be a problem.

Another area of concern is the potential of advertising to offend consumers. This is an area where the government is not involved and clear-cut standards cannot be generated to regulate these factors in advertising. What is offensive to some consumers may be perfectly acceptable and even enjoyable for others. A 2014 study at the Missouri School of Journalism found sharp differences in perceptions of video ads in terms of ethical dimensions (Duffy, Thorsen, Choi, & Karaliova, 2014). Nevertheless, it is wise for advertisers to heed concerns of the public, not only on ethical grounds, but because they risk alienating major market groups. Areas of concern include stereotyping on the basis of race, gender, and age; the presentation of violent images; and strong sexual content.

In addition to ad claims and copy, advertisers face ethical dilemmas in business transactions with clients, subcontractors, and partners, and with their own professional employees. These range from promises to clients made by an agency or campaign about what the agency can accomplish to what agencies charge for services. How advertisers treat clients and professionals, and how they are treated by clients and agencies, also present ethical dilemmas. The IAE premise to "Do the Right Thing" is directed to both professional employees and clients in their personal dealings.

Perhaps one of the toughest ethical dilemmas for advertising and PR professionals arises when a client or boss orders an employee to do something that is unethical. This can include falsifying or exaggerating the services provided or overbilling the client. For instance, a media buyer booking time on a particular network or station might be offered the incentive of a free vacation trip from the media company. However, the client may end up paying more for the media buy. Also, an agency might inappropriately obtain confidential information regarding a competitive agency's service that aids it in bidding for a client's business.

In our IAE Ad Ethics Certificate sessions, we take time for group discussions on "hypothetical" ethical dilemmas in the workplace. Here is an example: We've learned that one of our young professionals on a major account has lied to the client about what our agency can accomplish in our marketing plan. We are told that the client—not aware of the lie—wants and expects this to be accomplished. What are our ethical options with respect to interacting with the client and dealing with the young professional? What is your final recommendation as to the client and professional?

Another real-world dilemma could come to a young CEO of a small but growing ad agency in her response to a major client's order to do something unethical. On the one hand, it is "right" for her to say no. On the other hand, she may feel compelled to obey, fearful that she will lose the account and risk putting her employees out of work. She must consider that an unethical decision may have both short- and long-term consequences for her personally and for her employees.

The members of the IAE Advisory Council, who come from long and successful careers in the advertising and PR world, all emphasize the importance of ethics in resolving workplace dilemmas. David Bell, chair emeritus of IPG, urges that we find an ethical solution to provide the boss what he or she wants. At a 2012 American Academy of Advertising conference, he remarked, "If we can't find a way then we should confront the boss (or client) with the potential negative impact from the unethical conduct."

This section of the chapter concludes with a discussion of how we can inspire our professionals to practice enhanced advertising ethics. First, we need to create ethical cultures within our businesses that will guide and motivate our professionals. Turning to our experts in ethics, we learn first from Gene Ahner, who stresses, "A business organization is more than a group of people who happen to be contractually related to the company. We are, or must become, a community of shared values if we are to succeed" (Ahner, 2007, p. 55). Rush Kidder, who established the Institute for Global Ethics, puts it this way, "It is all about articulating shared values and developing a vision for the future— since that after all, is how consensus is built and gridlock broken" (Kidder, 2009, p.101). Agency values often come from the founder(s) and executive leaders. Again, Rich Stoddart cited Leo Burnett: "When a man [*sic*] knows deep in his bones what is right and keeps acting on it, he avoids the trap of compromise—he remains incorruptible (AAF Conference, 2012).

Company values should be written, posted, and distributed to all of the organization's members. A good example is Ketchum's Code of Business Conduct (2014). Ketchum, as a large organization with many employees, emphasizes the importance of its value system with a video directly from the CEO, teaches all new hires with a webinar in their first three months, and does a mandatory quiz annually to check that everyone knows the ethical values. Also, the Institute for Advertising Ethics encourages companies to "fully support" its Principles for Advertising Ethics and make them available to the company's professionals as part of the company values.

Next, it is crucial that ethical values are communicated throughout the company and to the company's subcontractors. Leo Burnett's ethical values are framed and adorn the hallways and offices of the agency. Smaller firms could do the same with live presentations by the executive leadership and one-on-one and small-group training.

Above all, we must create and sustain expectations that ethical concerns will be proactively expressed and discussed. We know this is difficult in a fast paced and competitive environment. But with consumers having online access, it is too late to deal with most ethical concerns after the fact. Our Institute for Advertising Ethics Principle 8 provides: "Advertisers and their agencies, and online and offline media, should discuss privately potential ethical concerns, and members of the team creating ads should be given permission to express internally their ethical concerns."

The point about giving permission to express ethical concerns is essential to the practice of enhanced ethics. It is critical that our professionals know they can express ethical concerns about ads or client interactions and that they are expected to do so, or they just might not do so.

Finally, David Bell's statement offers a powerful conclusion for this article. In an interview at the American Academy of Advertising Conference in 2012, he was asked how to inspire advertising professionals. He emphatically answered, "Tell them stories." He said that everyone in an organization should hear stories about the ethical dilemmas faced by the agency and let them feel the importance of being ethical. He said further, "Make it emotional, and then we react—not just rationally with rules."

With the awareness and practice of enhanced advertising ethics everyone benefits. First, enhanced ethics complements and supports our industry's excellent self-regulation programs. Second, improved ethics helps advertising and public relations as industries to win the trust of consumers in order to do the best job of building brand loyalty. Third, high ethical standards for practitioners provide a strong framework for individuals who want "To Do the Right Thing" in business and personally. And finally, enhanced advertising ethics benefits consumers who can more confidently purchase and use the products and services they seek.

References

AD Reviews "Geomean" Evidence (2014). Recommends Dyson Modify, Discontinue Claims for 2 Vacuum Cleaners; Finds Certain Claims Supported. Retrieved January 19, 2015 from: http://www.asrcreviews.org/2014/11/nad-reviews-geomean-evidence-recommends-dyson-modify-discontinue-claims-for-2-vacuum-cleaners-finds-certain-claims-supported/

Ahner, E. C. (2007). *Business Ethics: Making a Life, Not Just a Living*. Maryknoll, NY: Orbis Books.

Auto safety crusader Ralph Nader testifies before Congress (1966). Retrieved January 19, 2015 from http://www.history.com/this-day-in-history/auto-safety-crusader-ralph-nader-testifies-before-congress

CARU Finds Telebrands' 'Phantom Saucer' Ad Accurately Depicts Toy's Capabilities, Recommends Additional Disclosure (2014). Retrieved January 19, 2015 from http://www.asrcreviews.org/2014/08/caru-finds-telebrands-phantom-saucer-ad-accurately-depicts-toys-capabilities-recommends-additional-disclosure/

CARU Recommends IHOP Modify 'IHOP.com' Website to Better Disclose Advertising Within Game (2012). Retrieved January 19, 2015 from http://www.asrcreviews.

org/2012/09/caru-recommends-ihop-modify-ihop-com-website-to-better-disclose-advertising-within-game/

CBAI (2015). Retrieved January 20, 2015 from http://www.bbb.org/globalassets/local-bbbs/council-113/media/cfbai/program-and-core-principles_for-online-access.pdf

Duffy, M., Thorson, E., Choi, H., & Karaliova, T. (2014). A Mutualist Theory of Processing PSAs and Ethically Problematic Commercials. Accepted for presentation at the Digital Disruption to Journalism and Mass Communication Conference, October 3, Brussels.

Elliott, S. (2013). A message that tries to blend in. *The New York Times*, Dec. 12. Retrieved January 14, 2014 from http://www.nytimes.com/2013/12/13/business/media/a-message-that-tries-to-blend-in.html?_r=0

E-Marketer (2013, June 22). Seventy-three percent of online publishers offer native advertising. Retrieved January 14 from http://marketingland.com/73-of-online-publishers-offer-native-advertising-just-10-still-sitting-on-the-sidelines-emarketer-52506

Ethics and Principles, AAF (2015). Retrieved January 19, 2015 from http://www.aaf.org/institute-advertising-ethics

FCC. (2014, September 3). Verizon to pay $7.4 million to settle consumer privacy investigation. FCC. Retrieved January 17, 2015 from: http://www.fcc.gov/document/verizon-pay-74m-settle-privacy-investigation-0

FTC Approves Final Consent Settling Charges that Home Security Company ADT's Endorsements Deceived Consumers (2014). Retrieved January 17, 2015 from http://www.ftc.gov/news-events/press-releases/2014/06/ftc-approves-final-consent-settling-charges-home-security-company. Retrieved from http://www.oyez.org/cases/1970–1979/1975/1975_74_895

FTC Investigation of Ad Claims that Rice Krispies Benefits Children's Immunity Leads to Stronger Order Against Kellogg (2010). Retrieved January 19, 2015 from: http://www.ftc.gov/news-events/press-releases/2010/06/ftc-investigation-ad-claims-rice-krispies-benefits-childrens

FTC Seeks to Halt 10 Operators of Fake News Sites from Making Deceptive Claims About Acai Berry Weight Loss Products (2011). Retrieved January 19, 2015 from http://www.ftc.gov/news-events/press-releases/2011/04/ftc-seeks-halt-10-operators-fake-news-sites-making-deceptive

Google Will Pay $22.5 Million to Settle FTC Charges it Misrepresented Privacy Assurances to Users of Apple's Safari Internet Browser (2012, August. 9). Retrieved January 16, 2015 from http://www.ftc.gov/news-events/press-releases/2012/08/google-will-pay-225-million-settle-ftc-charges-it-misrepresented

Institute for Advertising Ethics (2011). Reynolds Journalism Institute. Retrieved January 19, 2015 from http://www.rjionline.org/institute-for-advertising-ethics

Ketchum's Code of Business Conduct (2014). Retrieved January 19, 2015 from http://www.ketchum.com/sites/default/files/2013_ungc_ketchum_report_-_04.18.14.pdf

Kidder, R. (2009). *How Good People Make Tough Choices.* New York: Harper.

Marketing and direct-to-consumer advertising (DTCA) of pharmaceuticals (2013). Blog on the National Conference of State Legislatures. Retrieved September 17, 2015 from http://www.ncsl.org/research/health/marketing-and-advertising-of-pharmaceuticals.aspx

Missouri School of Journalism Research. (2014). Retrieved January 19, 2015 from http://www.rjionline.org/institute-for-advertising-ethics

NARB Panel Recommends BP Lubricants Discontinue 'Stronger' Claims Based on Company's 'Torture' Test (2014). Retrieved January 19, 2015 from http://www. asrcreviews.org/2014/06/narb-panel-recommends-bp-lubricants-discontinue-stronger-claims-based-on-companys-torture-test/

Pfizer, Inc. (1972). 3 Trade Reg. Rep. 20,056 FTC, July 11, 1972.

Sony Computer Entertainment America To Provide Consumer Refunds To Settle FTC Charges Over Misleading Ads For PlayStation Vita Gaming Console (2014). Retrieved Jan. 19, 2015 from http://www.ftc.gov/news-events/press-releases/2014/11/sony-computer-entertainment-america-provide-consumer-refunds

The importance of being ethical (2000). *Inc.* Magazine, Nov. 30. Retrieved January 19, 2015 from http://www.inc.com/articles/2000/11/14278.html

Virginia Pharmacy Board v. Virginia Consumer Council (1976). Docket No.74–895. Retrieved January 14, 2015 from http://www.oyez.org/cases/1970–1979/1975/1975_74_895

Winkler, R. (2014). Ads tied to web searches criticized as deceptive. *Wall Street Journal*, Oct. 13. Retrieved January 16, 2015 from http://www.wsj.com/articles/ads-tied-to-web-searches-criticized-as-deceptive-1413226602

16 The Minimum and Maximums of Professional Ethics Codes

Chris Roberts

CHAPTER SUMMARY

Now here at "The Rock" we have two basic rules. Memorize them so that you can say them in your sleep. The first rule is: Obey all rules. Secondly: Do not write on the walls, as it takes a lot of work to erase writing off of the walls.
—Dep. Barney Fife, *The Andy Griffith Show*
"The Big House"—Season 3, Episode 32, May 6, 1963

Almost every corporation, news outlet, and promotional agency has codes of ethics, mission statements, and vision and values. Sometimes these codes are rigorously followed and are part of the culture of the organization. Often, however, they are statements posted on boardroom walls that have little application in the day-to-day life of employees and other stakeholders. This chapter points out what's wrong and what's right with ethics codes for media persuaders. What's wrong includes ethics statements that are loaded with contradictions, those written in abstract and fuzzy generalities, those that are really window dressing and not taken seriously, are out of date, and those that make little difference in the real world of the industry. However, codes of ethics can be meaningful in many ways. They can remind practitioners about the balance of loyalties and responsibilities to clients, their colleagues, publics, and themselves. Regular updates of codes can help practitioners deal with changing ethical challenges and mores. Most important, good ethical guidelines can remind us of what we value and what's important in our working lives. Put simply, identifying what is and what should be important to us offers guides for action.

Introduction

Many ethics codes read like Deputy Barney Fife's rules to new prisoners at the Mayberry Courthouse Jail—painfully obvious, a little silly, and little help to anyone but fools and youngsters who have never been told that it is wrong to scribble on someone else's walls. Yet nearly every professional organization for media persuaders has its own ethics code, as do many individual advertising and public relations firms. Indeed, a professional group without an ethics code may not be perceived as a "professional" group at all (Frankel, 1989). As this chapter will argue, codes of ethics are helpful because they give practitioners, the industry, and the public a starting point in thinking about the obvious wrongs and multiple gray areas of persuasion ethics. But as it also will argue, some persuasion-focused codes have inherent limitations, because they are focused more on law than ethics, making them of little practical use when applied to thorny ethical issues. Sometimes codes may even be dangerous when misunderstood and misused.

Problems with Organizational Ethics Codes

Plenty of reasons exist to dismiss ethics codes as relics that "probably should be relegated to a framed wall hanging" to be ignored by media practitioners "who have advanced beyond their internships," as *Journal of Mass Media Ethics* editors Jay Black and Ralph Barney wrote in the journal's inaugural issue (1985, p. 27).[1] As they and others have noted (for examples see Bivins, 2009; Black & Roberts, 2011; Johannesen, 2002), ethics codes aimed for persuasion-focused communicators:

- Reek in contradictions. The fundamental ethical quandary for persuasion-based communicators centers on to whom final loyalty is owed—to the client paying the bills or to the public. Yet the Public Relations Society of America's code says its members "are faithful to those we represent, while honoring our obligation to serve the public interest," with no insight on who wins and who loses when those competing loyalties conflict. As another example, the International Public Relations Association's (2011) Code of Conduct says practitioners have duties to be both transparent and to maintain confidentialities, with no insight on which becomes the actual duty (Ross, 1930) when those competing values conflict. As this chapter will discuss, codes ultimately do not answer gray questions that require black-or-white decisions of loyalties and obligations.
- Do not always explain what they mean. While every media code calls for practitioners to tell the "truth," different lines of work have different working definitions of truth that go undefined in their codes (see, for example, Bivins, 2009, p. 116). This chapter will discuss this concern in greater detail.
- Come across as self-serving. Some industry codes pay lip service to "the public good" but also serve a purpose of protecting the industry's own interests. An example may be in Principle 8 of the Institute for Advertising Ethics, which says advertisers and agencies "should discuss privately potential ethical concerns, and members of the team creating ads should be given permission to express internally their ethical concerns" (American Advertising Federation, 2011). Some might interpret the "discuss privately" and "express internally" statements to be really about limiting

public embarrassment and limiting transparency. At the very least, it seems less demanding than the code of the Society of Professional Journalists. Its 1996 code told members to "[e]xpose unethical practices of journalists and the news media." The 2014 code goes even further, telling members to "expose unethical conduct in journalism, including within their organizations."

- Are really about persuading the public that persuaders are not evil. Simply having a code of ethics has a public relations value, as it sends the signal that you thought enough about ethics to write down your thoughts. However, having a code does not foster adherence or attention to ethics in an ethically questionable group. Pirates had ethics codes (Berderman, 2008), as does the Mafia (Pisa, 2007) and the porn industry (Free Speech Coalition, n.d.).
- Often are decrees tossed from upon high by the bosses, not real-world documents that bubble up from the people who do the real work and face new ethical issues.
- Seek conformity, as they often have an underlying assumption of "professionalism" that comes when everyone follows the same rules. Such codes can limit people who might realize that "professional" behavior is not a high-enough standard.
- Mix highfalutin maxims with "no-duh" legal requirements and moral absolutes without distinguishing among them. Again, from the PRSA code: "Disclose promptly any existing or potential conflict of interest to affected clients or organizations" seems to be a rule, but it shares the same code as the aspirational, "We respect all opinions and support the right of free expression."
- Sometimes remain static in a changing world, which is of significant concern as new digital technologies bring new (or at least speeded-up) ethical challenges to practitioners and their audiences.
- Are ultimately unenforceable when coming from professional organizations. The worst a group can do is kick out a bad guy.
- Become an enforceable employment contract—not an ethics code—when required by management. Should a boss be able to fire workers who fail to meet an aspirational goal on every occasion, especially when the goal includes fuzzy language? Take, for example, the code of ethics for Hill+Knowlton Strategies' Spain operations (n.d.), which says the firm will communicate information on its business "in a clear and precise" manner. So does the first long-winded sentence get an employee suspended or fired?
- Make little real-world difference in the industry, as studies have shown no relationship in the actions of organizations with and without ethics codes. A typical worker rarely takes a second look at an ethics code, much less consults it when making decisions (Bowen, 2007).
- Cannot persuade the public that practitioners are ethical. Despite their codes of ethics, advertising practitioners continue to rank low in Gallup's

annual public rankings of ethics in professions (2014). The most recent ranking said 42% of respondents thought ad practitioners had low or very low ethics; just 10% thought ad practitioners had high or very high ethical standards. That was down from 14% in 2013 when only car sales-people, politicians, and lobbyists ranked worse. (Public relations prac-titioners should not think they get off easy here. PR is not a job listed in the poll but remember that lobbyists are in the PR business (Hanson, 2014, p. 294).)

- Cannot replace an ultimate goal of ethics—for individuals to move beyond rules imposed by others, to grow morally and intellectually, to expand their empathy, and to think for themselves. Codes give us that starting point, but Aristotle, Kant, and others said we may not ultimately be ethical beings until we make up our own minds and then live by our principles. For example, a truly ethical PR practitioner never "intentionally leaks pro-prietary information to the detriment of some other party" not because the code (Public Relations Society of America, 2000) says it is a no-no but because a morally developed person keeps promises. But that practitioner also knows not to make deals to stay silent when it is clear that silence will be deadly to the public.

These criticisms of professional organization ethics codes do not mean you should shoot down every ethics code you see. As others have pointed out, codes serve important purposes despite their many limitations. Codes can be tools to train neophytes, providing an educational function. They justify their profession to the public, telling others that we take ethics seriously. (Or, more cynically, they serve as public relations tools in hopes of persuading the public that we must be good because we "have" ethics, or at least an ethics codes.) They remind practitioners about the profession's ideals, providing fundamen-tal statements about the principles, values, and loyalties to be held dear. In public relations, codes can remind practitioners to make decisions that con-sider the delicate balance between loyalties to their clients, the public, other practitioners, their employers, and to themselves. In advertising, codes can help practitioners move "beyond obligation" to their clients and produce cam-paigns that "align the clients' best interests with those of the world with which we communicate" (Griffin & Morrison, 2008, p. 280).

The process of making a code, or updating a current code, forces writers to wrestle with both continuing and emerging issues in the industry. Even as bedrock ethical principles remain unchanged, the ethics codes that espouse those ideals must change to consider new laws, new-and-better thinking about ethics, and new standards and practices for this era of new communication technologies. This is especially true in this new millennium. Pre-Internet mass communication was a one-way street; today mass communicators compete in a bumper-car world of communication where everyone can shout as loudly as everyone else can. As a result, ethics codes are being updated across media pro-fessions. The Society of Professional Journalists members approved an update of their famous code in mid-2014 with an eye toward including the concept of transparency and describing ethics in an age of falling revenue and rising social media. In 2011, the International Public Relations Association (2011) introduced a single code of conduct that updated codes originally published in 1961, 1965, and 2007, creating the document that aspires to describe ethical PR across countries and cultures. That same year, the American Association of Advertising Agencies (2011) updated its standards and practices documents, and the American Advertising Federation (2011) released updated principles and practices in conjunction with the Institute for Advertising Ethics at the University of Missouri (2011). The new code replaced an older code, providing insight into such things as online privacy marketing techniques that did not exist in the pre-Internet era when the previous code was written.

In Advertising, Emphasizing the Minimums

For all their lack of teeth, ethics codes have a bite—particularly for persuasion communicators operating in nations with a "co-regulation" approach to curbing abuses of commercial speech (Spence & Van Heekeren, 2005, p. 22). America is among the nations where the government sets basic rules, has courts and agencies to sanction the most egregious sinners, but also gives industry-sponsored agencies the power to deal with other cases.

Co-regulation, however, collides with First Amendment freedoms; after all, its promise that Congress shall make no law abridging the freedom of the press comes with no mention of any obligation to be fair. In fact, the First Amendment was born amid a partisan press that bickered with itself, played favorites, and had no sense of objectivity. But as concerns about social responsibility cropped up in the 20th century, there were efforts to create formal media accountability systems. Those systems, especially for journalism, did not take root. Journalism, which revels in having few government-enforced regulations, experimented with press councils to let people who feel they had been wronged take their complaints to independent fact-finding groups instead of suing in federal and state courts. The National News Council lasted nearly a decade in the 1970s; the final press council, in Washington state, closed in May 2014, a victim of tough economic times for the news industry and news gatherers who refused to participate in a process that second-guessed their decisions (Connelly, 2014). On the other hand, the U.S. public relations industry, which shares the First Amendment freedom of journalists, has never had an outside council to hear complaints.

The advertising industry, however, has much less freedom of speech than journalism and public relations, as the government has created laws restricting the claims that can be made in commercial speech and agencies, such as the Food and Drug Administration and the Federal Trade Commission, that enforce those rules. (This is why, for example, you don't see tobacco ads on television.) As a result, the industry has turned to co-regulation as its best hope to control its standards and practices. The result is the national Advertising

Self-Regulatory Council (2012), the new name for the National Advertising Review Council administered by the Council of Better Business Bureaus. It oversees an alphabet-soup collection of organizations that handle self-regulation among general advertisers, those who market to children, electronic retailing, and online ads. Advertisers generally prefer the self-regulation approach because it is faster, cheaper, and keeps out the government. An added benefit for advertisers is a process that is not fully transparent, because only the decision is released, not the information collected during an investigation that could be embarrassing or taken out of context.

Advertising industry ethics codes have become part of the social contract for co-regulation. However, these codes can blur aspirational goals and minimum expectations, which can be problematic when applied in quasi-legal proceedings. As an example, take the "online behavioral advertising" industry—companies that use "cookies" and other software techniques to track what you do online and then use that information to target specific ads at you. What they do can be useful, as advertisers do not waste money carpet bombing the world and instead aim ads at you, peddling products consumers are more likely to care about. (This can backfire, of course—a few years ago, when working on Chapter 7 of a book, a colleague using Gmail received ads for bankruptcy assistance because Google read his e-mail and thought he was talking about Chapter 7 bankruptcy.)

A few months after the Federal Trade Commission (2009) revised its policies regarding industry practices, the industry[2] produced "Self-Regulatory Principles for Online Behavioral Advertising." One industry group, the Direct Marketing Association, touted in a press release that it built those principles into its "Guidelines for Ethical Business Practice" required of all of its members (Interactive Advertising Bureau, 2010). The seven principles are written as aspirational goals—educating the public about online advertising, being transparent in disclosing what data they collect from online consumers, how they keep that data secure, having consumers understand major changes in data collection policies, being sensitive in collecting data from children, and keeping companies accountable. These are all useful standards, but it is important to not confuse these principles with what they really are—accepting the government's minimum standards in a veneer of ethical principles in hopes of keeping the government out of the nuts and bolts of regulating the industry.

The word "ethics" does not appear anywhere in the 48-page document. What matters in the document are the technical definitions and the specific practices that online advertisers can and cannot do. Failure to follow those principles can earn a slap on the wrist from self-regulators, such as its May 2014 "recommendation" that Tablooa LLC not use labels such as "recommended videos" or "more in the news" to link people to its advertising (Advertising Self-Regulatory Council, 2014). Those same self-regulators, however, said that marketers can use the phrase "sponsored content" instead of (in this writer's opinion, the more precise word) "advertisement," because there is no evidence that consumers "do not understand the words 'sponsored content' or 'promoted content' to mean 'paid content.'"[3] (Its press release did not mention whether there has been any studies to see if audiences confuse the terms; there is a difference between saying "no evidence" and saying "no evidence because no one has looked for evidence.")

The National Advertising Division is one part of the Advertising Self-Regulatory Council, and it works to review factual statements in national ads and to mediate disputes between advertisers that could easily have become messy and expensive court battles. The Division notes that its job is to ensure that ad claims "convey truth and accurate messages to consumers," while the job of government regulators is to ensure that products sold are safe and effective. It is a distinction with a difference. Ultimately, however, the advertising industry's definitions and practices are tied directly to government agencies, such as the Food and Drug Administration and Federal Trade Commission, which make rules and enforce them. The industry's self-regulation has its limits. While Tablooa may be unethical when using the phrase "more in the news" to link to an ad, Google paid a $22.5 million fine after the FTC caught the company, whose motto is "Don't be evil," fiddling with privacy settings in Apple's web browser to deliver its ads to Safari users (Miller, 2012). It was a breach not adjudicated by the Advertising Self-Regulatory Council, even though its "educating" and "transparency" principles frown upon the practice, the detailed guidelines mention "cookies," and Google is an active member of industry groups with Council ties.

Google, in fact, has a great deal of need for both the Council and federal regulators, because some of its customers are advertisers who push the edges of law and ethics (see, for example, Perez, 2010). In 2014, Google said it disabled 524 million evil ads placed by its advertising customers who were selling counterfeit goods, linking to malware and spyware, or tricking consumers clicking a link. Google banned 214,000 bad advertisers and kicked out 33,000 merchants who broke its Google Shopping rules (Marvin, 2015; Google, 2015, February 3).

Advertising Codes Do Value the Law

Codes of ethics are designed to remind us what should be important to us. Codes are statements of "values," the abstract principles that people or groups believe to be of worth. Values often compete with one another for primacy, and humans tend to sort our values (whether knowingly or not) into a ranked hierarchy. Our belief system leads to specific behaviors. Social psychology says those bedrock values guide our system of beliefs, which in turn determine our attitudes, which ultimately lead to the actions that we take (for more information, see Pojman, 1995, Chapter 5). If you possess the physical and mental capabilities, then you act in ways that are (whether knowingly or not) consistent with your values. Put more simply: If you want to know what is important to you, then track how you spend your time and your money. So if you tell a professor, "I didn't have time to read the chapter you assigned to be read before class," what you are implicitly saying is, "Your assignment wasn't important to me because I don't value your class as much as I value other things."

Looking at the Comparative Codes of Ethics

Because codes of ethics are fundamental statements about values, it is useful to analyze those codes to look for patterns of values and to compare those values and patterns to other industries. This author did that a few years ago (Roberts, 2012), describing values found in 15 media ethics codes for journalists, bloggers, advertisers, and PR practitioners. For this chapter, the analysis was updated to 232 values in communication codes after replacing an older code from the International Public Relations Association's older code with its 2011 Code of Conduct.

The value descriptions were derived from categories described by social psychologist Shalom Schwartz (1992) who spent years defining and comparing values of people all across the globe. He and researchers who followed (Rohan, 2000) described two pairs of competing motivational dimensions—a tension between values that focus on society versus those that focus on individual outcomes, and a tension between values that focus on organization (and "conservation") versus those that focus on individual "opportunity" and openness to change.

Inside of those four higher-type values are a total of 44 values that cluster into 10 value types. These value types compete with one another. For example, the value type of "benevolence," which has general society as its focus, would often conflict with the value type of "hedonism," which is the focus in individual outcomes. And the value type "self-direction," inside general focus on opportunity, competes with the value type "conformity," which is inside the organization focus. More simply put: If you're a conformer, you're not self-directed because you're following others.

Advertising Codes are Insufficient in Many Ways

The analysis included five codes from marketing and advertising groups—the "advertising principles of American business" from the American Advertising Federation (1984), the 1990 statement of principles from the American Association of Advertising Agencies (2011), the American Marketing Association's statement of ethics (2008), the "standards of practice" from the Institute for Advertising Ethics (2011), and the Word of Mouth Marketing Association's code of ethics (2011). As Table 16.1 shows, those five codes have a combined 49 values.

The key takeaway from the analysis is not surprising—ethics codes mostly talk about how we should treat other people. In every case, a majority of values in media ethics codes focus on "social context outcomes," the values that reflect our "self-transcendence" as we think about others more than ourselves. Nearly two-thirds of the value statements in media codes fit neatly into categories of "universalism" (described as "understanding, appreciation, tolerance,

Table 16.1 Values in ethics codes by value category and code types (N = 232)

Larger Focus/ Value Category	News (n = 93)	Blogging (n = 12)	Advertising/ Marketing (n = 49)	Public Relations (n = 78)
Social context outcomes				
Universalism	38%	67%	27%	13%
Benevolence	32%	25%	29%	47%
Individual outcomes				
Achievement	–	–	6%	7%
Power	–	–	–	10%
Organization				
Conformity	13%	8%	37%	17%
Tradition	2%	–	–	3%
Security	–	–	–	
Opportunity				
Self–direction	15%	–	2%	4%
Stimulation	–	–	–	
Hedonism	–	–	–	

Note: Advertising/marketing rounds up to 101%.

and protection for the welfare of all people and for nature") or "benevolence (described as "preservation and enhancement of the welfare of people with whom one is in frequent personal contact" (Schwartz, 1992).

Advertising codes had the lowest percentage of values in social outcome categories—still a majority of all values at 56% but lower than blogging (92%), journalism (70%), and PR (60%). It may be because the ad codes have other things they need to talk about—or that at its core advertising is more self-focused than other forms of communication. Having said that, ad codes have plenty of statements about serving society. Typical is the second sentence from the AAAA's principles, which says "advertising agencies must recognize an obligation, not only to their clients, but to the public, the media they employ, and to each other." Every advertising code has a sentence like this to remind practitioners to reach for a higher moral plain and take other people into consideration when making decisions. A code that does not mention duty to outsiders would not be an ethics code at all, hardly different from the self-serving codes of pirates and Mafioso.

Where ad codes differed from other media industries was that 37% of its values related to "conformity," described as "restraint of actions, inclinations, and impulses likely to upset or harm others and violate social expectations or norms." This is the largest single category for ad codes and more than twice as high as any other industry. The AAAA and American Advertising Federation codes had single mentions of good taste and decency, which connect with the value of "politeness." But most striking were the 15 mentions in ad codes related to "obedience," described by Kaptein & Schwartz (2008) as being dutiful and meeting obligations. Essentially, these were values in codes that told advertising practitioners to obey the law. The AAAA's "creative code" specifically says members should not knowingly create ads with:

a) False or misleading statements or exaggerations, visual or verbal.
b) Testimonials that do not reflect the real opinion of the individual(s) involved.
c) Price claims that are misleading.
d) Claims insufficiently supported or that distort the true meaning or practicable application of statements made by professional or scientific authority.

Similarly, the Institute for Advertising Ethics' 2011 code says advertisers should "follow federal, state and local advertising laws," which sounds a great deal like Deputy Fife's not-so-helpful first rule: "Obey all rules." Each of these is a minimum standard, an appeal to advertising professionals to obey the many laws that when broken lead to trouble with government regulators. People and organizations who obey minimum standards that, if violated would lead to punishment, do not deserve praise. (When was the last time you received a blue ribbon because you had not stabbed anyone just for giggles?) Perhaps one reason why the Gallup poll (2014) shows that ad practitioners are held in low esteem is because of this appeal to minimum standards—and because the public see ads that may not technically break laws but certainly fail to meet high ethical standards related to stereotyping, sexism, greed, or conspicuous consumption. This is a strong and important critique.

You're perhaps saying to yourself, "Only a louse would break such cut-and-dried laws." However, laws are bent and broken from time to time. A recent example is "Lice Shield," a line of products designed to help with *pediculosis capitis*, the personal- and community-health issue related to the blood-sucking parasites that infest 6 million to 12 million Americans each year (Ohio Department of Health, 2014). The company approved ads with the tag line "Don't Get Lice, Get Lice Shield," which implies that the shampoo and other products would "prevent or reduce the risk of" head lice. Lice Shield's print ads included a scientific chart claiming that using its products produced an 86% repellency rate compared to doing nothing. The U.S. Federal Trade Commission (2014) was having none of that, writing that in "truth and in fact, scientific tests do not prove that, when used as directed, Lice Shield products significantly reduce the likelihood or chance of a head lice infestation." Lornamead Inc., the products' maker, was ordered to pay $500,000 for the ads and told to provide at least one real scientific study on humans before making its claims (2014).

Lice Shield's ad makers drew legal sanction and ethical condemnation for failing to meet the federal rules that are reflected in the minimum standards of advertising codes of ethics. But do advertisers who meet these low standards deserve praise? Maybe not. It is easy to think of many advertisers, politicians, businesspeople, journalists, and others who justify an unethical decision by saying "I followed the law." A concern about such law-driven, minimalist codes is that they can confuse young practitioners into thinking that obeying laws is all there is to ethics or when using PR documents to bamboozle the public into thinking that practitioners are ethical when they are merely following legal rules or other minimum standards.

Public Relations Codes Value Gaining, Maintaining, and Using Power

Like their advertising cousins, codes for public relations practitioners also have a jumble of highs and lows. There are high-minded maximums, such as the Canadian Public Relations Society's edict that members "shall practice public relations according to the highest professional standards" (2014). There also are minimums, such as the reminder from the International Public Relations Association that members should "[n]either directly nor indirectly offer nor give any financial or other inducement to public representatives or the media, or other stakeholders" (2011). Translation: Don't bribe anybody.

An analysis of those two PR codes, plus codes from the Public Relations Society of America (2000) and Association of Business Communicators (2014), shows a different dynamic at work. PR codes reveal the industry's dual concerns about power—the need to pursue power in order to be able to influence leaders of organizations who use PR, as well as the understanding that practitioners have power as they shape public agendas and provide the voice for the powerful organizations that use them.

To be powerful, PR practitioners must be heard and respected. The author's analysis showed 10% of code statements were related to social power, defined as "control over others." Codes specifically mentioned the need to "enhance the profession" (PRSA) and "not engage in professional or personal conduct that will bring discredit to themselves, the Society or the practice of public relations" (Canadian Public Relations Society), which are related to individualistic outcomes. The PRSA code says this is necessary to "strengthen the public's trust in the profession," which is related to how the PR industry questions itself about whether it has its own image problem (Callison, 2001) and its own legitimacy (Merkelsen, 2011). It also is related to the need for PR practitioners to be perceived as valuable counsel by corporate executives who ultimately decide the messages and strategies of their organizations, as well as the need for practitioners to serve as a "corporate conscience" to their bosses (Bowen, 2008). PR founding father Edward Bernays created the term "PR counsel," taking the term purposely from "legal counsel" in hopes of equating the need for PR experts to the need for lawyers in the minds of business executives (Ewen, 1996, p. 163.)

While codes in other media professions remind practitioners to do right, they do not always state why. These PR statements provide the reason—that doing wrong harms the image of PR, which is a tacit understanding of the need to gain and maintain social power. Perhaps the writers of PR codes deserve praise for admitting what codes in other professions do not admit, that ethics has a relationship with perception.

The second discussion of power in PR is about the positions of strength from which practitioners work when compared to their audiences. PR codes rated lowest among media codes for "universalism" at 13%. The International Public Relations Association is the most universal, with multiple mentions of the United Nations' charter and declaration of human rights. And while PR codes discuss values of broad-mindedness and social justice, those mentions show up at half the rate of advertising (27%) and far behind journalism (38%). At the end of the day, it can be argued that PR's broad-mindedness and social justice do not require it to become advocates for those who are not its clients in the marketplace of ideas. By this definition of values, the argument can be made that, just as an ethical defense lawyer has no obligation to argue for the prosecution, PR practitioners can be ethical while serving their own clients and still have no obligation to argue for others. The PR-counsel-as-lawyer comparison goes only so far; unlike the checks and balances in the legal system, such as discovery and equal opportunity to make arguments, PR practitioners have no such rules of fairness in the court of public opinion (Black & Roberts, 2011, p. 276).

Concerns of power reveal themselves in the value category of "benevolence," which at 47% of all values statements in PR codes ranks the highest of any industry. These values are connected to both intramural relationships with the public (including general audiences, news media, governments, etc.) and intermural relationships with clients and fellow practitioners. In both cases, the strength comes from the power of information that practitioners may or may not reveal to others. For external audiences, benevolence values are related to honesty (such as the IRPA's reminder to "take all reasonable steps to ensure the truth and accuracy of all information provided), the related value of transparency in not hiding their hands as they seek to set public agendas, and in showing respect to the public (such PRSA code's reminder to build "mutual understanding, credibility, and relationships among a wide array of institutions and audiences." The IRPA code goes even further, reminding practitioners that they should respect "the rights of all parties involved to state their case and express their views," which would suggest that PR may be unfair when it silences others to win instead of winning by having better (and better-told) arguments than competing voices.

The codes also give a great deal of attention to concerns that PR practitioners should work and play well with each other. Among advertising codes, only the American Association of Advertising Agencies discusses proprieties among inside-the-industry players, which is unsurprising because it is in the best interest of these players to act respectfully among themselves. Among other guidelines, the codes include specific sections on competition, the need to not steal ideas from each other, reminders that practitioners ought not spread rumors about each other, to not promise results they cannot deliver, and to protect proprietary information they glean while doing business. The Public Relations Society of America code is especially inward focused, with intramural statements folded into the sections related to practitioner expertise, fair competition among firms, safeguarding confidences, conflicts of interest, and enhancing the PR profession.

Loyalties and Truth—Where Persuasion Ethics Codes Fall Short

Without diving too deeply into metaethics, the study of the definitions of what morality itself is, it is safe to say that key concerns of ethics are the nature of loyalty and the definition of truth. Many ethical decisions require practitioners to determine who deserves the higher loyalty when there is competition between those who deserve your loyalty—your clients, the public, the government that regulates you, your boss, your fellow workers, others in your profession, your family, and yourself. They can be divided into two categories of loyalties. One is unsentimental loyalties, which are transitory and based on professional relationships. (A surgeon generally has a moral obligation to operate on me even if that surgeon does not like me personally. After being loyal and repairing me, any loyalty ends.) Other loyalties are sentimental, which are generally less transitory loyalties based on bloodlines, gratitude, or voluntary association. (I am loyal to you because you have been good to me or because you are my mother.) True professionals distinguish among these loyalty types and work to meet obligations in both.

When loyalties conflict, the test of ethics is deciding who deserves top loyalty and then acting upon it. For example, for a college student, it may be the competition of going to work even when he or she does not want to (an unsentimental loyalty to the boss) or to hang out with friends (a sentimental loyalty.) In the world of practitioners, troubles will erupt when clients ask you to do something unethical to keep their business, to disseminate incorrect information, or otherwise create a campaign that takes advantage of the public by treating them as means to your and your client's ends.

Even thornier is the notion of truth, which for professional communicators has been defined along a continuum of uppercase TRUTH to blatant lies (Deaver, 1990). This continuum places journalist news (defined as the intent to inform accurately and without bias) above public relations and advertising, which is the intent to persuade by telling the truth but not the whole truth. As Bivins (2009) wrote, the work that persuasion practitioners do is ethical: "Unless the claim is absolutely false or the information inaccurate, the truth is not being altered—the message is merely being selectively presented" (p. 119). The business of persuading is not inherently unethical, but this allowance for an "incomplete truth" leads to decisions that practitioners must make in every instance of deciding what "truth" to present.

For advertising, "truth" can be defined as both a binary state of "accurate/inaccurate." As the Lice Shield example shows, the government requires that measurable claims be accurate. The literature of epistemology would suggest that Lice Shield fell short in its use of a "correspondence" theory of truth, the notion that a statement has a true or false relationship to objective reality. But advertising has another working definition of "truth," a purposeful fuzziness designed to support what it hopes will be presumed true by audiences regardless of objective reality. The industry calls it "puffery"—defined by the *Oxford Dictionary of English* as "exaggerated or false praise"—a practice intentionally fuzzy and perfectly legal. Even though Pizza Hut tried, it could not convince federal courts that Papa John's "Better Ingredients. Better Pizza" slogan was a proposal of fact that could therefore be proven factually inaccurate. A court ruled that "better" is so vague as to be an opinion, which is why that claim remains on pizza boxes (Guarnani & Talati, 2008). That sort of truth may be described under the "coherence" theory of truth, which says truth must connect with other things we believe to be true. (The problem is making sure that our version of truth matches external reality.)

For PR, truth can lie somewhere in the middle, aided by the post-structuralist argument that all truth is "socially and contestable" (Weaver, Motion, & Roper, 2006, p. 8) and the goal of public relations to help shape a society's beliefs about individual truths. There is too much to be said about the nature of truth in public relations to put in this chapter or to describe that fine line where selective truth telling veers into lies. While each case differs, it is fair to say that ethical lapses begin when audience members lose their autonomy because they have been misled by the information provided (or not provided) by the speaker.

Codes of ethics fall particularly short in helping practitioners make decisions when dilemmas of truth and loyalty occur. In every case, codes remind practitioners to be loyal and to tell the truth. But those reminders are not particularly helpful. We could pick any of several codes, but for this example we chose the code from the Public Relations Society of America (2000), which says: "We are faithful to those we represent, while honoring our obligation to serve the public interest." Anyone in the PR business, however, can describe plenty of situations where it is impossible to serve both masters, and the code does not say who deserves the higher loyalty when conflict occurs. The PRSA's code and pledge use the word "truth" four times, but never defines it. So what happens when larger truth collides with the competing interests of the client and the public? The code offers no advice.

A Case Study: What Help Can Codes Provide?

Ethical issues appear at all levels, from the lowest intern deciding what to tell the boss to the corporation itself deciding who to accept as clients. While some ethical concerns are well above an intern's pay grade (assuming interns are paid, which is a corporate ethical issue), think about what assistance a code of ethics can and cannot provide in the following case study:

Ketchum Inc. is one of the United States' largest public relations, marketing, and advertising firms, with more than 2,000 employees working in 70 countries (Ketchum Inc., 2014) after merging with a German company in 2009. Its clients have included many U.S. federal agencies, including the army and the Internal Revenue Service. Among its clients is the Russian Federation, which has been paid at least $10 million to handle that nation's public relations efforts in the United States (Elliott, 2013), even as the United States and other nations have condemned the Russian government for restricting free speech among citizens, for jailing dissidents, for anti-gay laws, and for its military forays into Crimea and Ukraine.

Among its work, Ketchum pitched a column under Vladimir Putin's byline (2013) published in the *New York Times*. The paper's editorial page editor justified publication in order to fulfill the paper's mission of providing points of view to readers, including those "contrary to *The Times's* own point of view" (Sullivan, 2013). Max Fisher of the *Washington Post* questioned the truthfulness of a Ketchum spokesperson who said Putin wrote it himself (2013a) and also said the piece had "a number of valid and even compelling points, but there is an undeniable hypocrisy and even some moments of dishonesty between the lines" (2013b).

The company also runs www.ThinkRussia.com, an English-language site that "offers news and shares perspectives on Russia, from global and domestic policy matters to the country's quality of life and economic and social modernization." It claims to provide "a space to identify opportunities and challenges, and focus on the plans and steps underway to address them" (ThinkRussia. com, 2015). But missing from the promised news, perspectives, and challenges about Russia is some harsh truth. Readers at the site in late May 2014 could learn of Russian aid to flood victims in the Balkans (ThinkRussia.com, 2014), for example, but not find a substantial mention of Ukraine in more than a year. They could find dozens of stories and videos about the 2014 Winter Olympics in Sochi, but no mention that the G8 economic summit became the G7 summit (without Russia) when leaders of other nations moved the June 2014 meetings from Sochi to protest actions in Crimea and Ukraine.

The company has sought to justify its actions through statements when journalists question its relationship with Russia. The company notes that is follows U.S. law, which requires it to register as a foreign agent representing another nation, including the amount of money it receives from the Russian government and Gazprom, the government-owned natural gas company. The company notes that it does not advise the Russian Federation on foreign policy and has obeyed rules related to U.S. sanctions against Russia. "Our work continues to focus on supporting economic development and investment in the country and facilitating the relationship between representatives of the Russian Federation and the Western media," Ketchum told the *Washington Post* when asked about its Russian dealings (Yeager, 2014).

The case brings to mind many questions centering on loyalties and truth:

- Should the firm be representing Russia to U.S. publics? Should a firm represent both the U.S. government and an oppositional foreign government? If so, at what point should lines be drawn?
- Should Ketchum employees be allowed to refuse to work on the account for ethical reasons, and without sanction?

- While Ketchum notes that it is working on economic/development matters but not foreign policy for Russia, is that a distinction without a difference?
- What obligations do PR practitioners providing content for ThinkRussia. com have in telling a larger truth that goes beyond the happy stories. Should the site claim to report "news" that others would say is fluff that embarrassingly ignores the reality?

These are difficult questions, and the PRSA code provides little help beyond pointing out where ethical dilemmas may lie.

For loyalties, the PRSA code says practitioners should be "faithful to those we represent, while honoring our obligation to serve the public interest." The loyalty-to-client edict, followed directly by the public interest reminder, encapsulates public relations' fundamental loyalty issues. With no definition of "public interest," practitioners are left to create their own in a marketplace that, by definition, assumes that people will have varied interests.

The loyalty discussion in the PRSA code says firms should "decline representation of clients or organizations that urge or require actions contrary to" the code, but it provides few guidelines about what in the code matters. The code's credo that practitioners "support the right of free expression" might say Russia shouldn't be a client because it systematically (and, sometimes, violently) limits free speech among its citizens, but the credo that practitioners "provide a voice in the marketplace of ideas, facts, and viewpoints to aid informed public debate" would argue in favor of keeping the client.

For questions of truth, the PRSA code is even less helpful. It never fully defines truth, never stating whether the code is discussing an objective truth assumed in media practices such as journalism, the truth required by federal regulators, or the selected truth telling that is common as PR promotes and protects its clients. The code says practitioners should "adhere to the highest standards of accuracy and truth in advancing the interests of those we represent and in communicating with the public," another conundrum. The truth-telling edict, immediately followed by a reminder that practitioners work for their clients, encapsulates the fundamental ethical issue of persuasion ethics and the key flaw in ethics codes. Parts of the code discuss elements of truth—the transparency required to allow the public to know the source of the communication, the need for honesty and for correcting mistakes—are contained elsewhere in the code. But they still help little in this case.

Conclusion

This chapter shows that ethics codes, for all their utility in defining key ethical issues and describing values for persuasion-focused communicators, are useful for many reasons but ultimately are not sufficient for decision making. In as far as they help newcomers, serve a public relations purpose, provide a path in self-regulation, go beyond the silly "obey all rules" rules, then codes deserve a place on our walls as they assure the public and inspire the industry's professionals.

It is clear from the analysis here, however, that you should not expect persuasion-organization codes to provide a clear guide to solving real-life dilemmas that go beyond the minimum expectations of government, society, and the industry. Codes of ethics must become a balanced part of a complete ethical framework for individual practitioners. To be truly ethical, practitioners must move beyond blind obedience, a technocratic allegiance to rules, and reliance on the industry's long-standing conventions. Ultimately, ethics is about thinking for yourself, making decisions that may go against the status quo or cost an account, and commitment to living up to your decisions.

Notes

1. This author was a graduate student in the late 1980s under Dr. Black, and more than two decades later we published a book together: *Doing Ethics in Media: Theories and Practical Applications* (Black & Roberts, 2011). He once told me the story of the "case against" paper, which was part of the inaugural issue of the *Journal of Mass Media Ethics* and devoted to academic thinking about ethics codes during a time when the Society of Professional Journalist's code was being revised. The "case against" paper, he said, was written late and quickly by the journal's co-editors because they thought somebody needed to make a reasoned case against codes. As Dr. Black was instrumental in the SPJ code revision, his paper served more as a devil's advocate argument than about his personal beliefs at the time.
2. The "Self-Regulatory Principles for Online Behavioral Advertising" was developed by the American Association of Advertising Agencies, Association of National Advertisers, Council of Better Business Bureaus, Direct Marketing Association, and Interactive Advertising Bureau. These industry organizations represent a large majority of key advertisers, but by no means do they include every agency that advertises online.
3. While journalism is beyond the scope of this chapter, it is worth noting that the print news industry (which has seen revenues fall by half from 2007 to 2013) is also struggling with blurring the line between news and "advertorial" or other "sponsored content."

References

Advertising Self-Regulatory Council (2012). ARSC snapshot. Retrieved May 13, 2014 from http://www.asrcreviews.org/about-us/

Advertising Self-Regulatory Council (2014). NAD reviews Taboola's native ad widget, recommends clearer disclosures. Retrieved May 20, 2014 from http://www.asrcreviews.org/2014/05/nad-reviews-taboolas-native-ad-widget-recommends-clearer-disclosures/

American Advertising Federation (1984). Advertising principles of American business. Retrieved May 12, 2014, from http://www.aafspokane.com/22/aaf

American Advertising Federation (2011). Institute for Advertising Ethics. Retrieved May 12, 2014 from http://www.aaf.org/default.asp?id=1236

American Association of Advertising Agencies (2011). Standards of practice. Retrieved May 8, 2014 from http://www.aaaa.org/about/association/pages/standardsofpractice.aspx

American Marketing Association (2008). Statement of ethics. Retrieved March 10, 2010 from www.marketingpower.com/AboutAMA/Pages/Statement%20of%20Ethics.aspx

Berderman, D. J. (2008). The pirate code. Retrieved May 11, 2014 from http://www. law.emory.edu/fileadmin/journals/eilr/22/22.2/Bederman.pdf

Bivins, T. (2009). *Mixed Media: Moral Distinctions in Advertising, Public Relations, and Journalism* (2nd edition). New York: Routledge.

Black, J., & Barney, R. D. (1985). The case against mass media codes of ethics. *Journal of Mass Media Ethics*, 1(1), 27–36.

Black, J., & Roberts, C. (2011). *Doing Ethics in Media: Theories and Practical Applications*. New York: Routledge.

Bowen, S. A. (2007). Ethics and public relations. Retrieved May 13, 2014 from http:// www.instituteforpr.org/topics/ethics-and-public-relations/

Bowen, S. A. (2008). A state of neglect: Public relations as 'corporate conscience' or ethics counsel. *Journal of Public Relations Research*, 20(3), 271–96. doi: 10.1080/ 10627260801962749

Callison, C. (2001). Do PR practitioners have a PR problem?: The effect of associating a source with public relations and client-negative news on audience perception of credibility. *Journal of Public Relations Research*, 13(3), 219–34.

Canadian Public Relations Society (2014). Code of ethics. Retrieved May 10, 2014 from www.cprs.ca/aboutus/code_ethic.aspx

Connelly, J. (2014). The Washington News Council is going out of business. Retrieved September 15, 2015 from http://blog.seattlepi.com/seattlepolitics/2014/04/10/the-washington-news-council-is-going-out-of-business/

Deaver, F. (1990). On defining truth. *Journal of Mass Media Ethics*, 5(3), 168–77.

Elliott, J. (2013, September 12). From Russia with PR. Retrieved May 12, 2014 from http://www.propublica.org/article/from-russia-with-pr-ketchum-cnbc

Ewen, S. (1996). *PR! A Social History of Spin*. New York: Basic Books.

Federal Trade Commission (2009). FTC staff report: Self-regulatory principles for online behavorial advertising. Retrieved May 12, 2014 from http://www.ftc.gov/ sites/default/files/documents/reports/federal-trade-commission-staff-report-self-regulatory-principles-online-behavioral-advertising/p085400behavadreport.pdf

Fisher, M. (2013a). Is it possible that Putin wrote the New York Times op-ed himself? Retrieved May 30, 2014 from http://www.washingtonpost.com/blogs/worldviews/ wp/2013/09/13/is-it-possible-that-putin-wrote-the-new-york-times-op-ed-himself/

Fisher, M. (2013b). Vladimir Putin's New York Times op-ed, annotated and fact-checked. Retrieved May 30, 2014 from http://www.washingtonpost.com/blogs/worldviews/ wp/2013/09/12/vladimir-putins-new-york-times-op-ed-annotated-and-fact-checked/

Frankel, M. S. (1989). Professional codes: Why, how, and with what impact? *Journal of Business Ethics*, 8(2/3), 109–15. doi: 10.2307/25071878

Free Speech Coalition (n.d.). FCS code of ethics. Retrieved May 10, 2014 from http:// fscblogger.wordpress.com/fsc-code-of-ethics/

Gallup Inc. (2014). Honesty/Ethics in professions. Retrieved February 3, 2015 from http://www.gallup.com/poll/1654/honesty-ethics-professions.aspx

Google (2015, February 3). Fighting bad advertising practices on the Web—2014 year in review. Retrieved February 4, 2015 from http://adwords.blogspot.com/2015/02/ fighting-bad-advertising-practices-on.html

Griffin, W. G., & Morrison, D. K. (2008). Beyond obligation: Advertising's grand potential to do good. In T. Reichert (Ed.) *Issues in American Advertising: Media, Society, and a Changing World* (pp. 265–81). Chicago: The Copy Workshop.

Guarnani, A. K., & Talati, A. R. (2008). The world's most trusted article on puffery: Non-actionable puffery or misleading? *Update: Food and Law Drug Institute*. Retrieved

May 12, 2014 from http://www.americanbar.org/content/dam/aba/administrative/litigation/materials/2012_food_supplements_2nd_annual_cle_wrkshp/2012_aba_panel3_the_worlds_most_trusted.authcheckdam.pdf

Hanson, R. E. (2014). *Mass Communication: Living in a Media World* (Vol. 4th): Sage.

Hill+Knowlton Strategies (n.d.). Our ethics and conduct. Retrieved May 11, 2014 from http://hkstrategies.es/en/About-Us/Our-Ethics-and-Conduct

Institute for Advertising Ethics at the University of Missouri (2011). Principles and practices for advertising ethics. Retrieved February 4, 2015 from www.rjionline.org/institute-for-advertising-ethics

Interactive Advertising Bureau (2010). Major marketing/media trade groups launch program to give consumers enhanced control over collection and use of Web viewing data for online behavioral advertising. Retrieved May 14, 2014 from http://www.iab.net/about_the_iab/recent_press_releases/press_release_archive/press_release/pr-100410

International Association of Business Communicators (2014). IABC code of ethics for professional communicators. Retrieved February 4, 2015 from http://www.iabc.com/about-us/leaders-and-staff/code-of-ethics/

International Public Relations Association (2011). IRPA Code of Conduct. Retrieved May 12, 2014 from http://www.ipra.org/about/ipra-codes

Johannesen, R. L. (2002). *Ethics in human communication* (5th ed.). Long Grove, IL: Waveland Press.

Kaptein, M., & Schwartz, M. S. (2008). The effectiveness of business codes: A critical examination of existing studies and the development of an integrated research model. *Journal of Business Ethics*, 77(2), 111–27.

Ketchum Inc. (2014). Quick facts about Ketchum. Retrieved May 19, 2014 from http://www.ketchum.com/quick-facts

Marvin, G. (2015). Google issues its 2014 "bad ads" report: disabled more than half a billion ads. Retrieved September 15, 2015 from http://searchengineland.com/google-issues-2014-bad-ads-report-disabled-half-billion-ads-214056

Merkelsen, H. (2011). The double-edged sword of legitimacy in public relations. *Journal of Communication Management*, 15(2), 125–43.

Miller, C. C. (2012, August 9). F.T.C. fines Google $22.5 million for Safari privacy violations. *The New York Times*. Retrieved from http://bits.blogs.nytimes.com/2012/08/09/f-t-c-fines-google-22-5-million-for-safari-privacy-violations/

Ohio Department of Health (2014). Pediculosis. Retrieved May 30, 2014 from http://www.odh.ohio.gov/pdf/IDCM/pedic.pdf

Perez, J. C. (2010). Google sues allegedly rogue prescription drug advertisers. *PC World.* Retrieved September 15, 2015 from http://www.pcworld.com/article/206008/Google_Sues_Allegedly_Rogue_Prescription_Drug_Advertisers.html

Pisa, N. (2007, November 8). Police discover mafia's secret code of conduct on Godfather. *Evening Standard*, p. 26. Retrieved September 15, 2015 from http://www.dailymail.co.uk/news/article-492449/Police-discover-Mafias-Ten-Commandments-arresting-Godfather.html

Pojman, L. P. (1995). *Ethics: Discovering Right and Wrong* (Vol. 2nd). Belmont, CA: Wadsworth.

Public Relations Society of America (2000). Public Relations Society of America (PRSA) member code of ethics. Retrieved March 10, 2014 from www.prsa.org/AboutPRSA/Ethics/CodeEnglish/index.html

Putin, V. (2013, September 12). A plea for caution from Russia: What Putin has to say to America about Syria. *The New York Times*, p. A31. Retrieved from http://www.nytimes.com/2013/09/12/opinion/putin-plea-for-caution-from-russia-on-syria.html

Roberts, C. (2012). Identifying and defining values in media codes of ethics. *Journal of Mass Media Ethics*, 27(2), 115–29. doi: 10.1080/08900523.2012.669289

Rohan, M. (2000). A rose by any name? The values construct. *Personality and Social Psychology Review*, 4(3), 255.

Ross, W. D. (1930). *The Right and the Good*. Oxford: Oxford University Press.

Schwartz, S. H. (1992). Universals in the content and structure of values. In M. P. Zanna (Ed.) *Advances in Experimental Social Psychology*, 25, 1–65.

Society of Professional Journalists (1996). Code of Ethics. Retrieved May 10, 2014 from www.spj.org/ethicscode.asp

Society of Professional Journalists (2014). Code of Ethics. Retrieved February 4, 2015 from www.spj.org/ethicscode.asp

Spence, E., & Van Heekeren, B. (2005). *Advertising Ethics*. Upper Saddle River, NJ: Pearson Prentice Hall.

Sullivan, M. (2013). The story behind the Putin op-ed article in the Times. Retrieved May 30, 2014 from http://publiceditor.blogs.nytimes.com/2013/09/12/the-story-behind-the-putin-op-ed-article-in-the-times/

ThinkRussia.com. (2014). Russian provides aid to the flood-stricken Balkans. Retrieved May 28, 2014 from http://www.thinkrussia.com/policy-initiatives/russia-provides-aid-flood-stricken-balkans

ThinkRussia.com. (2015). About us. Retrieved May 30, 2014 from http://www.think russia.com/about

U. S. Federal Trade Commission (2014). In the matter of Lornamead, Inc., a corporation. Retrieved May 30, 2014 from http://www.ftc.gov/system/files/documents/cases/140527lornameadcmpt.pdf

Weaver, C. K., Motion, J., & Roper, J. (2006). From propaganda to discourse (and back again): Truth, power, the public interest and public relations. In J. L'Etang & M. Pieczka (Eds.) *Public Relations: Critical Debates and Contemporary Practice* (pp. 7–21). New York: Taylor & Francis.

Word of Mouth Marketing Association (2011). Code of ethics and standards of conduct. Retrieved May 10, 2014 from http://www.womma.org/ethics/womma-code-of-ethics

Yeager, H. (2014, March 7). Who would work for Russia? These people. Retrieved May 30, 2014 from http://www.washingtonpost.com/blogs/the-fix/wp/2014/03/07/who-would-lobby-for-russia-these-people/

17 What Do Students Think of Business Ethics? Three Decades of Research

Richard F. Beltramini

CHAPTER SUMMARY

College students will graduate and become the business, professional, and political leaders of the future. You yourself have probably given some thought about the rightness and wrongness of organizations and government entities, and you have likely been aware of moral breaches that revealed law breaking or behaviors you might characterize as immoral in some way. Student beliefs about ethics and morals in business settings are likely to shape their beliefs and activities in the future. This chapter surveyed students in a wide range of disciplines, including business, the humanities, engineering, and the sciences. The results of three studies are found in this chapter. Encouragingly, all three studies revealed awareness of the importance of ethics and interestingly, women were found to be more concerned about ethics than men were. However, the last two studies showed that students were more pessimistic about the state of business ethics than in the first study. Are these concerns rising because students have greater awareness of ethical issues? Or, on the other hand, are instances of bad behavior significantly more frequent or egregious thus spurring greater worries on the parts of students?

Introduction

In the 1980s, my colleagues and I began assessing national student attitudes toward business ethics (the moral right and wrong arising in the context of business practice). Clearly such attitudes would influence the ethical behaviors of future business leaders. Although the subject of "business ethics" had been addressed before then, our research represented the first national, empirical study focusing on students. We felt it important to employ such a focus, in that the next generation of business workers, executives, and policy makers alike were being shaped in the nation's colleges and universities. And, obviously, understanding such a phenomenon represented the first step in potentially influencing future ethical marketplace conduct.

The First Study

In addition to allowing for national representativeness, we felt it important to assess student ethical concerns across majors—not just business, but also liberal arts, social sciences, engineering, and physical sciences. Again, the issue of future ethical behavior reflects the aggregate of educational formation across multiple disciplines, and our goal was to provide broad applicability.

Finally, although an expansive array of ethical problem issues were available at the time, we sought to focus on student-defined concerns. That is, we wanted to first identify ethical concerns from students' perspectives, specifically, rather than to assume they were the same as professionals.

We used a pretest to identify in a broad sample of two hundred students who were nationally representative of concerns students had about business ethics. We then identified the top-10 concerns. These top-10 concerns were then presented to a national sample of nearly 3,000 students attending 28 different universities located in 23 different states. Based on how they each rated the 10 concerns, we were able to order them from "high" to "low" and to assess potential differences across academic classification, major, and gender.

The results revealed students were generally concerned over business ethics, with improving ethics in business rated more highly than, for example, blaming business managers versus government workers for management problems. Students were similarly concerned with the extent to which ethical standards meet the needs of society and business. And more broadly, they were concerned over the future deterioration of business ethics. They were excited about the possibility of improving ethics in business.

We found this youthful idealism did not differ meaningfully across classifications, with the exception of gender. Indeed, as we stated at the time (Beltramini, Peterson, & Kozmetsky, 1984), "There was a consistent tendency for the females in the sample to express more concern than the males in the sample, regardless of the issue." While unanticipated, this finding alone garnered more speculative interpretation than other findings, particularly given the growing presence of females in business at the time. The potential for a new moral force in tomorrow's business world was regarded as particularly noteworthy amidst changing societal patterns. If indeed business ethics were to improve in the years to come, these future business leaders, particularly women, seemed to accept the challenge of playing their role.

The findings of this first study had important implications, not only for the business community but also for the educational community as well. Colleges and universities had evidence of a growing need to incorporate ethical coverage across disciplines. The importance of monitoring trends in ethical concerns among students was established.

The Second Study

Following our 1984 *Journal of Business Ethics* benchmark, the next decade witnessed a heightened awareness of business ethics in all segments of society, as business practices became more closely scrutinized. The 1990s were also different because the distinction between legal and ethical decision making became clearer, especially in the face of mergers and acquisitions, environmental pollution, and the meltdown in the savings and loan industry. The media trumpeted the need for improved business ethics in an era seemingly challenged by ethical standards, from Jim and Tammy Baker to Michael Milken to AIDS and pollution. Furthermore, universities, faced with alleged increases in student cheating, scrambled to introduce ethics courses to stem the tide of rampant unethical behaviors (rather than providing scant coverage as a capstone afterthought in a single class session),

This period of seemingly increased challenges to ethical concerns motivated us to replicate our earlier work as a comparison with our earlier benchmark. Again, our goal was to secure nationally projectable results, so we returned to 16 of the original 28 universities we had studied and surveyed 1,681 students. We preserved those ethical concerns still relevant to the current time period and eliminated those no longer relevant. And, given the changes in academic majors from a decade earlier, we weighted proportions of majors to reflect those changes and facilitate accurate comparisons.

Our results (Peterson, Beltramini, & Kozmetsky, 1991) revealed that college students at the end of the 1980s reported being somewhat more concerned about each business ethics issue investigated than college students were at the beginning of the decade. Further, responses to the issue of whether business ethics will get better or worse in the future evidenced statistically significant differences from the benchmark study. So not only did students continue to report heightened concerns over business ethics, but these results showed a potential concern that ethics had actually deteriorated over the past decade. Nevertheless, their youthful idealism seemingly remained intact, and they reported sensing an opportunity to improve the situation with them at the helm.

When we analyzed results by academic major, year of school, and gender, once again the only substantive difference found was that female students reported significantly greater ethical concerns than their male counterparts did. Although males did evidence an increase in their concerns over business ethics, the level of females' concerns showed the gap had widened since our earlier study.

Thus this second wave of assessment both corroborated our earlier findings and demonstrated a trend in increasing concern among college students regarding business ethics. At the same time as the gender balance in business was shifting toward more women, and while academic institutions were enhancing coverage of ethical issues, it seemed that even greater attention to ethics was called for. Ironically, it was students reporting this growing level of concern and calling for this increased emphasis when paradoxically some reported an alarming trend in unethical student behavior (cheating). Indeed, this evidence of a 'double standard' seemingly supported the need for ongoing monitoring of this trend.

The Third Study

In the years leading up to the third study, we found ourselves in the midst of another spate of ethical lapses, from Enron to Martha Stewart to the collapse of the financial industry and environmental disasters. And again sensing the need to weigh in on the trend in student concerns over business ethics, we developed the third and most recent wave in our ongoing monitoring (Drover, Franczak, & Beltramini, 2012). Motivated by the potential to better understand, and hence predict, ethical decision making among business leaders and policy makers alike, our goal was to maintain a national focus with a broad sample and provide relevant comparisons with our earlier work.

This time, however, we wanted to both maintain the same basic ethical issues studied in our first two waves for comparison purposes and yet add potential concerns that may have arisen in the intervening years, attributable to unprecedented changes in technology, globalization, and regulation/enforcement. Therefore, we again used the same pretest approach as earlier to identify the top potential ethical concerns that had emerged in the first study, contributing an additional five issues to the ongoing list of ten issues assessed in the first two waves.

In 2011, we surveyed 2,009 students from 23 universities, including schools from the earlier waves, and again focused broadly on the identical educational demographics as before. There were no significant differences found in comparison to the demographic profiles of the two prior waves.

The top-five concerns that emerged from the 2012 pre-study were included with the original 10 items from the 1980 and 1991 studies, yielding a total of 15 student concerns. Again, students indicated the extent to which they were concerned about the 15 issues. Table 17.1 shows both the levels of concern and the statistical significance of changes observed in comparison to the studies in 1980 and 1991.

In general, this three-decade assessment of student concerns over business ethics revealed a steady upward trend, from 74.1% in 1980, to 79.7% in 1991, to 82.4% in 2011. This result alone may be interpreted in multiple ways. Perhaps it is the case that business ethical practice has become more problematic and hence student concern has grown. Or, alternatively, perhaps it is the case that student ethical awareness has increased, perhaps as a result of increased emphasis on ethics in classrooms across the country.

More specifically, each of the five "new" issues revealed somewhat surprisingly high levels of concern. A total of 79% expressed concern about business ethics policies where the issue was invading personal Internet privacy, and 80% expressed concern about decisions that were likely to have a negative effect on the environment. Although today's students are far more Internet savvy than those in the earlier two waves, environmental concerns have evidenced a three-decade staying power.

A total of 82% level of concern was found regarding increased pressure to participate in unethical business practices in order to succeed, 84% over the impact of lower ethical standards on the overall economy, and 85% with lower ethical standards affecting personal financial positions (personal savings, retirement funds, etc.). This last finding in particular revealed a more personal nature of business ethical concerns—the highest percentage of all 15 issues posed to the national sample of students in the current wave of study.

The wave-to-wave comparisons across the three decades were also enlightening. Asked about current ethical standards meeting the needs of business, 67% (1980) grew significantly to 73% (1991) and again grew significantly to

75% in 2011. Similarly, a 74% level of concern (1980) regarding the deterioration of business ethics over the years grew significantly to 79% (1991) and remained high in 2011 (79%). Clearly students have continued to perceive the problematic lag between growing ethical challenges in business and the perceived level of standards of reality. This perceived deterioration in business ethics merits further assessment.

When asked about the improvement or decline of business ethics in the future, results revealed a 76% level of concern in the 1980 wave, which grew significantly to 83% in the 1991 wave before declining slightly in the 2011 wave to 82%. These results parallel results related to the issue that current ethical standards are meeting the needs of society in general at 77% (1980), growing significantly to 81% (1991) and again dipping slightly to 80% in 2011. These results are consistent with the others in evidencing not only a potential deterioration but perhaps suggesting a sense of futility over how business ethics are succeeding. Although this interpretation is speculative, further support is provided by the results concerning the possibility of improving ethics in business. The 1980 level of 77% agreement grew significantly to 83% in 1991 and declined significantly to 78% in 2011. This further seems to indicate that students see business ethics somewhat more pessimistically than did students in earlier waves.

Conclusions

At this point it is possible to provide several broader conclusions based on the results observed in the replications of this study over three decades. The most recent results reveal today's students' top concern is how lower ethical standards may influence their individual financial position. Their second concern is that poor ethics will have a negative impact on the overall economy. Students' third concern is over the increased pressure for them to act unethically to maintain individual success in business. Self-interest now trumps general business or societal benefit, albeit with lesser expression over privacy and environmental concerns.

It is troubling that the largest decline evidenced in the three decades is the possibility of improving ethics in business. Less idealistic over potential business/societal change, the most recent study showed students perceive a high need to look out for themselves. This could be a reflection of economic practicality in today's postrecession environment. Nevertheless, the focus on impact on self of business ethics issues is troublesome.

Today's business ethics may well be characterized as "not great, but good enough," but students do not seem to be giving up in this regard. Accepting ethical challenges may be viewed as inevitable, along with a troublesome corresponding need to act unethically to protect one's self-interest. Students' potential disillusionment with having watched whistle-blowers suffer undesirable, instantaneous media exposure may be making today's student "gun shy" and lacking in the personal courage to express individual viewpoints versus preserving individual economic well-being.

The bottom line, however, is that student concern over business ethics was found to be at a 30-year high in the 2011 study based on the research reported in our three waves of study. Whether or not students will accept ethical transgressions or continue to work to rectify business ethics remains a topic worth monitoring further.

References

Beltramini, R.F., Peterson, R.A., & Kozmetsky, G. (1984). Concerns of college students regarding business ethics. *Journal of Business Ethics*, 3, 195–200. Reprinted in A.C. Michalos & D.C. Poff (Eds.) *Citation Classics from the Journal of Business Ethics: Celebrating the First Thirty Years of Publication* (pp. 419–26). New York: Springer.

Drover, W., Franczak, J., & Beltramini, R.F. (2012). A 30 Year historical examination of ethical concerns regarding business ethics: Who's concerned? *Journal of Business Ethics*, 111, 431–38.

Peterson, R.A., Beltramini, R.F., & Kozmetsky, G. (1991). Concerns of college students regarding business ethics: A replication. *Journal of Business Ethics*, 10, 733–38.

Table 17.1 Top ethical concerns and comparisons

	% Concerned 1980	% Concerned 1991	% Concerned 2011
** **Lower ethical standards affecting personal financial positions (personal savings, retirement funds, etc.).**			84.5
** **The impact of lower ethical standards on the overall economy.**			83.5
** **Increased pressure to participate in unethical business practices in order to succeed.**			82.1
The improvement or decline of business ethics in the future.	75.8	82.6a	81.9b
** **Ethical decisions negatively impacting environmental concerns.**			80.0
Current ethical standards meeting the needs of society.	76.8	80.8a	79.8
** **Business ethics policies invading personal Internet privacy.**			79.3
The deterioration of business ethics over the years.	74.1	79.4a	78.5b
The possibility of improving ethics in business.	77.0	83.0a	77.7c
Current ethical standards meeting the needs of business.	67.0	72.6a	74.8b
OVERALL % CONCERNED (top 5)	74.1	79.7	82.4

Notes:

** Indicates new concern from open-ended portion of 2011 data

a. 1980–1991 concerns difference statistically significant at $p < .05$
b. 1980–2011 concerns difference statistically significant at $p < .05$
c. 1991–2011 concerns difference statistically significant at $p < .05$

18 Marbles in the Soup and Crushed Volvos

Ethical Choices on the Advertising Ethics Battlefield

Esther Thorson and Margaret Duffy

CHAPTER SUMMARY

Marbles in the soup and crushed Volvos refer to two famous examples of what most people consider to be deceptive advertising (Horovitz, 1991; Michlin, 2008). Some years ago, it was revealed that Campbell's made its soup look chunkier and substantial in its advertising photographs by putting marbles in soup bowls. (The company said that the real vegetables in the soup sunk to the bottom of the bowl and thus didn't properly show the true texture of the product). The Volvo ads presumably showed a car that was so strong that it could survive a monster truck being driven over it. In fact, workers had reinforced the car well beyond its usual construction. In the view of critics, these actions violated ethical norms.

Introduction

Every day, people working in advertising and marketing communication confront ethical dilemmas. Some have to do with making decisions about the form and content of campaigns. Some have to do with loyalties to a company, a client, to customers, potential customers, and the public interest.

Ethical dilemmas may include truthfulness in campaigns and ads, fake blogs, invasion of privacy, the potential for harm in use of certain products, ads that are in poor taste, dangerous products, depictions of dangerous activities such as hazardous driving, deceptive product portrayals, disguised authorship of publicity materials, behavioral targeting, targeting vulnerable segments such as children, and stereotyping. In addition, the challenges of global marketing could include government officials or buyers who demand personal payments to them from marketers as a requirement for doing business.

In this book, we looked at philosophical principles and ethical standpoints that offer norms for proper behavior and methods to arrive at those behaviors. In addition, we have addressed many of the practical problems communicators face in their jobs. Ethical questions are not just something for ethicists and philosophers to discuss in ivory towers. Instead, they are part of the everyday fabric of our professional lives. They have real consequences for real people, including you.

At their core, ethical dilemmas are rooted in conflicts about who benefits and who might be hurt by certain decisions and actions. It's important that we first recognize and acknowledge ethical issues and then develop critical processes to evaluate the right course of action in an ethical conundrum. The TARES construct, the Potter Box (chapter 14), Veil of Ignorance (chapter 14), Ross's Moral Theory (chapter 3), and the Golden Rule (chapter 13), are all processes we can use when we're unsure of the right course of action. We don't propose to give you ironclad rules that apply in every situation. Instead, we hope you'll see these approaches as practical problem-solving tools that apply to both professional and personal decision making.

Tension and Conflict

Analyze any ethical situation and you'll likely be able to locate the tension at the heart of the problem. Something that benefits you or your well-being may have the potential to injure others. Something that benefits a large number of people may also severely damage a vulnerable minority. Something that calls upon your loyalty to an individual (a friend, a boss, or a client, for instance) may conflict with your loyalty to your community or society.

Let's examine some of these possibilities.

Creepy Rob Lowe

In 2015, a series of commercials by DirectTV featured actor Rob Lowe and compared the suave, good-looking "real-life" person with creepy and weird characters also played by the actor. The cool Rob Lowe is presented as a DirectTV customer, while the strange and even perverted Rob Lowe is presented as a loser cable customer. Of course, the message is that you can decide if you want to be smooth, popular, and sophisticated or weird, friendless, and decidedly unattractive.

The claims in the ads suggest that DirectTV has better signal reliability, better audio and video quality, that customers rank it as first in satisfaction, it offers more sports programming, and quicker responses on service calls. Comcast, the cable giant, evidently didn't take kindly to being classified as a loser and filed a complaint with the National Advertising Division (NAD) of the Better Business Bureau and challenged DirectTV's claims. However, DirectTV could not definitively substantiate those claims. (The NAD is part of the advertising industry's self-regulation program, and its decisions are not binding. However, if an agency or company has generally committed to the NAD voluntary process, they usually will abide by its decisions.)

The Tension

DirectTV argued that the company "continues to believe that the various Rob Lowe advertisements are so outlandish and exaggerated that no reasonable

Figure 18.1 Cool Rob Lowe alongside creepy Rob Lowe in a DirecTV commercial

consumer would believe that the statements being made by the alter-ego characters are comparative or need to be substantiated" (NAD, 2015).

But the NAD disagreed, saying that while they understood humor as an
effective strategy for advertisers, it "does not relieve an advertiser of the obligation to support messages that their advertisement might reasonably convey—
especially if the advertising disparages a competitor's product" (NAD, 2015).
Both researchers and advertisers generally find that humor in advertisements
is highly effective in gaining attention, increasing audiences' liking for ads,
and increasing brand awareness (Weinberger & Gulas, 1992). However, other
research suggests that humor can frequently be used to mask deceptive claims
(Shabbir & Thwaites, 2007). Lee Wilkins, in Chapter 3, writes that advertising,
like journalism, is information. If persuasive messages are, indeed, information,
then they may have genuine consequences, even if they appear on the surface to
be silly and unimportant. In fact, Rance Crain, in an editorial in the industry's
premiere journal reporting on the ad business writes: "It's a well-established
advertising self-regulatory principle that humor and hyperbole don't relieve an
advertiser of the obligation to support messages that their ads might reasonably
convey—especially if the advertising disparages a competitive product" (Crain,
2015). Clearly Crain, along with the NAD, believed that information conveyed
in a humorous way didn't relieve the advertiser of the responsibility of providing false or misleading information. It is also important to note that the campaign resulted in substantial increases in subscribers, thus indicating that people
did, indeed, believe that the claims were accurate (Crain, 2015).

Momma, Am I Fat?

In the American Academy of Advertising Ethics courses developed by Wally Snyder, he provides another important example of an ethical conundrum. The state of Georgia sought to address an increasing problem of childhood obesity: Some 25% of the state's children are obese, thus endangering their health and well-being. The state has tried several strategies, including positive messaging about cutting calories and encouraging exercise. However, these approaches have not shown any significant results.

In a change of tactics, Georgia officials announced a hard-edged campaign aimed directly at the obese children. It shows photos of the children in an attempt to get them to "see" their obesity problem. One of the ads shows a young obese boy around age 10 standing next to his obese mother. He asks, "Momma, am I fat?" Another ad features an overweight child with the message, "WARNIING. It's hard to be a little girl if you're not."

Tension

Several children's advocacy groups came out against the campaign and urged the state to use public service announcements (PSAs) directed to the parents/guardians to encourage them to cut back on the children's food consumption. Snyder points out that this is a "right versus right" ethical dilemma. It is right to protect the children from ridicule by other children based on the campaign, but it is also right to find a way to more effectively influence the obese children to improve their health. Is it ethical to stigmatize certain groups and make them feel bad about their bodies in an effort to address a health problem from which they are suffering? Seow Ting Lee, in Chapter 14 of this book, might say "no." As she discussed, a focus on teleology (the outcomes of an act) doesn't necessarily address a message's intrinsic moral worth. If you applied the TARES construct to such a campaign, you might conclude that it violates the principle of respect for the person being persuaded.

Another way to examine this campaign is through the lens of framing as Geise and Colman discuss in Chapter 12. They argue that any campaign or health messaging that causes emotional distress, guilt, or embarrassment is intrinsically unethical, pointing out that such approaches stigmatize people who may not be able to control the circumstances leading to their health or behavioral issues. They also note that visuals can often be more persuasive than text and lead to easy and unconscious adoption of the persuaders' frames. Similarly, Page and Duffy (Chapter 13) offer evidence that visual representations can "shortcut" our evaluations of messages and evoke visceral but superficial conclusions as well as unintended consequences. As you can see from the example in this campaign, the frame defines the problem and, most important, make moral judgments. Despite the persuaders' intentions, frames result in viewers assigning blame for a condition on individuals suffering from that condition rather than on social or economic factors.

Figure 18.2 Public service announcement from the state of Georgia

Suicide Bomber or Doctor?

In 2010, Lt. Col. Allen McCormick, a former Procter & Gamble executive, developed a campaign as part of the army's psychological operations aimed at reducing suicide bombing with positive images, including that of an Afghani baby boy. He deliberately chose a male-centric strategy that would likely reso-nate with the male-dominated culture of that country (Thorson & Duffy, 2012).

Suicide Bomber. Or Doctor?

What will you make of Massoud Sanjeer?
Will you teach him to take lives?
Or Save Them?
You are what he sees.
Your actions what he copies.
He will be what you make him.
If you build him a garden,
he will plant roses.
If you build him a battlefield
he will die a casualty.
And if you do nothing.
So will he.
You have that Power. Each of you.
As parents. And as citizens.
Hope is first born then nurtured.
If you want a new Afghanistan,
Build one for this new Afghan.
Build it for Massoud Sanjeer.
He is new life for us all.

A New Afghan. **A New Afghanistan.**

Figure 18.3 Example of an advertising campaign aimed at Afghan citizens and sponsored by the U.S. military

Source: Ad created by Allen McCormick.

In many Western cultures, the notion of a campaign focused only around boy babies would be questionable at best. Executed in both Dari and Pashtu, the copy begins, "What will you make of Massoud Sanjeer? Will you teach him to take lives? Or Save Them?"

The Tension

Does such a campaign perpetuate stereotypes about the worth of men over women in a culture that many say is not only unequal but also abusive? In Afghanistan, women are not only low-status individuals, but they can be prosecuted for "moral crimes," including running away from an abusive family member. Amnesty International (2014) reported that "huge numbers" of women suffer domestic violence, and education of women and girls is constantly under threat or attack. Boy babies are prized and wives are often blamed for having girls. Women who give birth to boys are given special foods and treatment, while those who do not are ostracized by family and tribe (Najibullah & Shaheeda, 2012).

Bivins (Chapter 5) and Frith (Chapter 6) explore the stereotyping and potential for harm in quick categorizations of individuals that do not provide full context for human beings who may be slotted into those categories. Nevertheless, as Carrie La Ferle points out in Chapter 11, persuasion can't be successful without taking culture into account, whether it's regional or national. Culture is crucially linked to the values or enduring beliefs people hold, and people usually internalize them by the age of 10. Furthermore, these values are unlikely to change much over time (de Mooij, 2014).

From a pragmatic and utilitarian viewpoint, customization of a campaign to conform to the culture of the target audience would seem necessary. However, considering this from the standpoint of Kantian ethics, the message itself must be judged on its intrinsic worth, not on potential "good" outcomes.

Yellow 5 and Yellow 6

For an ethics assignment in her class, Missouri professor Jamie Flink provided this case study. Yellow 5 and yellow 6 are food coloring agents said by some to be linked to allergies, ADHD, and even cancer (Goyanes, 2013). Some activists claim that Kraft Macaroni & Cheese, frequently marketed toward families and children, has petroleum-based ingredients. Some of those ingredients are said to be carcinogenic and have also been linked with hyperactivity in children.

Your boss has assigned you to this account. For several years, the company has been under pressure to remove these artificial dyes and other ingredients from its products. The dyes add color and brightness to the product, and some of the meals have pasta in shapes designed to be appealing to kids, including cartoon characters.

Your agency conducted considerable qualitative and quantitative research, and it became clear that the children greatly preferred the brighter traditional recipe. In the research, parents also indicated that the most important factor in choosing foods for their children was "foods my child prefers." In addition, for parents, the factor "better for my child's health" was significantly less important than price and convenience.

The Tension

In this case, conflicting loyalties are in play: loyalty to client, loyalty to your employer, loyalty to the concept of responsibility for the well-being of others, and loyalty to yourself and your family. You're concerned enough about the issues that you won't allow your own children to consume the product. You point out to your boss that your agency's code of ethics talks about showing respect for the public, serving the public interest, and being transparent in communication. She replies that the product and its ingredients are legal, they're listed on the box, and that having this account is very important for your agency's success.

Chris Roberts in Chapter 16, points out that while codes of ethics are important, they often fall short in "helping practitioners make decisions when dilemmas of truth and loyalty occur" (p. 273). As the lead account manager on the account, what do you recommend? Do you accept the assignment and do your best to sell more of a product that you think may potentially offer harm?

Postscript: Under pressure from consumer groups and slowing sales as consumers began to opt for what they perceived as healthier and more natural foods, Kraft Foods reformulated its macaroni and cheese product. The company eliminated synthetic dyes and certain preservatives (Reuters, 2015).

My Opponent Hates Babies and Puppies

Of course, this is a tongue-in-cheek reference to some of the outrageous negative advertising we see in most political campaigns. The 2012 U.S. presidential election featured many negative or attack ads, including the ones that follow. In 2015, the U.S. Supreme Court ruled that spending on political campaigns was free speech protected by the First Amendment to the Constitution. This case, Citizens United versus the Federal Election Commission (FEC) vastly increased spending by outside groups and rich donors and resulted not only in more political ads but more negative political ads (Lane, 2015).

The Tension

Weber and Laczniak (Chapter 8) suggest that there are real consequences for democratic processes as candidates increasingly rely on ads that attack opponents. They cite increased polarization among citizens who then have less tolerance and appreciation for opposing views, the potential that good candidates may be deterred from running for office as they anticipate a barrage of personal attacks, and increasing cynicism and mistrust of government. Others argue that negative advertising helps voters see the records and mistakes of candidates, that such advertising is legal, and that candidates are on a level playing field with each having the opportunity to make her case and point out the weaknesses of the opponent. Still others say that not all negative ads should be characterized as harmful and that the "best" negative ads can raise "legitimate" questions and in America we should always err on the side of free speech (Penn, 2012).

Weber and Laczniak argue that while free speech in the United States should remain unfettered, political marketers and policy makers should examine the ethical implications of such practices. They point out that certain NPAs are exploitative and result in voters merely being used as a "means to an end," which is a violation of Kant's categorical imperative. They further write that these ads are contrary to the principle of "virtue ethics" and are violations of the values of fairness and honesty.

The Pregnancy Predictor

An angry father stormed into a Minnesota Target with coupons his high-school-aged daughter received, coupons that promoted cribs and other baby items. He accused the store manager of attempting to encourage his teenager to get pregnant with these promotions. The manager apologized at the time and later called the father to extend further apologies. However, the father said "I had a talk with my daughter. It turns out there's been some activities in my house I haven't been completely aware of. She's due in August. I owe you an apology" (Duhigg, 2012, p. 13).

If this story makes you uneasy, you aren't alone. Everything Target did was entirely legal, and yet such purchase predictions clearly have privacy and ethics implications. While identifying prospective parents is potentially a lucrative strategy, it is not a simple process. Using an array of data including an in-house baby registry, Target's analysts determined that at each stage of a pregnancy, parents buy different types of products and even developed a "pregnancy prediction" score (Duhigg, 2012, p. 12). With this information, the retailer can send optimally timed coupons and promotions that will map pregnancy stage product needs with considerable precision.

You probably have used various "loyalty cards" that grocery stores, drugstores, and other retailers use to offer you points, special deals, and sales. These customer cards also serve to help analysts track your buying behaviors and preferences, and they often are able to link them with highly personal information about you, including your online behaviors, your marital status, age, home ownership data, and even your political beliefs (Duhigg, 2012). If you're like most people, you don't give much thought to the data being gathered about you and how it might be used or misused.

In addition, marketers work very hard to understand and predict consumer behavior and to identify important life milestones, such a home buying, marriage, and becoming parents. In an intensively competitive retail environment, marketers also strive to entice consumers undergoing a life-changing event to go to their stores first to buy these new necessities of life. In particular, pregnancy is a game changer, as prospective parents have a whole new set of priorities for purchase, including clothing, maternity needs, and all sorts of baby paraphernalia.

By being the first store prospective parents think of for baby needs, retailers know that their stores are more likely to continue to be the spot for routine purchases and thus enhance a customer's "lifetime value." Lifetime value calculates how much it costs to acquire you as a customer through various promotional costs and how much you are likely to spend over time (Gupta, et al., 2006). This calculation includes the calculation of customer equity or, in other words, how valuable you are to the company. As you can see, catching a soon-to-be parent is an important goal for marketers and can be a significant boost to customer equity over many years.

The Tension

Several forces are in play in this situation. The first involves the marketers' need to compete in a challenging retail environment with both online and brick-and-mortar firms vying for customers' loyalty and dollars. The second involves genuine customer needs and their interest in receiving valuable information and money-saving opportunities for products they want and need. The third is, of course, the importance of individuals' private information about sensitive matters and, more important, their awareness and knowledge that they are giving up information that may be used in many ways. Most information is likely used in benign ways, but others have the potential for real harm, particularly in the wrong hands. In Chapter 10, Shoenberger mentions the Target case and other instances of potential privacy problems through the use of "big data" and sophisticated analytics. She suggests that it will become increasingly important that brands are transparent and consumers have a clearer idea of what private information they may be giving up in return for a perceived benefit, as well as what risks they may be taking. Unethical use of big data analytics may lead to erosion of trust in institutions on the part of citizens. Lack of clear guidelines at firms and agencies for what constitutes ethical uses of data may lead employees to fall back on legalistic rationales or personal codes of conduct.

As you can see, persuasion ethics in today's world involve a vast range of situations and complex challenges for professional persuaders, marketers, customers, and individuals. We hope you have come to see that persuasion is not inherently unethical, but it is inherently inevitable in human interactions. Through persuasion we work together and human beings can avoid relying on coercion or other questionable means to gain people's cooperation. Professional persuasion in advertising, public relations, and promotion are essential to Western economies; may bring down prices; and provide information about products, services, and ideas that people want and need (Plumer, 2012). Nevertheless, you've seen that ethics in persuasion is fraught with tensions and conflicting loyalties. However, it is crucial that as individuals we act with integrity as Davidson (1986) defines it: having the courage of our convictions and being willing to act upon them. Davidson writes:

> Those who have integrity have discovered something that the rest of the world must know: that integrity, which many look upon as being composed of sacrifice, struggle, and non-advantageous decision making, actually makes life easier, joyful, and powerful.

(p. 24)

We have the responsibility as persuaders with integrity to act with care and concern toward those with whom we communicate and to "focus on a fundamental desire of individuals to be treated with respect and fairness and the fact that when people are so treated they react well" (Robin & Reidenbach, 1987). Integrity in persuasion is possible *and* essential.

References

Amnesty International (2014). Women's rights in Afghanistan. Retrieved May 15, 2015 from http://www.amnesty.org.uk/issues/Women's-rights-in-Afghanistan

Crain, R. (2015). If DirecTV's ads were too silly to be believed, then why run them? April 22. *AdAge*. Retrieved May 20, 2015 from http://adage.com/print/298157

Davidson, J. P. (1986). The elusive nature of integrity: People know it when they see it, but can't explain it. Marketing News, 20(23), 24.

de Mooij, M. (2014). *Global Marketing and Advertising: Understanding Cultural Paradoxes*. Thousand Oaks, CA: Sage Publications.

Duhigg, C. (2012). How companies learn your secrets. *The New York Times*, Feb. 19. Retrieved May 1, 2015 from http://www.nytimes.com/2012/02/19/magazine/shopping-habits.html

Goyanes, C. (2013). Nine common foods that contain toxic ingredients. *Shape Magazine*, March 16. Retrieved May 16, 2015 from http://www.shape.com/healthy-eating/diet-tips/9-common-foods-contain-toxic-ingredients/slide/2

Gupta, S., Hanssens, D., Hardie, B., Kahn, W., Kumar, V., Lin, N., & Ravishander, N. (2006). Modeling lifetime customer value. *Journal of Service Research*, 9(2), 139–55.

Horvitz, B. (1991). Volvo, agency fined $150,000 each for TV ad : Commercials: A spot showing a monster truck crushing all but the European car was misleading, the Federal Trade Commission says. *Los Angeles Times*, August 22. Retrieved May 1, 2015 from http://articles.latimes.com/1991-08-22/business/fi-1522_1_federal-trade-commission

Lane, A. (2015). How Citizens United has changed politics in five years. *U.S. News and World Report*, Jan. 21. Retrieved May 1, 2015 from http://www.usnews.com/news/articles/2015/01/21/5-years-later-citizens-united-has-remade-us-politics

Michlin, S. (2008). Marbles in the Soup: Companies that depict food in their ads often have a fine line to walk. *D Ceo*, May. Retrieved May 1, 2015 from http://www.dmagazine.com/publications/d-ceo/2008/may/marbles-in-the-soup

NAD (2015). NAD recommends DirecTV discontinue certain claims in Rob Lowe ads following Comcast challenge. Retrieved May 1, 2015 from http://www.asrcreviews.org/2015/04/nad-recommends-directv-discontinue-certain-claims-in-rob-lowe-ads-following-comcast-challenge-directv-to-appeal/

Najibullah, F., & Shaheeda, H. (2012). Baby girls seen as mixed blessing in Afghanistan. Radio Free Europe, February 2. Retrieved May 15, 2015 from http://www.rferl.org/content/baby_girls_seen_as_mixed_blessing_in_afghanistan/24476659.html

Penn, M. (2012). The case for negative ads. *Time Magazine*, May 23. Retrieved May 1, 2015 from http://ideas.time.com/2012/05/23/the-case-for-negative-campaign-ads-2/

Plumer, B. (2012). Does advertising help or harm the economy? *Washington Post*, Nov. 27. Retrieved May 27, 2015 at http://www.washingtonpost.com/blogs/wonkblog/wp/2012/11/27/does-advertising-help-or-harm-the-economy/

Reuters (2015). Kraft to drop preservatives from its macaroni and cheese. *The New York Times*, April 20. Retrieved May 1, 2015 from http://www.nytimes.com/2015/04/21/business/kraft-to-drop-preservatives-from-its-macaroni-and-cheese.html

Robin, D. P., & Reidenbach, E. R. (2007). Social responsibility, ethics, and marketing strategy: Closing the gap between concept and application. *Journal of Marketing*, Jan.1987, 51(1), 44–58.

Shabbir, H., & Thwaites, D. (2007). The use of humor to mask deceptive advertising. *Journal of Advertising*, 36(2), 75–85.

Weinberger, M. G., & Gulas, C. S. (1992). The impact of humor in advertising: A Review. *Journal of Advertising*, 21, 45–59.

Index